Merriam-Webster's easy learning Complete French

MW01027742

Merriam-Webster, Incorporated
Springfield, Massachusetts, USA

DEVELOPED IN ASSOCIATION WITH Collins

HarperCollins Publishers
Westerhill Road
Bishopbriggs
Glasgow
G64 2QT
Great Britain

First Edition 2011

Reprint 10 9 8 7 6 5 4 3 2 1 0

© HarperCollins Publishers 2011

ISBN 978-0-87779-566-7

Collins® is a registered trademark of
HarperCollins Publishers Limited

www.collinslanguage.com

Typeset by Davidson Pre-Press, Glasgow, UK

Printed in the USA by RR Donnelley

Acknowledgements
We would like to thank those authors and
publishers who kindly gave permission
for copyright material to be used in the
Collins Word Web. We would also like to
thank Times Newspapers Ltd for providing
valuable data.

All rights reserved. No part of this
publication may be reproduced, stored in a
retrieval system or transmitted, in any form
or by any means, electronic, mechanical,
photocopying, recording or otherwise,
without the prior permission of the
publisher. This book is sold subject to the
conditions that it shall not, by way of trade
or otherwise, be lent, re-sold, hired out or
otherwise circulated without the publisher's
prior consent in any form of binding or cover
other than that in which it is published and
without a similar condition including this
condition being imposed on the subsequent
purchaser.

Entered words that we have reason to believe
constitute trademarks have been designated
as such. However, neither the presence nor
absence of such designation should be
regarded as affecting the legal status of
any trademark.

SERIES EDITOR
Rob Scriven

MANAGING EDITOR
Gaëlle Amiot-Cadey

PROJECT CO-ORDINATOR
Genevieve Gerrard

Contents

Foreword for language teachers

Merriam-Webster's Easy Learning Complete French is designed to be used by both young and adult learners, as a study group reference book to complement your textbook in class, or as a recommended text for self-study and homework/coursework.

The text is intended for learners from beginner to intermediate and advanced levels, and therefore its content and vocabulary have been matched to the needs of students at each level.

The approach aims to develop knowledge and understanding of grammar and your students' ability to apply it by:

- defining parts of speech at the beginning of each major section with examples in English to clarify concepts
- minimizing the use of grammar terminology and providing clear explanations of terms both within the text and in the **Glossary**
- illustrating all points with examples (and their translations) based on topics and contexts which are relevant to beginner and intermediate course content

The text helps you develop positive attitudes toward the study of grammar in your classes by:

- giving clear, easy-to-follow explanations
- prioritizing content according to level of complexity
- sequencing points to reflect course topics, e.g. verb tenses
- highlighting useful **Tips** to deal with common difficulties
- summarizing **Key points** at the end of sections to reinforce learning

In addition to fostering success and building a thorough foundation in French grammar, the optional **Grammar Extra** sections will encourage and challenge your students to further their studies to more advanced levels.

The blue pages in the middle section of the book contain **Verb Tables** and a **Verb Index** which students can use as a reference in their work.

Finally the **Vocabulary** section in the last part of the book provides thematic vocabulary lists which can either be used for self-study or as an additional teaching resource.

Introduction for students

Whether you are learning French for the very first time, brushing up on topics you have learned in class, or studying to improve your mastery of the language, *Merriam-Webster's Easy Learning Complete French* is here to help.

Newcomers can sometimes struggle with the technical terms they come across when they start to explore the grammar of a new language. This book explains how to get a good handle on all the parts of speech you will need to know, using simple language and cutting out jargon.

The text is divided into sections, each dealing with a particular area of grammar. Each section can be studied individually, as numerous cross-references in the text direct you to relevant direct in other sections of the book for further information.

Every major section begins with an explanation of the area of grammar covered on the following pages. For quick reference, these definitions are also collected together on pages viii–xii, in a glossary of essential grammar terms.

> **What is a verb?**
> A **verb** is a "doing" word which describes what someone or something does, what someone or something is, or what happens to them, for example, *be*, *sing*, *live*.

Each grammar point in the text is followed by simple examples of real French, complete with English translations, to help you understand the rules. Underlining has been used in examples throughout the text to highlight the grammatical point being explained.

➤ If you are talking about a part of your body, you usually use a word like *my* or *his* in English, but in French you usually use the definite article.

Tourne <u>la</u> tête à gauche.	Turn your head to the left.
Il s'est cassé <u>le</u> bras.	He broke his arm.
J'ai mal à <u>la</u> gorge.	I have a sore throat.

In French, as with any foreign language, there are certain pitfalls which have to be avoided. **Tips** and **Information** notes throughout the text are useful reminders of the things that often trip students up.

Tip

If you are not sure which form of *you* to use, it is safest to use **vous** so that you will not offend anybody.

Key points sum up all the important facts about a particular area of grammar, to save you time when you are studying and help you focus on the main grammatical points.

Key points

✔ With masculine singular nouns → use **un**.

✔ With feminine singular nouns → use **une**.

✔ With plural nouns → use **des**.

✔ **un**, **une** and **des** → change to **de** or **d'** in negative sentences.

✔ The indefinite article is not usually used when you say what jobs people do, or in exclamations with **quel**.

If you think you would like to take your French studies to a higher level, check out the **Grammar Extra** sections. These are intended for advanced students who want to know a little more about the structures they will come across as they widen their exposure to the language.

Grammar Extra!

If you want to use an adjective after **quelque chose**, **rien**, **quelqu'un** and **personne**, you link the words with **de**.

quelqu'un **d'**important	someone important
quelque chose **d'**intéressant	something interesting
rien **d'**amusant	nothing funny

The blue pages in the middle of the book contain **Verb Tables**, where 115 important French verbs (both regular and irregular) are declined in full. Examples show you how to use these verbs in a sentence. You can look up any common verbs in the **Verb Index** on pages 436–446 to find either the conjugation of the verb itself, or a cross-reference to a model verb, which will show you the patterns that verb follows.

Finally, the **Vocabulary** section at the end of the book is divided into 50 topics, followed by a list of supplementary vocabulary.

Glossary of grammar terms

ABSTRACT NOUN a word used to refer to a quality, idea, feeling, or experience, rather than a physical object, for example, *size, reason, happiness*. Compare with **concrete noun**.

ADJECTIVE a "describing" word that tells you more about a person or thing, such as their appearance, color, size, or other qualities, for example, *pretty, blue, big*.

ADVERB a word usually used with verbs, adjectives or other adverbs that gives more information about when, where, how, or in what circumstances something happens, for example, *quickly, happily, now*.

AGREE (with) to change word endings according to whether you are referring to masculine, feminine, singular, or plural people or things.

AGREEMENT changing word endings according to whether you are referring to masculine, feminine, singular, or plural people or things.

APOSTROPHE s an ending ('s) added to a noun to show who or what someone or something belongs to, for example, *Danielle's dog, the doctor's wife, the book's cover*.

ARTICLE a word like *the, a*, and *an*, which is used in front of a noun. See also **definite article, indefinite article** and **partitive article**.

AUXILIARY VERB a verb such as *be, have*, and *do* when it is used with a main verb to form tenses, negatives and questions.

BASE FORM the form of the verb without any endings added to it, for example, *walk, have, be, go*. Compare with **infinitive**.

CARDINAL NUMBER a number used in counting, for example, *one, seven, ninety*. Compare with **ordinal number**.

CLAUSE a group of words containing a verb.

COMPARATIVE an adjective or adverb with *-er* on the end of it or *more* or *less* in front of it that is used to compare people, things, or actions, for example, *slower, less important, more carefully*.

COMPOUND NOUN a word for a living being, thing, or idea, which is made up of two or more words, for example, *old-fashioned, subway station*.

CONCRETE NOUN a word that refers to an object you can touch with your hand, rather than to a quality or idea, for example, *ball, map, apples*. Compare with **abstract noun**.

CONDITIONAL a verb form used to talk about things that would happen or would be true under certain conditions, for example, *I would help you if I could*. It is also used to say what you would like or need, for example, *Could you give me the bill?*

CONJUGATE to give a verb different endings according to whether you are referring to *I, you, they*, and so on, and according to whether you are referring to past, present, or future, for example, *I have, she had, they will have*.

CONJUGATION a group of verbs which have the same endings as each other or change according to the same pattern.

CONJUNCTION a word such as *and*, *because*, or *but* that links two words or phrases of a similar type or two parts of a sentence, for example, *Diane _and_ I have been friends for years.*; *I left _because_ I was bored.*

CONSONANT a letter of the alphabet which is not a vowel, for example, *b*, *f*, *m*, *s*, *v* etc. Compare with **vowel**.

CONSTRUCTION an arrangement of words together in a phrase or sentence.

DEFINITE ARTICLE the word *the*. Compare with **indefinite article**.

DEMONSTRATIVE ADJECTIVE one of the words *this*, *that*, *these*, and *those* used with a noun to point out a particular person or thing, for example, *_this_ woman, _that_ dog*.

DEMONSTRATIVE PRONOUN one of the words *this*, *that*, *these*, and *those* used instead of a noun to point out people or things, for example, *_That_ looks fun*.

DIRECT OBJECT a noun referring to the person or thing affected by the action described by a verb, for example, *She wrote _her name_.*; *I shut _the window_*. Compare with **indirect object**.

DIRECT OBJECT PRONOUN a word such as *me*, *him*, *us*, and *them* which is used instead of a noun to stand in for the person or thing most directly affected by the action described by the verb. Compare with **indirect object pronoun**.

EMPHATIC PRONOUN a word used instead of a noun when you want to emphasize something, for example,

Is this for _me_?; *"Who broke the window?"* – *"_He_ did."* Also called **stressed pronoun**.

ENDING a form added to a verb, for example, *go* → *goes*, and to adjectives and nouns depending on whether they refer to masculine, feminine, singular, or plural things.

EXCLAMATION a word, phrase or sentence that you use to show you are surprised, shocked, angry, and so on, for example, *Wow!; How dare you!; What a surprise!*

FEMININE a form of noun, pronoun or adjective that is used to refer to a living being, thing, or idea that is not classed as masculine.

FUTURE a verb tense used to talk about something that will happen or will be true.

GENDER the masculine or feminine category to which a noun, pronoun, or adjective belongs.

IMPERATIVE the form of a verb used when giving orders and instructions, for example, *Shut the door!; Sit down!; Don't go!*

IMPERFECT one of the verb tenses used to talk about the past, especially in descriptions, and to say what was happening or used to happen, for example, *I used to walk to school.; It was sunny during the weekend*. Compare with **perfect**.

IMPERSONAL VERB one which does not refer to a real person or thing and where the subject is represented by *it*, for example, *It's going to rain.; It's 10 o'clock*.

INDEFINITE ADJECTIVE one of a small group of adjectives used to talk about people or things in a general way, without saying who or what they are, for example, *several*, *all*, *every*.

INDEFINITE ARTICLE the words *a* and *an*. Compare with **definite article**.

INDEFINITE PRONOUN a small group of pronouns such as *everything*, *nobody*, and *something*, which are used to refer to people or things in a general way, without saying exactly who or what they are.

INDIRECT OBJECT a noun used with verbs that take two objects. For example, in *I gave the carrot to the rabbit*, *the rabbit* is the indirect object and *carrot* is the direct object. Compare with **direct object**.

INDIRECT OBJECT PRONOUN when a verb has two objects (a direct one and an indirect one), the indirect object pronoun is used instead of a noun to show the person or the thing the action is intended to benefit or harm, for example, *me* in *He gave me a book* and *Can you get me a towel?* Compare with **direct object pronoun**.

INDIRECT QUESTION used to tell someone else about a question and introduced by a verb such as *ask*, *tell*, or *wonder*, for example, *He asked me what time it was.; I wonder who he is.*

INFINITIVE the form of the verb with *to* in front of it and without any endings added, for example, *to walk*, *to have*, *to be*, *to go*. Compare with **base form**.

INTERROGATIVE ADJECTIVE a question word used with a noun to ask *who?*, *what?*, or *which?*, for example, *What instruments do you play?; Which shoes do you like?*

INTERROGATIVE PRONOUN one of the words *who*, *whose*, *whom*, *what*, and *which* when they are used instead of a noun to ask questions, for example, *What's happening?; Who's coming?*

INVARIABLE used to describe a form which does not change.

IRREGULAR VERB a verb whose forms do not follow a general pattern or the normal rules. Compare with **regular verb**.

MASCULINE a form of noun, pronoun or adjective that is used to refer to a living being, thing, or idea that is not classed as feminine.

NEGATIVE a question or statement which contains a word such as *not*, *never*, or *nothing*, and is used to say that something is not happening, is not true or is absent, for example, *I never eat meat.; Don't you love me?*

NOUN a "naming" word for a living being, thing, or idea, for example, *woman*, *desk*, *happiness*, *Andrew*.

NUMBER used to say how many things you are referring to or where something goes in a sequence. See also **ordinal number** and **cardinal number**.

OBJECT a noun or pronoun which refers to a person or thing that is affected by the action described by the verb. Compare with **direct object**, **indirect object**, and **subject**.

OBJECT PRONOUN one of the set of pronouns including *me*, *him*, and *them*, which are used instead of the noun as the object of a verb or preposition. Compare with **subject pronoun**.

ORDINAL NUMBER a number used to indicate where something goes in an order or sequence, for example, *first, fifth, sixteenth.* Compare with **cardinal number**.

PART OF SPEECH a word class, for example, *noun, verb, adjective, preposition, pronoun*.

PARTITIVE ARTICLE the words *some* or *any*, used to refer to part of a thing but not all of it, for example, *Do you have any money?; I'm going to buy some bread.*

PASSIVE a form of the verb that is used when the subject of the verb is the person or thing that is affected by the action, for example, *we were told.*

PAST PARTICIPLE a verb form which is used to form perfect and pluperfect tenses and passives, for example, *watched, swum.* Some past participles are also used as adjectives, for example, *a broken watch.*

PERFECT one of the verb tenses used to talk about the past, especially about actions that took place and were completed in the past. Compare with **imperfect**.

PERSON one of the three classes: the first person (*I, we*), the second person (*you* singular and *you* plural), and the third person (*he, she, it* and *they*).

PERSONAL PRONOUN one of the group of words including *I, you,* and *they* which are used to refer to yourself, the people you are talking to, or the people or things you are talking about.

PLUPERFECT one of the verb tenses used to describe something that had happened or had been true at a point in the past, for example, *I'd forgotten to finish my homework.*

PLURAL the form of a word which is used to refer to more than one person or thing. Compare with **singular**.

POSSESSIVE ADJECTIVE one of the words *my, your, his, her, its, our,* or *their,* used with a noun to show that one person or thing belongs to another.

POSSESSIVE PRONOUN one of the words *mine, yours, hers, his, ours,* or *theirs,* used instead of a noun to show that one person or thing belongs to another.

PREPOSITION is a word such as *at, for, with, into,* or *from,* which is usually followed by a noun, pronoun or, in English, a word ending in *-ing.* Prepositions show how people and things relate to the rest of the sentence, for example, *She's at home.; a tool for cutting grass; It's from David.*

PRESENT a verb form used to talk about what is true at the moment, what happens regularly, and what is happening now, for example, *I'm a student.; I travel to college by train.; I'm studying Language.*

PRESENT PARTICIPLE a verb form ending in *-ing* which is used in English to form verb tenses, and which may be used as an adjective or a noun, for example, *What are you doing?; the setting sun; Swimming is easy!*

PRONOUN a word which you use instead of a noun, when you do not need or want to name someone or something directly, for example, *it, you, none.*

PROPER NOUN the name of a person, place, organization, or thing. Proper nouns are always written with a capital letter, for example, *Kevin, Boston, Europe, Newsweek*.

QUESTION WORD a word such as *why, where, who, which* or *how* which is used to ask a question.

REFLEXIVE PRONOUN a word ending in *-self* or *-selves*, such as *myself* or *themselves*, which refers back to the subject, for example, *He hurt himself.; Take care of yourself.*

REFLEXIVE VERB a verb where the subject and object are the same, and where the action "reflects back" on the subject. A reflexive verb is used with a reflexive pronoun such as *myself, yourself, herself*, for example, *I washed myself.; He shaved himself.*

REGULAR VERB a verb whose forms follow a general pattern or the normal rules. Compare with **irregular verb**.

RELATIVE PRONOUN a word such as *that, who*, or *which*, when it is used to link two parts of a sentence together.

SENTENCE a group of words which usually has a verb and a subject. In writing, a sentence has a capital letter at the beginning and a period, question mark or exclamation mark at the end.

SINGULAR the form of a word which is used to refer to one person or thing. Compare with **plural**.

STEM the main part of a verb to which endings are added.

STRESSED PRONOUN used instead of a noun when you want to emphasize something, for example, *Is this for me?; "Who broke the window?" – "He did."* Also called **emphatic pronoun**.

SUBJECT the noun in a sentence or phrase that refers to the person or thing that does the action described by the verb or is in the state described by the verb, for example, *My cat doesn't drink milk.* Compare with **object**.

SUBJECT PRONOUN a word such as *I, he, she*, and *they* which carries out the action described by the verb. Pronouns stand in for nouns when it is clear who is being talked about, for example, *My brother isn't here at the moment. He'll be back in an hour.* Compare with **object pronoun**.

SUBJUNCTIVE a verb form used in certain circumstances to express some sort of feeling, or to show doubt about whether something will happen or whether something is true. It is only used occasionally in modern English, for example, *If I were you, I wouldn't bother.; So be it.*

SUPERLATIVE an adjective or adverb with *-est* on the end of it or *most* or *least* in front of it that is used to compare people, things, or actions, for example, *thinnest, most quickly, least interesting*.

SYLLABLE consonant+vowel units that make up the sounds of a word, for example, *ca-the-dral* (3 syllables), *im-po-ssi-ble* (4 syllables).

TENSE the form of a verb which shows whether you are referring to the past, present, or future.

VERB a "doing" word which describes what someone or something does, what someone or something is, or what happens to them, for example, *be, sing, live*.

VOWEL one of the letters *a, e, i, o*, or *u*. Compare with **consonant**.

Nouns

> **What is a noun?**
> A **noun** is a "naming" word for a living being, thing, or idea, for example, *woman*, *happiness*, *Andrew*.

Using nouns

➤ In French, all nouns are either <u>masculine</u> or <u>feminine</u>. This is called their <u>gender</u>. Even words for things have a gender.

➤ Whenever you are using a noun, you need to know whether it is masculine or feminine as this affects the form of other words used with it, such as:

- adjectives that describe it
- articles (such as **le** or **une**) that go before it
- pronouns (such as **il** or **elle**) that replace it

➡ *For more information on **Adjectives**, **Articles** or **Pronouns**, see pages 25, 12 and 42.*

➤ You can find information about gender by looking the word up in a dictionary. When you come across a new noun, always learn the word for *the* or *a* that goes with it to help you remember its gender.

- **le** or **un** before a noun tells you it is masculine
- **la** or **une** before a noun tells you it is feminine

➤ We refer to something as <u>singular</u> when we are talking about just one of them, and as <u>plural</u> when we are talking about more than one. The singular is the form of the noun you will usually find when you look a noun up in the dictionary. As in English, nouns in French change their form in the plural.

➤ Adjectives, articles and pronouns are also affected by whether a noun is singular or plural.

> *Tip*
> Remember that you have to use the right word for *the*, *a* and so on according to the gender of the French noun.

2 Nouns

Gender

1 Nouns referring to people

➤ Most nouns referring to men and boys are <u>masculine</u>.

<u>un</u> homme	a man
<u>un</u> roi	a king

➤ Most nouns referring to women and girls are <u>feminine</u>.

<u>une</u> fille	a girl
<u>une</u> reine	a queen

➤ When the same word is used to refer to either men/boys or women/girls, its gender usually changes depending on the sex of the person it refers to.

<u>un</u> camarade	a (male) friend
<u>une</u> camarade	a (female) friend
<u>un</u> Belge	a Belgian (man)
<u>une</u> Belge	a Belgian (woman)

Grammar Extra!

Some words for people have only <u>one</u> possible gender, whether they refer to a male or a female.

<u>un</u> bébé	a (male or female) baby
<u>un</u> guide	a (male or female) guide
<u>une</u> personne	a (male or female) person
<u>une</u> vedette	a (male or female) star

➤ In English, we can sometimes make a word masculine or feminine by changing the ending, for example, English<u>man</u> and English<u>woman</u>, or prince and prin<u>cess</u>. In French, very often the ending of a noun changes depending on whether it refers to a man or a woman.

<u>un</u> Anglais	an Englishman
<u>une</u> Anglaise	an Englishwoman
<u>un</u> prince	a prince
<u>une</u> prin<u>cess</u>e	a princess
<u>un</u> employé	a (male) employee
<u>une</u> employée	a (female) employee

⇨   *For more information on **Masculine and feminine forms of words**, see page 7.*

For further explanation of grammatical terms, please see pages viii-xii.

2 Nouns referring to animals

➤ In English we can choose between words like *bull* or *cow*, depending on the sex of the animal we are referring to. In French too there are sometimes separate words for male and female animals.

<u>un</u> taureau	a bull
<u>une</u> vache	a cow

➤ Sometimes, the same word with different endings is used for male and female animals.

<u>un</u> chien	a (male) dog
<u>une</u> chienne	a (female) dog

> *Tip*
> When you do not know or care what sex the animal is, you can usually use the masculine form as a general word.

➤ Words for other animals do not change according to the sex of the animal. Just learn the French word with its gender, which is always the same.

<u>un</u> poisson	a fish
<u>une</u> souris	a mouse

3 Nouns referring to things

➤ In English, we call all things – for example, *table, car, book, apple* – "<u>it</u>." In French, however, things are either <u>masculine</u> or <u>feminine</u>. As things do not divide into sexes the way humans and animals do, there are no physical clues to help you with their gender in French. Try to learn the gender as you learn the word.

➤ There are lots of rules to help you:

- words ending in -e are usually <u>feminine</u> (**une boulangeri<u>e</u>** a bakery; **une banqu<u>e</u>** a bank)

- words ending in a consonant (any letter except *a, e, i, o,* or *u*) are usually <u>masculine</u> (**un aéropor<u>t</u>** an airport; **un fil<u>m</u>** a movie)

➤ There are some exceptions to these rules, so it is best to check in a dictionary if you are unsure.

4 Nouns

➤ These endings are often found on <u>masculine nouns</u>.

Masculine ending	Examples
-age	<u>un</u> vill<u>age</u> a village <u>un</u> voy<u>age</u> a journey <u>un</u> ét<u>age</u> a floor <u>le</u> from<u>age</u> cheese BUT: <u>une</u> image a picture <u>une</u> page a page <u>la</u> plage the beach
-ment	<u>un</u> apparte<u>ment</u> an apartment <u>un</u> bâti<u>ment</u> a building <u>le</u> ci<u>ment</u> cement <u>un</u> vête<u>ment</u> a piece of clothing
-oir	<u>un</u> mir<u>oir</u> a mirror <u>un</u> coul<u>oir</u> a corridor <u>le</u> s<u>oir</u> the evening <u>un</u> mouch<u>oir</u> a handkerchief
-sme	<u>le</u> touri<u>sme</u> tourism <u>le</u> raci<u>sme</u> racism
-eau	<u>un</u> cad<u>eau</u> a present <u>un</u> chap<u>eau</u> a hat <u>un</u> gât<u>eau</u> a cake <u>le</u> rid<u>eau</u> the curtain BUT: <u>la</u> peau skin <u>l'</u>eau water
-eu	<u>un</u> j<u>eu</u> a game
-ou	<u>un</u> ch<u>ou</u> a cabbage <u>le</u> gen<u>ou</u> the knee
-ier	<u>le</u> cah<u>ier</u> the notebook <u>un</u> quart<u>ier</u> an area <u>un</u> escal<u>ier</u> a staircase
-in	<u>un</u> magas<u>in</u> a store <u>un</u> jard<u>in</u> a garden <u>un</u> dess<u>in</u> a drawing <u>le</u> v<u>in</u> the wine BUT: <u>la</u> fin the end <u>une</u> main a hand

For further explanation of grammatical terms, please see pages viii-xii.

-on	un champignon a mushroom
	un ballon a ball
	le citron the lemon
	BUT:
	une maison a house
	la saison the season

➤ The following types of words are also masculine:

- names of the days of the week, and the months and seasons of the year

le lundi	Monday
septembre prochain	next September
le printemps	Spring

- the names of languages

le français	French
le portugais	Portuguese
Tu apprends le français depuis combien de temps ?	How long have you been learning French?

- most metric weights and measures

un gramme	a gram
un mètre	a meter
un kilomètre	a kilometer

- English nouns used in French

le football	soccer
un tee-shirt	a T-shirt
un sandwich	a sandwich

➤ These endings are often found on <u>feminine nouns</u>.

Feminine ending	Examples
-ance -anse -ence -ense	la chance luck, chance une danse a dance la patience patience la défense defense BUT: le silence silence
-ion	une région a region une addition a bill une réunion a meeting la circulation traffic BUT: un avion a plane
-té -tié	une spécialité a specialty la moitié half BUT: un été a summer le pâté pâté

Grammar Extra!

A few words have different meanings depending on whether they are masculine or feminine. These are the most common:

Masculine	Meaning	Example	Feminine	Meaning	Example
<u>un</u> livre	a book	un livre de poche a paperback	<u>une</u> livre	a pound	une livre de beurre a pound of butter
<u>un</u> mode	a method	le mode d'emploi the directions for use	<u>la</u> mode	fashion	à la mode in fashion
<u>un</u> poste	a set (*TV/radio*); a position (*job*); an extension (*phone*)	un poste de professeur a teaching job	<u>la</u> poste	the mail; the post office	mettre quelque chose à la poste to mail something
<u>un</u> tour	a walk	faire un tour to go for a walk	<u>une</u> tour	tower	la tour Eiffel the Eiffel Tower

Key points

✔ Most nouns referring to men, boys, and male animals are <u>masculine</u>; most nouns referring to women, girls, and female animals are <u>feminine</u>. The ending of a French noun often changes depending on whether it refers to a male or a female.

✔ Generally, words ending in -e are feminine and words ending in a consonant are masculine, though there are many exceptions to this rule.

✔ These endings are often found on masculine nouns: -age, -ment, -oir, -sme, -eau, -eu, -ou, -ier, -in and -on.

✔ These endings are often found on feminine nouns: -ance, -anse, -ence, -ense, -ion, -té, -tié.

✔ Days of the week, months, and seasons of the year are masculine. So are languages, most metric weights and measures, and English nouns used in French.

For further explanation of grammatical terms, please see pages viii-xii.

4 Masculine and feminine forms of words

➤ In French there are sometimes very different words for men and women, and for male and female animals, just as in English.

un homme	a man
une femme	a woman
un taureau	a bull
une vache	a cow
un neveu	a nephew
une nièce	a niece

➤ Many masculine French nouns can be made feminine simply by changing the ending. This is usually done by adding an -e to the masculine noun to form the feminine.

un ami	a (male) friend
une amie	a (female) friend
un employé	a (male) employee
une employée	a (female) employee
un Français	a Frenchman
une Française	a Frenchwoman

➤ If the masculine singular form already ends in -e, no further e is added.

un élève	a (male) student
une élève	a (female) student
un camarade	a (male) friend
une camarade	a (female) friend
un collègue	a (male) colleague
une collègue	a (female) colleague

Tip

If a masculine noun ends in a vowel, its pronunciation does not change when an -e is added to form the feminine. For example, ami and amie (meaning *friend*) are pronounced the same.

If a masculine noun ends with a consonant that is not pronounced, for example, -d, -s, -r, or -t, you DO pronounce that consonant when an -e is added in the feminine. For example, in étudiant (meaning *student*), you cannot hear the t; in étudiante, you can hear the t.

> ## Tip
>
> Some masculine nouns, such as **voisin** (meaning *neighbor*), end in what is called a <u>nasal vowel</u> and an **-n**. With these words, you pronounce the vowel "through your nose" but DO NOT say the **n**. When an **-e** is added in the feminine – for example, **voisine** – the vowel becomes a normal one instead of a nasal vowel and you DO pronounce the **n**.

5 Some other patterns

➤ Some changes to endings from masculine to feminine are a little more complicated but still fall into a regular pattern.

Masculine ending	Feminine ending	Example	Meaning
-f	-ve	<u>un</u> veu<u>f</u>/<u>une</u> veu<u>ve</u>	a widower/a widow
-x	-se	<u>un</u> épou<u>x</u>/<u>une</u> épou<u>se</u>	a husband/a wife
-eur	-euse	<u>un</u> dans<u>eur</u>/ <u>une</u> dans<u>euse</u>	a (male) dancer/ a (female) dancer
-teur	-teuse -trice	<u>un</u> chan<u>teur</u>/ <u>une</u> chan<u>teuse</u> <u>un</u> ac<u>teur</u>/<u>une</u> ac<u>trice</u>	a (male) singer/ a (female) singer an actor/an actress
-an	-anne	<u>un</u> pays<u>an</u>/ <u>une</u> pays<u>anne</u>	a (male) farmer/ a (female) farmer
-ien	-ienne	<u>un</u> Paris<u>ien</u>/ <u>une</u> Paris<u>ienne</u>	a (male) Parisian/ a (female) Parisian
-on	-onne	<u>un</u> li<u>on</u>/<u>une</u> li<u>onne</u>	a lion/a lioness
-er	-ère	<u>un</u> étrang<u>er</u>/ <u>une</u> étrang<u>ère</u>	a (male) foreigner/ a (female) foreigner
-et	-ette	<u>le</u> cad<u>et</u>/<u>la</u> cad<u>ette</u>	the youngest (male) child the youngest (female) child
-el	-elle	<u>un</u> professionn<u>el</u>/ <u>une</u> professionn<u>elle</u>	a (male) professional/ a (female) professional

> ### Key points
> ✔ Many masculine French nouns can be made to refer to females by adding an **-e**. If the masculine singular form already ends in **-e**, no further **e** is added.
> ✔ The pronunciation of feminine nouns is sometimes different from that of the corresponding masculine nouns.
> ✔ Other patterns include:
>
> | | | |
> |---|---|---|
> | -f → -ve | -teur → -teuse or -trice | -er → -ère |
> | -x → -se | -an, -en, and -on → -anne | -et → -ette |
> | -eur → -euse | -enne and -onne | -el → -elle |

For further explanation of grammatical terms, please see pages viii-xii.

Forming plurals

1 Plurals ending in -s

➤ In English, we usually make nouns plural by adding an -s to the end (*garden* → *gardens*; *house* → *houses*), although we do have some nouns which are <u>irregular</u> and do not follow this pattern (*mouse* → *mice*; *child* → *children*).

> *Tip*
>
> Remember that you have to use **les** with plural nouns in French. Any adjective that goes with the noun has to agree with it, as does any pronoun that replaces it.
>
> ⇨ For more information on **Adjectives**, **Articles** and **Pronouns**, see pages 25, 12 and 42.

➤ Most French nouns also form their plural by adding an -s to their singular form.

un jardin	a garden
des jardin<u>s</u>	gardens
une voiture	a car
des voiture<u>s</u>	cars
un hôtel	a hotel
des hôtel<u>s</u>	hotels

➤ If the singular noun ends in -s, -x, or -z, no further -s is added in the plural.

un fils	a son
des fils	sons
une voix	a voice
des voix	voices
un nez	a nose
des nez	noses

2 Plurals ending in -x

➤ The following nouns add an -x instead of an -s in the plural:

- nouns ending in -eau

un chapeau	a hat
des chapeau<u>x</u>	hats

- most nouns ending in **-eu**

un jeu	a game
des jeux	games

- a FEW nouns ending in **-ou** (MOST nouns ending in **-ou** add **-s** as usual)

un bijou	a jewel
des bijoux	jewels
un caillou	a pebble
des cailloux	pebbles
un chou	a cabbage
des choux	cabbages
un genou	a knee
des genoux	knees
un hibou	an owl
des hiboux	owls
un joujou	a toy
des joujoux	toys
un pou	a louse
des poux	lice

Tip

Adding an **-s** or **-x** to the end of a noun does not usually change the way the word is pronounced. For example, **professeur** and **professeurs** and **chapeau** and **chapeaux** sound just the same when you say them out loud.

➤ If the singular noun ends in **-al** or **-ail**, the plural usually ends in **-aux**.

un journal	a newspaper
des journaux	newspapers
un animal	an animal
des animaux	animals
un travail	a job
des travaux	jobs

For further explanation of grammatical terms, please see pages viii-xii.

> **Tip**
>
> The plural of **un œil** (*an eye*) is **des yeux** (*eyes*).

3 Plural versus singular

➤ A few words relating to clothing are plural in English but <u>NOT</u> in French.

<u>un</u> slip	panties
<u>un</u> short	shorts
<u>un</u> pantalon	pants

➤ A few common words are plural in French but <u>NOT</u> in English.

<u>les</u> affaires	business
<u>les</u> cheveux	hair
<u>des</u> renseignements	information

Grammar Extra!

When nouns are made up of two separate words, they are called <u>compound nouns</u>, for example, **les grands-parents** (meaning *grandparents*), **des ouvre-boîtes** (meaning *can openers*). The rules for forming the plural of compound nouns are complicated, and it is best to check in a dictionary to see what the plural is.

Key points

✔ Most French nouns form their plural by adding an **-s** to their singular form. If the singular noun ends in **-s**, **-x**, or **-z**, no further **-s** is added in the plural.

✔ Most nouns ending in **-eau** or **-eu** add an **-x** in the plural.

✔ Most nouns ending in **-ou** take an **-s** in the plural, with a few exceptions.

✔ If the singular noun ends in **-al** or **-ail**, the plural usually ends in **-aux**.

✔ Adding an **-s** or **-x** to the end of a noun does not generally affect the way the word is pronounced.

✔ A few common words are plural in English but not in French, and vice versa.

Articles

> **What is an article?**
> In English, an **article** is one of the words *the*, *a*, and *an* which is given in front of a noun.

Different types of articles

➤ There are three types of articles:

- the <u>definite</u> article: *the* in English. This is used to identify a particular thing or person.

  I'm going to <u>the</u> supermarket.
  That's <u>the</u> woman I was talking to.

- the <u>indefinite</u> article: *a* or *an* in English, *some* or *any* (or no word at all) in the plural. This is used to refer to something nonspecific, or that you do not really know about.

  Is there <u>a</u> supermarket near here?
  I need <u>a</u> day off.

- the <u>partitive</u> article: *some* or *any* (or no word at all) in English. This is used to talk about quantities or amounts.

  Can you lend me <u>some</u> sugar?
  Did you buy <u>any</u> wine?
  Do you like chocolate?

The definite article: le, la, l' and les

1 The basic rules

➤ In English we only have <u>one</u> definite article: *the*. In French, there is more than one definite article to choose from. All French nouns are either masculine or feminine and, just as in English, they can be either singular or plural. The word you choose for *the* depends on whether the noun it is used with is masculine or feminine, singular or plural. This may sound complicated, but it is not too difficult.

⟹ *For more information on **Nouns**, see page 1.*

	with masculine noun	with feminine noun
Singular	le (l')	la (l')
Plural	les	les

> *Tip*
>
> le and la change to l' when they are used in front of a word starting with a vowel and most words starting with h.

➤ le is used in front of <u>masculine singular nouns</u>.

<u>le</u> roi	the king
<u>le</u> chien	the dog
<u>le</u> jardin	the garden

➤ la is used in front of <u>feminine singular nouns</u>.

<u>la</u> reine	the queen
<u>la</u> souris	the mouse
<u>la</u> porte	the door

➤ l' is used in front of <u>singular nouns that start with a vowel</u> (*a*, *e*, *i*, *o*, or *u*), whether they are masculine or feminine.

<u>l'</u>ami (*masculine*)	the friend
<u>l'</u>eau (*feminine*)	the water
<u>l'</u>étage (*masculine*)	the floor

ⓘ Note that l' is also used in front of most words starting with h but some others take le or la instead.

<u>l'</u>hôpital	the hospital
<u>le</u> hamster	the hamster
<u>la</u> hi-fi	the stereo

> **Tip**
>
> It is a good idea to learn the <u>article</u> or the <u>gender</u> with the noun when you come across a word for the first time, so that you know whether it is masculine or feminine. A good dictionary will also give you this information.

➤ **les** is used in front of <u>plural nouns</u>, whether they are masculine or feminine and whatever letter they start with.

<u>les</u> chiens	the dogs
<u>les</u> portes	the doors
<u>les</u> amis	the friends
<u>les</u> hôtels	the hotels

i Note that you have to make the noun plural too, just as you would in English. In French, as in English, you usually add an **-s**.

⇨ *For more information on* **Forming plurals**, *see page* 9.

> **Tip**
>
> When **les** is used in front of a word that starts with a consonant, you DO NOT say the **s** on the end of **les**: **les chiens** *the dogs*.
>
> When **les** is used in front of a word that starts with a vowel, most words starting with **h**, and the French word **y**, you DO pronounce the **s** on the end of **les**. It sounds like the **z** in the English word *zipper*: **le<u>s</u> amis** *the friends*, **le<u>s</u> hôtels** *the hotels*.

2 **Using à with le, la, l', and les**

➤ The French word **à** is translated into English in several different ways, including *at* or *to*. There are special rules when you use it together with **le** and **les**.

⇨ *For more information on the preposition à, see page* 163.

➤ When **à** is followed by **le**, the two words become **au**.

<u>au</u> cinéma	to/at the movies
<u>aux</u> professeurs	to the teachers

➤ When à is followed by **les**, the two words become **aux**.

    aux maisons   to the houses
    aux étudiants   to the students

➤ When à is followed by **la** or **l'**, the words do not change.

    à la bibliothèque   to/at the library
    à l'hôtel   to/at the hotel

> *Tip*
>
> **le** and **la** change to **l'** when they are used in front of a word starting with a vowel and most words starting with **h**.

3 | Using **de** with **le, la, l', and les**

➤ The French word **de** is translated into English in several different ways, including *of* and *from*. There are special rules when you use it together with **le** and **les**.

⇨ *For more information on the preposition de, see page 166.*

➤ When **de** is followed by **le**, the two words become **du**.

    du cinéma   from/of the movies
    des professeurs   from/of the teachers

➤ When **de** is followed by **les**, the two words become **des**.

    des maisons   from/of the houses
    des étudiants   from/of the students

➤ When **de** is followed by **la** or **l'**, the words do not change.

    de la bibliothèque   from/of the library
    de l'hôtel   from/of the hotel

> *Tip*
>
> **le** and **la** change to **l'** when they are used in front of a word starting with a vowel and most words starting with **h**.

> ### Key points
> ✔ With masculine singular nouns → use **le**.
> ✔ With feminine singular nouns → use **la**.
> ✔ With nouns starting with a vowel, most nouns beginning with **h**, and the French word **y** → use **l'**.
> ✔ With plural nouns → use **les**.
> ✔ à + le = au
>   à + les = aux
>   de + le = du
>   de + les = des

4 Using the definite article

➤ The definite article in French (**le**, **la**, **l'**, and **les**) is used in more or less the same way as we use *the* in English, but it is also used in French in a few places where you might not expect it.

➤ The definite article is used with words like *prices*, *life* and *time* that describe qualities, ideas, or experiences (called <u>abstract nouns</u>) rather than something that you can touch with your hand. Usually, *the* is left out in English with this type of word.

<u>Les</u> prix montent.	Prices are rising.
<u>La</u> vie est courte.	Life is short.
Je n'ai pas <u>le</u> temps.	I don't have time.

ⓘ Note that there are some set phrases using **avoir**, **avec**, or **sans** followed by a noun, where the definite article is <u>NOT</u> used.

avoir faim	to be hungry (*literally: to have hunger*)
avec plaisir	with pleasure
sans doute	probably (*literally: without doubt*)

➤ You also use the definite article when you are talking about things like *coffee* or *computers* that you can touch with your hand (called <u>concrete nouns</u>) if you are talking generally about that thing. Usually, *the* is left out in English with this type of word.

Je n'aime pas <u>le</u> café.	I don't like coffee.
<u>Les</u> ordinateurs coûtent très cher.	Computers are very expensive.
<u>Les</u> professeurs ne gagnent pas beaucoup.	Teachers don't earn very much.

➤ If you are talking about a part of your body, you usually use a word like *my* or *his* in English, but in French you usually use the definite article.

Tourne <u>la</u> tête à gauche.	Turn your head to the left.
Il s'est cassé <u>le</u> bras.	He broke his arm.
J'ai mal à <u>la</u> gorge.	I have a sore throat.

➤ In French you have to use the definite article in front of the names of countries, continents and regions.

<u>la</u> Bretagne	Brittany
<u>l'</u>Europe	Europe
<u>La</u> France est très belle.	France is very beautiful.
J'ai acheté ce poster <u>au</u> Japon.	I bought this poster in Japan.
Je viens <u>des</u> États-Unis.	I come from the United States.

[*i*] Note that if the name of the country comes after the French word **en**, meaning *to* or *in*, you do not use the definite article. **en** is used with the names of countries, continents and regions that are feminine in French.

Je vais <u>en Écosse</u> le mois prochain.	I'm going to Scotland next month.
Il travaille <u>en Allemagne</u>.	He works in Germany.

⇨ *For more information on the preposition en, see page 168.*

➤ You often use the definite article with the name of school subjects, languages, and sports.

Tu aimes <u>les</u> maths ?	Do you like math?
J'apprends <u>le</u> français depuis trois ans.	I've been learning French for three years.
Mon sport préféré, c'est <u>le</u> foot.	My favorite sport is soccer.

[*i*] Note that the definite article is not used after **en**.

Comment est-ce qu'on dit "fils" <u>en anglais</u> ?	How do you say 'fils' in English?
Sophie est nulle <u>en chimie</u>.	Sophie's not any good at Chemistry.

➤ When you use the verb **parler** (meaning *to speak*) in front of the name of the language, you do not always need to use the definite article in French.

Tu parles espagnol ?	Do you speak Spanish?
Il parle bien <u>l'</u>anglais.	He speaks English well.

➤ You use **le** with dates, and also with the names of the days of the week and the seasons when you are talking about something that you do regularly or that is a habit.

Elle part le 7 mai.	She's leaving on May seventh.
Je vais chez ma grand-mère le dimanche.	I go to my grandmother's on Sundays.

i Note that you do not use the definite article after **en**.

En hiver nous faisons du ski.	In the winter we go skiing.

➤ You often find the definite article in phrases that tell you about prices and rates.

6 euros le kilo	6 euros a kilo
3 euros la pièce	3 euros each
On roulait à 100 kilomètres à l'heure.	We were doing 100 kilometers an hour.

Key points

✔ The definite article is used in French with:
- abstract nouns
- concrete nouns (*when you are saying something that is true about a thing in general*)
- parts of the body
- countries, continents, and regions
- school subjects, languages, and sports
- dates
- days of the week and the seasons (*when you are talking about something that you do regularly or that is a habit*)
- prices and rates

The indefinite article: un, une and des

1 The basic rules

➤ In English, we have the indefinite article *a*, which changes to *an* in front of a word that starts with a vowel. In the plural we say either *some*, *any*, or nothing at all.

➤ In French, you choose from **un**, **une**, and **des**, depending on whether the noun is masculine or feminine, and singular or plural.

	with masculine noun	with feminine noun
Singular	un	une
Plural	des	des

➤ **un** is used in front of <u>masculine singular nouns</u>.

un roi	a king
un chien	a dog
un jardin	a garden

➤ **une** is used in front of <u>feminine singular nouns</u>.

une reine	a queen
une souris	a mouse
une porte	a door

➤ **des** is used in front of <u>plural nouns</u>, whether they are masculine or feminine, and whatever letter they start with.

des chiens	(some/any) dogs
des souris	(some/any) mice
des amis	(some/any) friends

i Note that **des** is also a combination of **de + les** and has other meanings, such as saying who something belongs to or where something is from.

➪ *For more information on **des**, see page 166.*

> ## Tip
>
> When **des** is used in front of a word that starts with a consonant (any letter except *a*, *e*, *i*, *o*, or *u*), you DO NOT say the **s** on the end of **des**: **des chiens** *(some/any) dogs*.
>
> When **des** is used in front of a word that starts with a vowel, and most words starting with **h**, you DO pronounce the **s** on the end.
> It sounds like the **z** in the English word *zipper*: **des amis** *(some/any) friends*, **des hôtels** *(some/any) hotels*.

2 The indefinite article in negative sentences

➤ In English we use words like *not* and *never* to indicate that something is not happening or is not true. The sentences that these words are used in are called <u>negative</u> sentences.

> I <u>don't</u> know him.
> I <u>never</u> do my homework on time.

➤ In French, you use word pairs like **ne ... pas** (meaning *not*) and **ne ... jamais** (meaning *never*) to say that something is not happening or not true. When **un**, **une**, or **des** is used after this type of expression, it has to be changed to **de**.

> Je <u>n</u>'ai <u>pas</u> <u>de</u> vélo.   I don't have a bike.
> Nous <u>n</u>'avons <u>pas</u> <u>de</u> cousins.   We don't have any cousins.

⇨ *For more information on **Negatives**, see page 138.*

Tip

de changes to **d'** in front of a word starting with a vowel and most words starting with **h**.

> Je n'ai pas <u>d</u>'ordinateur.   I don't have a computer.
> Il n'y a pas <u>d</u>'horloge dans la salle.   There isn't a clock in the room.

Grammar Extra!

There are some very common adjectives, like **beau**, **bon**, and **petit**, that can come <u>BEFORE</u> the noun instead of after it. When an adjective comes before a plural noun, **des** changes to **de**.

> J'ai reçu <u>de</u> beaux cadeaux.   I got some beautiful presents.
> Cette région a <u>de</u> très jolis   This area has some very pretty
> villages.   villages.

⇨ *For more information on **Word order with adjectives**, see page 32.*

---

3 The meaning of <u>des</u>

➤ **des** can mean different things in English, depending on the sentence. *Some* is often the best word to use.

> J'ai un chien, deux chats et   I have a dog, two cats, and
> <u>des</u> souris.   <u>some</u> mice.
> Tu veux <u>des</u> chips ?   Would you like <u>some</u> chips?

For further explanation of grammatical terms, please see pages viii-xii.

➤ In questions and negative sentences **des** means *any*, or is not translated at all.

Tu as <u>des</u> frères ?	Do you have <u>any</u> brothers?
Il n'y a pas <u>d'</u>œufs.	There aren't <u>any</u> eggs.
Avez-vous <u>des</u> timbres ?	Do you have stamps?

Tip

As an English speaker, you will know what sounds right in your own language. The important thing to remember is that **des** can <u>NEVER</u> be left out in French, even if there is no word in English.

---

4 Using the indefinite article

➤ The indefinite article is used in French in much the same way as we use *a*, *some*, and *any* in English, but there are two places where the indefinite article is <u>NOT</u> used:

- with the adjective **quel** (meaning *what a*), in sentences like

Quel dommage !	What <u>a</u> shame!
Quelle surprise !	What <u>a</u> surprise!
Quelle bonne idée !	What <u>a</u> good idea!

⇨ *For more information on* **quel**, *see page 148.*

- when you say what jobs people do

Il est professeur.	He's <u>a</u> teacher.
Ma mère est infirmière.	My mother's <u>a</u> nurse.

Tip

When you use **c'est** (to mean *he/she is*), you <u>DO</u> use **un** or **une**. When you use **ce sont** (to mean *they are*), you <u>DO</u> use **des**.

C'est <u>un</u> médecin.	He's/She's a doctor.
Ce sont <u>des</u> acteurs.	They're actors.

⇨ *For more information on* **c'est** *and* **ce sont**, *see page 65.*

Key points

✔ With masculine singular nouns → use **un**.
✔ With feminine singular nouns → use **une**.
✔ With plural nouns → use **des**.
✔ **un**, **une**, and **des** → change to **de** or **d'** in negative sentences.
✔ The indefinite article is not usually used when you say what jobs people do, or in exclamations with **quel**.

The partitive articles: du, de la, de l', and des

1 The basic rules

➤ du, de la, de l', and des can all be used to give information about the amount or quantity of a particular thing. They are often translated into English as *some* or *any*.

➤ In French, you choose between du, de la, de l', and des, depending on whether the noun is masculine or feminine, singular or plural.

	with masculine noun	with feminine noun
Singular	du (de l')	de la (de l')
Plural	des	des

> *Tip*
>
> de + le and de la change to de l' when they are used in front of a word starting with a vowel, most words starting with h, and the French word y.

➤ du is used in front of <u>masculine singular nouns</u>.

| <u>du</u> beurre | (some/any) butter |
| <u>du</u> jus d'orange | (some/any) orange juice |

i Note that du is also a combination of de + le and has other meanings, such as saying who something belongs to or where something is from.

⇨ *For more information on du, see page 166.*

➤ de la is used in front of <u>feminine singular nouns</u>.

| <u>de la</u> viande | (some/any) meat |
| <u>de la</u> margarine | (some/any) margarine |

➤ de l' is used in front of <u>singular nouns that start with a vowel</u> and most nouns starting with h, whether they are masculine or feminine.

<u>de l'</u>argent (*masculine*)	(some/any) money
<u>de l'</u>eau (*feminine*)	(some/any) water
<u>de l'</u>herbe (*feminine*)	(some/any) grass

➤ **des** is used in front of <u>plural nouns</u>, whether they are masculine or feminine and whatever letter they start with.

<u>des</u> gâteaux	(some/any) cakes
<u>des</u> lettres	(some/any) letters
<u>des</u> hôtels	(some/any) hotels

i Note that **des** is also a combination of **de + les** and has other meanings, such as saying who something belongs to or where something is from.

⮕ *For more information on des, see page 166.*

2 The partitive article in negative sentences

➤ In French, you use word pairs like **ne ... pas** (meaning *not*) and **ne ... jamais** (meaning *never*) to say that something is not happening or not true. In this type of expression, **du, de la, de l'**, and **des** all change to **de**.

Nous n'avons pas de beurre.	We don't have any butter.
Je ne mange jamais de viande.	I never eat meat.
Il n'y a pas de timbres.	There aren't any stamps.

⮕ *For more information on **Negatives**, see page 138.*

> ### Tip
> **de** changes to **d'** in front of a word starting with a vowel and most nouns starting with **h**.
>
> | | |
> |---|---|
> | Il n'a pas <u>d'</u>argent. | He doesn't have any money. |
> | Il n'y a pas <u>d'</u>horloge dans la salle. | There isn't a clock in the room. |

Grammar Extra!

There are some very common adjectives, like **beau, bon**, and **petit**, that can come <u>BEFORE</u> the noun instead of after it. When an adjective comes before a plural noun, **des** changes to **de**.

J'ai reçu de beaux cadeaux.	I got some beautiful presents.
Cette région a de très jolis villages.	This area has some very pretty villages.

⮕ *For more information on **Word order with adjectives**, see page 32.*

3 The meaning of du, de la, de l', and des

➤ du, de la, de l', and des are often translated into English as *some* or *any*, but there are times when no word is used in English to translate the French.

Il me doit de l'argent.	He owes me (some) money.
Je vais acheter de la farine et du beurre pour faire un gâteau.	I'm going to buy (some) flour and butter to make a cake.
Est-ce qu'il y a des lettres pour moi ?	Are there any letters for me?
Elle ne veut pas de beurre.	She doesn't want any butter.
Je ne prends pas de lait.	I don't take milk.

Tip

Remember that du, de la, de l', and des can <u>NEVER</u> be left out in French, even if there is no word in English.

Key points

✔ With masculine singular nouns → use du.

✔ With feminine singular nouns → use de la.

✔ With singular nouns starting with a vowel and some nouns beginning with h → use de l'.

✔ With plural nouns → use des.

✔ du, de la, de l', and des → change to de or d' in negative sentences.

Adjectives

> **What is an adjective?**
> An **adjective** is a "describing" word that tells you more about a person or thing, such as their appearance, color, size, or other qualities, for example, *pretty*, *blue*, *big*.

Using adjectives

➤ Adjectives are words like *clever*, *expensive*, and *silly* that tell you more about a noun (a living being, thing, or idea). They can also tell you more about a pronoun, such as *he* or *they*. Adjectives are sometimes called "describing words." They can be used right next to a noun they are describing, or can be separated from the noun by a verb like *be*, *look*, *feel* and so on.

>   a clever girl
>   an expensive coat
>   a silly idea
>   He's just being silly.

⇨   *For more information on **Nouns** and **Pronouns**, see pages 1 and 42.*

➤ In English, the only time an adjective changes its form is when you are making a comparison.

>   She's cleverer than her brother.
>   That's the silliest idea I ever heard!

➤ In French, however, most adjectives agree with what they are describing. This means that their endings change depending on whether the person or thing you are referring to is masculine or feminine, and singular or plural.

un mot français	a French word
une chanson française	a French song
des traditions françaises	French traditions

➤ In English we put adjectives <u>BEFORE</u> the noun they describe, but in French you usually put them <u>AFTER</u> it.

      un chat <u>noir</u>   a <u>black</u> cat

⇨ *For further information, see **Word order with adjectives** on page 32.*

> ### Key points
> ✔ Most French adjectives change their form according to whether the person or thing they are describing is masculine or feminine, singular or plural.
> ✔ In French, adjectives usually go after the noun they describe.

Making adjectives agree

1 The basic rules

➤ In dictionaries, regular French adjectives are usually shown in the masculine singular form. You need to know how to change them to make them agree with the noun or pronoun that they are describing.

➤ To make an adjective agree with the noun or pronoun it describes, you simply add the following endings in most cases:

	with masculine noun	with feminine noun
Singular	-	-e
Plural	-s	-es

un chat <u>noir</u>	a black cat
une chemise <u>noire</u>	a black shirt
des chats <u>noirs</u>	black cats
des chemises <u>noires</u>	black shirts

2 Making adjectives feminine

➤ With most adjectives you add an -e to the masculine singular form to make it feminine.

un chat noir a black cat → une chemise noir<u>e</u> a black shirt
un sac lourd a heavy bag → une valise lourd<u>e</u> a heavy suitcase

➤ If the adjective already ends in an -e in the masculine, you do not add another -e.

un sac jaune a yellow bag → une chemise jaune a yellow shirt
un garçon sage a good boy → une fille sage a good girl

➤ Some changes to endings are a little more complicated but still follow a regular pattern. Sometimes you have to double the consonant as well as add an -e. On the next page there is a table showing these changes.

Masculine ending	Feminine ending	Example	Meaning
-f	-ve	neuf/neuve	new
-x	-se	heureux/heureuse	happy
-er	-ère	cher/chère	dear, expensive
-an	-anne	paysan/paysanne	farming, country
-en	-enne	européen/européenne	European
-on	-onne	bon/bonne	good, right
-el	-elle	cruel/cruelle	cruel
-eil	-eille	pareil/pareille	similar
-et	-ette	net/nette	clear
	-ète	complet/complète	complete, full

un **bon** repas a good meal → de **bonne** humeur in a good mood

un homme **cruel** a cruel man → une remarque **cruelle** a cruel remark

Tip

If a masculine adjective ends in a vowel (*a*, *e*, *i*, *o*, or *u*), its pronunciation does not change when an -**e** is added to form the feminine. For example, **joli** and **jolie** are both pronounced the same.

If a masculine adjective ends with a consonant that is not pronounced, such as -**d**, -**s**, or -**t**, you DO pronounce that consonant when an -**e** is added in the feminine. For example, in **chaud** (meaning *hot*, *warm*), you cannot hear the **d** when it is said out loud; in the feminine form **chaude**, you can hear the **d** sound.

This is also true when you have to double the consonant before the -**e** is added, for example, **gros** (meaning *big*, *fat*), where you cannot hear the **s**, and the feminine form **grosse**, where you can hear the **s** sound.

Some masculine adjectives, such as **bon** (meaning *good*) or **italien** (meaning *Italian*), end in what is called a nasal vowel and an -**n**. With these words, you pronounce the vowel "through your nose" but do not say the **n**. When the consonant is doubled and an -**e** is added in the feminine – **bonne**, **italienne** – the vowel becomes a normal one instead of a nasal vowel and you do pronounce the **n**.

Adjectives 29

➤ Some very common adjectives have irregular feminine forms.

Masculine form	Feminine form	Meaning
blanc	blanche	white, blank
doux	douce	soft, sweet, mild, gentle
faux	fausse	untrue
favori	favorite	favorite
frais	fraîche	fresh, chilly, cool
gentil	gentille	nice, kind
grec	grecque	Greek
gros	grosse	big, fat
long	longue	long
nul	nulle	useless
roux	rousse	red, red-haired
sec	sèche	dry, dried
turc	turque	Turkish

mon sport <u>favori</u> my favorite sport → ma chanson <u>favorite</u> my favorite song

un ami <u>grec</u> a Greek (male) friend → une amie <u>grecque</u> a Greek (female) friend

➤ A very small group of French adjectives have an <u>extra</u> masculine singular form that is used in front of words that begin with a vowel (*a, e, i, o,* or *u*) and most words beginning with h. These adjectives also have an irregular feminine form.

Masculine form in front of a word beginning with a consonant	Masculine form in front of a word beginning with a vowel or most words beginning with h	Feminine form	Meaning
beau	bel	belle	lovely, beautiful, good-looking, handsome
fou	fol	folle	crazy
nouveau	nouvel	nouvelle	new
vieux	vieil	vieille	old

un <u>bel</u> appartement   a beautiful apartment
le <u>Nouvel</u> An   New Year's
un <u>vieil</u> arbre   an old tree

3 Making adjectives plural

➤ With most adjectives you add an -s to the masculine singular or feminine singular form to make it plural.

un chat noir a black cat → **des chats noirs** black cats

une valise lourde a heavy suitcase → **des valises lourdes** heavy suitcases

> ### Tip
> When an adjective describes a masculine and a feminine noun or pronoun, use the masculine plural form of the adjective.
>
> | | |
> |---|---|
> | **La maison et le jardin sont beaux.** | The house and garden are beautiful. |
> | **Sophie et son petit ami sont très gentils.** | Sophie and her boyfriend are very nice. |

➤ If the masculine singular form already ends in an -s or an -x, you do not add an -s.

un fromage français a French cheese → **des fromages français** French cheeses

un homme dangereux a dangerous man → **des hommes dangereux** dangerous men

➤ If the masculine singular form ends in -eau or -al, the masculine plural is usually -eaux or -aux.

le nouveau professeur the new teacher → **les nouveaux professeurs** the new teachers

le rôle principal the main role → **les rôles principaux** the main roles

> ### Tip
> Adding an -s or an -x does not change the pronunciation of a word. For example, **noir** and **noirs** sound just the same, as do **nouveau** and **nouveaux**.
>
> When the -s or -x ending comes before a word starting with a vowel or most words starting with h, you have to pronounce the s or x on the end of the adjective. It sounds like the z in the English word zipper.
>
> | | |
> |---|---|
> | **les anciens élèves** | the former students |
> | **de grands hôtels** | big hotels |

4 Invariable adjectives

➤ A small number of adjectives (mostly relating to colors) do not change in the feminine or plural. They are called <u>invariable</u> because their form <u>NEVER</u> changes, no matter what they are describing. These adjectives are often made up of more than one word – for example, **bleu marine** (meaning *navy blue*), or else come from the names of fruit or nuts – for example, **orange** (meaning *orange*), **marron** (meaning *brown*).

des chaussures <u>marron</u>	brown shoes
une veste <u>bleu marine</u>	a navy blue jacket

Key points

✔ To make an adjective agree with a feminine singular noun or pronoun, you usually add -e to the masculine singular. If the adjective already ends in an -e, no further -e is added.

✔ Several adjectives ending in a consonant double their consonant as well as adding -e in the feminine.

✔ beau, fou, nouveau, and vieux have an irregular feminine form and an extra masculine singular form that is used in front of words that begin with a vowel and most words beginning with h: bel, fol, nouvel, vieil.

✔ To make an adjective agree with a masculine plural noun or pronoun, you usually add -s to the masculine singular. If the adjective already ends in an -s or an -x, no further -s is added.

✔ If the adjective ends in -eau or -al, the masculine plural is usually -eaux or -aux.

✔ To make an adjective agree with a feminine plural noun or pronoun, you usually add -es to the masculine singular.

✔ Some adjectives relating to colors never change their form.

Word order with adjectives

1 The basic rules

➤ When adjectives are used right beside the noun they are describing, they
go <u>BEFORE</u> it in English. French adjectives usually go <u>AFTER</u> the noun.

| l'heure <u>exacte</u> | the <u>correct</u> time |
| la page <u>suivante</u> | the <u>following</u> page |

➤ Adjectives describing colors, shapes, or nationalities always go <u>AFTER</u>
the noun.

des cravates <u>rouges</u>	red ties
une table <u>ronde</u>	a round table
un mot <u>français</u>	a French word

➤ Some very common adjectives usually come <u>BEFORE</u> the noun.

beau	lovely, beautiful, good-looking, handsome
bon	good, right
court	short
grand	tall, big, long, great
gros	big, fat
haut	high
jeune	young
joli	pretty
long	long
mauvais	bad, poor
meilleur	better
nouveau	new
petit	small, little
premier	first
vieux	old
une belle journée	a lovely day
Bonne chance !	Good luck!

➤ There is a small group of common adjectives whose meaning changes
depending on whether they come before the noun or go after it.

Adjective	Example before noun	Meaning	Example after noun	Meaning
ancien	un ancien collègue	a <u>former</u> colleague	un fauteuil ancien	an <u>antique</u> chair
cher	Chère Julie	<u>Dear</u> Julie	une robe chère	an <u>expensive</u> dress
propre	ma propre chambre	my <u>own</u> bedroom	un mouchoir propre	a <u>clean</u> handkerchief

For further explanation of grammatical terms, please see pages viii-xii.

Tip

dernier (meaning *last*) and prochain (meaning *next*) go <u>AFTER</u> nouns relating to time, for example, semaine (meaning *week*) and mois (meaning *month*). Otherwise they go <u>BEFORE</u> the noun.

la semaine <u>dernière</u>	last week
la <u>dernière</u> fois que je t'ai vu	the last time I saw you
la semaine <u>prochaine</u>	next week
la <u>prochaine</u> fois que j'y vais	the next time I go there

Grammar Extra!

When certain adjectives are used with certain nouns, they take on a meaning you cannot always guess. You may need to look these up in your dictionary and learn them. Here are a few:

mon petit ami	my boyfriend
les petits pois	peas
les grandes vacances	summer vacation
une grande personne	an adult, a grown-up

2 Using more than one adjective

➤ In French you can use more than one adjective at a time to describe someone or something. If one of the adjectives usually comes <u>BEFORE</u> the noun and the other usually goes <u>AFTER</u> the noun, the word order follows the usual pattern.

une <u>jeune</u> femme <u>blonde</u>	a young blonde woman
un <u>nouveau</u> film <u>intéressant</u>	an interesting new movie

➤ If both adjectives usually come <u>AFTER</u> the noun, they are joined together with et (meaning *and*).

un homme mince <u>et</u> laid	a thin, ugly man
une personne intelligente <u>et</u> drôle	an intelligent, funny person

Key points

✔ Most French adjectives go after the noun they describe.
✔ Some very common adjectives usually come before the noun: bon/mauvais, court/long, grand/petit, jeune/nouveau/vieux, gros, haut, beau, joli, premier, meilleur.
✔ The meaning of some adjectives such as ancien, cher, and propre varies according to the position in the sentence.

Comparatives and superlatives of adjectives

1 Making comparisons using comparative adjectives

> **What is a comparative adjective?**
> A **comparative adjective** in English is one with *-er* on the end of it or *more* or *less* in front of it, that is used to compare people or things, for example, *slower*, *less important*, *more beautiful*.

➤ In French, to say that something is *easier*, *more expensive* and so on, you use **plus** (meaning *more*) before the adjective.

Cette question est <u>plus</u> facile.	This question is easier.
Cette veste est <u>plus</u> chère.	This jacket is more expensive.

➤ To say something is *less expensive*, *less complicated* and so on, you use **moins** (meaning *less*) before the adjective.

Cette veste est <u>moins</u> chère.	This jacket is less expensive.
un projet <u>moins</u> compliqué	a less complicated plan

➤ To introduce the person or thing you are making the comparison with, use **que** (meaning *than*).

Elle est plus petite <u>que</u> moi.	She's smaller than me.
Cette question est plus facile <u>que</u> la première.	This question is easier than the first one.

➤ To say that something or someone is *as ... as* something or someone else, use **aussi ... que**.

Il est <u>aussi</u> inquiet <u>que</u> moi.	He's as worried as me.
Cette ville n'est pas <u>aussi</u> grande <u>que</u> Bordeaux.	This town isn't as big as Bordeaux.

2 Making comparisons using superlative adjectives

> **What is a superlative adjective?**
> A **superlative adjective** in English is one with *-est* on the end of it or *most* or *least* in front of it, that is used to compare people or things, for example, *thinnest*, *most beautiful*, *least interesting*.

➤ In French, to say that something or someone is *easiest*, *prettiest*, *most expensive* and so on, you use:

- **le plus** with <u>masculine singular</u> adjectives

For further explanation of grammatical terms, please see pages viii-xii.

- la plus with <u>feminine singular</u> adjectives
- les plus with <u>plural</u> adjectives (for both masculine and feminine)

le guide <u>le plus</u> utile	the <u>most</u> useful guidebook
la question <u>la plus</u> facile	the easi<u>est</u> question
<u>les plus</u> grands hôtels	the bigg<u>est</u> hotels
<u>les plus</u> petites voitures	the small<u>est</u> cars

➤ To say that something or someone is *the least easy, the least pretty, the least expensive* and so on, you use:

- le moins with <u>masculine singular</u> adjectives
- la moins with <u>feminine singular</u> adjectives
- les moins with <u>plural</u> adjectives (for both masculine and feminine).

le guide <u>le moins</u> utile	the <u>least</u> useful guidebook
Cette question est <u>la moins</u> facile.	This question is the <u>least</u> easy (*or* the hard<u>est</u>).
les mois <u>les moins</u> agréables	the <u>least</u> pleasant months
<u>les moins</u> belles photos	the <u>least</u> attractive photos

> ## Tip
>
> When the adjective comes <u>AFTER</u> the noun, you repeat the definite article (le, la, or les).
>
> | | |
> |---|---|
> | les mois <u>les</u> moins agréables | the least pleasant months |
>
> When the adjective comes <u>BEFORE</u> the noun, you do not repeat the definite article.
>
> | | |
> |---|---|
> | les moins belles photos | the least attractive photos |
>
> ⇨ *For more information on **Word order with adjectives**, see page 32.*

➤ In phrases like *the biggest hotel in New York* and *the oldest person in the village*, you use de to translate *in*.

le plus grand hôtel <u>de</u> New York	the biggest hotel in New York
la personne la plus âgée <u>du</u> village	the oldest person in the village

⇨ *For more information on **de and du**, see page 166.*

3 Irregular comparative and superlative adjectives

➤ Just as English has some irregular comparative and superlative forms – *better* instead of "*more good*," and *worst* instead of "*most bad*" – French also has a few irregular forms.

36 Adjectives

Adjective	Meaning	Comparative	Meaning	Superlative	Meaning
bon	good	meilleur	better	le meilleur	the best
mauvais	bad	pire plus mauvais	worse	le pire le plus mauvais	the worst
petit	small	moindre plus petit	smaller, lesser	le moindre le plus petit	the smallest, the least, the slightest

J'ai une <u>meilleure</u> idée.   I have a <u>better</u> idea.

Il ne fait pas <u>le moindre</u> effort.   He doesn't make the <u>slightest</u> effort.

> ## Tip
> Choose the right form of the adjective to match the noun or pronoun, depending on whether it is masculine or feminine, singular or plural. Don't forget to change le to la or les too in superlatives.

Grammar Extra!

bien and its comparative and superlative forms mieux and le mieux can be both adjectives and adverbs.

> Il est <u>bien</u>, ce restaurant. (=adjective)   This restaurant is good.
> Elle va <u>mieux</u> aujourd'hui. (=adverb)   She's better today.

⇨ For more information on **Adverbs**, see page 152.

Key points
- ✔ To compare people or things in French you use plus + adjective, moins + adjective, or aussi ... que.
- ✔ *than* in comparatives corresponds to que.
- ✔ French superlatives are formed with le/la/les plus + adjective and le/la/les moins + adjective.
- ✔ *in* after superlatives corresponds to de.
- ✔ bon, mauvais and petit have irregular comparatives and superlatives: bon/meilleur/le meilleur, mauvais/pire/le pire, petit/moindre/le moindre.

Demonstrative adjectives ce, cette, cet, and ces

> **What is a demonstrative adjective?**
> A **demonstrative adjective** is one of the words *this*, *that*, *these*, and *those* used with a noun in English to point out a particular thing or person, for example, *this* woman, *that* dog.

➤ In French you use **ce** to point out a particular thing or person. Like all adjectives in French, **ce** changes its form depending on whether you are referring to a noun that is masculine or feminine, singular or plural.

	Masculine	Feminine	Meaning
Singular	ce (cet)	cette	this that
Plural	ces	ces	these those

Tip

cet is used in front of masculine singular nouns which begin with a vowel and most words beginning with **h**.

| cet oiseau | this/that bird |
| cet hôpital | this/that hospital |

➤ **ce** comes <u>BEFORE</u> the noun it refers to.

Combien coûte <u>ce</u> manteau ?	How much is this/that coat?
Comment s'appelle <u>cette</u> entreprise ?	What's this/that company called?
<u>Ces</u> livres sont très intéressants.	These/Those books are very interesting.
<u>Ces</u> couleurs sont jolies.	These/Those colors are pretty.

➤ If you want to emphasize the difference between something that is close to you and something that is farther away, you can add:

- -ci on the end of the noun for things that are closer
  Prends cette valise-<u>ci</u>.   Take this suitcase.

- -là on the end of the noun for things that are farther away

Est-ce que tu reconnais cette personne-**là** ?   Do you recognize that person?

Key points

✔ The adjective **ce** corresponds to *this* and *that* in the singular, and *these* and *those* in the plural.

✔ The forms are **ce** and **cette** in the singular, and **ces** in the plural. **cet** is used with masculine singular nouns beginning with a vowel and most words beginning with **h**.

✔ You can add -**ci** on the end of the noun for things that are closer, or -**là** for things that are farther away, to emphasize the difference between them.

Possessive adjectives

> **What is a possessive adjective?**
> In English a **possessive adjective** is one of the words *my, your, his, her, its, our,* or *their* used with a noun to show that one person or thing belongs to another.

➤ Here are the French possessive adjectives. Like all French adjectives, these agree with the noun they refer to.

with masculine singular noun	with feminine singular noun	with plural noun (masculine or feminine)	Meaning
mon	ma (mon)	mes	my
ton	ta (ton)	tes	your
son	sa (son)	ses	his her its one's
notre	notre	nos	our
votre	votre	vos	your
leur	leur	leurs	their

Tip

You use **mon, ton,** and **son** with feminine singular nouns in front of words that begin with a vowel and most words beginning with h. This makes them easier to say.

<u>mon</u> assiette	my plate
<u>ton</u> histoire	your story
<u>son</u> erreur	his/her mistake
<u>mon</u> autre sœur	my other sister

➤ Possessive adjectives come <u>BEFORE</u> the noun they describe.

Voilà <u>mon</u> mari.	There's my husband.
<u>Mon</u> frère et <u>ma</u> sœur habitent à Philadelphie.	My brother and sister live in Philadelphia.
Est-ce que <u>tes</u> voisins vendent <u>leur</u> maison ?	Are your neighbors selling their house?
Rangez <u>vos</u> affaires.	Put your things away.

> *Tip*
>
> Possessive adjectives agree with what they describe, <u>NOT</u> with the person who owns that thing. For example, sa can mean *his, her, its,* and *one's,* but can only ever be used with a feminine singular noun.
>
> | | |
> |---|---|
> | Paul cherche <u>sa</u> montre. | Paul's looking for <u>his</u> watch. |
> | Paul cherche <u>ses</u> lunettes. | Paul's looking for <u>his</u> glasses. |
> | Catherine a appelé <u>son</u> frère. | Catherine called <u>her</u> brother. |
> | Catherine a appelé <u>sa</u> sœur. | Catherine called <u>her</u> sister. |

➤ The equivalent of *your* in French is ton/ta/tes for someone you call tu, or votre/vos for someone you call vous.

⇨ *For more information on the difference between tu and vous, see page 43.*

ⓘ Note that possessive adjectives are <u>not</u> normally used with parts of the body. Use le, la, l', or les instead.

> J'ai mal <u>à la main</u>.   My hand hurts.

⇨ *For more information on **Articles**, see page 12.*

> **Key points**
> ✔ The French possessive adjectives are:
> - mon/ton/son/notre/votre/leur in the masculine singular
> - ma/ta/sa/notre/votre/leur in the feminine singular
> - mes/tes/ses/nos/vos/leurs in the plural
>
> ✔ Possessive adjectives come before the noun they refer to. They agree with what they describe, rather than with the person who owns that thing.
>
> ✔ You use mon, ton, and son with feminine singular nouns when the following word begins with a vowel. You also use them with most words beginning with h.
>
> ✔ Possessive adjectives are not normally used with parts of the body. Use le, la, l', or les instead.

Indefinite adjectives

> **What is an indefinite adjective?**
> An **indefinite adjective** is one of a small group of adjectives that are used to talk about people or things in a general way without saying exactly who or what they are, for example, *several*, *all*, *every*.

➤ In French, this type of adjective comes <u>BEFORE</u> the noun it refers to. Here are the most common French indefinite adjectives:

Masculine singular	Feminine singular	Masculine plural	Feminine plural	Meaning
autre	autre	autres	autres	other
chaque	chaque	-	-	every, each
même	même	mêmes	mêmes	same
-	-	quelques	quelques	some, a few
tout	toute	tous	toutes	all, every

J'ai d'<u>autres</u> projets.	I have other plans.
J'y vais <u>chaque</u> année.	I go every year.
J'ai le <u>même</u> manteau.	I have the same coat.
Il a <u>quelques</u> amis à Paris.	He has some friends in Paris.
Il reste <u>quelques</u> bouteilles.	There are a few bottles left.
Il travaille <u>tout</u> le temps.	He works all the time.

> *Tip*
> You can also use **tout** to talk about how often something happens.
>
> | | |
> |---|---|
> | **tous les jours** | every day |
> | **tous les deux jours** | every other day |

i Note that these words can also be used as <u>pronouns</u>, standing in place of a noun instead of being used with one. **chaque** and **quelques** have a slightly different form when they are used in this way.

⇨ *For more information on **Pronouns**, see page 42.*

> **Key points**
> ✔ The most common French indefinite adjectives are **autre**, **chaque**, **même**, **quelques**, and **tout**.
> ✔ They come before the noun when they are used in this way.

Pronouns

What is a pronoun?
A **pronoun** is a word you use instead of a noun when you do not need or want to name someone or something directly, for example, *it*, *you*, *none*.

➤ There are several different types of pronouns:

- <u>Personal pronouns</u> such as *I*, *you*, *he*, *her*, and *they*, which are used to refer to yourself, the person you are talking to, or other people and things. They can be either <u>subject pronouns</u> (*I*, *you*, *he* and so on) or <u>object pronouns</u> (*him*, *her*, *them* and so on).

- <u>Possessive pronouns</u> like *mine* and *yours*, which show who someone or something belongs to.

- <u>Indefinite pronouns</u> like *someone* or *nothing*, which refer to people or things in a general way without saying exactly who or what they are.

- <u>Relative pronouns</u> like *who*, *which*, or *that*, which link two parts of a sentence together.

- <u>Demonstrative pronouns</u> like *this* or *those*, which point things or people out.

- <u>Reflexive pronouns</u>, a type of object pronoun that forms part of French reflexive verbs like **se laver** (meaning *to wash*) or **s'appeler** (meaning *to be called*).

⇨ *For more information on **Reflexive verbs**, see page 88.*

- The two French pronouns, **en** and **y**, which are used in certain constructions.

- The pronouns **qui ?** (meaning *who?*, *whom?*), **que ?** (meaning *what?*), **quoi ?** (meaning *what?*) and **lequel ?** (meaning *which one?*), which are used when asking questions.

⇨ *For more information on **Questions**, see page 142.*

➤ Pronouns often stand in for a noun to avoid repeating it.
> I finished my homework and gave <u>it</u> to my teacher.
> Do you remember Jack? I saw <u>him</u> over the weekend.

➤ Word order with personal pronouns is usually different in French and English.

For further explanation of grammatical terms, please see pages viii-xii.

Personal pronouns: Subject

> **What is a subject pronoun?**
> A **subject pronoun** is a word such as *I*, *he*, *she*, and *they*, which performs the action expressed by the verb. Pronouns stand in for nouns when it is clear who is being talked about, for example, *My brother isn't here at the moment. He'll be back in an hour.*

1 Using subject pronouns

➤ Here are the French subject pronouns:

Singular	Meaning	Plural	Meaning
je (j')	I	nous	we
tu	you	vous	you
il	he it	ils	they (*masculine*)
elle	she it	elles	they (*feminine*)
on	one (we/you/they)		

Je pars en vacances demain.   I'm going on vacation tomorrow.
Nous habitons à Nice.   We live in Nice.

> *Tip*
> je changes to **j'** in front of words beginning with a vowel, most words beginning with **h**, and the French word **y**.
> **J'arrive!**   I'm coming!
> **Bon, j'y vais.**   OK, I'm off.

2 tu or vous?

➤ In English we have only <u>one</u> way of saying *you*. In French, there are <u>two</u> words: **tu** and **vous**. The word you use depends on:

- whether you are talking to one person or more than one person
- whether you are talking to a friend or family member, or someone else

➤ If you are talking to one person you know well, such as a friend, a young person, or a relative, use **tu**.

Tu me prêtes ce CD ?   Will you lend me this CD?

➤ If you are talking to one person <u>you do not know very well</u>, such as your teacher, your boss, or a stranger, use **vous**.

> <u>Vous</u> pouvez entrer.   You may come in.

> *Tip*
> If you are not sure which form of *you* to use, it is safest to use **vous** so that you will not offend anybody.

➤ If you are talking to <u>more than one person</u>, you have to use **vous**, no matter how well you know them.

> <u>Vous</u> comprenez, les enfants ?   Do you understand, children?

[*i*] Note that the adjectives you use with **tu** and **vous** have to agree in the feminine and plural forms.

> Vous êtes <u>certain</u>, Monsieur   Are you sure, Mr. Leclerc?
> Leclerc ? (*masculine singular*)
>
> Vous êtes <u>certains</u>, les enfants ?   Are you sure, children?
> (*masculine plural*)

Grammar Extra!

Any past participles (the form of the verb ending in -é, -i, or -u in French) used with **être** in tenses such as the perfect also have to agree in the feminine and plural forms.

> Vous êtes <u>partie</u> quand, Estelle ?   When did you leave, Estelle?
> (*feminine singular*)
>
> Estelle et Sophie – vous êtes   Estelle and Sophie – when did you
> <u>parties</u> quand ? (*feminine plural*)   leave?

⇨ *For more information on the **Past participle**, see page 111.*

---

3 il/elle **and** ils/elles

➤ In English, we generally refer to things (such as *table, book, car*) only as *it*. In French, **il** (meaning *he, it*) and **elle** (meaning *she, it*) are used to talk about a thing, as well as about a person or an animal. You use **il** for <u>masculine nouns</u> and **elle** for <u>feminine nouns.</u>

> <u>Il</u> est déjà parti.   He's already left.
>
> <u>Elle</u> est actrice.   She's an actress.
>
> <u>Il</u> mord, ton chien ?   Does your dog bite?
>
> Prends cette chaise. <u>Elle</u> est   Take this chair. It's more
> plus confortable.   comfortable.

For further explanation of grammatical terms, please see pages viii-xii.

➤ **il** is also used to talk about the weather, the time, and in certain other set phrases, often in the same way as some phrases with *it* in English.

Il pleut.	It's raining.
Il est deux heures.	It's two o'clock.
Il faut partir.	We/You have to go.

➤ **ils** (meaning *they*) and **elles** (meaning *they*) are used in the plural to talk about things, as well as about people or animals. Use **ils** for <u>masculine nouns</u> and **elles** for <u>feminine nouns</u>.

Ils vont appeler ce soir.	They're going to call tonight.
"Où sont Anne et Rachel ?" – "**Elles** sont à la piscine."	"Where are Anne and Rachel?" – "They're at the swimming pool."
"Est-ce qu'il reste des billets ?" – "Non, **ils** sont tous vendus."	"Are there are any tickets left?" – "No, they're sold out."
"Tu aimes ces chaussures ?" – "Non, **elles** sont affreuses !"	"Do you like those shoes?" – "No, they're horrible!"

➤ If you are talking about a masculine and a feminine noun, use **ils**.

Que font <u>ton père et ta mère</u> quand <u>ils</u> partent en vacances ?	What do your father and mother do when they go on vacation?
"Où sont <u>le poivre et la moutarde</u> ?" – "<u>Ils</u> sont déjà sur la table."	"Where are the pepper and the mustard?" – "They're already on the table."

4 on

➤ **on** is frequently used in informal, everyday French to mean *we*.

On va à la plage demain.	We're going to the beach tomorrow.
On y va ?	Shall we go?

➤ **on** can also have the sense of *someone* or *they*.

On m'a volé mon porte-monnaie.	Someone has stolen my wallet.
On vous demande au téléphone.	There's a phone call for you.

> **Tip**
>
> **on** is often used to avoid a passive construction in French.
>
> On m'a dit que tu étais malade.   I was told you were sick.
>
> ⟹ *For more information on the **Passive**, see page 122.*

46 Pronouns

➤ You can also use **on** as we use *you* in English when we mean people in general.

On peut visiter le château en été.	You can visit the castle in the summer.
D'ici **on** peut voir les côtes françaises.	From here you can see the French coast.

Tip

The form of the verb you use with **on** is the same as the **il/elle** form.

⇨ *For more information on **Verbs**, see pages 69–137.*

Key points

✔ The French subject pronouns are: **je (j')**, **tu**, **il**, **elle**, **on** in the singular, and **nous**, **vous**, **ils**, **elles** in the plural.

✔ To say *you* in French, use **tu** if you are talking to one person you know well or to a young person. Use **vous** if you are talking to one person you do not know very well or to more than one person.

✔ **il/ils** (masculine singular/plural) and **elle/elles** (feminine singular/plural) are used to refer to things, as well as to people or animals. **il** is also used in certain set phrases.

✔ If there is a mixture of masculine and feminine nouns, use **ils**.

✔ **on** can mean *we*, *someone*, *you*, *they*, or people in general. It is often used instead of a passive construction.

Personal pronouns: Direct object

> **What is a direct object pronoun?**
> A **direct object pronoun** is a word such as *me*, *him*, *us*, and *them*, which is used instead of the noun to stand in for the person or thing most directly affected by the action expressed by the verb.

1 Using direct object pronouns

➤ Direct object pronouns stand in for nouns when it is clear who or what is being talked about, and avoid having to repeat the noun.

>   I lost my glasses. Have you seen <u>them</u>?
>   "Have you met Jo?" – "Yes, I really like <u>her</u>!"

➤ Here are the French direct object pronouns:

Singular	Meaning	Plural	Meaning
me (m')	me	nous	us
te (t')	you	vous	you
le (l')	him it	les	them (*masculine and feminine*)
la (l')	her it		

Ils vont <u>nous</u> aider.	They're going to help us.
Je <u>la</u> vois.	I can see her/it.
"Tu aimes les carottes ?" – "Non, je <u>les</u> déteste !"	"Do you like carrots?" – "No, I hate them!"

[i] Note that you cannot use direct object pronouns after a preposition like à or de, or when you want to emphasize something.

➪ *For more information on **Emphatic pronouns**, see page 51.*

Tip

me changes to m', te to t', and le/la to l' in front of words beginning with a vowel, most words beginning with h, and the French word y.

Je <u>t'</u>aime.	I love you.
Tu m'entends ?	Can you hear me?

➤ In orders and instructions telling someone to do something, **moi** is used instead of **me**, and **toi** is used instead of **te**.

> **Aidez-moi !** — Help me!
> **Assieds-toi.** — Sit down.

➤ **le** is sometimes used to refer back to an idea or information that has already been given. The word *it* is often left out in English.

> "**Ta chemise est très sale.**" – "Your shirt's very dirty." –
> "**Je le sais.**" – "I know."

2 Word order with direct object pronouns

➤ The direct object pronoun usually comes <u>BEFORE</u> the verb.

> **Je t'aime.** — I love you.
> **Les voyez-vous ?** — Can you see them?
> **Elle ne nous connaît pas.** — She doesn't know us.

i Note that in orders and instructions telling someone to do something, the direct object pronoun comes <u>AFTER</u> the verb.

> **Asseyez-vous.** — Sit down.

➤ In tenses like the perfect that are formed with **avoir** or **être** and the past participle (the part of the verb that ends in -**é**, -**i**, or -**u** in French), the direct object pronoun comes <u>BEFORE</u> the part of the verb that comes from **avoir** or **être**.

> **Il m'a vu.** — He saw me.

➤ When a verb like **vouloir** (meaning *to want*) or **pouvoir** (meaning *to be able to, can*) is followed by another verb in the infinitive (the "*to*" form of the verb), the direct object pronoun comes <u>BEFORE</u> the infinitive.

> **Il voudrait la revoir.** — He'd like to see her again.
> **Puis-je vous aider ?** — Can I help you?

> **Key points**
> ✔ The French direct object pronouns are: **me (m')**, **te (t')**, **le/la (l')** in the singular, and **nous**, **vous**, **les** in the plural.
> ✔ Except in orders and instructions telling someone to do something, the direct object pronoun comes before the verb.

Personal pronouns: Indirect object

What is an indirect object pronoun?
When a verb has two objects (a <u>direct</u> one and an <u>indirect</u> one), the **indirect object pronoun** is used instead of a noun to show the person or thing the action is intended to benefit or harm, for example, *me* in *He gave <u>me</u> a book.; Can you get <u>me</u> a towel?*

1 Using indirect object pronouns

➤ It is important to understand the difference between direct and indirect object pronouns in English, as they can have different forms in French:

- an <u>indirect object</u> answers the question *who to/for?* or *to/for what?*

  He gave me a book. → *Who did he give the book to?* → me (=*indirect object pronoun*)

  Can you get me a towel? → *Who can you get a towel for?* → me (=*indirect object pronoun*)

- if something answers the question *what* or *who*, then it is the <u>direct object</u> and <u>NOT</u> the indirect object

  He gave me a book. → *What did he give me?* → a book (=*direct object*)

  Can you get me a towel? → *What can you get me?* → a towel (=*direct object*)

➤ Here are the French indirect object pronouns:

Singular	Meaning	Plural	Meaning
me (m')	me, to me, for me	nous	us, to us, for us
te (t')	you, to you, for you	vous	you, to you, for you
lui	him, to him, for him it, to it, for it	leur	them, to them, for them *(masculine and feminine)*
lui	her, to her, for her it, to it, for it		

Il <u>nous</u> écrit tous les jours.   He writes to us every day.
Ils <u>te</u> cachent quelque chose.   They're hiding something from you.

> ### Tip
>
> **me** changes to **m'** and **te** to **t'** in front of words beginning with a vowel, most words beginning with **h**, and the French word **y**.
>
> | | |
> |---|---|
> | Il <u>m'</u>a donné un livre. | He gave me a book. |
> | Tu <u>m'</u>apportes une serviette ? | Can you get me a towel? |

➤ The pronouns shown in the table are used instead of the preposition **à** with a noun.

J'écris <u>à Suzanne</u>. I'm writing to Suzanne. → Je <u>lui</u> écris. I'm writing to her.
Donne du lait <u>au chat</u>. Give the cat some milk. → Donne-<u>lui</u> du lait. Give it some milk.

➤ Some French verbs like **demander à** (meaning *to ask*) and **téléphoner à** (meaning *to call*) take an <u>indirect object</u> even though English uses a <u>direct object</u>.

Il <u>leur</u> téléphone tous les soirs. He calls <u>them</u> every evening.

➤ On the other hand, some French verbs like **attendre** (meaning *to wait for*), **chercher** (meaning *to look for*) and **regarder** (meaning *to look at*) take a <u>direct object</u> even though English uses an <u>indirect object</u>.

Je <u>les</u> attends devant la gare. I'll wait for <u>them</u> outside the station.

2 Word order with indirect object pronouns

➤ The indirect object pronoun usually comes <u>BEFORE</u> the verb.

Dominique <u>vous</u> écrit une lettre.	Dominique's writing you a letter.
Il ne <u>nous</u> parle pas.	He doesn't speak to us.
Il ne veut pas <u>me</u> répondre.	He won't answer me.

[*i*] Note that in orders and instructions telling someone to do something, the indirect object pronoun comes <u>AFTER</u> the verb.

Donne-<u>moi</u> ça ! Give me that!

> ### Key points
> ✔ The French indirect object pronouns are: **me (m')**, **te (t')**, **lui** in the singular, and **nous**, **vous**, **leur** in the plural.
> ✔ Except in orders and instructions telling someone to do something, the direct object pronoun comes <u>before</u> the verb.

Emphatic pronouns

> **What is an emphatic pronoun?**
> An **emphatic pronoun** is used instead of a noun when you want to
> emphasize something, for example *Is this for me?*

1 Using emphatic pronouns

➤ In French, there is another set of pronouns which you use after prepositions,
when you want to emphasize something and in certain other cases. These are
called <u>emphatic pronouns</u> or <u>stressed pronouns</u>.

Singular	Meaning	Plural	Meaning
moi	I me	nous	we us
toi	you	vous	you
lui	he him	eux	they (*masculine*) them
elle	she her	elles	they (*feminine*) them
soi	oneself (yourself, ourselves)		

Je pense souvent à <u>toi</u>.	I often think about you.
C'est pour <u>moi</u> ?	Is this for me?
Venez avec <u>moi</u>.	Come with me.
Il a besoin de <u>nous</u>.	He needs us.

➤ **soi** (meaning *oneself*) is used with the subject pronoun **on** and with words like
tout le monde (meaning *everyone*) or **chacun** (meaning *each one*).

Il faut avoir confiance en <u>soi</u>.	You have to have confidence in yourself.
Tout le monde est rentré chez <u>soi</u>.	Everyone went home.

2 When to use emphatic pronouns

➤ Emphatic pronouns are used in the following circumstances:
- after a preposition

C'est <u>pour moi</u> ?	Is this for me?

- for emphasis, especially where a contrast is involved

<u>Toi</u>, tu ressembles à ton père, mais <u>elle</u> non.	You look like your father, she doesn't.
Il m'énerve, <u>lui</u> !	He's getting on my nerves!

- on their own without a verb

"Qui a cassé la fenêtre ?" – "<u>Lui</u>."	"Who broke the window?" – "He did."
"Je suis fatiguée." – "<u>Moi</u> aussi."	"I'm tired." – "Me too."

- after c'est and ce sont (meaning *it is*)

C'est <u>toi</u>, Simon ?	Is that you, Simon?
Ce sont <u>eux</u>.	It's them.

⮕ *For more information on c'est and ce sont, see page* 65.

- in comparisons

Tu es plus jeune que <u>moi</u>.	You're younger than me.
Il est moins grand que <u>toi</u>.	He's smaller than you (are).

- when the subject of the sentence is made up of two pronouns, or of a pronoun and a noun

<u>Mon père et elle</u> ne s'entendent pas.	My father and she don't get along.

Grammar Extra!

You can add -même or -mêmes to the emphatic pronouns when you particularly want to emphasize something. These forms correspond to English *myself, ourselves* and so on.

Form with -même	Meaning
moi-même	myself
toi-même	yourself
lui-même	himself, itself
elle-même	herself, itself
soi-même	oneself (yourself, ourselves)
nous-mêmes	ourselves
vous-même vous-mêmes	yourself yourselves
eux-mêmes	themselves (*masculine*)
elles-mêmes	themselves (*feminine*)

Je l'ai fait <u>moi-même</u>.	I did it myself.
Elle l'a choisi <u>elle-même</u>.	She chose it herself.

Key points

✔ The French emphatic pronouns are: moi, toi, lui, elle, soi in the singular, and nous, vous, eux, elles in the plural.

✔ They are used:
- after a preposition
- for emphasis
- on their own without a verb
- after c'est and ce sont
- in comparisons
- when the subject of the sentence is made up of two pronouns, or of a pronoun and a noun

✔ You can add -même or -mêmes to the emphatic pronouns when you particularly want to emphasize something.

Possessive pronouns

> **What is a possessive pronoun?**
> A **possessive pronoun** is one of the words *mine, yours, hers, his, ours*, or *theirs*, which are used instead of a noun to show that one person or thing belongs to another, for example, *Ask Carole if this pen is <u>hers</u>*.

➤ Here are the French possessive pronouns:

Masculine singular	Feminine singular	Masculine plural	Feminine plural	Meaning
le mien	la mienne	les miens	les miennes	mine
le tien	la tienne	les tiens	les tiennes	yours
le sien	la sienne	les siens	les siennes	his hers
le nôtre	la nôtre	les nôtres	les nôtres	ours
le vôtre	la vôtre	les vôtres	les vôtres	yours
le leur	la leur	les leurs	les leurs	theirs

Ces CD-là, ce sont <u>les miens</u>. — Those CDs are mine.
Heureusement que tu as tes clés. J'ai oublié <u>les miennes</u>. — It's lucky you have your keys. I forgot mine.

Tip

In French, possessive pronouns agree with what they describe, <u>NOT</u> with the person who owns that thing. For example, **le sien** can mean *his* or *hers*, but can only be used to replace a masculine singular noun.

"C'est <u>le vélo</u> de Paul ?" – "Oui, c'est <u>le sien</u>." — "Is that Paul's bike?" – "Yes, it's <u>his</u>."
"C'est <u>le vélo</u> d'Isabelle ?" – "Oui, c'est <u>le sien</u>." — "Is that Isabelle's bike?" – "Yes, it's <u>hers</u>."

Grammar Extra!

Remember that à with the definite article le becomes au, and à with les becomes aux, so:

> à + le mien → au mien
> à + les miens → aux miens
> à + les miennes → aux miennes

> **Tu préfères ce manteau <u>au mien</u> ?**   Do you prefer this coat to mine?

Remember that de with the definite article le becomes du, and de with les becomes des, so:

> de + le mien → du mien
> de + les miens → des miens
> de + les miennes → des miennes

> **J'ai oublié mes clés. J'ai besoin <u>des tiennes</u>.**   I've forgotten my keys. I need yours.

➪ *For more information on **Articles**, see page 12.*

Key points

✔ The French possessive pronouns are **le mien, le tien, le sien** for singular subject pronouns, and **le nôtre, le vôtre** and **le leur** for plural subject pronouns. Their forms change in the feminine and the plural.

✔ In French, the pronoun you choose has to agree with the noun it replaces, and <u>not</u> with the person who owns that thing.

en and y

➤ en and y do not usually refer to people. How we translate them into English depends on where en and y are found in French.

[1] en

➤ en is used with verbs and phrases normally followed by de to avoid repeating the same word.

Si tu as un problème, tu peux m'<u>en</u> parler.	If you have a problem, you can talk to me about it. (*en replaces de in parler* <u>*de quelque chose*</u>)
Est-ce que tu peux me prêter ce livre ? J'<u>en</u> ai besoin.	Can you lend me that book? I need it. (*en replaces de in avoir besoin* <u>*de quelque chose*</u>)
Il a un beau jardin et il <u>en</u> est très fier.	He has a beautiful garden and is very proud of it. (*en replaces de in être fier* <u>*de quelque chose*</u>)

➤ en can also replace the <u>partitive article</u> (du, de la, de l', des).

Je n'ai pas d'argent. Tu <u>en</u> as ?	I don't have any money. Do you have any?
"Tu peux me prêter des timbres ?" – "Non, je dois <u>en</u> acheter."	"Can you lend me some stamps?" – "No, I have to buy some."

⤷ *For more information on the **Partitive article**, see page 22.*

➤ en is also used:
- as a preposition
- with the present participle of verbs

⤷ *For more information on **Prepositions** and the **Present participle**, see pages 162 and 125.*

➤ When en is used with avoir, with il y a, or with numbers, it is often not translated in English but can <u>NEVER</u> be left out in French.

"Est-ce que tu as un dictionnaire ?" – "Oui, j'<u>en</u> ai un."	"Do you have a dictionary?" – "Yes, I have one."
"Combien d'élèves y a-t-il dans ta classe ?" – "Il y <u>en</u> a trente."	"How many students are there in your class?" – "There are thirty."
J'<u>en</u> veux deux.	I want two (of them).

2 y

➤ y is used with verbs and phrases normally followed by à to avoid repeating the same word.

"Je pensais à l'examen." – "Mais arrête d'y penser !"

"I was thinking about the exam." – "Well, stop thinking about it!" (y replaces à in penser à quelque chose)

"Je ne m'attendais pas à ça." – "Moi, je m'y attendais."

"I wasn't expecting that." – "Well, I was expecting it." (y replaces à in s'attendre à quelque chose)

➤ y can also mean *there*. It can be used to replace phrases that would use prepositions such as dans (meaning *in*) and sur (meaning *on*).

Elle y passe tout l'été.

She spends the whole summer there.

Regarde dans le tiroir. Je pense que les clés y sont.

Look in the drawer. I think the keys are in there.

3 Word order with en and y

➤ en and y usually come <u>BEFORE</u> the verb.

J'en veux.	I want some.
Elle en a parlé avec moi.	She talked with me about it.
En êtes-vous content ?	Are you pleased with it/them?
Comment fait-on pour y aller ?	How do you get there?
N'y pense plus.	Don't think about it any more.

➤ In orders and instructions telling someone to do something, en or y come <u>AFTER</u> the verb and are attached to it with a hyphen (-).

Prenez-en.	Take some.
Restez-y.	Stay there.

Tip

The final -s of -er verbs is usually dropped in the tu form used for orders and instructions. When an -er verb in the tu form is used before en or y, however, the -s is not dropped, to make it easier to say.

Donne des bonbons à ton frère.	Give some candy to your brother.
Donnes-en à ton frère.	Give some to your brother.
Va dans ta chambre !	Go to your room!
Vas-y !	Go on!

⇨ For more information on the **Imperative**, see page 85.

➤ **en** and **y** come <u>AFTER</u> other direct or indirect object pronouns.

> Donnez-<u>leur-en</u>.   Give them some.
> Il <u>m'en</u> a parlé.   He spoke to me about it.

⇨ *For more information on **Direct object pronouns** and **Indirect object pronouns**, see pages 47 and 49.*

Key points

✔ **en** is used with verbs and expressions normally followed by **de** to avoid repeating the same word.

✔ **en** can also replace the partitive article.

✔ When **en** is used with **avoir** and **il y a** or with numbers, it is often not translated in English but can never be left out in French.

✔ **y** is used with verbs and expressions normally followed by **à** to avoid repeating the same word.

✔ **y** can also mean *there* and may replace expressions that would be used with **dans** and **sur** or some other preposition indicating a place.

✔ **en** and **y** usually come before the verb, except in orders and instructions telling someone to do something, when **en** or **y** follows the verb and is attached to it with a hyphen.

✔ **en** and **y** come after other direct or indirect object pronouns.

Using different types of pronouns together

➤ Sometimes you find a direct object pronoun and an indirect object pronoun in the same sentence.

> He gave <u>me</u> (*indirect object*) <u>them</u> (*direct object*).
> He gave <u>them</u> (*direct object*) to <u>me</u> (*indirect object*).

➤ When this happens in French, you have to put the indirect and direct object pronouns in a certain order.

Indirect	Direct	Indirect	
me	le		
te	la	lui	en
nous	les	leur	y
vous			

Dominique <u>vous l'</u>envoie demain.	Dominique's sending it to you tomorrow.
Il <u>te les</u> a montrés ?	Has he shown them to you?
Je <u>les lui</u> ai lus.	I read them to him/her.
Ne <u>la leur</u> donne pas.	Don't give it to them.
Elle ne <u>m'en</u> a pas parlé.	She didn't speak to me about it.

Key points
✔ If a direct and an indirect object pronoun are used in the same sentence, you usually put the indirect object pronoun before the direct object pronoun.
✔ With **lui** and **leur**, this order is reversed and you put the direct object pronoun before the indirect object pronoun.

Indefinite pronouns

> **What is an indefinite pronoun?**
> An **indefinite pronoun** is one of a small group of pronouns such as *everything*, *nobody*, and *something* which are used to refer to people or things in a general way without saying exactly who or what they are.

➤ Here are the most common French indefinite pronouns:

- chacun (*masculine singular*)/chacune (*feminine singular*) each, everyone

Nous avons <u>chacun</u> donné dix euros.	We each gave ten euros.
<u>Chacun</u> fait ce qu'il veut.	Everyone does what they want.
Toutes les villas ont <u>chacune</u> leur piscine.	Each villa has its own swimming pool.

- personne nobody/no one, anybody/anyone

Il <u>n'</u>y a <u>personne</u> à la maison.	There's no one at home.
Elle <u>ne</u> veut voir <u>personne</u>.	She doesn't want to see anybody.

⇨ *For more information on **Negatives**, see page 138.*

> *Tip*
> You can use **personne** on its own to answer a question.
> Qui sait la réponse ? <u>Personne</u>.   Who knows the answer? No one.
> If the sentence contains a verb you have to use **ne** with it.
> Personne <u>n'</u>est venu.   Nobody came.

- quelque chose something, anything

J'ai <u>quelque chose</u> pour toi.	I have something for you.
Avez-vous <u>quelque chose</u> à déclarer ?	Do you have anything to declare?

- quelqu'un somebody/someone, anybody/anyone

Il y a <u>quelqu'un</u> à la porte.	There's someone at the door.
<u>Quelqu'un</u> a vu mon parapluie ?	Has anybody seen my umbrella?

- rien nothing, anything

Elle n'a <u>rien</u> dit.	She didn't say anything.
<u>Rien</u> n'a changé.	Nothing's changed.

⇨ *For more information on **Negatives**, see page 138.*

> *Tip*
>
> You can use **rien** on its own to answer a question.
>
> "Qu'est-ce tu as acheté ?" –   "What did you buy?" –
> "**Rien**."   "Nothing."
>
> If the sentence contains a verb you have to use **ne** with it.
>
> Il **n'a** **rien** mangé.   He's eaten nothing.

- **tout** everything

  Il organise **tout**.   He's organizing everything.

  Tout va bien ?   Is everything OK?

- **tous** (*masculine plural*)/**toutes** (*feminine plural*) all

  Je les connais **tous**.   I know them all.

  Elles sont **toutes** arrivées ? Are they all here?

➤ You can use **quelque chose de/rien de** and **quelqu'un de/personne de**
  with adjectives if you want to say *nothing interesting*, *something new* and so on.

  rien d'intéressant   nothing interesting

Key points

✔ **rien** and **personne** can be used on their own to answer questions,
but need to be used with **ne** when there is a verb in the sentence.

✔ **quelque chose/rien** and **quelqu'un/personne** can be followed by
de + adjective.

Relative pronouns: qui, que, lequel, auquel, duquel

> **What is a relative pronoun?**
> In English, a **relative pronoun** is one of the words *who*, *which*, and *that* (and the more formal *whom*) which can be used to introduce information that makes it clear which person or thing is being talked about, for example, *The man <u>who</u> has just come in is Ann's boyfriend; The vase <u>that</u> you broke was very valuable.*
> Relative pronouns can also introduce further information about someone or something, for example, *Peter, <u>who</u> is a brilliant painter, wants to study art; Jane's house, <u>which</u> was built in 1890, needs a lot of repairs.*

➤ In French, the relative pronouns are qui, que, lequel, auquel, and duquel.

1 **qui and que**

➤ qui and que can both refer to people or things.

	Relative pronoun	Meaning
Subject	qui	who which that
Direct object	que	who, whom which that

Mon frère, <u>qui</u> a vingt ans, est à l'université.	My brother, who's twenty, is in college.
Est-ce qu'il y a un bus <u>qui</u> va au centre-ville ?	Is there a bus that goes downtown?
Les amis <u>que</u> je vois le plus sont Léa et Mehdi.	The friends (that) I see most are Léa and Mehdi.
Voilà la maison <u>que</u> nous voulons acheter.	That's the house (which) we want to buy.

> *Tip*
> que changes to qu' in front of a word beginning with a vowel and most words beginning with h.

➤ qui is also used after a preposition such as à, de, or pour to talk about <u>people</u>.

la personne <u>à qui</u> il parle	the person he is speaking to
les enfants <u>pour qui</u> j'ai acheté des bonbons	the children I bought candy for

> ### Tip
> In English we often leave out the object pronouns who, which, and that. For example, we can say both *the friends <u>that</u> I see most*, or *the friends I see most*, and *the house <u>which</u> we want to buy*, or *the house we want to buy*. In French you can <u>NEVER</u> leave out **que** or **qui** in this way.

2 lequel, laquelle, lesquels, lesquelles

➤ **lequel** (meaning *which*) is used after a preposition such as à, de, or pour to talk about <u>things</u>. It has to agree with the noun it replaces.

	Masculine	Feminine	Meaning
Singular	lequel	laquelle	which
Plural	lesquels	lesquelles	which

le livre <u>pour lequel</u> elle est connue	the book she is famous for
la table <u>sur laquelle</u> j'ai mis mon sac	the table I put my bag on

➤ Remember that à and de combine with the definite article le to become au and du, and with les to become aux and des. lequel/lesquels/lesquelles combine with à and de as shown in the table. laquelle doesn't change.

	+ lequel	+ laquelle	+ lesquels	+ lesquelles	Meaning
à	auquel	à laquelle	auxquels	auxquelles	to which
de	duquel	de laquelle	desquels	desquelles	of which

⇨ *For more information on à and de, see pages 14 and 15.*

Grammar Extra!

dont means *whose, of whom, of which, about which* and so on. It can refer to people or things, but its form <u>NEVER</u> changes.

la femme <u>dont</u> la voiture est en panne	the woman whose car has broken down
les films <u>dont</u> tu parles	the movies you're talking about

Key points

✔ qui and que can both refer to people or things: qui is the subject of the part of the sentence it is found in; que is the object.

✔ In English, we often leave out the object pronouns *who*, *which*, and *that*, but in French you can <u>never</u> leave out que or qui.

✔ After a preposition you use qui if you are referring to people, and lequel if you are referring to things – lequel agrees with the noun it replaces.

✔ à + lequel → auquel
à + lesquels → auxquels
à + lesquelles → auxquelles

✔ de + lequel → duquel
de + lesquels → desquels
de + lesquelles → desquelles

For further explanation of grammatical terms, please see pages viii-xii.

Demonstrative pronouns: ce, cela/ça, ceci, celui

> **What is a demonstrative pronoun?**
> In English, a **demonstrative pronoun** is one of the words *this*, *that*, *these*, and *those* used instead of a noun to point people or things out, for example, *That* looks fun.

1 | ce

➤ ce is usually used with the verb être (meaning *to be*) in the expressions c'est (meaning *it's*, *that's*), c'était (meaning *it was*, *that was*), ce sont (meaning *it's*, *that's*) and so on.

C'est moi.	It's me.
C'était mon frère.	That was my brother.
Ce sont eux.	It's them.

> ## Tip
> ce becomes c' when it is followed by a part of the verb that starts with e or é.
> ce becomes ç' when it is followed by a part of the verb that starts with a.
>
> | | |
> |---|---|
> | Ç'a été difficile. | It was difficult. |
>
> Note that after c'est and ce sont and so on you have to use the emphatic form of the pronoun, for example, moi instead of je, eux instead of ils and so on.
>
> | | |
> |---|---|
> | C'est moi. | It's me. |
>
> ⇨ *For more information on* **Emphatic pronouns**, *see page* 51.

➤ ce is used:

- with a noun or a question word to identify a person or thing

Qui est-ce ?	Who is it?, Who's this/that?
Ce sont des professeurs.	They're teachers.
Qu'est-ce que c'est ?	What's this/that?
C'est un ouvre-boîte.	It's a can opener.

- with an adjective to refer to a statement, idea and so on that cannot be classed as either masculine or feminine

<u>C'</u>est très intéressant.	That's/It's very interesting.
<u>C'</u>est dangereux.	That's/It's dangerous.
<u>Ce</u> n'est pas grave.	It doesn't matter.

- for emphasis

<u>C'</u>est moi qui ai téléphoné.	It was me who called.
<u>Ce</u> sont les enfants qui ont fait le gâteau.	It was the children who made the cake.

2 | cela, ça, and ceci

➤ cela and ça mean *it, this,* or *that*. Both refer to a statement, an idea, or an object. ça is used instead of cela in everyday, informal French.

<u>Ça</u> ne fait rien.	It doesn't matter.
Écoute-moi <u>ça</u> !	Listen to this!
<u>Cela</u> dépend.	That/It depends.
Je n'aime pas <u>cela</u>.	I don't like that.
Donne-moi <u>ça</u> !	Give me that!

> ### Tip
> ça and cela are used in a more general way than il and elle, which are usually linked to a noun that has already been mentioned.
>
> | | |
> |---|---|
> | <u>Ça</u> te plaît d'aller à l'étranger ? | Do you like going abroad? |
> | <u>Elle</u> te plaît, <u>ma nouvelle voiture</u> ? | Do you like my new car? |

➤ ceci means *this* and is not as common as cela and ça. It is used to talk about something that has not yet been mentioned.

Lisez <u>ceci</u>.	Read this.

➤ ceci is also used to hand or show someone something.

Prends <u>ceci</u>. Tu en auras besoin.	Take this. You'll need it.

3 | celui, celle, ceux, celles

➤ celui and celle mean *the one*; ceux and celles mean *the ones*. The form you choose depends on whether the noun it is replacing is masculine or feminine, and singular or plural.

	Masculine	Feminine	Meaning
Singular	celui	celle	the one
Plural	ceux	celles	the ones

➤ celui and its other forms are used before:

- qui, que, or dont

  "Quelle robe préférez-vous ?"
  – "Celle qui est en vitrine."

  "Which dress do you like best?"
  – "The one in the window."

  Prends ceux que tu préfères.

  Take the ones you like best.

  celui dont je t'ai parlé

  the one I told you about

- prepositions like à, dans and so on.

  celui proche de la fontaine

  the one near the fountain

➤ celui and its other forms can be used with de to show who something belongs to. In English, we would use 's.

  Je n'ai pas d'appareil photo mais je peux emprunter celui de ma sœur.

  I don't have a camera, but I can borrow my sister's.

  Comparez vos réponses à celles de votre voisin.

  Compare your answers with your neighbor's.

➤ You can add the endings -ci and -là to celui and its other forms to emphasize the difference between something that is close to you and something that is farther away.

- use -ci for something that is closer to you
- use -là for something that is farther away

	Masculine	Feminine	Meaning
Singular	celui-ci	celle-ci	this, this one
	celui-là	celle-là	that, that one
Plural	ceux-ci	celles-ci	these
	ceux-là	celles-là	those

  On prend quel fromage ? Celui-ci ou celui-là ?

  Which cheese shall we get? This one or that one?

  Ces chemises ont deux poches mais celles-là n'en ont pas.

  These shirts have two pockets, but those have none.

Key points

✔ ce is often found in the expressions c'est, ce sont and so on.

✔ ce is also used:
- to identify a person or thing
- to refer to a statement, idea and so on that cannot be classed as either masculine or feminine
- for emphasis

✔ cela and ça mean *it, this,* or *that*; ceci means *this*, but is not as common.

✔ celui and celle mean *the one*; ceux and celles mean *the ones*. They are often found with the endings -ci and -là and are used to distinguish between things that are close and things that are farther away.

Verbs

> **What is a verb?**
> A **verb** is a "doing" word which describes what someone or something does, what someone or something is, or what happens to them, for example, *be*, *sing*, *live*.

The three conjugations

➤ Verbs are usually used with a noun, with a pronoun such as *I*, *you*, or *she*, or with somebody's name. They can relate to the present, the past, and the future; this is called their <u>tense</u>.

⇨ *For more information on* **Nouns** *and* **Pronouns**, *see pages 1 and 42.*

➤ Verbs are either:
  - <u>regular</u>; their forms follow the normal rules
  - <u>irregular</u>; their forms do not follow the normal rules

➤ Regular English verbs have a <u>base form</u> (the form of the verb without any endings added to it, for example, *walk*). The base form can have *to* in front of it, for example, *to walk*. This is called the <u>infinitive</u>. You will find one of these forms when you look up a verb in your dictionary.

➤ French verbs also have an infinitive, which ends in **-er**, **-ir**, or **-re**, for example, **donner** (meaning *to give*), **finir** (meaning *to finish*), **attendre** (meaning *to wait*). <u>Regular</u> French verbs belong to one of these three verb groups, which are called <u>conjugations</u>. We will look at each of these three conjugations in turn on the next few pages.

➤ English verbs have other forms apart from the base form and infinitive: a form ending in *-s* (*walks*), a form ending in *-ing* (*walking*), and a form ending in *-ed* (*walked*).

➤ French verbs have many more forms than this, which are made up of endings added to a <u>stem</u>. The stem of a verb can usually be worked out from the infinitive.

➤ French verb endings change depending on who you are talking about: **je** (*I*), **tu** (*you*), **il/elle/on** (*he/she/one*) in the singular, or **nous** (*we*), **vous** (*you*), and **ils/elles** (*they*) in the plural. French verbs also have different forms depending on whether you are referring to the present, future, or past.

➤ Some verbs in French do not follow the normal rules, and are called <u>irregular verbs</u>. These include some very common and important verbs like **avoir** (meaning *to have*), **être** (meaning *to be*), **faire** (meaning *to do, to make*), and **aller** (meaning *to go*). There is information on many of these irregular verbs in the following sections.

⇨ *For **Verb tables**, see supplement.*

> **Key points**
> ✔ French verbs have different forms depending on what noun or pronoun they are used with, and on their tense.
> ✔ They are made up of a stem and an ending. The stem is usually based on the infinitive.
> ✔ Regular verbs fit into one of three patterns or conjugations: -er, -ir, or -re verbs.
> ✔ Irregular verbs do not follow the normal rules.

The present tense

> **What is the present tense?**
> The **present tense** is used to talk about what is true at the moment, what happens regularly, and what is happening now, for example, *I'm a student.*; *I travel to college by train.*; *I'm studying Language.*

➤ You use a verb in the present tense to talk about:

- things that are happening now
  It's raining.
  The phone's ringing.

- things that happen all the time or at certain intervals, or things that you do as a habit
  It always snows in January.
  I play baseball on Saturdays.

- things that are true at the present time:
  She's not very well.
  It's a beautiful house.

➤ There is more than one way to express the present tense in English. For example, you can say either *I give*, *I am giving*, or occasionally *I do give*. In French you use the same form (**je donne**) for all of these!

➤ In English you can also use the present tense to talk about something that is going to happen in the near future. You can do the same in French.

Je **vais** en France le mois prochain.	I'm going to France next month.
Nous **prenons** le train de dix heures.	We're getting the ten o'clock train.

> *Tip*
> Although English sometimes uses parts of the verb *to be* to form the present tense of other verbs (for example, *I am listening*, *she's talking*), French **NEVER** uses the verb **être** in this way.

72 Verbs

The present tense: Regular -er (first conjugation) verbs

➤ If an infinitive in French ends in -er, it means the verb belongs to the <u>first conjugation</u>, for example, donner, aimer, parler.

➤ To know which form of the verb to use in French, you need to work out what the stem of the verb is and then add the correct ending. The stem of -er verbs in the present tense is formed by taking the <u>infinitive</u> and chopping off -er.

Infinitive	Stem (without -er)
donner (to give)	donn-
aimer (to like, to love)	aim-
parler (to speak, to talk)	parl-

➤ Now that you know how to find the stem of a verb, you can add the correct ending. Which one you choose will depend on whether you are referring to je, tu, il, elle, on, nous, vous, ils, or elles.

⇨ *For more information on **Pronouns**, see page 42.*

➤ Here are the present tense endings for -er verbs:

Pronoun	Ending	Add to stem, e.g. donn-	Meanings
je (j')	-e	je donne	I give I am giving
tu	-es	tu donnes	you give you are giving
il elle on	-e	il donne elle donne on donne	he/she/it/one gives he/she/it/one is giving
nous	-ons	nous donnons	we give we are giving
vous	-ez	vous donnez	you give you are giving
ils elles	-ent	ils donnent elles donnent	they give they are giving

Marie <u>regarde</u> la télé.   Marie is watching TV.
Le train <u>arrive</u> à deux heures.   The train arrives at 2 o'clock.

For further explanation of grammatical terms, please see pages viii-xii.

> **Tip**
>
> je changes to j' in front of a word starting with a vowel (*a, e, i, o,* or *u*), most words starting with h, and the French word y.

i Note that there are a few regular -**er** verbs that are spelled slightly differently from what you might expect.

⇨ *For more information on **Spelling changes in -er verbs**, see page 78.*

Key points

✔ Verbs ending in -**er** belong to the first conjugation and form their present tense stem by losing the -**er** from the infinitive.

✔ The present tense endings for -**er** verbs are:
-**e**, -**es**, -**e**, -**ons**, -**ez**, -**ent**.

The present tense: Regular -ir (second conjugation) verbs

➤ If an infinitive ends in -ir, it means the verb belongs to the <u>second conjugation</u>, for example, **finir**, **choisir**, **remplir**.

➤ The stem of -ir verbs in the present tense is formed by taking the <u>infinitive</u> and chopping off -ir.

Infinitive	Stem (without -ir)
finir (to finish)	fin-
choisir (to choose)	chois-
remplir (to fill, to fill out)	rempl-

➤ Now add the correct ending, depending on whether you are referring to **je**, **tu**, **il**, **elle**, **on**, **nous**, **vous**, **ils**, or **elles**.

⇨ For more information on **Pronouns**, see page 42.

➤ Here are the present tense endings for -ir verbs:

Pronoun	Ending	Add to stem, e.g. fin-	Meanings
je (j')	-is	je fin<u>is</u>	I finish I am finishing
tu	-is	tu fin<u>is</u>	you finish you are finishing
il elle on	-it	il fin<u>it</u> elle fin<u>it</u> on fin<u>it</u>	he/she/it/one finishes he/she/it/one is finishing
nous	-issons	nous fin<u>issons</u>	we finish we are finishing
vous	-issez	vous fin<u>issez</u>	you finish you are finishing
ils elles	-issent	ils fin<u>issent</u> elles fin<u>issent</u>	they finish they are finishing

Le cours <u>finit</u> à onze heures.　　The lesson finishes at eleven o'clock.
Je <u>finis</u> mes devoirs.　　I'm finishing my homework.

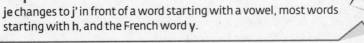

> **Tip**
> je changes to j' in front of a word starting with a vowel, most words
> starting with h, and the French word y.

➤ The **nous** and **vous** forms of **-ir** verbs have an extra syllable.

　　tu fi|nis　　　　(*two syllables*)
　　vous fi|ni|ssez　(*three syllables*)

> **Key points**
> ✔ Verbs ending in **-ir** belong to the second conjugation and form their
> present tense stem by losing the -ir from the infinitive.
> ✔ The present tense endings for -ir verbs are:
> **-is, -is, -it, -issons, -issez, -issent**.
> ✔ Remember the extra syllable in the **nous** and **vous** forms.

The present tense: Regular -re (third conjugation) verbs

➤ If an infinitive ends in -re, it means the verb belongs to the <u>third conjugation</u>, for example, **attendre**, **vendre**, **entendre**.

➤ The stem of -re verbs in the present tense is formed by taking the <u>infinitive</u> and chopping off -re.

Infinitive	Stem (without -re)
attendre (to wait)	attend-
vendre (to sell)	vend-
entendre (to hear)	entend-

➤ Now add the correct ending, depending on whether you are referring to **je**, **tu**, **il**, **elle**, **on**, **nous**, **vous**, **ils**, or **elles**.

⇨   For more information on **Pronouns**, see page 42.

➤ Here are the present tense endings for -re verbs:

Pronoun	Ending	Add to stem, e.g. attend-	Meanings
je (j')	-s	j'attend<u>s</u>	I wait I am waiting
tu	-s	tu attend<u>s</u>	you wait you are waiting
il elle on	-	il attend elle attend on attend	he/she/it/one waits he/she/it/one is waiting
nous	-ons	nous attend<u>ons</u>	we wait we are waiting
vous	-ez	vous attend<u>ez</u>	you wait you are waiting
ils elles	-ent	ils attend<u>ent</u> elles attend<u>ent</u>	they wait they are waiting

J'<u>attends</u> ma sœur.   I'm waiting for my sister.

Chaque matin nous <u>attendons</u>   Every morning we wait for the train
le train ensemble.   together.

> ### Tip
>
> **je** changes to **j'** in front of a word starting with a vowel, most words starting with **h**, and the French word **y**.

Key points

✔ Verbs ending in **-re** belong to the third conjugation and form their present tense stem by losing the **-re** from the infinitive.

✔ The present tense endings for **-re** verbs are:
  -s, -s, -, -ons, -ez, -ent.

The present tense: Spelling changes in -er verbs

➤ Learning the patterns shown on pages 72–73 means you can now work out the forms of most -er verbs. A few verbs, though, involve a small spelling change. This usually has to do with how a word is pronounced. In the tables below the form(s) with irregular spelling is/are <u>underlined</u>.

1 Verbs ending in -cer

➤ With verbs such as **lancer** (meaning *to throw*), which end in **-cer**, c becomes ç before an a or an o. This is so the letter c is still pronounced as in the English word *ice*.

Pronoun	Example verb: lancer
je	lance
tu	lances
il elle on	lance
nous	<u>lançons</u>
vous	lancez
ils elles	lancent

2 Verbs ending in -ger

➤ With verbs such as **manger** (meaning *to eat*), which end in **-ger**, g becomes ge before an a or an o. This is so the letter g is still pronounced like the s in the English word *leisure*.

Pronoun	Example verb: manger
je	mange
tu	manges
il elle on	mange
nous	<u>mangeons</u>
vous	mangez
ils elles	mangent

3 | Verbs ending in -eler

➤ With verbs such as **appeler** (meaning *to call*), which end in **-eler**, the **l** doubles before **-e**, **-es**, and **-ent**. The double consonant (**ll**) affects the pronunciation of the word. In **appeler**, the first **e** sounds like the vowel sound at the end of the English word *teacher*, but in **appelle** the first **e** sounds like the one in the English word *pet*.

Pronoun	Example verb: appeler
j'	<u>appelle</u>
tu	<u>appelles</u>
il elle on	<u>appelle</u>
nous	appelons
vous	appelez
ils elles	<u>appellent</u>

➤ The exceptions to this rule are **geler** (meaning *to freeze*) and **peler** (meaning *to peel*), which change in the same way as **lever** (*see page 81*).

➤ Verbs like this are sometimes called "<u>1, 2, 3, 6 verbs</u>" because they change in the first person singular (**je**), second person singular (**tu**), and third person singular and plural (**il/elle/on** and **ils/elles**).

4 | Verbs ending in -eter

➤ With verbs such as **jeter** (meaning *to throw*), which end in **-eter**, the **t** doubles before **-e**, **-es**, and **-ent**. The double consonant (**tt**) affects the pronunciation of the word. In **jeter**, the first **e** sounds like the vowel sound at the end of the English word *teacher*, but in **jette** the first **e** sounds like the one in the English word *pet*.

Pronoun	Example verb: jeter
je	<u>jette</u>
tu	<u>jettes</u>
il elle on	<u>jette</u>
nous	jetons
vous	jetez
ils elles	<u>jettent</u>

➤ The exceptions to this rule include **acheter** (meaning *to buy*), which changes in the same way as **lever** (*see page 81*).

➤ Verbs like this are sometimes called "1, 2, 3, 6 verbs."

5 Verbs ending in -yer

➤ With verbs such as **nettoyer** (meaning *to clean*), which end in -yer, the y changes to i before -e, -es, and -ent.

Pronoun	Example verb: nettoyer
je	nettoie
tu	nettoies
il elle on	nettoie
nous	nettoyons
vous	nettoyez
ils elles	nettoient

➤ Verbs ending in -ayer, such as **payer** (meaning *to pay*) and **essayer** (meaning *to try*), can be spelled with either a y or an i. So **je paie** and **je paye**, for example, are both correct.

➤ Verbs like this are sometimes called "1, 2, 3, 6 verbs."

6 Changes involving accents

➤ With verbs such as **lever** (meaning *to raise*), **peser** (meaning *to weigh*) and **acheter** (meaning *to buy*), e changes to è before the consonant + -e, -es, and -ent. The accent changes the pronunciation too. In **lever** the first e sounds like the vowel sound at the end of the English word *teacher*, but in **lève** and so on the first e sounds like the one in the English word *pet*.

Pronoun	Example verb: lever
je	lève
tu	lèves
il elle on	lève
nous	levons
vous	levez
ils elles	lèvent

➤ With verbs such as **espérer** (meaning *to hope*), **régler** (meaning *to adjust*), and **préférer** (meaning *to prefer*), é changes to è before the consonant + -e, -es, and -ent.

Pronoun	Example verb: espérer
j'	espère
tu	espères
il elle on	espère
nous	espérons
vous	espérez
ils elles	espèrent

➤ Verbs like this are sometimes called "1, 2, 3, 6 verbs."

> **Key points**
> ✔ In verbs ending in -cer and -ger:
>   c → ç and g → ge in the nous form.
> ✔ In verbs ending in -eler and -eter:
>   l → ll and t → tt in all but the nous and vous forms.
> ✔ In verbs ending in -yer:
>   y → i in all but the nous and vous forms (optional in -ayer verbs).

The present tense: Irregular verbs

➤ Some verbs in French do not follow the normal rules. These verbs include some very common and important verbs like **avoir** (meaning *to have*), **être** (meaning *to be*), **faire** (meaning *to do, to make*), and **aller** (meaning *to go*). The present tense of these four verbs is given in full below.

⇨ For **Verb tables**, see supplement.

1 The present tense of avoir

Pronoun	avoir	Meaning: *to have*
j'	ai	I have
tu	as	you have
il elle on	a	he/she/it/one has
nous	avons	we have
vous	avez	you have
ils elles	ont	they have

J'<u>ai</u> deux sœurs.	I have two sisters.
Il <u>a</u> les yeux bleus.	He has blue eyes.
Elle <u>a</u> trois ans.	She's three.
Qu'est-ce qu'il y <u>a</u> ?	What's the matter?

2 The present tense of être

Pronoun	être	Meaning: *to be*
je	suis	I am
tu	es	you are
il elle on	est	he/she/it/one is
nous	sommes	we are
vous	êtes	you are
ils elles	sont	they are

Je <u>suis</u> heureux.	I'm happy.
Mon père <u>est</u> instituteur.	My father's an elementary school teacher.
Il <u>est</u> deux heures.	It's two o'clock.

For further explanation of grammatical terms, please see pages viii-xii.

3 **The present tense of** faire

Pronoun	faire	Meaning: *to do, to make*
je	fais	I do/make I am doing/making
tu	fais	you do/make you are doing/making
il elle on	fait	he/she/it/one does/makes he/she/it/one is doing/making
nous	faisons	we do/make we are doing/making
vous	faites	you do/make you are doing/making
ils elles	font	they do/make they are doing/making

Je <u>fais</u> un gâteau.	I'm making a cake.
Qu'est-ce que tu <u>fais</u> ?	What are you doing?
Il <u>fait</u> chaud.	It's hot.
Ça ne <u>fait</u> rien.	It doesn't matter.

4 **The present tense of** aller

Pronoun	aller	Meaning: *to go*
je	vais	I go I am going
tu	vas	you go you are going
il elle on	va	he/she/it/one goes he/she/it/one is going
nous	allons	we go we are going
vous	allez	you go you are going
ils elles	vont	they go they are going

Je <u>vais</u> à New York.	I'm going to New York.
"Comment <u>allez</u>-vous ?" – "Je <u>vais</u> bien."	"How are you?" – "I'm fine."
"Comment ça <u>va</u> ?" – "Ça <u>va</u> bien."	"How are you?" – "I'm fine."

5 Irregular -ir verbs

➤ Many irregular verbs that end in -ir, such as **partir** (meaning *to go*) and **tenir** (meaning *to hold*), have a common pattern in the singular. The **je** and **tu** forms often end in -s, and the **il/elle/on** form often ends in -t.

Pronoun	partir	tenir
je	par<u>s</u>	tien<u>s</u>
tu	par<u>s</u>	tien<u>s</u>
il/elle/on	par<u>t</u>	tien<u>t</u>

Je <u>pars</u> demain.	I'm leaving tomorrow.
Elle <u>tient</u> le bébé.	She is holding the baby.

⇨ For **Verb tables**, see supplement.

Key points

✔ Some very important French verbs are irregular, including **avoir**, **être**, **faire**, and **aller**. They are worth learning in full.

✔ The -s, -s, -t pattern occurs frequently in irregular -ir verbs.

The imperative

> **What is the imperative?**
> An **imperative** is a form of the verb used when giving orders and
> instructions, for example, *Shut the door!; Sit down!; Don't go!*

1 Using the imperative

➤ In French, there are two forms of the imperative that are used to give
instructions or orders to someone. These correspond to **tu** and **vous**.

➡ *For more information on the difference between* tu *and* vous, *see page 43.*

➤ There is also a form of the imperative that corresponds to **nous**. This means
the same as *let's* in English. It is not used as often as the **tu** and **vous** forms.

2 Forming the present tense imperative

➤ For regular verbs, the imperative is the same as the **tu**, **nous**, and **vous** forms
of the present tense, except that you do not say the pronouns **tu**, **nous**, and
vous. Also, in the **tu** form of -er verbs like **donner**, the final **-s** is dropped.

Pronoun	-er verbs: donner	Meaning	-ir verbs: finir	Meaning	-re verbs: attendre	Meaning
tu	donne	give	finis	finish	attends	wait
nous	donnons	let's give	finissons	let's finish	attendons	let's wait
vous	donnez	give	finissez	finish	attendez	wait

<u>Donne</u>-moi ça !	Give me that!
<u>Finissez</u> vos devoirs et <u>allez</u> vous coucher.	Finish your homework and go to bed.
<u>Attendons</u> le bus.	Let's wait for the bus.

> *Tip*
>
> When a **tu** imperative comes before **en** or **y**, the final **-s** is kept to
> make the words easier to pronounce. The **s** is pronounced like the **z** in
> the English word *zipper*:
>
> | | |
> |---|---|
> | **Vas**-<u>y</u> ! | Go on! |
> | **Donne**<u>s</u>-en à ton frère. | Give some to your brother. |

86 Verbs

3 Where to put the object pronoun

➤ An object pronoun is a word like **la** (meaning *her/it*), **me/moi** (meaning *me*), or **leur** (meaning *to them*) that is used instead of a noun as the object of a sentence. In orders and instructions, the position of these object pronouns in the sentence changes depending on whether you are telling someone <u>TO DO</u> something or <u>NOT TO DO</u> something.

⇨ *For more information on **Object pronouns**, see page 47.*

➤ If you are telling someone <u>NOT TO DO</u> something, you put the object pronouns <u>BEFORE</u> the verb.

Ne <u>me</u> dérange pas.	Don't disturb me.
Ne <u>leur</u> parlons pas.	Let's not speak to them.
Ne <u>le</u> regardez pas.	Don't look at him/it.

➤ If you are telling someone <u>TO DO</u> something, you put the object pronouns <u>AFTER</u> the verb and join the two words with a hyphen. The word order is the same as in English.

Excusez-<u>moi</u>.	Excuse me.
Aide-<u>nous</u>.	Help us.
Attendons-<u>la</u>.	Let's wait for her/it.

➤ Orders and instructions telling someone to do something may contain <u>direct object</u> and <u>indirect object pronouns</u>. When this happens, the pronouns go in this order:

DIRECT		INDIRECT
le		moi
la	BEFORE	toi
les		lui
		nous
		vous
		leur

Prête-<u>les moi</u> !	Lend them to me! *or* Lend me them!
Donnez-<u>la-nous</u> !	Give it to us!

⇨ *For imperatives using **Reflexive verbs**, see page 90.*

For further explanation of grammatical terms, please see pages viii-xii.

4 | Imperative forms of irregular verbs

➤ avoir (meaning *to have*), être (meaning *to be*), savoir (meaning *to know*), and vouloir (meaning *to want*) have irregular imperative forms.

Pronoun	avoir	être	savoir	vouloir
tu	aie	sois	sache	veuille
nous	ayons	soyons	sachons	veuillons
vous	ayez	soyez	sachez	veuillez

<u>Sois</u> sage.   Be good.

<u>Veuillez</u> fermer la porte.   Please shut the door.

Key points
✔ The imperative has three forms: tu, nous, and vous.

✔ The forms are the same as the tu, nous, and vous forms of the present tense, except that the final -s is dropped in the tu form of -er verbs.

✔ Object pronouns go before the verb when you are telling someone not to do something, but after the verb with a hyphen when you are telling someone to do something.

✔ avoir, être, savoir, and vouloir have irregular imperative forms.

Reflexive verbs

> **What is a reflexive verb?**
> A **reflexive verb** is one where the subject and object are the same, and where the action "reflects back" on the subject. It is used with a reflexive pronoun such as *myself*, *yourself*, and *herself* in English, for example, *I washed myself; He shaved himself.*

1 Using reflexive verbs

➤ In French, reflexive verbs are much more common than in English, and many are used in everyday French. They are shown in dictionaries as **se** plus the infinitive (**se** means *himself, herself, itself, themselves,* or *oneself*). **se** is called a reflexive pronoun.

> *Tip*
> **se** changes to **s'** in front of a word starting with a vowel, most words starting with **h**, and the French word **y**.

➤ Reflexive verbs are often used to describe things you do (to yourself) every day or that involve a change of some kind (going to bed, sitting down, getting angry, going to sleep). Some of the most common French reflexive verbs are listed here:

s'amuser	to play, to enjoy oneself
s'appeler	to be called
s'arrêter	to stop
s'asseoir	to sit down
se baigner	to go swimming
se coucher	to go to bed
se dépêcher	to hurry
s'habiller	to get dressed
s'intéresser à quelque chose	to be interested in something
se laver	to wash, to wash up
se lever	to get up, to rise, to stand up
se passer	to take place, to happen, to go
se promener	to go for a walk
se rappeler	to remember
se réveiller	to wake up
se trouver	to be (situated)

For further explanation of grammatical terms, please see pages viii-xii.

Qu'est-ce qui <u>se passe</u> ?	What's happening?
Le soleil <u>se lève</u> à cinq heures.	The sun rises at five o'clock.
<u>Asseyez-vous</u> !	Sit down!

i Note that **se** and **s'** are very rarely translated as *himself* and so on in English.

➤ Some French verbs can be used with a reflexive pronoun or without a reflexive pronoun, for example, the verbs **appeler** and **s'appeler**, and **arrêter** and **s'arrêter**. Sometimes, however, their meaning may change.

<u>Appelle</u> le chien.	<u>Call</u> the dog.
Je <u>m'appelle</u> Jacques.	<u>I'm called</u> Jacques.
Il <u>arrête</u> le moteur.	He <u>turns off</u> the engine.
Elle <u>s'arrête</u> devant une vitrine.	She <u>stops</u> in front of a store window.

2 Forming the present tense of reflexive verbs

➤ To use a reflexive verb in French, you need to decide which reflexive pronoun to use. The forms shown in brackets in the table are used before a word starting with a vowel, most words starting with **h**, or the French word **y**.

Subject pronoun	Reflexive pronoun	Meaning
je	me (m')	myself
tu	te (t')	yourself
il elle on	se (s')	himself herself itself oneself
nous	nous	ourselves
vous	vous	yourself (*singular*) yourselves (*plural*)
ils elles	se (s')	themselves

Je <u>me lève</u> tôt.	I get up early.
Elle <u>s'habille</u>.	She's getting dressed.
Ils <u>s'intéressent</u> beaucoup aux animaux.	They're very interested in animals.

➤ The present tense forms of a reflexive verb work in exactly the same way as an ordinary verb, except that the reflexive pronoun is used as well.

Reflexive forms	Meaning
je me lave	I wash (myself)
tu te laves	you wash (yourself)
il se lave elle se lave on se lave	he washes (himself) she washes (herself) it washes (itself) one washes (oneself)
nous nous lavons	we wash (ourselves)
vous vous lavez	you wash (yourself) (*singular*) you wash (yourselves) (*plural*)
ils se lavent elles se lavent	they wash (themselves)

➤ Some reflexive verbs, such as **s'asseoir** (meaning *to sit down*), are irregular. Some of these irregular verbs are shown in the **Verb tables**.

⇨ For **Verb tables**, see supplement.

3 Where to put the reflexive pronoun

➤ In the present tense, the reflexive pronoun almost always comes <u>BEFORE</u> the verb.

Je <u>me</u> couche tôt.	I go to bed early.
Comment <u>t'</u>appelles-tu ?	What's your name?

➤ When telling someone <u>NOT TO DO</u> something, you put the reflexive pronoun <u>BEFORE</u> the verb as usual.

Ne <u>te</u> lève pas.	Don't get up.
Ne <u>vous</u> habillez pas.	Don't get dressed.

➤ When telling someone <u>TO DO</u> something, you put the reflexive pronoun <u>AFTER</u> the verb and join the two words with a hyphen.

Lève-<u>toi</u> !	Get up!
Dépêchez-<u>vous</u> !	Hurry up!
Habillons-<u>nous</u>.	Let's get dressed.

Tip

When you are telling someone <u>TO DO</u> something, te or t'
changes to toi.

    Assieds-<u>toi</u>.   Sit down.

When you are telling someone <u>NOT TO DO</u> something, te or t' is used,
not toi.

    Ne te lève pas.   Don't get up.

⇨ *For more information on the **Imperative**, see page 85.*

4 *Each other* and *one another*

➤ We use *each other* in English when we are talking about two people, and *one another* when we are talking about three or more people. The French reflexive pronouns nous, vous, and se can all mean two or more people.

Nous <u>nous</u> parlons tous les jours.	We speak to <u>each other</u> every day.
On <u>se</u> voit demain ?	Shall we see <u>each other</u> tomorrow?
Les trois pays <u>se</u> ressemblent beaucoup.	The three countries are really similar to <u>one another</u>.

Key points

✔ A reflexive verb is made up of a reflexive pronoun and a verb.

✔ The reflexive pronouns are: me, te, se, nous, vous, se (m', t', s', nous, vous, s' before a vowel, most words beginning with h, and the French word y).

✔ The reflexive pronoun comes before the verb, except when you are telling someone to do something.

The imperfect tense

> **What is the imperfect tense?**
> The **imperfect tense** is one of the verb tenses used to talk about the past, especially in descriptions, and to say what used to happen, for example, *I used to walk to school*; *It was sunny during the weekend*.

1 Using the imperfect tense

➤ The imperfect tense is used:

- to describe what things were like and how people felt in the past

  I _was_ very sad when she left.

  It _was pouring_ rain.

- to say what used to happen or what you used to do regularly in the past

  We _used to get up_ very early in those days.

  I never _used to like_ milk.

- to indicate things that were happening or something that was true when something else took place

  I _was watching_ TV when the phone rang.

  As we _were looking_ out of the window, we saw someone walk across the lawn.

i Note that if you want to talk about an event or action that took place and was completed in the past, you use the _perfect tense_.

  ⇨ *For more information on the **Perfect tense**, see page 111.*

➤ You can often recognize an imperfect tense in English because it uses a form like *were looking* or *was raining*. The words *used to* also show an imperfect tense.

> *Tip*
> Remember that you <u>NEVER</u> use the verb **être** to translate *was* or *were* in forms like *was raining* or *were looking* and so on. You change the French verb ending instead.

2 Forming the imperfect tense of -er verbs

➤ To form the imperfect tense of **-er** verbs, you use the same stem of the verb as for the present tense. Then you add the correct ending, depending on whether you are referring to **je**, **tu**, **il**, **elle**, **on**, **nous**, **vous**, **ils**, or **elles**.

Pronoun	Ending	Add to stem, e.g. donn-	Meanings
je (j')	-ais	je donn**ais**	I gave I was giving I used to give
tu	-ais	tu donn**ais**	you gave you were giving you used to give
il elle on	-ait	il donn**ait** elle donn**ait** on donn**ait**	he/she/it/one gave he/she/it/one was giving he/she/it/one used to give
nous	-ions	nous donn**ions**	we gave we were giving we used to give
vous	-iez	vous donn**iez**	you gave you were giving you used to give
ils elles	-aient	ils donn**aient** elles donn**aient**	they gave they were giving they used to give

Il <u>portait</u> toujours un grand chapeau noir.	He always wore a big black hat.
Nous <u>habitions</u> à Paris à cette époque.	We were living in Paris at that time.
Pour gagner un peu d'argent, je <u>donnais</u> des cours de français.	To earn a little money I used to give French lessons.

Tip

je changes to j' in front of a word starting with a vowel, most words starting with h, and the French word y.

3 Forming the imperfect tense of -ir verbs

➤ To form the imperfect tense of -ir verbs, you use the same stem of the verb as for the present tense. Then you add the correct ending, depending on whether you are referring to je, tu, il, elle, on, nous, vous, ils, or elles.

Pronoun	Ending	Add to stem, e.g. fin-	Meanings
je (j')	-issais	je finissais	I finished I was finishing I used to finish
tu	-issais	tu finissais	you finished you were finishing you used to finish
il elle on	-issait	il finissait elle finissait on finissait	he/she/it/one finished he/she/it/one was finishing he/she/it/one used to finish
nous	-issions	nous finissions	we finished we were finishing we used to finish
vous	-issiez	vous finissiez	you finished you were finishing you used to finish
ils elles	-issaient	ils finissaient elles finissaient	they finished they were finishing they used to finish

Il finissait souvent ses devoirs avant le dîner.

He often finished his homework before dinner.

Cet après-midi-là ils choisissaient une bague de fiançailles.

That afternoon they were choosing an engagement ring.

4 Forming the imperfect tense of -re verbs

➤ To form the imperfect tense of -re verbs, you use the same stem of the verb as for the present tense. Then you add the correct ending, depending on whether you are referring to je, tu, il, elle, on, nous, vous, ils, or elles. These endings are the same as for -er verbs.

Pronoun	Ending	Add to stem, e.g. attend-	Meanings
j' (j')	-ais	j'attend<u>ais</u>	I waited I was waiting I used to wait
tu	-ais	tu attend<u>ais</u>	you waited you were waiting you used to wait
il elle on	-ait	il attend<u>ait</u> elle attend<u>ait</u> on attend<u>ait</u>	he/she/it/one waited he/she/it/one was waiting he/she/it/one used to wait
nous	-ions	nous attend<u>ions</u>	we waited we were waiting we used to wait
vous	-iez	vous attend<u>iez</u>	you waited you were waiting you used to wait
ils elles	-aient	ils attend<u>aient</u> elles attend<u>aient</u>	they waited they were waiting they used to wait

Christine m'<u>attendait</u> tous les soirs à la sortie.

Christine used to wait for me every evening at the exit.

Je <u>vivais</u> seule après mon divorce.

I was living alone after my divorce.

5 Spelling changes in -er verbs

➤ As with the present tense, a few -er verbs change their spellings slightly when they are used in the imperfect tense. The forms with spelling changes have been <u>underlined</u> in the tables.

➤ With verbs such as **lancer** (meaning to throw), which end in **-cer**, c becomes ç before an a or an o. This is so that the letter c is still pronounced as in the English word ice.

Pronoun	Example verb: lancer
je	<u>lançais</u>
tu	<u>lançais</u>
il elle on	<u>lançait</u>
nous	lancions
vous	lanciez
ils elles	<u>lançaient</u>

➤ With verbs such as **manger** (meaning *to eat*), which end in **-ger**, g becomes **ge** before an **a** or an **o**. This is so the letter **g** is still pronounced like the *s* in the English word *leisure*.

Pronoun	Example verb: manger
je	mangeais
tu	mangeais
il elle on	mangeait
nous	mangions
vous	mangiez
ils elles	mangeaient

➤ These verbs follow the 1,2,3,6 pattern. That is, they change in the first, second and third person singular, and in the third person plural.

6 Reflexive verbs in the imperfect tense

➤ The imperfect tense of reflexive verbs is formed exactly as for ordinary verbs, except that you add the reflexive pronoun (**me**, **te**, **se**, **nous**, **vous**, **se**).

Subject pronoun	Reflexive pronoun	Example with laver	Meaning
je	me (m')	lavais	I washed I was washing I used to wash
tu	te (t')	lavais	you washed you were washing you used to wash
il elle on	se (s')	lavait	he/she/it/one washed he/she/it/one was washing he/she/it/one used to wash
nous	nous	lavions	we washed we were washing we used to wash
vous	vous	laviez	you washed you were washing you used to wash
ils elles	se (s')	lavaient	they washed they were washing they used to wash

> ***Tip***
> **me** changes to **m'**, **te** to **t'**, and **se** to **s'** before a vowel, most
> words starting with **h**, and the French word **y**.

7 | Irregular verbs in the imperfect tense

➤ The only verb that is irregular in the imperfect tense is **être**.

Pronoun	être	Meaning
j'	étais	I was
tu	étais	you were
il elle on	était	he/she/it/one was
nous	étions	we were
vous	étiez	you were
ils elles	étaient	they were

J'<u>étais</u> heureux.   I was happy.

Mon père <u>était</u> instituteur.   My father was an elementary school
teacher.

> **Key points**
> ✔ The imperfect tense endings for **-er** and **-re** verbs are:
> **-ais, -ais, -ait, -ions, -iez, -aient**.
> ✔ The imperfect tense endings for **-ir** verbs are:
> **-issais, -issais, -issait, -issions, -issiez, -issaient**.
> ✔ In verbs ending in **-cer** and **-ger**:
> **c → ç** and **g → ge** in all but the **nous** and **vous** forms.
> ✔ **être** is irregular in the imperfect tense.

The future tense

> **What is the future tense?**
> The **future tense** is a verb tense used to talk about something that will happen or will be true.

1 Using the future tense

➤ In English the future tense is often shown by *will* or its shortened form *'ll*.

> What <u>will</u> you do?
> The weather <u>will</u> be warm and dry tomorrow.
> He<u>'ll</u> be here soon.
> I<u>'ll</u> give you a call.

➤ Just as in English, you can use the present tense in French to refer to something that is going to happen in the future.

> Je <u>prends</u> le train de dix heures.   I'm taking the ten o'clock train.
> Nous <u>allons</u> à Paris la semaine   We're going to Paris next week.
> prochaine.

➤ In English we often use *going to* followed by an infinitive to talk about something that will happen in the immediate future. You can use the French verb **aller** (meaning *to go*) followed by an infinitive in the same way.

> Tu <u>vas tomber</u> si tu continues.   You're going to fall if you keep it up.
> Il <u>va manquer</u> le train.   He's going to miss the train.

> *Tip*
> Remember that French has no direct equivalent of the word *will* in verb forms like *will rain* or *will look* and so on. You change the French verb ending instead to form the future tense.

2 Forming the future tense

➤ To form the future tense in French, you use:
- the <u>infinitive</u> of -er and -ir verbs, for example, **donner**, **finir**
- the <u>infinitive without the final e</u> of -re verbs: for example, **attendr-**

➤ Then add the correct ending to the stem, depending on whether you are talking about **je**, **tu**, **il**, **elle**, **on**, **nous**, **vous**, **ils**, or **elles**. The endings are the same for -er, -ir, and -re verbs.

i Note that apart from the **nous** and **vous** forms, the endings are the same as the present tense of **avoir**.

⇨ *For the present tense of avoir, see page 82.*

Pronoun	Ending	Add to stem, e.g. donner-, finir-, attendr-	Meanings
je (j')	-ai	je donner<u>ai</u> je finir<u>ai</u> j'attendr<u>ai</u>	I will give I will finish I will wait
tu	-as	tu donner<u>as</u> tu finir<u>as</u> tu attendr<u>as</u>	you will give you will finish you will wait
il elle on	-a	il/elle/on donner<u>a</u> il/elle/on finir<u>a</u> il/elle/on attendr<u>a</u>	he/she/it/one will give he/she/it/one will finish he/she/it/one will wait
nous	-ons	nous donner<u>ons</u> nous finir<u>ons</u> nous attendr<u>ons</u>	we will give we will finish we will wait
vous	-ez	vous donner<u>ez</u> vous finir<u>ez</u> vous attendr<u>ez</u>	you will give you will finish you will wait
ils elles	-ont	ils/elles donner<u>ont</u> ils/elles finir<u>ont</u> ils/elles attendr<u>ont</u>	they will give they will finish they will wait

Elle te <u>donnera</u> mon adresse. — She'll give you my address.
Le cours <u>finira</u> à onze heures. — The class will finish at eleven o'clock.
Nous t'<u>attendrons</u> devant le cinéma. — We'll wait for you in front of the movie theater.

Tip
je changes to **j'** in front of a word starting with a vowel, most words starting with **h**, and the French word **y**.

3 Spelling changes in -er verbs

➤ As with the present and imperfect tenses, a few **-er** verbs change their spellings slightly in the future tense. The forms with spelling changes have been <u>underlined</u> in the tables.

➤ With verbs such as **appeler** (meaning *to call*), which end in **-eler**, the l doubles throughout the future tense. The double consonant (**ll**) affects the pronunciation of the word. In **appeler**, the first e sounds like the vowel sound at the end of the English word *teacher*, but in **appellerai** the first e sounds like the one in the English word *pet*.

Pronoun	Example verb: appeler
j'	appellerai
tu	appelleras
il elle on	appellera
nous	appellerons
vous	appellerez
ils elles	appelleront

➤ The exceptions to this rule are **geler** (meaning *to freeze*) and **peler** (meaning *to peel*), which change in the same way as **lever** (*see page 101*).

➤ With verbs such as **jeter** (meaning *to throw*), that end in **-eter**, the t doubles throughout the future tense. The double consonant (**tt**) affects the pronunciation of the word. In **jeter**, the first e sounds like the vowel sound at the end of the English word *teacher*, but in **jetterai** the first e sounds like the one in the English word *pet*.

Pronoun	Example verb: jeter
je	jetterai
tu	jetteras
il elle on	jettera
nous	jetterons
vous	jetterez
ils elles	jetteront

➤ The exceptions to this rule include **acheter** (meaning *to buy*), which changes in the same way as **lever** (*see page 101*).

➤ With verbs such as **nettoyer** (meaning *to clean*), that end in **-yer**, the **y** changes to **i** throughout the future tense.

Pronoun	Example verb: nettoyer
je	nettoierai
tu	nettoieras
il elle on	nettoiera
nous	nettoierons
vous	nettoierez
ils elles	nettoieront

➤ Verbs ending in **-ayer**, such as **payer** (meaning *to pay*) and **essayer** (meaning *to try*), can be spelled with either a **y** or an **i**. So **je paierai** and **je payerai**, for example, are both correct.

➤ With verbs such as **lever** (meaning *to raise*), **peser** (meaning *to weigh*) and **acheter** (meaning *to buy*), **e** changes to **è** throughout the future tense. In **lever** the first **e** sounds like the vowel sound at the end of the English word *teacher*, but in **lèverai** and so on the first **e** sounds like the one in the English word *pet*.

Pronoun	Example verb: lever
je	lèverai
tu	lèveras
il elle on	lèvera
nous	lèverons
vous	lèverez
ils elles	lèveront

4 Reflexive verbs in the future tense

➤ The future tense of reflexive verbs is formed in exactly the same way as for ordinary verbs, except that you have to remember to give the reflexive pronoun (me, se, nous, vous, se).

Subject pronoun	Reflexive pronoun	Example with laver	Meaning
je	me (m')	laverai	I will wash
tu	te (t')	laveras	you will wash
il elle on	se (s')	lavera	he/she/it/one will wash
nous	nous	laverons	we will wash
vous	vous	laverez	you will wash
ils elles	se (s')	laveront	they will wash

> **Tip**
>
> me changes to m', te to t', and se to s' before a vowel, most words starting with h, and the French word y.

5 Irregular verbs in the future tense

➤ There are some verbs that <u>do not</u> use their infinitives as the stem for the future tense, including avoir, être, faire, and aller, which are shown in full on pages 103–104.

➤ Other irregular verbs include:

Verb	Meaning	je	tu	il/elle/on	nous	vous	ils/elles
devoir	to have to, must	devrai	devras	devra	devrons	devrez	devront
pouvoir	to be able to, can	pourrai	pourras	pourra	pourrons	pourrez	pourront
savoir	to know	saurai	sauras	saura	saurons	saurez	sauront
tenir	to hold	tiendrai	tiendras	tiendra	tiendrons	tiendrez	tiendront
venir	to come	viendrai	viendras	viendra	viendrons	viendrez	viendront
voir	to see	verrai	verras	verra	verrons	verrez	verront
vouloir	to want	voudrai	voudras	voudra	voudrons	voudrez	voudront

For further explanation of grammatical terms, please see pages viii–xii.

➤ **il faut** becomes **il faudra** (meaning *it will be necessary to*).

➤ **il pleut** becomes **il pleuvra** (meaning *it will rain*).

➤ This is the future tense of **avoir**:

Pronoun	avoir	**Meaning:** *to have*
j'	aurai	I will have
tu	auras	you will have
il elle on	aura	he/she/it/one will have
nous	aurons	we will have
vous	aurez	you will have
ils elles	auront	they will have

➤ This is the future tense of **être**:

Pronoun	être	**Meaning:** *to be*
je	serai	I will be
tu	seras	you will be
il elle on	sera	he/she/it/one will be
nous	serons	we will be
vous	serez	you will be
ils elles	seront	they will be

➤ This is the future tense of **faire**:

Pronoun	faire	**Meaning:** *to do, to make*
je	ferai	I will do/make
tu	feras	you will do/make
il elle on	fera	he/she/it/one will do/make
nous	ferons	we will do/make
vous	ferez	you will do/make
ils elles	feront	they will do/make

➤ This is the future tense of **aller**:

Pronoun	aller	Meaning: *to go*
j'	irai	I will go
tu	iras	you will go
il elle on	ira	he/she/it/one will go
nous	irons	we will go
vous	irez	you will go
ils elles	iront	they will go

⇨ *For **Verb tables**, see supplement.*

Key points

✔ You can use a present tense in French to talk about something that will happen or be true in the future, just as in English.

✔ You can use **aller** with an infinitive to refer to things that will happen in the immediate future.

✔ The stem is the same as the infinitive for -er, -ir, and -re verbs, except that the final -e of -re verbs is lost.

✔ The future tense endings are the same for -er, -ir, and -re verbs: -ai, -as, -a, -ons, -ez, -ont.

✔ In verbs ending in -eler and -eter:
l → ll and t → tt throughout the future tense.

✔ In verbs ending in -yer:
y → i throughout the future tense (optional in -ayer verbs).

✔ Some verbs are irregular in the future tense. It is worth learning these in full.

The conditional

> **What is the conditional?**
> The **conditional** is a verb form used to talk about things that would happen
> or that would be true under certain conditions, for example, I _would_ help you
> _if I could_.
> It is also used to say what you would like or need, for example, _Could_ you give
> me the bill?

1 Using the conditional

➤ You can often recognize a conditional in English by the word _would_ or its
shortened form _'d_.

I _would_ be sad if you left.
If you asked him, he_'d_ help you.

➤ You use the conditional for:

- asking for something formally and politely, especially in a store
  I_'d_ like a pound of pears, please.
- saying what you would like
  I_'d_ like to go to Paris.
- making a suggestion
  I _could_ come and pick you up.
- giving advice
  You _should_ say you're sorry.

> _Tip_
> There is no direct French translation of _would_ in verb forms like
> _would be_, _would like_, _would help_ and so on. You change the French verb
> ending instead.

2 Forming the conditional

➤ To form the conditional in French, you have to use:

- the infinitive of **-er** and **-ir** verbs, for example, **donner-**, **finir-**
- the infinitive without the final **e** of **-re** verbs, for example, **attendr-**

➤ Then add the correct ending to the stem, depending on whether you are
talking about **je**, **tu**, **il**, **elle**, **on**, **nous**, **vous**, **ils**, or **elles**. The endings are the
same for all verbs. In fact, they are the same as the **-er** and **-re** endings for the
IMPERFECT TENSE, but the stem is the same as the FUTURE TENSE.

⇨ _For more information on the **Imperfect tense** and the **Future tense**, see pages 92 and 98._

Pronoun	Ending	Add to stem, e.g. donner-, finir-, attendr-	Meanings
je (j')	-ais	je donnerais je finirais j'attendrais	I would give I would finish I would wait
tu	-ais	tu donnerais tu finirais tu attendrais	you would give you would finish you would wait
il elle on	-ait	il/elle/on donnerait il/elle/on finirait il/elle/on attendrait	he/she/it/one would give he/she/it/one would finish he/she/it/one would wait
nous	-ions	nous donnerions nous finirions nous attendrions	we would give we would finish we would wait
vous	-iez	vous donneriez vous finiriez vous attendriez	you would give you would finish you would wait
ils elles	-aient	ils/elles donneraient ils/elles finiraient ils/elles attendraient	they would give they would finish they would wait

J'<u>aimerais</u> aller à Paris.   I'd like to go to Paris.

Tip

je changes to j' in front of a word starting with a vowel, most words starting with h, and the French word y.

[i] Note that you have to be careful not to mix up the future tense and the conditional. They look very similar.

FUTURE	CONDITIONAL
je donnerai	je donnerais
je finirai	je finirais
j'attendrai	j'attendrais
j'aimerai	j'aimerais
je voudrai	je voudrais
je viendrai	je viendrais
je serai	je serais

3 | **Spelling changes in -er verbs**

➤ As with the future tense, a few **-er** verbs change their spellings slightly in the conditional. The forms with spelling changes have been <u>underlined</u> in the tables below.

➤ With verbs such as **appeler** (meaning *to call*), which end in **-eler**, the **l** doubles throughout the conditional. The double consonant (**ll**) affects the pronunciation of the word. In **appeler**, the first **e** sounds like the vowel sound at the end of the English word *teacher*, but in **appellerais** the first **e** sounds like the one in the English word *pet*.

Pronoun	Example verb: appeler
j'	<u>appellerais</u>
tu	<u>appellerais</u>
il elle on	<u>appellerait</u>
nous	<u>appellerions</u>
vous	<u>appelleriez</u>
ils elles	<u>appelleraient</u>

➤ The exceptions to this rule are **geler** (meaning *to freeze*) and **peler** (meaning *to peel*), which change in the same way as **lever** (*see page 108*).

➤ With verbs such as **jeter** (meaning *to throw*), which end in **-eter**, the **t** doubles throughout the conditional. The double consonant (**tt**) affects the pronunciation of the word. In **jeter**, the first **e** sounds like the vowel sound at the end of the English word *teacher*, but in **jetterais** the first **e** sounds like the one in the English word *pet*.

Pronoun	Example verb: jeter
je	<u>jetterais</u>
tu	<u>jetterais</u>
il elle on	<u>jetterait</u>
nous	<u>jetterions</u>
vous	<u>jetteriez</u>
ils elles	<u>jetteraient</u>

➤ The exceptions to this rule include **acheter** (meaning *to buy*), which changes in the same way as **lever** (*see page 108*).

➤ With verbs such as **nettoyer** (meaning *to clean*), that end in **-yer**, the y changes to i throughout the conditional.

Pronoun	Example verb: nettoyer
je	nettoierais
tu	nettoierais
il elle on	nettoierait
nous	nettoierions
vous	nettoieriez
ils elles	nettoieraient

➤ Verbs ending in **-ayer**, such as **payer** (meaning *to pay*) and **essayer** (meaning *to try*), can be spelled with either a y or an i. So **je paierais** and **je payerais**, for example, are both correct.

➤ With verbs such as **lever** (meaning *to raise*), **peser** (meaning *to weigh*), and **acheter** (meaning *to buy*), e changes to è throughout the conditional. In **lever** the first e sounds like the vowel sound at the end of the English word *teacher*, but in **lèverais** and so on the first e sounds like the one in the English word *pet*.

Pronoun	Example verb: lever
je	lèverais
tu	lèverais
il elle on	lèverait
nous	lèverions
vous	lèveriez
ils elles	lèveraient

4 Reflexive verbs in the conditional

➤ The conditional of reflexive verbs is formed in exactly the same way as for ordinary verbs, except that you have to remember to give the reflexive pronoun (me, te, se, nous, vous, se).

Subject pronoun	Reflexive pronoun	Example with laver	Meaning
je	me (m')	laverais	I would wash
tu	te (t')	laverais	you would wash
il elle on	se (s')	laverait	he/she/it would wash
nous	nous	laverions	we would wash
vous	vous	laveriez	you would wash
ils elles	se (s')	laveraient	they would wash

Tip

me changes to m', te to t', and se to s' before a vowel, most words starting with h, and the French word y.

5 Irregular verbs in the conditional

➤ The same verbs that are irregular in the future tense are irregular in the conditional, including: avoir, être, faire, aller, devoir, pouvoir, savoir, tenir, venir, voir, vouloir.

➪ For more information on **Irregular verbs in the future tense**, see page 102.

➤ To form the conditional of an irregular verb, use the same stem as for the future tense, for example:

avoir → aur-
être → ser-

➤ Then add the usual endings for the conditional.

Infinitive	Future stem	Conditional endings	Conditional form
avoir	aur-	-ais, -ais, -ait, -ions, -iez, -aient	j'aurais, tu aurais, il/elle/on aurait, nous aurions, vous auriez, ils/elles auraient
être	ser-	-ais, -ais, -ait, -ions, -iez, -aient	je serais, tu serais, il/elle/on serait, nous serions, vous seriez, ils/elles seraient
faire	fer-	-ais, -ais, -ait, -ions, -iez, -aient	je ferais, tu ferais, il/elle/on ferait nous ferions, vous feriez, ils/elles feraient
aller	ir-	-ais, -ais, -ait, -ions, -iez, -aient	j'irais, tu irais, il/elle/on irait, nous irions, vous iriez, ils/elles iraient

J'irais si j'avais le temps.	I would go if I had time.
Je voudrais un kilo de poires, s'il vous plaît.	I'd like a kilo of pears, please.
Tu devrais t'excuser.	You should say you're sorry.

Key points

✔ The conditional endings are the same for -er, -ir, and -re verbs: -ais, -ais, -ait, -ions, -iez, -aient.

✔ The conditional endings are the same as the endings for the imperfect tense of -er and -re verbs, but the stem is the same as the stem of the future tense.

✔ In verbs ending in -eler and -eter:
l → ll and t → tt throughout the conditional.

✔ In verbs ending in -yer:
y → i throughout the conditional (optional in -ayer verbs).

✔ The same verbs that are irregular in the future are irregular in the conditional. It is worth learning these in full.

The perfect tense

> **What is the perfect tense?**
> The **perfect** is one of the verb tenses used to talk about the past, especially about actions that took place and were completed in the past.

1 Using the perfect tense

➤ You can often recognize the perfect tense in English by a form like *I gave*, *I have finished*.

> I <u>gave</u> her my phone number.
> I <u>have finished</u> my soup.

> *Tip*
> The perfect tense is the tense you will need most to talk about things that have happened or were true in the past. It is used to talk about actions that took place and <u>WERE COMPLETED</u> in the past.
> Use the <u>imperfect tense</u> for regular events and in most descriptions.
>
> ⇨ *For more information on the **Imperfect tense**, see page 92.*

2 Forming the perfect tense

➤ The imperfect, future and conditional tenses in French are made up of just <u>one</u> word, for example, **je donne**, **tu finissais**, or **il attendra**. The perfect tense has <u>TWO</u> parts to it:

- the <u>present</u> tense of the verb **avoir** (meaning *to have*) or **être** (meaning *to be*)
- a part of the main verb called the <u>past participle</u>, like *given*, *finished*, and *done* in English

➤ In other words, the perfect tense in French is like the form *I have done* in English.

⇨ *For more information on forming the present tense of **avoir** and **être**, see page 82.*

3 Forming the past participle

➤ To form the past participle of regular verbs, you use the <u>infinitive</u> of the verb:

- For **-er** verbs, you replace the **-er** at the end of the infinitive with **é**.

Infinitive	Take off -er	Add -é
donner (*to give*)	donn-	donn<u>é</u>
tomber (*to fall*)	tomb-	tomb<u>é</u>

- For **-ir** verbs, you replace the **-ir** at the end of the infinitive with **-i**.

Infinitive	Take off -ir	Add -i
finir (*to finish*)	fin-	fin<u>i</u>
partir (*to leave, to go*)	part-	part<u>i</u>

- For **-re** verbs, you replace the **-re** at the end of the infinitive with **-u**.

Infinitive	Take off -re	Add -u
attendre (*to wait*)	attend-	attend<u>u</u>
descendre (*to go down, to come down, to get off*)	descend-	descend<u>u</u>

4 | **Verbs that form their perfect tense with** <u>avoir</u>

➤ Most verbs form their perfect tense with **avoir**, for example **donner**:

Pronoun	avoir	Past participle	Meaning
j'	ai	donné	I gave I have given
tu	as	donné	you gave you have given
il elle on	a	donné	he/she/it/one gave he/she/it/one has given
nous	avons	donné	we gave we have given
vous	avez	donné	you gave you have given
ils elles	ont	donné	they gave they have given

Elle <u>a donné</u> son numéro de téléphone à Claude.

She gave Claude her phone number.

Il <u>a acheté</u> un ordinateur.

He's bought a computer.

Je n'<u>ai</u> pas <u>regardé</u> la télé hier.

I didn't watch TV yesterday.

For further explanation of grammatical terms, please see pages viii-xii.

> *Tip*
> je changes to j' in front of a word starting with a vowel, most words starting with h, and the French word y.

➤ The perfect tense of -ir verbs like finir is formed in the same way, except for the past participle: j'ai fini, tu as fini and so on.

➤ The perfect tense of -re verbs like attendre is formed in the same way, except for the past participle: j'ai attendu, tu as attendu and so on.

5 avoir or être?

➤ MOST verbs form their perfect tense with avoir; these include donner as shown on page 112.

➤ There are two main groups of verbs which form their perfect tense with être instead of avoir:

- all reflexive verbs

⇨ *For more information on **Reflexive verbs**, see page 88.*

- a group of verbs that are mainly used to talk about movement or a change of some kind, including these:

aller	to go
venir	to come
arriver	to arrive, to happen
partir	to leave, to go
descendre	to go down, to come down, to get off
monter	to go up, to come up
entrer	to go in, to come in
sortir	to go out, to come out
mourir	to die
naître	to be born
devenir	to become
rester	to stay
tomber	to fall

Je <u>suis allé</u> au match de football hier.	I went to the soccer game match yesterday.
Il <u>est sorti</u> acheter un journal.	He's gone out to buy a newspaper.
Vous <u>êtes descendu</u> à quelle station ?	Which station did you get off at?

Grammar Extra!

Some of the verbs on the previous page take avoir when they are used with a direct object, for example:

descendre quelque chose	to get something down, to bring something down, to take something down
monter quelque chose	to go up something, to come up something
sortir quelque chose	to take something out
Est-ce que tu <u>as descendu</u> les bagages ?	Did you bring the bags down?
Elle <u>a monté</u> les escaliers.	She went up the stairs.
Elle <u>a sorti</u> son porte-monnaie de son sac.	She took her wallet out of her purse.

⇨ For more information on **Direct objects**, see page 47.

---

6 | **Verbs that form their perfect tense with <u>être</u>**

➤ When a verb takes être, the past participle <u>ALWAYS</u> agrees with the subject of the verb; that is, the endings change in the feminine and plural forms.

	Masculine endings	Examples	Feminine endings	Examples
Singular	-	tombé parti descendu	-e	tombé<u>e</u> parti<u>e</u> descendu<u>e</u>
Plural	-s	tombé<u>s</u> parti<u>s</u> descendu<u>s</u>	-es	tombé<u>es</u> parti<u>es</u> descendu<u>es</u>

Est-ce que ton frère est <u>allé</u> à l'étranger ?	Did your brother go abroad?
Elle est <u>venue</u> avec nous.	She came with us.
Ils sont <u>partis</u> à six heures.	They left at six o'clock.
Mes cousines sont <u>arrivées</u> hier.	My cousins arrived yesterday. (*The cousins are female.*)

For further explanation of grammatical terms, please see pages viii-xii.

➤ Here are the perfect tense forms of **tomber** in full:

Pronoun	avoir	Past participle	Meaning
je	suis	tombé (*masculine*) tombée (*feminine*)	I fell/I have fallen
tu	es	tombé (*masculine*) tombée (*feminine*)	you fell/you have fallen
il	est	tombé	he/it fell, he/it has fallen
elle	est	tombée	she/it fell, she/it has fallen
on	est	tombé (*singular*) tombés (*masculine plural*) tombées (*feminine plural*)	one fell/one has fallen, we fell/we have fallen
nous	sommes	tombés (*masculine*) tombées (*feminine*)	we fell/we have fallen
vous	êtes	tombé (*masculine singular*) tombée (*feminine singular*) tombés (*masculine plural*) tombées (*feminine plural*)	you fell/you have fallen
ils	sont	tombés	they fell/they have fallen
elles	sont	tombées	they fell/they have fallen

Grammar Extra!

When **on** means *we*, the past participle can agree with the subject of the sentence, but it is optional.

On est <u>arrivés</u> en retard.   We arrived late. (*masculine*)

**On est <u>rentrées</u> toutes les deux   We both came in at the same time.
à la même heure.**   (*feminine*)

➤ The perfect tense of **-ir** verbs like **partir** is formed in the same way, except for the past participle: **je suis parti(e)**, **tu es parti(e)** and so on.

➤ The perfect tense of **-re** verbs like **descendre** is formed in the same way, except for the past participle: **je suis descendu(e)**, **tu es descendu(e)** and so on.

Grammar Extra!

When a verb takes **avoir**, the past participle usually stays in the masculine singular form, as shown in the table for **donner**, and does not change for the feminine or plural forms.

Il a <u>fini</u> sa dissertation.	He finished his essay.
Elles ont <u>fini</u> leur dissertation.	They've finished their essay.

In one particular case, however, the past participle of verbs with **avoir** does change in the feminine and plural forms. In the sentences above, **dissertation** is the direct object of the verb **finir.** When the direct object comes <u>AFTER</u> the verb, as it does in the examples above, then the past participle doesn't change. If the direct object comes <u>BEFORE</u> the verb, however, the past participle has to change to agree with that direct object.

<u>la</u> dissertation qu'il a fini<u>e</u> hier	the essay that he finished yesterday
<u>la</u> dissertation qu'elles ont fini<u>e</u> hier	the essay that they finished yesterday

Since object pronouns usually come BEFORE the verb, the past participle changes to agree with the pronoun.

Il a bu son thé ? – Oui, il <u>l'</u>a <u>bu</u>.	Did he drink his tea? – Yes, he drank it.
Il a bu sa limonade ? – Oui, il <u>l'</u>a <u>bue</u>.	Did he drink his lemonade? – Yes, he drank it.

> *Tip*
>
> Remember that with verbs taking **être**, it is the <u>subject</u> of the verb that tells you what ending to add to the past participle. Compare this with the rule for verbs taking **avoir** that have a direct object; in their case, it is the <u>direct object</u> coming before the verb that tells you what ending to add to the past participle.

7 The perfect tense of reflexive verbs

➤ Here is the perfect tense of the reflexive verb **se laver** (meaning *to wash (oneself), to wash up, to get washed*) in full. Remember that all reflexive verbs take **être**, and so the past participle of reflexive verbs usually agrees with the subject of the sentence.

Subject pronoun	Reflexive pronoun	Present tense of être	Past participle	Meaning
je	me	suis	lavé (*masculine*) lavée (*feminine*)	I washed myself
tu	t'	es	lavé (*masculine*) lavée (*feminine*)	you washed yourself
il	s'	est	lavé	he washed himself one washed oneself
elle	s'	est	lavée	she washed herself
on	s'	est	lavé (*singular*) lavés (*masculine plural*) lavées (*feminine plural*)	one washed oneself we washed ourselves
nous	nous	sommes	lavés (*masculine*) lavées (*feminine*)	we washed ourselves
vous	vous	êtes	lavé (*masculine singular*) lavée (*feminine singular*) lavés (*masculine plural*) lavées (*feminine plural*)	you washed yourself (*singular*) you washed yourselves (*plural*)
ils	se	sont	lavés	they washed themselves
elles	se	sont	lavées	they washed themselves

Tip

When **on** means *we*, the past participle can agree with the subject of the sentence, but it is optional.

On s'est <u>lavées</u> l'une après l'autre.

We washed ourselves one after the other. (*feminine*)

Grammar Extra!

The past participle of reflexive verbs <u>DOES NOT</u> change if the direct object (**la jambe** in the example below) <u>FOLLOWS</u> the verb.

Elle s'<u>est cassé</u> la jambe.   She broke her leg.

---

8 Irregular verbs in the perfect tense

➤ Some past participles are irregular. There aren't too many, so try to learn them.

avoir (meaning *to have*)	→ **eu**
devoir (meaning *to have to, must*)	→ **dû**
dire (meaning *to say, to tell*)	→ **dit**
être (meaning *to be*)	→ **été**
faire (meaning *to do, to make*)	→ **fait**
mettre (meaning *to put*)	→ **mis**
pouvoir (meaning *to be able to, can*)	→ **pu**
prendre (meaning *to take*)	→ **pris**
savoir (meaning *to know*)	→ **su**
tenir (meaning *to hold*)	→ **tenu**
venir (meaning *to come*)	→ **venu**
voir (meaning *to see*)	→ **vu**
vouloir (meaning *to want*)	→ **voulu**

➤ **il pleut** becomes **il a plu** (*it rained*).

➤ **il faut** becomes **il a fallu** (*it was necessary*).

Key points

✔ The perfect tense describes things that happened and were completed in the past. It is not used for things that happened regularly or in descriptions.

✔ The perfect tense is formed with the present tense of **avoir** or **être** and a past participle.

✔ Most verbs take **avoir** in the perfect tense. All reflexive verbs and a small group of verbs referring to movement or change take **être**.

✔ The past participle ends in -é for -er verbs, in -i for -ir verbs, and in -u for -re verbs.

✔ With verbs that take **avoir**, the past participle does not usually change. With verbs that take **être**, including reflexive verbs, the past participle changes in the feminine and plural.

For further explanation of grammatical terms, please see pages viii-xii.

Grammar Extra!

The pluperfect tense

> **What is the pluperfect tense?**
> The **pluperfect** is a verb tense which describes something that <u>had</u> happened or <u>had</u> been true at a point in the past, for example, *I'd forgotten to finish my homework.*

1 Using the pluperfect tense

➤ You can often recognize a pluperfect tense in English by a form like *I had arrived, you'd fallen*.

Elle <u>avait essayé</u> des douzaines de pulls.	She <u>had tried on</u> dozens of sweaters.
Nous <u>avions</u> déjà <u>commencé</u> à manger quand il est arrivé.	We<u>'d</u> already <u>started</u> eating when he arrived.
J'<u>étais arrivée</u> la première.	I <u>had arrived</u> first.
Mes parents <u>s'étaient couchés</u> tôt.	My parents <u>had gone</u> to bed early.

2 Forming the pluperfect tense

➤ Like the perfect tense, the pluperfect tense in French has <u>two</u> parts to it:
  - the <u>imperfect</u> tense of the verb **avoir** (meaning *to have*) or **être** (meaning *to be*)
  - the past participle

➤ If a verb takes **avoir** in the perfect tense, then it will take **avoir** in the pluperfect too. If a verb takes **être** in the perfect, then it will take **être** in the pluperfect too.

⇨ *For more information on the **Imperfect tense** and the **Perfect tense**, see pages 92 and 111.*

3 Verbs taking avoir

➤ Here are the pluperfect tense forms of **donner** (meaning *to give*) in full.

Pronoun	avoir	Past participle	Meaning
j'	avais	donné	I had given
tu	avais	donné	you had given
il elle on	avait	donné	he/she/it/one had given
nous	avions	donné	we had given
vous	aviez	donné	you had given
ils elles	avaient	donné	they had given

➤ The pluperfect tense of -ir verbs like **finir** (meaning *to finish*) is formed in the same way, except for the past participle: **j'avais fini, tu avais fini** and so on.

➤ The pluperfect tense of -re verbs like **attendre** (meaning *to wait*) is formed in the same way, except for the past participle: **j'avais attendu, tu avais attendu** and so on.

4 | Verbs taking être

➤ Here are the pluperfect tense forms of **tomber** (meaning *to fall*) in full. When a verb takes être in the pluperfect tense, the past participle <u>always</u> agrees with the subject of the verb; that is, the endings change in the feminine and plural forms.

Pronoun	être	Past participle	Meaning
j'	étais	tombé (*masculine*) tombée (*feminine*)	I had fallen
tu	étais	tombé (*masculine*) tombée (*feminine*)	you had fallen
il	était	tombé	he/it had fallen
elle	était	tombée	she/it had fallen
on	était	tombé (*singular*) tombés (*masculine plural*) tombées (*feminine plural*)	one had fallen we had fallen
nous	étions	tombés (*masculine*) tombées (*feminine*)	we had fallen
vous	étiez	tombé (*masculine singular*) tombée (*feminine singular*) tombés (*masculine plural*) tombées (*feminine plural*)	you had fallen
ils	étaient	tombés	they had fallen
elles	étaient	tombées	they had fallen

➤ The pluperfect tense of -ir verbs like **partir** (meaning *to leave*, *to go*) is formed in the same way, except for the past participle: **j'étais parti(e)**, **tu étais parti(e)** and so on.

➤ The pluperfect tense of -re verbs like **descendre** (meaning *to come down*, *to go down*, *to get off*) is formed in the same way, except for the past participle: **j'étais descendu(e)**, **tu étais descendu(e)** and so on.

> *Tip*
>
> When **on** means *we*, the past participle can agree with the subject of the sentence, but it is optional.
>
> **On était <u>tombées</u>.**   We had fallen. (*feminine*)

5 | Reflexive verbs in the pluperfect tense

➤ Reflexive verbs in the pluperfect tense are formed in the same way as in the perfect tense, but with the imperfect tense of the verb être (*see page 97*).

➡ *For more information on the **Perfect tense of reflexive verbs**, see page 117.*

6 **Irregular verbs in the pluperfect tense**

➤ Irregular past participles are the same as for the perfect tense (*see page 118*).

> **Key points**
> ✔ The pluperfect tense describes things that had happened or were true at a point in the past before something else happened.
> ✔ It is formed with the imperfect tense of **avoir** or **être** and the past participle.
> ✔ The rules for agreement of the past participle are the same as for the perfect tense.

The passive

> **What is the passive?**
> The **passive** is a form of the verb that is used when the subject of the verb is the person or thing that is affected by the action, for example, *I was given, we were told, it had been made.*

1 Using the passive

➤ In a normal or *active* sentence, the "subject" of the verb is the person or thing that carries out the action described by the verb. The "object" of the verb is the person or thing that the verb "happens" to.

Ryan *(subject)* hit *(active verb)* me *(object)*.

➤ In English, as in French, you can turn an <u>active</u> sentence around to make a <u>passive</u> sentence.

I *(subject)* was hit *(passive verb)* by Ryan *(agent)*.

➤ Very often, however, you cannot identify who is carrying out the action indicated by the verb.

I was hit in the face.

The trees will be chopped down.

I've been chosen to represent the school.

Tip

There is a very important difference between French and English in sentences containing an <u>indirect object</u>. In English, we can very easily turn a normal (active) sentence with an indirect object into a passive sentence.

Active

Someone *(subject)* gave *(active verb)* me *(indirect object)* a book *(direct object)*.

Passive

I *(subject)* was given *(passive verb)* a book *(direct object)*.

In French, an indirect object can <u>NEVER</u> become the subject of a passive verb.

⇨ For more information on **Direct** and **Indirect objects**, see pages 47 and 49.

For further explanation of grammatical terms, please see pages viii-xii.

2 Forming the passive

➤ In English we use the verb *to be* with the past participle (*was hit, was given*) to form the passive. In French the passive is formed in exactly the same way, using **être** and the past participle. The past participle agrees with the subject of the passive verb; that is, the endings change in the feminine and plural forms.

Elle <u>est encouragée</u> par ses parents.	She is encouraged by her parents.
Vous <u>êtes</u> tous bien <u>payés</u>.	You are all well paid. (*"you" refers to more than one person here*)
Les portes <u>ont été fermées</u>.	The doors have been closed.

➪ *For more information on the **Past participle**, see page 111.*

➤ Here is the present tense of the -er verb **aimer** (meaning *to like, to love*) in its passive form.

Pronoun	Present tense of être	Past participle	Meaning
je	suis	aimé (*masculine*) aimée (*feminine*)	I am loved
tu	es	aimé (*masculine*) aimée (*feminine*)	you are loved
il	est	aimé	he/it is loved
elle	est	aimée	she/it is loved
on	est	aimé (*singular*) aimés (*masculine plural*) aimées (*feminine plural*)	one is loved we are loved
nous	sommes	aimés (*masculine*) aimées (*feminine*)	we are loved
vous	êtes	aimé (*masculine singular*) aimée (*feminine singular*) aimés (*masculine plural*) aimées (*feminine plural*)	you are loved
ils	sont	aimés	they are loved
elles	sont	aimées	they are loved

➤ The passive of -ir verbs is formed in the same way, except that the past participle is different. For example, **elle est remplie** (meaning *it is full*).

➤ The passive of -re verbs is formed in the same way, except that the past participle is different. For example, **il est défendu** (meaning *it is forbidden*).

Grammar Extra!

When **on** means *we*, the past participle can agree with the subject of the sentence, but it is optional.

> **On est <u>aimés</u> de tout le monde.**   We're loved by everyone. (*masculine*)

➤ You can form other tenses of the passive by changing the tense of the verb **être**.

> Imperfect: **j'étais aimé(e)** I was loved
> Future: **tu seras aimé(e)** you will be loved
> Perfect: **il a été aimé** he has been loved

⇨ *For more information on the **Imperfect**, **Future**, and **Perfect tenses**, see pages 92, 98 and 111.*

➤ Irregular past participles are the same as for the perfect tense (*see page 118*).

3 Avoiding the passive

➤ Passives are not as common in French as in English. There are <u>two</u> main ways that French speakers express the same idea.

- by using the pronoun **on** (meaning *someone* or *they*) with a normal, active verb

> **<u>On</u> leur a envoyé une lettre.**   They were sent a letter. (*literally: Someone sent them a letter.*)
>
> **<u>On</u> m'a dit que tu ne venais pas.**   I was told that you weren't coming. (*literally: They told me you weren't coming.*)

⇨ *For more information on **Pronouns**, see page 42.*

- by using a reflexive verb

> **Les melons <u>se vendent</u> 2 euros la pièce.**   Melons are sold for 2 euros each.

⇨ *For more information on **Reflexive verbs**, see page 88.*

> ### Key points
> ✔ The present tense of the passive is formed by using the present tense of **être** with the past participle.
> ✔ The past participle always agrees with the <u>subject</u> of the passive verb.
> ✔ You can sometimes avoid a passive construction by using a reflexive verb or the pronoun **on**.

For further explanation of grammatical terms, please see pages viii-xii.

Grammar Extra!

The present participle

> **What is a present participle?**
> The **present participle** is a verb form ending in *-ing* which is used in English to
> form verb tenses, and which may be used as an adjective and a noun, for example,
> *What are you doing?; the setting sun; Swimming is easy!*

1 Using the present participle

➤ Present participles are not as common in French as in English, because they are not
used to form tenses. The main uses of the present participle in French are:

- as a verb, on its own, corresponding to the English *-ing* form. It <u>DOES NOT</u> agree
  with the subject of the verb when it is used in this way.

<u>Habitant</u> près de Paris, je vais assez souvent en ville.	Living close to Paris, I go into town fairly often.
Ils m'ont suivi, <u>criant</u> mon nom.	They followed me, shouting my name.

- as a verb, after the preposition **en**. The present participle <u>DOES NOT</u> agree with
  the subject of the verb when it is used in this way. The subject of the two parts of
  the sentence is always the same. **en** can be translated in a number of different
  ways.

<u>En attendant</u> sa sœur, Richard s'est endormi.	While waiting for his sister, Richard fell asleep.
Appelle-nous <u>en arrivant</u> chez toi.	Call us when you get home.
<u>En appuyant</u> sur ce bouton, on peut imprimer ses documents.	By pressing this button, you can print your documents.
Il s'est blessé <u>en essayant</u> de sauver un chat.	He hurt himself trying to rescue a cat.

⇨ *For more information on the preposition en, see page 168.*

- as an adjective, like in English. As with all adjectives in French, the ending <u>DOES</u>
  change in the feminine and plural forms.

le soleil <u>couchant</u>	the setting sun
l'année <u>suivante</u>	the following year
Ces enfants sont <u>énervants</u>.	Those children are annoying.
des chaises <u>pliantes</u>	folding chairs

> ### Tip
>
> The French present participle is <u>NEVER</u> used to translate English verb forms like *I was walking, we are leaving*.
>
> ⇨ *For more information on the* **Imperfect tense** *and the* **Present tense**, *see pages 92 and 111.*

➤ English verbs describing movement that are followed by an adverb such as *out* or *down*, or a preposition such as *across* or *up* are often translated by a verb + en + present participle.

Il <u>est sorti en courant</u>.	He ran out. (*literally: He came out running.*)
J'<u>ai traversé</u> la rue <u>en boîtant</u>.	I limped across the street. (*literally: I crossed the street limping.*)

2 | Forming the present participle

➤ To form the present participle of regular -er, -ir, and -re verbs, you use the **nous** form of the present tense and replace the -**ons** ending with -**ant**.

nous form of present tense	Take off -ons	Add -ant
donnons	donn-	donnant
lançons	lanç-	lançant
mangeons	mange-	mangeant
finissons	finiss-	finissant
partons	part-	partant
attendons	attend-	attendant
descendons	descend-	descendant

3 | Irregular verbs

➤ Three verbs have an irregular present participle:

    avoir (meaning *to have*) → ayant
    être (meaning *to be*) → étant
    savoir (meaning *to know*) → sachant

> ### Key points
>
> ✔ Present participles are never used to form tenses in French, but they can be used as verbs, either on their own or after en.
> ✔ They can also be used as adjectives, in which case they agree with the noun they describe.
> ✔ They are formed by taking the nous form of the present tense and replacing the -ons ending with -ant. The exceptions are avoir, être, and savoir.

For further explanation of grammatical terms, please see pages viii-xii.

Impersonal verbs

> **What is an impersonal verb?**
> An **impersonal verb** is one that does not refer to a real person or thing and where the subject is represented by *it*, for example, *It's going to rain; It's ten o'clock.*

➤ Impersonal verbs are only used with **il** (meaning *it*) and in the infinitive. They are called impersonal verbs because **il** does not really refer to a real person, animal or thing, just like *it* and *there* in English in the examples below.

Il pleut.	It's raining.
Il va pleuvoir.	It's going to rain.
Il y a un problème.	There's a problem.
Il pourrait y avoir un problème.	There could be a problem.

➤ There are also some very common verbs that can be used in this way in addition to their normal meanings, for example, **avoir**, **être**, and **faire**.

Infinitive	Expression	Meaning
avoir + noun	il y a	there is (*singular*) there are (*plural*)
être + time	il est	it is
faire + noun	il fait jour il fait nuit	it's daylight it's dark
falloir + noun	il faut	we/you *etc.* need it takes
falloir + infinitive	il faut	we/you *etc.* have to
manquer	il manque	there is ... missing (*singular*) there are ... missing (*plural*)
paraître	il paraît que	it appears that it seems that
rester + noun	il reste	there is ... left (*singular*) there are ... left (*plural*)
sembler	il semble que	it appears that it seems that
valoir mieux + infinitive	il vaut mieux	it would be better to

Il y a quelqu'un à la porte.	There's somebody at the door.
Il est deux heures.	It's two o'clock.
Il faut partir.	I/We *etc.* have to go.
Il manque cent euros.	100 euros are missing.
Il reste du pain.	There's some bread left.
Il vaut mieux ne rien dire.	It would be better to say nothing.

➤ Several impersonal verbs relate to the weather.

Infinitive	Expression	Meaning
faire + adjective	il fait beau il fait mauvais	the weather's fine the weather's bad
faire + noun	il fait du vent il fait du soleil	it's windy it's sunny
geler	il gèle	it's freezing
neiger	il neige	it's snowing
pleuvoir	il pleut	it's raining

Grammar Extra!

There is another group of useful expressions that start with an impersonal il. These are followed by a form of the verb called the <u>subjunctive</u>.

il faut que
Il faut que je <u>parte</u>.   I have to go.

il est nécessaire que
Il est nécessaire qu'on le <u>fasse</u>. ·   We have to do it.

il est possible que
Il est possible qu'il <u>vienne</u>.   He might come.

il est dommage que
Il est dommage que tu ne   It's a shame you didn't see him.
l'<u>aies</u> pas vu.

⇨ *For more information on the **Subjunctive**, see page 129.*

> ### Key points
> ✔ Impersonal verbs can only be used in the infinitive and the il form.
> ✔ il faut, il y a, il est, and il fait with expressions relating to the weather are very common.

Grammar Extra!

The subjunctive

> **What is the subjunctive?**
> The **subjunctive** is a verb form that is used in certain circumstances to express some kind of feeling, or to show there is doubt about whether something will happen or whether something is true. It is only used occasionally in modern English, for example, *If I were you, I wouldn't bother.; So be it.*

1 Using the subjunctive

➤ In French the subjunctive is used after certain verbs and conjunctions when two parts of a sentence have different subjects.

I'm afraid <u>he</u> won't come back.
(The subject of the first part of the sentence is "I;" the subject of the second part of the sentence is "he.")

➤ Sometimes, in a sentence like *We want her to be happy.*, you use the infinitive of the verb in English (*to be*). This is <u>NOT</u> possible in French when there is a different subject in the two parts of the sentence (*we* and *her*). You have to use a subjunctive for the second verb.

Nous voulons être heureux. We want to be happy.
(No change of subject, so you can just use an infinitive – être – in French.)

Nous voulons qu'elle soit heureuse. We want her to be happy.
(Subject changes from nous to elle, so you have to use a subjunctive – soit – in French.)

➤ You can only use the infinitive instead of the subjunctive in French with impersonal verbs.

Il faut que tu <u>viennes</u> à l'heure. → **Il faut <u>venir</u> à l'heure.**
   (using subjunctive)   *(using infinitive)*
You have to come on time.

Il vaut mieux que tu <u>restes</u> chez toi. → **Il vaut mieux <u>rester</u> chez toi.**
   (using subjunctive)   *(using infinitive)*
It's better that you stay at home.

2 Coming across the subjunctive

➤ The subjunctive has several tenses, but you are only likely to come across the present subjunctive occasionally in your reading.

➤ You may see a subjunctive after certain verbs that you use when you are:

- wishing something: **vouloir que** and **désirer que** (meaning *to wish that, to want*), **aimer que** (meaning *to like that*), **aimer mieux que** and **préférer que** (meaning *to prefer that*)
- fearing something: **avoir peur que** (meaning *to be afraid that*)
- giving your opinion: **croire que** (meaning *to think that*)

- saying how you feel: **regretter que** (meaning *to be sorry that*), **être content que** (meaning *to be pleased that*), **être surpris que** (meaning *to be surprised that*) and so on

> Je suis content que vous les <u>aimiez</u>.

> I'm pleased you like them.

> J'ai peur qu'il ne <u>revienne</u> pas.

> I'm afraid he won't come back.

➤ You may see a subjunctive after certain verbal expressions starting with **il**, such as **il faut que** (meaning *it is necessary that*) and **il vaut mieux que** (meaning *it is better that*).

> Il faut que je vous <u>parle</u>.

> I need to speak to you.

⇨ *For a list of some expressions requiring the subjunctive, see page 128.*

3 | Forming the present subjunctive of -er verbs

➤ To form the stem of the present subjunctive you take the <u>infinitive</u> and chop off -er, just as for the present tense. Then you add the correct ending, depending on whether you are referring to **je, tu, il, elle, on, nous, vous, ils**, or **elles**.

➤ For -er verbs the endings are the same as for the ordinary present tense, apart from the **nous** and **vous** forms, which have an extra **i**, as in the imperfect tense.

Pronoun	Ending	Add to stem, e.g. donn-	Meanings
je (j')	-e	je donne	I give
tu	-es	tu donn<u>es</u>	you give
il elle on	-e	il donne elle donn<u>e</u> on donne	he/she/it/one gives
nous	-ions	nous donn<u>ions</u>	we give
vous	-iez	vous donn<u>iez</u>	you give
ils elles	-ent	ils donn<u>ent</u> elles donn<u>ent</u>	they give

> *Tip*
>
> **je** changes to **j'** in front of a word starting with a vowel, most words starting with **h**, and the French word **y**.

4 Forming the present subjunctive of -ir verbs

➤ To form the stem of the present subjunctive you take the <u>infinitive</u> and chop off **-ir**, just as for the present tense. Then you add the correct ending, depending on whether you are referring to to **je, tu, il, elle, on, nous, vous, ils,** or **elles.**

Pronoun	Ending	Add to stem, e.g. fin-	Meanings
je (j')	-isse	je fin<u>isse</u>	I finish
tu	-isses	tu fin<u>isses</u>	you finish
il elle on	-isse	il fin<u>isse</u> elle fin<u>isse</u> on fin<u>isse</u>	he/she/it/one finishes
nous	-issions	nous fin<u>issions</u>	we finish
vous	-issiez	vous fin<u>issiez</u>	you finish
ils elles	-issent	ils fin<u>issent</u> elles fin<u>issent</u>	they finish

> *Tip*
>
> **je** changes to **j'** in front of a word starting with a vowel, most words starting with **h**, and the French word **y**.

5 Forming the present subjunctive of -re verbs

➤ To form the stem of the present subjunctive you take the <u>infinitive</u> and chop off **-re**, just as for the present tense. Then you add the correct ending, depending on whether you are referring to **je, tu, il, elle, on, nous, vous, ils,** or **elles.**

Pronoun	Ending	Add to stem, e.g. attend-	Meanings
je (j')	-e	j'attend<u>e</u>	I wait
tu	-es	tu attend<u>es</u>	you wait
il elle on	-e	il attend<u>e</u> elle attend<u>e</u> on attend<u>e</u>	he/she/it/one waits
nous	-ions	nous attend<u>ions</u>	we wait
vous	-iez	vous attend<u>iez</u>	you wait
ils elles	-ent	ils attend<u>ent</u> elles attend<u>ent</u>	they wait

> *Tip*
>
> **je** changes to **j'** in front of a word starting with a vowel, most words starting with **h**, and the French word **y**.

6 Irregular verbs in the subjunctive

➤ Some important verbs have irregular subjunctive forms.

Verb	Meaning	je (j')	tu	il/elle/on	nous	vous	ils/elles
aller	to go	aille	ailles	aille	allions	alliez	aillent
avoir	to have	aie	aies	ait	ayons	ayez	aient
devoir	to have to, must	doive	doives	doive	devions	deviez	doivent
dire	to say, to tell	dise	dises	dise	disions	disiez	disent
être	to be	sois	sois	soit	soyons	soyez	soient
faire	to do, to make	fasse	fasses	fasse	fassions	fassiez	fassent
pouvoir	to be able to, can	puisse	puisses	puisse	puissions	puissiez	puissent
prendre	to take	prenne	prennes	prenne	prenions	preniez	prennent

(apprendre and comprendre also behave like this – j'apprenne, tu apprennes and so on)

Verb	Meaning	je (j')	tu	il/elle/on	nous	vous	ils/elles
savoir	to know	sache	saches	sache	sachions	sachiez	sachent
venir	to come	vienne	viennes	vienne	venions	veniez	viennent
vouloir	to want to	veuille	veuilles	veuille	voulions	vouliez	veuillent

Key points

✔ After certain verbs you have to use a subjunctive in French when there is a different subject in the two clauses. These verbs mostly relate to wishing, fearing, and saying what you think, what you feel and that you are uncertain. A subjunctive is also found after certain verbal expressions that start with il.

✔ The stem of the present tense subjunctive is the same as the stem used for the ordinary present tense.

✔ The present tense subjunctive endings for -er and -re verbs are: -e, -es, -e, -ions, -iez, and -ent.

✔ The present tense subjunctive endings for -ir verbs are: -isse, -isses, -isse, -issions, -issiez, and -issent.

Verbs followed by an infinitive

1 Linking two verbs together

➤ Many verbs in French can be followed by another verb in the infinitive. The infinitive is the form of the verb that is found in the dictionary, such as **donner** (meaning *to give*), **finir** (meaning *to finish*), and **attendre** (meaning *to wait*).

➤ There are three main ways that verbs can be linked together:

- with no linking word

  Vous voulez attendre ?   Would you like to wait?
- with the preposition à

  J'apprends <u>à</u> nager.   I'm learning to swim.
- with the preposition de

  Essayez <u>de</u> venir.   Try to come.

⇨ *For more information on **Prepositions after adjectives** and on **Prepositions after verbs**, see pages 183 and 178.*

2 Verbs followed by an infinitive with no preposition

➤ A number of verbs and groups of verbs can be followed by an infinitive with no preposition. The following important group of verbs are all very irregular, but they crop up so frequently that they are worth learning in full:

- **devoir** (*to have to, must, to be due to*)

  Tu <u>dois être</u> fatiguée.   You must be tired.

  Elle <u>doit partir</u>.   She has to leave.

  Le nouveau centre commercial <u>doit ouvrir</u> en mai.   The new shopping center is due to open in May.
- **pouvoir** (*can, may*)

  Je <u>peux</u> t'<u>aider</u>, si tu veux.   I can help you, if you want.

  <u>Puis</u>-je <u>venir</u> vous voir samedi ?   May I come and see you on Saturday?
- **savoir** (*to know how to, can*)

  Tu <u>sais conduire</u> ?   Can you drive?

  Je <u>sais faire</u> les omelettes.   I know how to make omelets.
- **vouloir** (*to want*)

  Élise <u>veut rester</u> un jour de plus.   Élise wants to stay one more day.

  Ma voiture ne <u>veut</u> pas <u>démarrer</u>.   My car won't start.

  <u>Voulez</u>-vous <u>boire</u> quelque chose ?   Would you like something to drink?

  Je <u>voudrais acheter</u> un ordinateur.   I'd like to buy a computer.

➤ **falloir** (meaning *to be necessary*) and **valoir mieux** (meaning *to be better*) are only used in the infinitive and with **il**.

> **Il faut prendre** une décision.   We/you *etc.* have to make a decision.
> **Il vaut mieux téléphoner** avant.   It's better to call first.

⇨ *For more information on* **Impersonal verbs**, *see page 127.*

➤ The following common verbs can also be followed by an infinitive <u>without</u> a preposition:

adorer	to love
aimer	to like, to love
aimer mieux	to prefer
désirer	to want
détester	to hate
envoyer	to send
espérer	to hope
faire	to make, to have something done (*that is*, **faire faire quelque chose**)
laisser	to let
préférer	to prefer
sembler	to seem

> J'**espère** te <u>voir</u> la semaine prochaine.   I hope to see you next week.
> Ne me <u>fais</u> pas <u>rire</u> !   Don't make me laugh!
> J'<u>ai fait réparer</u> mes chaussures.   I've had my shoes repaired.
> Je <u>préfère manger</u> à la cantine.   I prefer to eat in the cafeteria.

➤ Some of these verbs combine with infinitives to make set phrases with a special meaning.

aller chercher quelque chose	to go get something
laisser tomber quelque chose	to drop something
vouloir dire quelque chose	to mean something

> <u>Va chercher</u> ton papa !   Go get your dad!
> Paul <u>a laissé tomber</u> le vase.   Paul dropped the vase.
> Qu'est-ce que ça <u>veut dire</u> ?   What does that mean?

➤ Verbs that relate to seeing or hearing, such as **voir** (meaning *to see*), **regarder** (meaning *to watch, to look at*), **écouter** (meaning *to listen to*), and **entendre** (meaning *to hear*) can be followed by an infinitive.

> Il nous <u>a vus arriver</u>.   He saw us arrive.
> On <u>entend chanter</u> les oiseaux.   You can hear the birds singing.

For further explanation of grammatical terms, please see pages viii-xii.

➤ Verbs that relate to movement of some kind and do not have a direct object, such as **aller** (meaning *to go*) and **venir** (meaning *to come*), can be followed by an infinitive.

Je <u>vais voir</u> Nicolas ce soir.	I'm going to see Nicolas tonight.
<u>Viens voir</u> !	Come see!

3 Verbs followed by à + infinitive

➤ There are some common verbs that can be followed by à and an infinitive.

s'amuser <u>à</u> faire quelque chose	to have fun doing something
apprendre <u>à</u> faire quelque chose	to learn to do something
commencer <u>à</u> faire quelque chose	to begin to do something
continuer <u>à</u> faire quelque chose	to go on doing something
s'habituer <u>à</u> faire quelque chose	to get used to doing something

J'apprends <u>à</u> skier.	I'm learning to ski.
Il a commencé <u>à</u> pleuvoir.	It began to rain.

➤ Some verbs can be followed by a person's name or by a noun relating to a person, and then by à and an infinitive. Sometimes you need to put à in front of the person too.

aider quelqu'un <u>à</u> faire quelque chose	to help someone do something
apprendre <u>à</u> quelqu'un <u>à</u> faire quelque chose	to teach someone to do something
inviter quelqu'un <u>à</u> faire quelque chose	to invite someone to do something

4 Verbs followed by de + infinitive

➤ There are some common verbs that can be followed by de and an infinitive.

arrêter <u>de</u> faire quelque chose, s'arrêter <u>de</u> faire quelque chose	to stop doing something
commencer <u>de</u> faire quelque chose	to start doing something
continuer <u>de</u> faire quelque chose	to go on doing something
décider <u>de</u> faire quelque chose	to decide to do something
se dépêcher <u>de</u> faire quelque chose	to hurry to do something
essayer <u>de</u> faire quelque chose	to try to do something
s'excuser <u>d'</u>avoir fait quelque chose	to apologize for doing something
finir <u>de</u> faire quelque chose	to finish doing something
oublier <u>de</u> faire quelque chose	to forget to do something
proposer <u>de</u> faire quelque chose	to suggest doing something
refuser <u>de</u> faire quelque chose	to refuse to do something
suggérer <u>de</u> faire quelque chose	to suggest doing something

J'<u>ai décidé de</u> lui écrire.	I decided to write to her.
Je leur <u>ai suggéré de</u> partir de bonne heure.	I suggested that they set off early.

➤ The following verbs meaning asking or telling are also followed by **de** and an infinitive. Sometimes you need to put **à** in front of the person you are asking or telling.

commander <u>à</u> quelqu'un <u>de</u> faire quelque chose	to order someone to do something
demander <u>à</u> quelqu'un <u>de</u> faire quelque chose	to ask someone to do something
dire <u>à</u> quelqu'un <u>de</u> faire quelque chose	to tell someone to do something
empêcher quelqu'un <u>de</u> faire quelque chose	to prevent someone from doing something
remercier quelqu'un <u>de</u> faire quelque chose	to thank someone for doing something

---

Grammar Extra!

If it is important to emphasize that something is going on at a particular time, you can use the phrase **être en train de faire quelque chose**.

Il <u>est en train de travailler</u>. Est-ce que vous pouvez rappeler plus tard ?	He's working. Can you call back later?

If you want to say you have just done something, you can use the phrase **venir de faire quelque chose**. In English you use the <u>PAST</u> tense, but in French you use the <u>PRESENT</u> tense.

Élisabeth <u>vient de partir</u>.	Élisabeth has just left.

Key points

✔ Many French verbs can be followed by another verb in the infinitive.

✔ The two verbs may be linked by nothing at all, or by the preposition **à** or **de**.

✔ The construction in French does not always match the English exactly. It's best to learn these constructions when you learn a new verb.

For further explanation of grammatical terms, please see pages viii-xii.

Other uses of the infinitive

➤ The infinitive can be used in many other ways:

- after certain adjectives

  content de happy to
  prêt à ready to

Il est toujours <u>prêt à rendre</u> service.	He's always ready to help.

- after certain prepositions

<u>Pour aller</u> à la gare ?	How do you get to the station?
Il est parti <u>sans dire</u> au revoir.	He left without saying goodbye.

- after certain set phrases involving a verb plus a noun

avoir envie de faire quelque chose	to feel like doing something
avoir besoin de faire quelque chose	to need to do something
avoir peur de faire quelque chose	to be frightened of doing something
J'ai besoin de <u>changer</u> de l'argent.	I need to change some money.

- in instructions that are aimed at the general public – for example, on signs or in cookbooks

<u>Ajouter</u> le sel et le poivre, et bien <u>mélanger</u>.	Add the salt and pepper, and mix well.
<u>Conserver</u> au frais.	Keep refrigerated.

- as the subject or object of a sentence, when the infinitive corresponds to the -ing form in English used as a noun

<u>Fumer</u> n'est pas bon pour la santé.	Smoking isn't good for your health.
J'adore <u>lire</u>.	I love reading.

> *Tip*
> You can use the verb **faire** with an infinitive to refer to something you are having done by someone else.
>
> | | |
> |---|---|
> | **Je dois <u>faire réparer</u> ma voiture.** | I have to get my car repaired. |

> **Key points**
> ✔ Infinitives are found after certain adjectives, prepositions and set phrases, and in instructions for the general public.
> ✔ They can also function like nouns, as the subject or object of another verb.

Negatives

> **What is a negative?**
> A **negative** question or statement is one which contains a word such as *not*, *never* or *nothing* and is used to say that something is not happening, is not true, or is absent.

1 Using negatives

➤ In English we use words like *not*, *no*, *nothing*, and *never* to show a negative.

I'm <u>not</u> very pleased.

Dan <u>never</u> called me.

Nothing <u>ever</u> happens here!

There's <u>no</u> milk left.

➤ *Not* is often combined with certain English verbs – for example, *can't*, *won't*, *didn't*, *hasn't*.

He <u>isn't</u> joking.

She <u>didn't</u> say.

➤ In French, if you want to make something negative, you usually use a pair of words, for example, **ne ... pas** (meaning *not*). The verb goes in the middle.

ne ... pas	not
ne ... rien	nothing, not ... anything
ne ... personne	nobody, no one, not ... anybody, not ... anyone
ne ... jamais	never, not ... ever
ne ... plus	no longer, no more, not ... any longer, not ... any more

Je <u>ne</u> fume <u>pas</u>.	I don't smoke.
<u>Ne</u> changez <u>rien</u>.	Don't change anything.
Je <u>ne</u> vois <u>personne</u>.	I can't see anybody.
Elle <u>n'</u>arrive <u>jamais</u> à l'heure.	She never arrives on time.
Il <u>ne</u> travaille <u>plus</u> ici.	He's no longer working here.

> *Tip*
>
> ne changes to n' in front of a word that starts with a vowel, most words beginning with h, and the French word y.

For further explanation of grammatical terms, please see pages viii-xii.

➤ In English, *did* is often used to make a statement negative.

> I went to his party. → I did<u>n't</u> go to his party.
> We saw David over the weekend. → We did<u>n't</u> see David over the weekend.

ℹ Note that the French verb **faire** is <u>NEVER</u> used in this way.

➤ **non plus** is the equivalent of English *neither* in phrases like *me neither, neither do I* and so on.

"Je n'aime pas les hamburgers." – "Moi <u>non plus</u>."	"I don't like hamburgers." – "Me neither."
Il n'y va pas et moi <u>non plus</u>.	He isn't going and neither am I.

➤ The French word **ne** is left out when negatives are used without a verb to answer a question.

"Qui a téléphoné ?" – "<u>Personne</u>."	"Who called?" – "Nobody."
"Qu'est-ce que tu fais cet après-midi ?" – "<u>Rien</u>."	"What are you doing this afternoon?" – "Nothing."

Tip

In everyday conversation French native speakers often leave out the word **ne**. Be careful about doing this yourself in formal situations.

Je peux pas venir ce soir.	I can't come tonight.
Il me l'a pas dit.	He didn't tell me.

Grammar Extra!

Sometimes you will find two of these negative expressions combined.

Ils ne font jamais rien d'intéressant.	They never do anything interesting.
Je ne connais plus personne à Nice.	I don't know anyone in Nice any more.

---

2 Word order with negatives

➤ Negative expressions in French "sandwich" the verb in the present tense and in other tenses that consist of just one word. **ne** goes before the verb and the other half of the expression comes after the verb.

Il <u>ne</u> boit <u>jamais</u> d'alcool.	He never drinks alcohol.
Il <u>ne</u> pleuvait <u>pas</u>.	It wasn't raining.

➤ In the perfect tense and other tenses that consist of two or more words such as the pluperfect, there are two possibilities:

- ne ... pas, ne ... rien, ne ... plus, and ne ... jamais follow the pattern:
  ne (n') + avoir or être + pas + past participle

Elle n'a pas fait ses devoirs.	She hasn't done her homework.
Je n'ai rien dit.	I didn't say anything.
Pierre n'est pas encore arrivé.	Pierre isn't here yet.

- ne ... personne follows the pattern:
  ne (n') + avoir or être + past participle + personne

Je n'ai vu personne.	I didn't see anybody.

⇨ *For more information on the **Perfect tense**, see page 111.*

➤ A negative sentence may also contain a pronoun such as te, le, lui and so on that is the direct or indirect object of the verb, or a reflexive pronoun. If so, ne comes before the pronoun.

Je ne t'entends pas.	I can't hear you.
Ne lui parle pas !	Don't speak to him/her!
Tu ne te rappelles pas de lui ?	Don't you remember him?
Il ne se lève jamais avant midi.	He never gets up before noon.

⇨ *For more information on **Direct** and **Indirect object pronouns** and on **Reflexive pronouns**, see pages 47, 49, and 89.*

➤ When a verb is in the infinitive, ne ... pas, ne ... rien, ne ... plus, and ne ... jamais are joined together before the infinitive.

Il essayait de ne pas rire.	He was trying not to laugh.
J'ai peur de ne pas réussir.	I'm afraid of not succeeding.

Tip

After these negative expressions, un, une, and des (the indefinite article) and du, de la, de l', and des (the partitive article) change to de.

⇨ *For more information on the **Indefinite article** and the **Partitive article**, see pages 19 and 22.*

3 non **and** pas

➤ non (meaning *no*) is the usual negative answer to a question. It can also correspond to *not* in English.

"Tu veux nous accompagner ?" – "**Non**, merci."	"Do you want to come with us?" – "**No** thanks."
Tu viens ou <u>non</u> ?	Are you coming or <u>not</u>?
J'espère que <u>non</u>.	I hope <u>not</u>.

➤ pas is generally used when a distinction is being made, or for emphasis. It often corresponds to *not* in English, too.

"Qui veut m'aider ?" – "**<u>Pas</u> moi !**"	"Who wants to help me?" – "<u>Not</u> me!"
"Est-il de retour ?" – "**<u>Pas</u> encore.**"	"Is he back?" – "<u>Not</u> yet."
"Tu as froid ?" – "**<u>Pas</u> du tout.**"	"Are you cold?" – "<u>Not</u> at all."
<u>Pas</u> question !	<u>No</u> way!

> ### Key points
> ✔ Negatives indicate when something is not happening or is not true. French uses set expressions or word pairs to indicate this.
> ✔ The two parts of these negative expressions "sandwich" the verb in tenses consisting of only one word.
> ✔ ne comes before any object pronouns or reflexive pronouns.
> ✔ Before infinitives, ne ... pas, ne ... rien, ne ... plus, and ne ... jamais are joined together.
> ✔ The articles un, une, des, du, de la, and de l' change to de after negatives.

Questions

> **What is a question?**
> A **question** is a sentence which is used to ask someone about something and which normally has the verb in front of the subject. A question word such as *why*, *where*, *who*, *which*, or *how* is used to ask a question.

How to ask a question in French

1 The basic rules

➤ There are four ways of asking questions in French:
- by making your voice go up at the end of the sentence
- by using the phrase **est-ce que**
- by changing around the order of words in a sentence
- by using a question word

2 Asking a question by making your voice go up

➤ If you are expecting the answer *yes* or *no*, there is a very straightforward way of asking a question. You can keep word order just as it would be in a normal sentence (subject then verb), but turn it into a question by making your voice go up at the end of the sentence. So to turn the sentence **Vous aimez la France** (meaning *You like France*) into a question, all you need to do is to add a question mark and make your voice go up at the end.

Vous (*subject*) **aimez** (*verb*) **la France ?**	Do you like France?
On part tout de suite.	We're leaving right away.
On part tout de suite ?	Are we leaving right away?
C'est vrai.	It's true.
C'est vrai ?	Is that true?
Tes parents sont en vacances.	Your parents are on vacation.
Tes parents sont en vacances ?	Are your parents on vacation?

> *Tip*
> French speakers use this way of asking a question in ordinary, everyday conversations.

3 | Asking a question by using est-ce que

➤ The phrase **est-ce que** is used to ask a question. Word order stays exactly the same as it would in an ordinary sentence. **Est-ce que** comes before the subject, and the verb comes after the subject. So to turn the sentence **Tu connais Marie** (meaning *You know Marie*) into a question, all you need to do is to add **est-ce que**.

<u>Est-ce que</u> tu *(subject)* **connais** *(verb)* **Marie ?**	Do you know Marie?
<u>Est-ce que</u> **vous allez en ville ?**	Are you going into town?
<u>Est-ce que</u> **ta sœur est vraiment heureuse ?**	Is your sister really happy?

4 | Asking a question by changing word order

➤ In ordinary sentences, the verb comes <u>AFTER</u> its subject. In this type of question, the verb is put <u>BEFORE</u> the subject. This change to normal word order is called <u>inversion</u>. You can do this when the subject is a pronoun such as **vous** or **il**. When you change the word order (or <u>invert</u>) in this way, you add a hyphen (-) between the verb and the pronoun.

Vous *(subject)* **aimez** *(verb)* **la France.**	You like France.
Aimez *(verb)*-**vous** *(subject)* **la France ?**	Do you like France?
Il écrit bien.	He writes well.
<u>Écrit-il</u> **bien ?**	Does he write well?
On part tout de suite.	We're leaving right away.
<u>Part-on</u> **tout de suite ?**	Are we leaving right away?

➾ *For more information on* **Pronouns**, *see page 42.*

> *Tip*
> This is a very formal way to ask a question.

➤ In the perfect tense and other tenses that consist of two or more words such as the pluperfect, the part of the verb that comes from **avoir** or **être** is the one that goes before the pronoun.

<u>As</u>-tu vu mon sac ?	Have you seen my bag?
<u>Est</u>-elle restée longtemps ?	Did she stay long?

➾ *For more information on the* **Perfect tense**, *see page 111.*

➤ When the verb ends in a vowel in the **il/elle** form, **-t-** is inserted before the pronoun to make the words easier to say.

Aime-**t**-il les chiens ?	Does he like dogs?
A-**t**-elle assez d'argent ?	Does she have enough money?

Tip

Unlike English there are two ways in French to answer *yes* to a question or statement. **oui** is the word you use to reply to an ordinary question.

"Tu l'as fait ?" – "Oui."	"Did you do it?" – "Yes."
"Elle est belle, n'est-ce pas ?" – "Oui."	"She's beautiful, isn't she?" – "Yes."

si is the word you use to reply to a question or statement that contains a negative expression like **ne ... pas**.

"Tu ne l'as pas fait ?" – "Si."	"Didn't you do it?" – "Yes (I did)."
"Elle n'est pas très belle." – "Mais si !"	"She isn't very beautiful." – "Yes, she is!"

Grammar Extra!

You can also form a question in this way with a noun or a person's name. If you do this, the noun or name comes first, then you add an extra pronoun after the verb and link them with a hyphen.

Jean-Pierre *(subject)* est*(verb)*-il *(pronoun)* là ?	Is Jean-Pierre there?
La pièce dure-t-elle longtemps ?	Does the play last long?

In less formal French, the pronoun may come before the verb, and the noun or name may come at the end of the sentence.

Il est là, Jean-Pierre ?	Is Jean-Pierre there?
Elle dure longtemps, la pièce ?	Does the play last long?

---

5 Asking a question by using a question word

➤ A question word is a word like *when* or *how* that is used to ask for information. The most common French question words are listed on pages 146-150.

➤ You can use a question word with one of the methods described above:

- you can make your voice go up at the end of the sentence. If you do this, the question word goes at the <u>END</u> of the sentence.

For further explanation of grammatical terms, please see pages viii-xii.

- you can use **est-ce que**. If you do this, the question word goes at the <u>BEGINNING</u> of the sentence.
- you can change word order so that the verb comes before the subject. If you do this, the question word goes at the <u>BEGINNING</u> of the sentence.

Vous arrivez <u>quand</u> ?
<u>Quand</u> est-ce que vous arrivez ?   <u>When</u> do you arrive?
<u>Quand</u> arrivez-vous ?

Tu prends <u>quel</u> train ?
<u>Quel</u> train est-ce que tu prends ?   <u>What</u> train are you taking?
<u>Quel</u> train prends-tu ?

Ils vont <u>où</u> ?
<u>Où</u> est-ce qu'ils vont ?   <u>Where</u> are they going?
<u>Où</u> vont-ils ?

⟳ *For more information on **Negatives**, see page 138.*

Key points

✔ You ask a question in French by making your voice go up at the end of the sentence, by using **est-ce que**, by changing normal word order, or by using a question word.

✔ When you put the verb in front of the subject, you join the two words with a hyphen. A **-t-** is used in the **il/elle** form if the verb ends in a vowel.

✔ You use **oui** to answer *yes* to an ordinary question, but **si** if there is a negative in the question or statement.

Question words

1 Common question words

➤ Listed below are some very common question words. que, quel, qui, quoi, and lequel are explained on pages 147–150.

- combien + *verb?* how much?, how many?
  combien de + *noun?* how much?, how many?

<u>Combien</u> coûte cet ordinateur ?	How much does this computer cost?
C'est <u>combien</u>, ce pantalon ?	How much are these pants?
Tu en veux <u>combien</u> ? Deux ?	How many do you want? Two?
<u>Combien de</u> personnes vas-tu inviter ?	How many people are you going to invite?

- comment ? how?

<u>Comment</u> va-t-elle ?	How is she?
<u>Comment</u> tu t'appelles ?	What's your name?

> ### Tip
> pardon is also used to ask someone to repeat something, and is the same as *Pardon?* in English. comment and quoi can mean the same thing, but are informal and are the same as *What?* in English.

- où ? where?

<u>Où</u> allez-vous ?	Where are you going?
<u>D'où</u> viens-tu ?	Where are you from?

> ### Tip
> Be careful not to mix up où, which means *where*, and ou (without an accent), which means *or*.

- pourquoi ? why?

<u>Pourquoi</u> est-ce qu'il ne vient pas avec nous ?	Why isn't he coming with us?

- quand ? when?

<u>Quand</u> est-ce que tu pars en vacances ?	When are you going on vacation?
<u>Depuis quand</u> est-ce que vous le connaissez ?	How long have you known him?

2 | qui ?, que ?, and quoi ?

➤ In questions, **qui**, **que**, and **quoi** are all pronouns. Which of them you choose depends on:

- whether you are referring to people or to things
- whether you are referring to the subject or object of the verb (the subject is the person or thing that is carrying out the action described by the verb; the object is the person or thing that "receives" the action)
- whether the word you use will come after a preposition such as **à**, **de**, or **en**

⇨ *For more information on **Pronouns** and **Prepositions**, see pages 42 and 62.*

➤ **qui ?** and **que ?** have longer forms, as shown in the table below. There is a difference in word order between the longer and shorter forms.

➤ **qui ?** is used for talking about people, and means *who?* or *whom?* in English. You can use *whom?* in formal English to refer to the object of a verb, though most people use *who?*. **qui ?** can be used after a preposition.

Who? Whom?	Referring to people	Meaning	Examples	Meaning
Subject	qui ? qui est-ce qui ?	who?	Qui vient ? Qui est-ce qui vient ?	Who's coming?
Object	qui ? qui est-ce que ?	who? whom?	Qui vois-tu ? Qui est-ce que tu vois ?	Who/Whom do you see?
After prepositions	qui ? qui est-ce que ?	who? whom?	De qui est-ce qu'il parle ? Pour qui est ce livre ? À qui avez-vous écrit ?	Who's he talking about? Who's this book for? Who did you write to?, To whom did you write?

Tip

que changes to **qu'** before a vowel, most words beginning with **h**, and the French word **y**.

⇨ *For more information on **que** and **qui**, see page 62.*

➤ **à qui** is the usual way of saying *whose* in questions.

| À qui est ce sac ? | Whose bag is this? |

➡ *For more information on using à to show possession, see page 165.*

➤ **que ?** and **quoi ?** are used for talking about things, and mean *what?* in English. **que ?** <u>cannot</u> be used after a preposition; you have to use **quoi ?** instead.

What?	Referring to things	Meaning	Examples	Meaning
Subject	qu'est-ce qui ?	what?	Qu'est-ce qui se passe ? Qu'est-ce qui t'inquiète ?	What's happening? What's worrying you?
Object	qu'est-ce que ?	what?	Qu'est-ce que vous faites ? Que faites-vous ?	What are you doing?
After prepositions	quoi ?	what?	À quoi penses-tu ? De quoi parlez-vous ?	What are you thinking about? What are you talking about?

Tip

It is possible to finish an English sentence with a preposition such as *about* or *of*, even though some people think this is not good grammar.
Who did you write <u>to</u>?
What are you talking <u>about</u>?
It is <u>NEVER</u> possible to end a French sentence with a preposition.

3 quel ?, quelle ?, quels ?, and quelles ?

➤ **quel ?** (meaning *who?, which?* or *what?*) can be used with a noun (as an <u>adjective</u>) or can replace a noun (as a <u>pronoun</u>). Compare this with **que ?** (and its longer forms) and **quoi ?**, which also mean *what?* but are <u>NEVER</u> used with nouns.

➡ *For more information on **Adjectives** and **Pronouns**, see pages 25 and 42.*

➤ **quel, quelle, quels,** and **quelles** are all forms of the same word. The form that you choose depends on whether you are referring to something that is masculine or feminine, singular or plural.

	Masculine	Feminine	Meaning
Singular	quel ?	quelle ?	who? what? which?
Plural	quels ?	quelles ?	who? what? which?

<u>Quel</u> est ton chanteur préféré ?	Who's your favorite singer?
<u>Quel</u> vin recommandez-vous ?	Which wine do you recommend?
<u>Quelle</u> est ta couleur préférée ?	What's your favorite color?
<u>Quelle</u> heure est-il ?	What time is it?
<u>Quels</u> sont tes chanteurs préférés ?	Who are your favorite singers?
Vous jouez de <u>quels</u> instruments ?	What instruments do you play?
<u>Quelles</u> sont tes couleurs préférées ?	What are your favorite colors?
<u>Quelles</u> chaussures te plaisent le plus ?	Which shoes do you like best?

⇨ *For more information on how quel in used in exclamations, see page 21.*

4 | <u>lequel</u> ?, <u>laquelle</u> ?, <u>lesquels</u> ?, and <u>lesquelles</u> ?

➤ In questions **lequel, laquelle, lesquels,** and **lesquelles** (meaning *which one/ones?*) are all forms of the same pronoun, and are used to replace nouns. The form that you choose depends on whether you are referring to something that is masculine or feminine, singular or plural.

	Masculine	Feminine	Meaning
Singular	lequel ?	laquelle ?	which? which one?
Plural	lesquels ?	lesquelles ?	which? which ones?

"J'ai choisi un livre." – "<u>Lequel</u> ?"	"I've chosen a book." – "Which one?"
<u>Laquelle</u> de ces valises est à Bruno ?	Which of these suitcases is Bruno's?

"Tu te souviens de mes amis ?"   "Do you remember my friends?" –
– "<u>Lesquels</u> ?"   "Which ones?"

<u>Lesquelles</u> de vos sœurs sont   Which of your sisters are married?
mariées ?

⇨   *For more information on lequel, see page 63.*

5   n'est-ce pas ? **and** non ?

➤ English speakers often tack on an expression like *isn't it?, don't they?, weren't we?,* or *will you?* to the end of a sentence to turn it into a question. French uses n'est-ce pas ? instead. This useful little phrase never changes, so it's very easy to use. You use it in questions when you expect the person you are talking to to agree with you.

Il fait chaud, <u>n'est-ce pas</u> ?   It's warm, <u>isn't it</u>?

Tu parles français, <u>n'est-ce pas</u> ?   You speak French, <u>don't you</u>?

Vous n'oublierez pas, <u>n'est-ce   You won't forget, <u>will you</u>?
pas</u> ?

➤ It is very common to use non (meaning *no*) in the same way in spoken French. hein ? means the same as *huh?* in English, and is only used in very informal conversations.

Il fait chaud, <u>non</u> ?   It's warm, isn't it?

Il fait chaud, <u>hein</u> ?   It's warm, huh?

Key points

✔ In questions qui ? means *who?*; que ? and quoi ? mean *what?*

✔ qui est-ce qui ? (*subject*) and qui est-ce que ? (*object*) are longer forms of qui ? Both mean *who?* The word order is different from qui.

✔ qu'est-ce qui ? (*subject*) and qu'est-ce que ? (*object*) are longer forms of que ? Both mean *what?* The word order is different from que.

✔ qui ? (for people) and quoi ? (for things) are used after prepositions.

✔ quel ? is both an adjective and a pronoun. It means *who?, what?,* or *which?* in questions, and is used with a noun or replaces a noun.

✔ lequel ? is a pronoun; it means *which?, which one?,* or *which ones?* in questions.

✔ n'est-ce pas ? or non ? can be tacked on to the end of sentences to turn them into questions.

Grammar Extra!

All the questions in the previous section are the actual words that someone uses when they are asking a question, and so they all end with a question mark. These are called <u>direct</u> questions. When you are telling someone else about a question that is being asked, you use an <u>indirect</u> question. Indirect questions never end with a question mark, and they are always introduced by a verb such as *to ask, to tell, to wonder, to know* and so on.

> He asked me what the time was. (His actual question was *What time is it?*)
>
> Tell me which way to go. (Your actual question was *Which way do I go?*)

Word order in indirect questions is generally the same as in English:
question word + subject verb.

Dites-moi quel (*question word*) **autobus** (*subject*) **va** (*verb*) **à la gare.**	Tell me which bus goes to the station.
Il m'a demandé combien d'argent j'avais.	He asked me how much money I had.
Je me demande s'il viendra ou pas.	I wonder if he'll come or not.

When the subject of the question is a noun and <u>NOT</u> a pronoun like **je** or **il**, the subject and verb that come after the question word are often switched around.

Je me demande où (*question word*) **sont** (*verb*) **mes clés** (*subject*).	I wonder where my keys are.
Demande-lui qui est venu.	Ask him who came.

Adverbs

What is an adverb?
An **adverb** is a word usually used with verbs, adjectives, or other adverbs that gives more information about when, how, where, or in what circumstances something happens, for example, *quickly, happily, now.*

How adverbs are used

➤ In general, adverbs are used together with:

- verbs (*act <u>quickly</u>, speak <u>strangely</u>, smile <u>cheerfully</u>*)
- adjectives (*<u>pretty</u> sick, <u>a lot</u> better, <u>deeply</u> sorry*)
- other adverbs (*<u>really</u> fast, <u>too</u> quickly, <u>very</u> well*)

➤ Adverbs can also relate to the whole sentence; they often tell you what the speaker is thinking or feeling.

> <u>Fortunately</u>, Jan had already left.
> <u>Actually</u>, I don't think I'll come.

How adverbs are formed

1 The basic rules

➤ Adverbs in French <u>NEVER</u> change their form, no matter what they refer to.

Il est <u>très</u> beau.	He's very handsome.
Elles sont <u>très</u> belles.	They're very beautiful.
J'y vais <u>souvent</u>.	I often go there.
Nous y allons <u>souvent</u>.	We often go there.

[i] Note that there is one exception to this rule. The word **tout** changes in certain phrases, for example, **tout seul** (meaning *all alone*).

Il est arrivé <u>tout seul</u>.	He arrived on his own.
Elle est souvent <u>toute seule</u>.	She's often by herself.

➤ Many English adverbs end in *-ly*, which is added to the end of the adjective (*quick → quickly; sad → sadly; frequent → frequently*). In French, many adverbs end in **-ment**. This is usually added to the end of the <u>feminine singular</u> form of the adjective.

Masculine adjective	Feminine adjective	Adverb	Meaning
heureux	heureuse	heureusement	fortunately
doux	douce	doucement	gently, slowly
seul	seule	seulement	only

➤ The adverb ending -ment is added to the <u>masculine</u> not the feminine form of the adjective if the masculine ends in -é, -i, or -u.

Masculine adjective	Feminine adjective	Adverb	Meaning
désespéré	désespérée	désespérément	desperately
vrai	vraie	vraiment	truly
absolu	absolue	absolument	absolutely

➤ If the adjective ends in -ant, the adverb ends in -amment. If the adjective ends in -ent, the adverb ends in -emment. The first vowel in the -emment and -amment endings is pronounced in the same way in both – like the *a* in the English word *cat*.

courant → couramment (*fluently*)
récent → récemment (*recently*)

[i] Note that an exception to this rule is the adverb **lentement** (meaning *slowly*), which comes from the adjective **lent** (meaning *slow*).

2 Irregular adverbs

➤ There are a number of common irregular adverbs.

Adjective	Meaning	Adverb	Meaning
bon	good	bien	well
gentil	nice, kind	gentiment	nicely, kindly
mauvais	bad	mal	badly
meilleur	better, best	mieux	better
petit	small	peu	little
pire	worse	pis	worse

Elle travaille <u>bien</u>. She works well.
C'est un emploi très <u>mal</u> payé. It's a very badly paid job.

3 Adjectives used as adverbs

➤ Certain adjectives are used as adverbs, mostly in set phrases:
● bon good
sentir bon to smell nice

- cher expensive
  coûter cher to be expensive
  payer cher to pay a lot

- droit straight
  aller tout droit to go straight on

- dur hard
  travailler dur to work hard

- fort loud
  parler plus fort to speak up

- mauvais bad
  sentir mauvais to smell bad

4 Adverbs made up of more than one word

➤ Adverbs can be made up of several words instead of just one. Here are some common ones:

bien sûr	of course
c'est-à-dire	that is
d'abord	first
d'habitude	usually
de temps en temps	from time to time
en général	usually
en retard	late
tout de suite	right away

Key points
✔ With the exception of tout, French adverbs do not change their form.
✔ The ending -ment is usually added to the feminine singular form of the corresponding adjective.
✔ If the masculine singular adjective ends in -é, -i, or -u, the -ment ending is added to that.
✔ If the adjective ends in -ant or -ent, the adverb ends in -amment or -emment (except for lentement).

Comparatives and superlatives of adverbs

1 Comparative adverbs

What is a comparative adverb?
A **comparative adverb** is one which, in English, has -er on the end of it or *more* or *less* in front of it, for example, *earlier, later, sooner, more/less frequently.*

➤ Adverbs can be used to make comparisons in French, just as they can in English. The comparative (*more often, faster*) of adverbs is formed using the same phrases as for adjectives.

- plus ... (que)   more ... (than)

Tu marches <u>plus</u> vite <u>que</u> moi.	You walk faster than me.
Elle chante <u>plus</u> fort <u>que</u> les autres.	She's singing louder than the others.

- moins ... (que)   less ... (than)

Parle <u>moins</u> vite !	Don't speak so fast! (*literally: Speak less fast!*)
Nous nous voyons <u>moins</u> souvent <u>qu'</u>avant.	We see each other less often than before.

- aussi ... que   as ... as

Je parle français <u>aussi</u> bien <u>que</u> toi !	I can speak French as well as you!
Viens <u>aussi</u> vite <u>que</u> possible.	Come as quickly as possible.

⟹ For more information on *Comparative adjectives*, see page 34.

2 Superlative adverbs

What is a superlative adverb?
A **superlative adverb** is one which, in English, has -est on the end of it or *most* or *least* in front of it, for example, *soonest, fastest, most/least frequently.*

➤ The superlative of adverbs (*the most, the fastest*) is formed using the same phrases as for adjectives, except that **le** <u>NEVER</u> changes to **la** or **les** in the feminine and plural with adverbs as it does with adjectives.

- le plus ... (que) the most ... (that)

Marianne parle <u>le plus</u> vite.	Marianne speaks fastest.

- le moins ... (que) the least ... (that)

C'est Gordon qui a mangé <u>le moins</u>.	Gordon ate the least.

⟹ For more information on *Superlative adjectives*, see page 34.

3 Adverbs with irregular comparatives and superlatives

➤ Some of the most common adverbs have irregular comparative and superlative forms.

Adverb	Meaning	Comparative	Meaning	Superlative	Meaning
beaucoup	a lot	plus	more	le plus	(the) most
bien	well	mieux	better	le mieux	(the) best
mal	badly	pis plus mal	worse	le pis le plus mal	(the) worst
peu	little	moins	less	le moins	(the) least

C'est lui qui danse <u>le mieux</u>.   He dances best.

> **Key points**
> ✔ Comparatives of adverbs are formed in the same way as comparatives of adjectives, using **plus … (que)**, **moins … (que)**, and **aussi … que**.
> ✔ Superlatives of adverbs are formed in the same way as superlatives of adjectives, using **le plus … (que)** and **le moins … (que)**.
> **le** never changes in the feminine and plural.
> ✔ Unlike adjectives, adverbs do not change their form to agree with the verb, adjective, or other adverb they relate to.

Some common adverbs

➤ Here are some common adverbs that do not end in **-ment**:

alors	then, so, at that time
après	afterward
après-demain	the day after tomorrow
aujourd'hui	today
assez	enough, fairly
aussi	also, too, as
avant-hier	the day before yesterday
beaucoup	a lot, much
bientôt	soon
cependant	however
dedans	inside
dehors	outside
déjà	already, before
demain	tomorrow
depuis	since
derrière	behind
devant	in front
encore	still, even, again
enfin	at last
ensemble	together
ensuite	then
environ	about
hier	yesterday
ici	here
jamais	never, ever

> ## Tip
>
> **jamais** can sometimes be used without **ne** to mean *never* or *ever*.
>
> "Est-ce que tu vas souvent au movies ?" – "Non, <u>jamais</u>."
>
> "Do you go to the movies a lot?" – "No, <u>never</u>."
>
> As-tu <u>jamais</u> revu ton père ?
>
> Did you <u>ever</u> see your father again?
>
> ➭ For more information on **Negatives**, see page 138.

là	there, here
là-bas	over there
loin	far, far off, a long time ago

longtemps	a long time
maintenant	now, nowadays
même	even
moins	less
où	where
parfois	sometimes
partout	everywhere
peu	not much, not very

Tip

Be careful not to confuse **peu**, which means *not much* or *not very*, with **un peu**, which means *a little* or *a bit*.

Il voyage <u>peu</u>.	He doe<u>sn't</u> travel <u>much</u>.
Elle est <u>un peu</u> timide.	She's <u>a bit</u> shy.

---

peut-être	perhaps
plus	more
presque	nearly
puis	then
quelquefois	sometimes
si	so
soudain	suddenly
souvent	often
surtout	especially, above all
tard	late
tôt	early
toujours	always, still
tout	all, very
très	very
trop	too much, too
vite	quick, fast, soon

Tip

vite and **rapide** can both mean *fast* or *quick*. Remember, though, that **vite** is an <u>adverb</u> and **rapide** is an <u>adjective</u>.

une voiture <u>rapide</u>	a fast car
Il roule trop <u>vite</u>.	He drives too fast.

For further explanation of grammatical terms, please see pages viii-xii.

➤ Some of the adverbs listed on pages 157 and 158 can be followed by **de** and used in front of a noun to talk about quantities or numbers of things or people:

- **assez de** enough

  Nous n'avons pas <u>assez de</u> temps.   We don't have enough time.

- **beaucoup de** a lot of

  Elle fait <u>beaucoup de</u> fautes.   She makes a lot of mistakes.

- **combien de** how much, how many

  <u>Combien de</u> personnes as-tu invitées ?   How many people have you invited?

- **trop de** too much, too many

  J'ai mangé <u>trop de</u> fromage.   I've eaten too much cheese.

➤ Several of the adverbs listed on pages 157 and 158 can also be used as prepositions: **après**, **avant**, **devant**, **derrière**, and **depuis**.

⇨ *For more information on **Prepositions**, see page 162.*

➤ The question words **combien** (meaning *how much, how many*), **comment** (meaning *how*), **pourquoi** (meaning *why*), and **quand** (meaning *when*) are described on page 146.

➤ **pas**, **plus**, and **jamais** are used in negative word pairs.

⇨ *For more information on **Negatives**, see page 138.*

> **Key points**
> ✔ Many very common adverbs do not end in -ment. They are worth learning.
> ✔ Several adverbs can be followed by de + noun and used to talk about quantities and numbers.

Word order with adverbs

1 Adverbs with verbs

➤ In English, adverbs can come in different places in a sentence.

> I'm <u>never</u> coming back.
> See you <u>soon</u>!
> <u>Suddenly</u> the phone rang.
> I'd <u>really</u> like to come.

➤ In French, the rules are more fixed. When an adverb goes with a verb that consists of just one word, such as a verb in the <u>present tense</u> or the <u>imperfect tense</u>, it usually goes <u>AFTER</u> that verb.

Il neige <u>toujours</u> en janvier.	It always snows in January.
Je pensais <u>souvent</u> à toi.	I often used to think about you.

➤ When an adverb goes with a verb that consists of more than one word, such as a verb in the <u>perfect tense</u>, it usually comes <u>BETWEEN</u> the part of the verb that comes from **avoir** or **être** and the past participle.

Il a <u>trop</u> mangé.	He's eaten too much.
Ils sont <u>déjà</u> partis.	They've already gone.

⇨ *For more information on the **Perfect tense**, see page 111.*

➤ The rule above covers most adverbs that tell you about quantity or time (apart from a few listed later), and some very common ones telling you how something is done.

beaucoup	a lot, much
bien	well
bientôt	soon
déjà	already, before
encore	still, even, again
enfin	at last
mal	badly
mieux	better
peu	not much, not very
rarement	rarely
souvent	often
toujours	always, still
trop	too much, too
vraiment	really

For further explanation of grammatical terms, please see pages viii-xii.

➤ Some adverbs <u>FOLLOW</u> the past participle of verbs that consist of more than one word. This rule covers most adverbs that tell you how or where something is done, and a few adverbs that tell you about time.

aujourd'hui	today
demain	tomorrow
hier	yesterday
loin	far, far off, a long time ago
longtemps	a long time
partout	everywhere
quelquefois	sometimes
tôt	early
tard	late
vite	quick, fast, soon

On les a vus <u>partout</u>.	We saw them everywhere.
Elle est revenue <u>hier</u>.	She came back yesterday.

2 | Adverbs with adjectives and other adverbs

➤ When an adverb goes with an <u>adjective</u>, it usually comes just <u>BEFORE</u> that adjective.

Ils ont une <u>très</u> belle maison.	They have a very nice house.
une femme <u>bien</u> habillée	a well-dressed woman

➤ When an adverb goes with another <u>adverb</u>, it usually comes just <u>BEFORE</u> that adverb.

C'est <u>trop</u> tard.	It's too late.
Fatima travaille <u>beaucoup plus</u> vite.	Fatima works much faster.

> **Key points**
> ✔ Adverbs follow verbs that consist of just one word.
> ✔ They usually go before the past participle of verbs that consist of two words when they relate to quantity or time.
> ✔ They usually go after the past participle of verbs that consist of two words when they relate to how or where something is done.
> ✔ When used with an adjective or another adverb, they generally come just before it.

Prepositions

What is a preposition?
A **preposition** is a word such as *at*, *for*, *with*, *into*, or *from*, which is usually followed by a noun, pronoun, or, in English, a word ending in *-ing*. Prepositions show how people and things relate to the rest of the sentence, for example, *She's <u>at</u> home.*; *a tool <u>for</u> cutting grass*; *it's <u>from</u> David*.

Using prepositions

➤ Prepositions are used in front of nouns and pronouns (such as *me*, *him*, *the man* and so on), and show the relationship between the noun or pronoun and the rest of the sentence. Some prepositions can be used before verb forms ending in *-ing* in English.

> I showed my ticket <u>to</u> the inspector.
> Come <u>with</u> me.
> This brush is really good <u>for</u> cleaning shoes.

⇨ For more information on **Nouns** and **Pronouns**, see pages 1 and 42.

➤ Prepositions are also used after certain adjectives and verbs and link them to the rest of the sentence.

> **Je suis très contente <u>de</u> te voir.**   I'm very happy to see you.
> **Tu aimes jouer <u>au</u> tennis ?**   Do you like playing tennis?

➤ In English it is possible to finish a sentence with a preposition such as *for*, *about*, or *on*, even though some people think this is not good grammar. You can <u>NEVER</u> end a French sentence with a preposition.

> **Le café au lait, c'est <u>pour</u> qui ?**   Who's the café au lait <u>for</u>?
> **<u>De</u> quoi parlez-vous ?**   What are you talking <u>about</u>?

> *Tip*
> The French preposition is not always the direct equivalent of the preposition that is used in English. It is often difficult to give just one English equivalent for French prepositions, as the way they are used varies so much between the two languages.

à, de, and en

1 à

➤ Be careful not to confuse the preposition à with the il/elle/on form of the verb avoir: il a (meaning *he has*) and so on.

> *Tip*
>
> When à is followed by le, the two words become au. Similarly, when à is followed by les, the two words become aux.
>
> ➪ *For more information on* **Articles***, see page 12.*

➤ à can mean *at*.

Les melons se vendent à 2 euros pièce.	Melons are selling <u>at</u> 2 euros each.
Nous roulions à 100 km à l'heure.	We were driving <u>at</u> 100 km an hour.
J'ai lancé une pierre à Chantal.	I threw a stone <u>at</u> Chantal.
Je suis à la maison.	I'm <u>at</u> home.

ⓘ Note that à la maison can also mean *to the house*.

Je rentre à la maison.	I'm going back to the house *or* back home.

➤ à can mean *in*.

Nous habitons à la campagne.	We live <u>in</u> the country.
Mon père est à Londres.	My father is <u>in</u> London.
Restez au lit.	Stay <u>in</u> bed.
Jean est entré, un livre à la main.	Jean came in with a book <u>in</u> his hand.

> *Tip*
>
> à is used to mean *in* with the names of towns and cities, and au (*singular*) or aux (*plural*) with the names of countries that are masculine in French.
>
> | | |
> |---|---|
> | J'habite <u>au</u> Mexique. | I live <u>in</u> Mexico. |
> | Elle est <u>aux</u> États-Unis. | She's <u>in</u> the States. |

➤ à can mean *to*.

Je vais <u>au</u> cinéma ce soir.	I'm going <u>to</u> the movies tonight.
Donne le ballon à ton frère.	Give the ball <u>to</u> your brother.

> *Tip*
>
> à is used to mean *to* with the names of towns and cities, and **au**
> (*singular*) or **aux** (*plural*) with the names of countries that are masculine
> in French.
>
> Je vais assez souvent <u>à</u> Paris.   I go <u>to</u> Paris quite often.
>
> Il va <u>aux</u> États-Unis la semaine   He's going <u>to</u> the States
> prochaine.   next week.

➤ à is also used with **de** to mean *from ... to ...*

le trajet <u>de</u> Londres <u>à</u> Paris   the journey <u>from</u> London <u>to</u> Paris

La banque est ouverte <u>de</u> 9   The bank is open <u>from</u> 9 <u>to</u> 12.
heures <u>à</u> midi.

Je suis en vacances <u>du</u> 21 juin   I'm on vacation <u>from</u> June 21 <u>to</u>
<u>au</u> 5 juillet.   July 5.

➤ à can mean *on.*

Il y a deux beaux tableaux <u>au</u>   There are two beautiful paintings
mur.   <u>on</u> the wall.

Le bureau se trouve <u>au</u> premier   The office is <u>on</u> the first floor.
étage.

Qu'est-ce qu'il y a <u>à la</u> télé ce   What's <u>on</u> TV tonight?
soir ?

[*i*] Note that à and sur can both mean *on* in English. **sur** usually means on
the top of something. **sur la télé** means *on top of the TV*, but **à la télé**
means *broadcast on TV*. Both can be translated as *on the TV* in English.
sur le mur means *on top of the wall*, but **au mur** means *hanging on the
wall*.

➤ à is often used to describe:

● what someone looks like or is wearing

la femme <u>au</u> chapeau vert   the woman with the green hat

un garçon <u>aux</u> yeux bleus   a boy with blue eyes

● how something is done

fait <u>à</u> la main   handmade

laver <u>à</u> la machine   to machine-wash

● what a type of food is made of

une tarte <u>aux</u> poires   a pear tart

un sandwich <u>au</u> jambon   a ham sandwich

pursuant to such retailer's or seller's return policy. Magazines, newspapers, eBooks, digital downloads, and used books are not returnable or exchangeable. Defective NOOKs may be exchanged at the store in accordance with the applicable warranty.

Returns or exchanges will not be permitted (i) after 14 days or without receipt or (ii) for product not carried by Barnes & Noble or Barnes & Noble.com.

Policy on receipt may appear in two sections.

Return Policy

With a sales receipt or Barnes & Noble.com packing slip, a full refund in the original form of payment will be issued from any Barnes & Noble Booksellers store for returns of undamaged NOOKs, new and unread books, and unopened and undamaged music CDs, DVDs and ~~~~~~~ ~~~~~ books made within 14 days of ~~~~~~~~~~~~~~ ~~~ & Noble Booksellers st~~~~~~~~~~~~~~~~~~~~~~ ~~e below

~~~~~~~~~~~~~~~~~~~~~~~~~~~~~~~~~~~~~~~ ssued (i)
~~~~~~~~~~~~~~~~~~~~~~~~~~~~~~~~~~~~~~~ prior to
~~~~~~~~~~~~~~~~~~~~~~~~~~~~~~~~~~~~~~~ sented
~~~~~~~~~~~~~~~~~~~~~~~~~~~~~~~~~~~~~~~ (iv) for
~~~~~~~~~~~~~~~~~~~~~~~~~~~~~~~~~~~~~~~ ollege
~~~~~~~~~~~~~~~~~~~~~~~~~~~~~~~~~~~~~~~ Noble

~~~~~~~~~~~~~~~~~~~~~~~~~~~~~~~~~~~~~~~ be
~~~~~~~~~~~~~~~~~~~~~~~~~~~~~~~~~~~~~~~ me
~~~~~~~~~~~~~~~~~~~~~~~~~~~~~~~~~~~~~~~ w
~~~~~~~~~~~~~~~~~~~~~~~~~~~~~~~~~~~~~~~ e

~~~~~~~~~~~~~~~~~~~~~~~~~~~~~~~~~~~~~~~ rried by

~~~~ may appear in two sections.

Barnes & Noble Booksellers #2574
420 W 47th Street
Kansas City, MO 64112
816-753-1313

STR:2574 REG:006 TRN:0694 CSHR:Brianna D

Merriam-Webster's Easy Learning Complete
    9780877795667   T1
    (1 @ 16.95)   16.95
DK Eyewitness Travel Guide: California
    9780756685607   T1
    (1 @ 30.00)   30.00

Subtotal   46.95
Sales Tax T1 (8.850%)   4.16
TOTAL   **51.11**
VISA   **51.11**
    Card#:   XXXXXXXXXXXXX5946
    Expdate: XX/XX
    Auth: 022588
    Entry Method: Swiped

A MEMBER WOULD HAVE SAVED   4.70

            Thanks for shopping at
              Barnes & Noble

101.32A   04/23/2014 09:16PM

            CUSTOMER COPY

- how you travel

On y va à pied ?	Shall we walk?
Il est venu à vélo.	He came on his bike.

> **Tip**
>
> Apart from **à vélo** and **à cheval** (meaning *on horseback*), the prepositions **en** and **par** are used with most other means of transportation.

➤ **à** can also show what something is used for.

une boîte **aux** lettres	a mailbox
une machine **à** laver	a washing machine
une tasse **à** café	a coffee cup

ⓘ Note that une tasse **à** café means a *coffee cup*, but une tasse **de** café means *a cup of coffee*. In the same way, un verre **à** vin means *a wine glass* but un verre **de** vin means *a glass of wine*.

➤ **à** is used with time, centuries, and the names of festivals.

à trois heures	at three o'clock
au vingtième siècle	in the twentieth century
à Noël	at Christmas
à Pâques	at Easter

➤ **à** is used to talk about distances and rates.

La maison est **à** 6 kilomètres d'ici.	The house is 6 kilometers from here.
C'est **à** deux minutes de chez moi.	It's two minutes from my place.
Je suis payé **à** l'heure.	I'm paid by the hour.

➤ **à** shows who owns something, or whose turn it is.

Ce cahier est **à** Paul.	This notebook is Paul's.
C'est **à** toi ?	Is this yours?
C'est **à** qui de nettoyer la salle de bains ?	Whose turn is it to clean the bathroom?

➤ If you want to say where something hurts, you use **à**.

J'ai mal **à** la tête.	I have a headache.
J'ai mal **aux** jambes.	My legs ache.
J'ai mal **à** la gorge.	I have a sore throat.

➤ à is used with certain adjectives.

> Son écriture est difficile à lire.   His/Her writing is difficult to read.
> Je suis prêt à tout.   I'm ready for anything.

⇨ *For more information about **Prepositions after adjectives**, see page 183.*

➤ à is used with certain verbs.

> s'intéresser à quelque chose   to be interested in something
> penser à quelque chose   to think about something

⇨ *For more information about **Prepositions after verbs**, see page 178.*

➤ Finally, some common ways of saying goodbye contain à.

> À bientôt !   See you soon!
> À demain !   See you tomorrow!
> À samedi !   See you Saturday!
> À tout à l'heure !   See you later!

2 de

➤ de is used as part of the <u>partitive article</u>, which is usually the equivalent of *some* or *any* in English.

⇨ *For more information on the **Partitive article**, see page 22.*

Tip

When de is followed by le, the two words become du. Similarly, when de is followed by les, the two words become des.

⇨ *For more information on **Articles**, see page 12.*

➤ de can mean *from*.

> Je viens d'Édimbourg.   I'm <u>from</u> Edinburgh.
> une lettre de Rachid   a letter <u>from</u> Rachid
> Je la vois de temps en temps.   I see her <u>from</u> time to time.

Tip

de changes to d' in front of a word starting with a vowel, most words starting with h, and the French word y.

➤ de is also used with à to mean *from ... to ...*

| le trajet de Londres à Paris | the journey <u>from</u> London <u>to</u> Paris |

le trajet de Londres à Paris   the journey <u>from</u> London <u>to</u> Paris
La banque est ouverte de 9   The bank is open <u>from</u> 9 <u>to</u> 12.
heures à midi.
Je suis en vacances du 21 juin   I'm on vacation <u>from</u> June 21 <u>to</u>
au 5 juillet.   July 5.

➤ de often shows who or what something belongs to.

un ami de la famille   a friend of the family
les fenêtres de la maison   the windows of the house
la voiture de Marie-Pierre   Marie-Pierre's car

➤ de can indicate what something contains, when it usually corresponds to *of* in English.

une boîte d'allumettes   a box <u>of</u> matches
deux bouteilles de vin   two bottles <u>of</u> wine
une tasse de café   a cup <u>of</u> coffee

> [i] Note that une tasse de café means *a cup of coffee* but une tasse à café means *a coffee cup*. In the same way, un verre à vin means *a wine glass* but un verre de vin means *a glass of wine*.

➤ de can describe what material something is made of.

une robe de coton   a cotton dress
une porte de bois   a wooden door

> *Tip*
> en can also be used to say what something is made of, and is used when it is important to stress the material.
> un bracelet <u>en</u> or   a gold bracelet

➤ You can use de to say what something is used for.

un sac de couchage   a sleeping bag
un terrain de foot   a soccer field
un arrêt de bus   a bus stop

➤ de is found after superlatives (*the most..., the biggest, the least ...* and so on).

la plus belle ville du monde   the most beautiful city in the world
le film le moins intéressant   the least interesting film in the
du festival   festival

⇨ For more information on **Superlative adjectives**, see page 34.

➤ **de** is used in phrases to talk about quantities.

> Elle fait <u>beaucoup de</u> fautes.   She makes a lot of mistakes.
> <u>Combien de</u> personnes as-tu invitées ?   How many people have you invited?

➤ **de** is used with certain adjectives.

> Je suis très surpris <u>de</u> te voir.   I'm very surprised to see you.
> Il est triste <u>de</u> partir.   He's sad to be leaving.

⇨ *For more information on **Prepositions after adjectives**, see page 183.*

Grammar Extra!

If you want to use an adjective after quelque chose, rien, quelqu'un, and personne, you link the words with de.

> quelqu'un <u>d</u>'important   someone important
> quelque chose <u>d</u>'intéressant   something interesting
> rien <u>d</u>'amusant   nothing funny

➤ **de** is found after certain verbs.

> dépendre <u>de</u> quelque chose   to depend on something
> parler <u>de</u> quelque chose   to talk about something

⇨ *For more information on **Prepositions after verbs**, see page 178.*

3 **en**

ℹ️ Note that en is never followed by an article such as le, du, or des.

➤ **en** is used to talk about a place. It can be the equivalent of the English *to* or *in*.

> Je vais <u>en</u> ville.   I'm going <u>to</u> town.
> Il a un appartement <u>en</u> ville.   He has an apartment <u>in</u> town.
> Nous allons <u>en</u> France cet été.   We're going <u>to</u> France this summer.
> Nous habitons <u>en</u> France.   We live <u>in</u> France.

> *Tip*
> en is used with the names of countries that are feminine in French. Use à with the names of towns and cities, and au or aux with masculine countries.

➤ **en** is used to talk about years and months, and to say how long something will take, when it is the equivalent of *in/within*:

<u>en</u> 1923	<u>in</u> 1923
<u>en</u> janvier	<u>in</u> January
Je le ferai <u>en</u> trois jours.	I'll do it <u>in</u> three days.

Grammar Extra!

en and **dans** can both be used in French to talk about a length of time, but the meaning is very different.

Je le ferai <u>dans</u> trois jours.	I'll do it in three days.
Je le ferai <u>en</u> trois jours.	I'll do it in three days.

Though both can be translated in the same way, the first sentence means that you'll do it in three days' time; the second means that it will take three days for you to do it.

➤ **en** is used with the names of the seasons, except for spring.

<u>en</u> été	in summer
<u>en</u> automne	in fall
<u>en</u> hiver	in winter
BUT: <u>au</u> printemps	in spring

➤ **en** is used for most means of transportation.

Je suis venu <u>en</u> voiture.	I came by car.
C'est plus rapide <u>en</u> train.	It's quicker by train.
Il est allé en Italie <u>en</u> avion.	He flew to Italy.

> ## Tip
> The prepositions **à** and **par** are also used with means of transport.

➤ Use **en** to say what language something is in.

une lettre écrite <u>en</u> espagnol	a letter written in Spanish
Dis-le <u>en</u> anglais.	Say it in English.

➤ **en** can be used to say what something is made of when you particularly want to stress the material.

un bracelet <u>en</u> or	a bracelet made of gold, a gold bracelet
un manteau <u>en</u> cuir	a coat made of leather, a leather coat

> **Tip**
> de can also be used to say what something is made of.
> une porte <u>de</u> bois   a wooden door

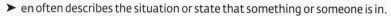

➤ en often describes the situation or state that something or someone is in.

Je suis <u>en</u> vacances.	I'm on vacation.
La voiture est <u>en</u> panne.	The car broke down.
Tu es toujours <u>en</u> retard !	You're always late!

➤ en is found before <u>present participles</u>, the form of the verb that ends in -*ing* in English and -**ant** in French.

Je fais mes devoirs <u>en regardant</u> la télé.	I do my homework while watching TV.
Il m'a vu <u>en passant</u> devant la porte.	He saw me as he went past the door.

For more information on the **Present participle**, see page 125.

> **Key points**
> ✔ à, de, and en are very frequent prepositions which you will use all the time.
> ✔ Each of them has several possible meanings, which depend on the context they are used in.

Some other common prepositions

[i] Note that some of these words are also adverbs, for example, **avant**, **depuis**.

➪ *For more information on the **Adverbs**, see page 152.*

➤ The following prepositions are also frequently used in French:

- **après** after

<u>après</u> le déjeuner	after lunch
<u>après</u> son départ	after he had left
la troisième maison <u>après</u> la mairie	the third house after the town hall
<u>Après</u> vous !	After you!

[i] Note that where English uses a verb in the perfect tense following *after*, French uses the infinitive **avoir** or **être** and a past participle.

Nous viendrons <u>après avoir fait</u> la vaisselle.	We'll come after we<u>'ve done</u> the dishes.

- **avant** before

Il est arrivé <u>avant</u> toi.	He arrived before you.
Tournez à gauche <u>avant</u> la poste.	Turn left before the post office.

[i] Note that where English uses a verb ending in *-ing* after *before*, French uses **de** followed by the infinitive.

Je préfère finir mes devoirs <u>avant de manger</u>.	I prefer to finish my homework <u>before eating</u>.

- **avec** with

<u>avec</u> mon père	with my father
une chambre <u>avec</u> salle de bain	a room with its own bathroom
Ouvre-la <u>avec</u> un couteau.	Open it with a knife.

- **chez**

Elle est <u>chez</u> Pierre.	She's at Pierre's house.
Elle va <u>chez</u> Pierre.	She's going to Pierre's house.
Je reste <u>chez</u> moi ce weekend.	I'm staying at home this weekend.
Je vais rentrer <u>chez</u> moi.	I'm going home.
Ils habitent près de <u>chez</u> moi.	They live near my house.

> *Tip*
>
> chez is also used with the name of jobs or professions to indicate a store or place of business.
>
> | Je vais <u>chez le médecin</u>. | I'm going to the doctor's. |

- contre against

| Ne mets pas ton vélo <u>contre</u> le mur. | Don't put your bike against the wall. |

- dans in, into

Il est <u>dans</u> sa chambre.	He's in his bedroom.
Nous passons une semaine <u>dans</u> les Alpes.	We're spending a week in the Alps.
<u>dans</u> deux mois	in two months' time
Il est entré <u>dans</u> mon bureau.	He came into my office.

Grammar Extra!

dans and en can both be used in French to talk about a length of time, but the meaning is very different.

| Je le ferai <u>dans</u> trois jours. | I'll do it in three days. |
| Je le ferai <u>en</u> trois jours. | I'll do it in three days. |

Though both can be translated in the same way, the first sentence means that you'll do it in three days' time; the second means that it will take three days for you to do it.

- depuis since, for

| Elle habite Paris <u>depuis</u> 1998. | She's been living in Paris since 1998. |
| Elle habite Paris <u>depuis</u> cinq ans. | She's been living in Paris for five years. |

i Note that French uses the <u>present tense</u> with depuis to talk about actions that started in the past and are still going on.

| Il <u>est</u> en France <u>depuis</u> le mois de septembre. | He's been in France since September. (*and he is still there*) |

If you are saying how long something has <u>NOT</u> happened for, you use the <u>perfect tense</u> with depuis.

| Nous ne l'<u>avons</u> pas <u>vu depuis</u> un mois. | We haven't seen him for a month. |

⇨ *For more information on the **Present tense** and the **Perfect tense**, see pages 71 and 111.*

- **derrière** behind

  <u>derrière</u> la porte

  behind the door

- **devant** in front of

  Il est assis <u>devant</u> moi.

  He's sitting in front of me.

- **entre ... et** between ... and

  Il est assis <u>entre</u> son père <u>et</u> son oncle.

  He's sitting between his father and his uncle.

  Le bureau est fermé <u>entre</u> 13 <u>et</u> 14 heures.

  The office is closed between 1 and 2 p.m.

- **jusque** as far as, until

  Je te raccompagne <u>jusque</u> chez toi.

  I'll go with you as far as your house.

  <u>Jusqu</u>'où vas-tu ?

  How far are you going?

  <u>Jusqu</u>'ici nous n'avons pas eu de problèmes.

  Until now we've had no problems.

  Je reste <u>jusqu</u>'à la fin du mois.

  I'm staying until the end of the month.

Tip

jusque changes to jusqu' before a word beginning with a vowel, most words starting with h, and the French word y.

- **par** by, with, per

  deux <u>par</u> deux

  two by two

  <u>par</u> le train

  by train

  <u>par</u> la poste

  by mail

  <u>par</u> e-mail

  by email

  Son nom commence <u>par</u> un H.

  His name begins with H.

  Prenez trois cachets <u>par</u> jour.

  Take three tablets per day.

  Le voyage coûte quatre cents euros <u>par</u> personne.

  The trip costs four hundred euros per person.

  Nous nous voyons une fois <u>par</u> mois.

  We see each other once a month.

  Il est tombé <u>par</u> terre.

  He fell down.

  Il y a beaucoup de touristes <u>par</u> ici.

  There are a lot of tourists around here.

> **Tip**
>
> The prepositions **à** and **en** are also used with means of transportation.

- **pendant** during, for

    | Ça s'est passé <u>pendant</u> l'été. | It happened during the summer. |
    | Il n'a pas pu travailler <u>pendant</u> plusieurs mois. | He couldn't work for several months. |

> **Tip**
>
> French uses the <u>perfect tense</u> with **pendant** to talk about actions in the past that are completed.
>
> | Nous <u>avons habité pendant</u> dix ans en Écosse. | We lived in Scotland for ten years. (*but don't any more*) |
>
> You can also miss out **pendant**.
>
> | Nous avons habité dix ans en Écosse. | We lived in Scotland for ten years. |
>
> **pendant** is also used to talk about something that will happen in the future.
>
> | Je <u>serai</u> à New York <u>pendant</u> un mois. | I'll be in New York for a month. |
>
> ⇨ For more information on the **Perfect tense**, see page 111.

- **pour** for (*who or what something is for, and where something or someone is going*)

    | C'est un cadeau <u>pour</u> toi. | It's a present for you. |
    | Nous voudrions une chambre <u>pour</u> deux nuits. | We'd like a room for two nights. |
    | le train <u>pour</u> Bordeaux | the train for Bordeaux |

[*i*] Note that **pour** can also be used with infinitives, when it has the meaning of *in order to*.

| Elle téléphone <u>pour savoir</u> à quelle heure on arrivera. | She's callilng to find out what time we'll get there. |
| <u>Pour aller</u> à Nice, s'il vous plaît ? | Which way is it to Nice, please? |

- **sans** without

Elle est venue <u>sans</u> son frère.	She came without her brother.
un café <u>sans</u> sucre	a coffee without sugar
un pull <u>sans</u> manches	a sleeveless sweater

> **[i]** Note that **sans** can also be used before infinitives in French. In English a verb form ending in *-ing* is used after *without*.
>
> | | |
> |---|---|
> | Elle est partie <u>sans dire</u> au revoir. | She left <u>without saying</u> goodbye. |

- **sauf** except

Tout le monde vient <u>sauf</u> lui.	Everyone's coming except him.

- **sous** under

<u>sous</u> la table	under the table
<u>sous</u> terre	underground

- **sur** on

Pose-le <u>sur</u> le bureau.	Put it down on the desk.
Ton sac est <u>sur</u> la table.	Your bag is on the table.
Vous verrez l'hôpital <u>sur</u> votre gauche.	You'll see the hospital on your left.
un livre <u>sur</u> la politique	a book on politics

> **[i]** Note that **à** and **sur** can both mean *on* in English. **sur** usually means on the top of something. **sur la télé** means *on top of the TV*, but **à la télé** means *broadcast on TV*. Both can be translated as *on the TV* in English. **sur le mur** means *on top of the wall*, but **au mur** means *hanging on the wall*.

Tip

With numbers and measurements **sur** can also mean *in*, *out of*, and *by*.

une personne <u>sur</u> dix	one person <u>in</u> ten
J'ai eu quatorze <u>sur</u> vingt en maths.	I got 14 <u>out of</u> 20 in Math.
La pièce fait quatre mètres <u>sur</u> deux.	The room measures four meters <u>by</u> two.

- **vers** towards (*a place*), at about

Il allait <u>vers</u> la gare.	He was going toward the station.
Je rentre chez moi <u>vers</u> cinq heures.	I go home at about 5 o'clock.

➤ **voici** (meaning *this is, here is*) and **voilà** (meaning *there is, that is*) are two very useful prepositions that French speakers often use to point things out.

<u>Voici</u> mon frère et <u>voilà</u> ma sœur.	This is my brother and that's my sister.
<u>Voici</u> ton sac.	Here's your bag.
Le <u>voici</u> !	Here he/it is!
Tiens! <u>Voilà</u> Paul.	Look! There's Paul.
Tu as perdu ton stylo ? En <u>voilà</u> un autre.	Did you lose your pen? Here's another one.
Les <u>voilà</u> !	There they are!

Prepositions consisting of more than one word

➤ Prepositions can also be made up of several words instead of just one.

au bord de	at the edge of, at the side of
au bout de	after
à cause de	because of
au-dessous de	below
au-dessus de	above
au fond de	at the bottom of, at the end of
au milieu de	in the middle of

<u>Au bout d</u>'un moment, il s'est endormi.	After a while, he fell asleep.
Nous ne pouvons pas sortir <u>à cause du</u> mauvais temps.	We can't go out because of the bad weather.
J'ai garé la voiture <u>au bord de</u> la route.	I parked the car on the side of the road.
Mon porte-monnaie est <u>au fond de</u> mon sac.	My wallet is at the bottom of my bag.
Place le vase <u>au milieu de</u> la table.	Put the vase in the middle of the table.

Prepositions after verbs

➤ Some French verbs can be followed by an <u>infinitive</u> (the *to* form of the verb) and linked to it by either **de** or **à**, or no preposition at all. This is also true of verbs and their <u>objects</u>: the person or thing that the verb "happens" to.

⇨ *For more information on **Verbs followed by an infinitive**, see page 133.*

> *Tip*
>
> The preposition that is used in French is not always the same as the one that is used in English. Whenever you learn a new verb, try to learn which preposition can be used after it too.

➤ The lists in this section concentrate on those French verbs that involve a different construction from the one that is used in English.

1 Verbs that are followed by à + object

➤ **à** is often the equivalent of the English word *to* when it is used with an indirect object after verbs like *send*, *give*, and *say*.

dire quelque chose <u>à</u> quelqu'un	to say something <u>to</u> someone
donner quelque chose <u>à</u> quelqu'un	to give something <u>to</u> someone
écrire quelque chose <u>à</u> quelqu'un	to write something <u>to</u> someone
envoyer quelque chose <u>à</u> quelqu'un	to send something <u>to</u> someone
montrer quelque chose <u>à</u> quelqu'un	to show something <u>to</u> someone

⇨ *For more information on **Indirect objects**, see page 49.*

> *Tip*
>
> There is an important difference between French and English with this type of verb. In English, you can say either *to give something <u>to</u> someone* or *to give someone something*; *to show something <u>to</u> someone* or *to show someone something*.
> You can <u>NEVER</u> leave out **à** in French in the way that you can sometimes leave out *to* in English.

➤ Here are some verbs taking à in French that have a different construction in English.

croire <u>à</u> quelque chose	to believe <u>in</u> something
s'intéresser <u>à</u> quelqu'un/quelque chose	to be interested <u>in</u> someone/something
jouer <u>à</u> quelque chose	to play something (sports, games)
obéir <u>à</u> quelqu'un	to obey someone
penser <u>à</u> quelqu'un/quelque chose	to think <u>about</u> someone/something
répondre <u>à</u> quelqu'un	to answer someone
téléphoner <u>à</u> quelqu'un	to call someone

Tip

When you are using **jouer** to talk about sports and games, you use **à**. When you are using **jouer** to talk about musical instruments, you use **de**.

jouer <u>au</u> tennis	to play tennis
jouer <u>aux</u> échecs	to play chess
jouer <u>de</u> la guitare	to play the guitar
jouer <u>du</u> piano	to play the piano

➤ **plaire** followed by **à** is a common way of saying you like something.

plaire <u>à</u> quelqu'un	to please someone
Ton cadeau me plaît beaucoup.	I like your present a lot.
Ce film plaît beaucoup aux jeunes.	This movie is very popular with young people.

Grammar Extra!

manquer à works very differently from its English equivalent, to miss. The English object is the French subject, and the English subject is the French object.

manquer <u>à</u> quelqu'un	to be missed by someone
Tu (subject) me (object) manques.	I (subject) miss you (object).
Mon pays (subject) me (object) manque beaucoup.	I (subject) miss my country (object) very much.

➤ There are also some verbs where you can put a direct object before **à**. The verb **demander** is the most common.

demander quelque chose <u>à</u> quelqu'un	to ask someone something, to ask someone for something

⇨ For more information on **Direct objects**, see page 47.

[*i*] Note that **demander** in French does <u>NOT</u> mean *to demand*. It means *to ask something* or *to ask for something*. If you want to say *demand* in French, use **exiger**.

> **Nous avons demandé notre chemin à un chauffeur de taxi.**
>
> We asked a taxi driver the way.
>
> **J'exige des excuses !**
>
> I demand an apology!

2 **Verbs that are followed by de + object**

➤ Here are some verbs taking **de** in French that have a different construction in English.

changer <u>de</u> quelque chose	to change something (*one's shoes and so on*)
dépendre <u>de</u> quelqu'un/ quelque chose	to depend <u>on</u> someone/something
s'excuser <u>de</u> quelque chose	to apologize <u>for</u> something
jouer <u>de</u> quelque chose	to play something
parler <u>de</u> quelque chose	to talk <u>about</u> something
se servir <u>de</u> quelque chose	to use something
se souvenir <u>de</u> quelqu'un/ quelque chose	to remember someone/something

> *Tip*
>
> When you are using **jouer** to talk about sports and games, you use **à**. When you are using **jouer** to talk about musical instruments, you use **de**.
>
> | | |
> |---|---|
> | jouer <u>au</u> tennis | to play tennis |
> | jouer <u>aux</u> échecs | to play chess |
> | jouer <u>de</u> la guitare | to play the guitar |
> | jouer <u>du</u> piano | to play the piano |

➤ Some common phrases using **avoir** also contain **de**.

<u>avoir</u> besoin <u>de</u> quelque chose	to need something
<u>avoir</u> envie <u>de</u> quelque chose	to want something
<u>avoir</u> peur <u>de</u> quelque chose	to be afraid of something

➤ There are also some verbs where you can put a direct object before **de**. **remercier** is the most common.

> remercier quelqu'un <u>de</u> quelque chose to thank someone for something

⇨ *For more information on **Direct objects**, see page 47.*

For further explanation of grammatical terms, please see pages viii-xii.

Grammar Extra!

The verb **se tromper de quelque chose** is often the equivalent of *to get the wrong ...*

Je me suis trompé de numéro.	I got the wrong number.
Je me suis trompé de maison.	I got the wrong house.

---

3 Verbs taking a direct object in French but not in English

➤ In English there are a few verbs that are followed by *for, on, in, to,* or *at* which, in French, are not followed by a preposition such as **à** or **de**. Here are the most common:

attendre quelqu'un/quelque chose	to wait <u>for</u> sb/sth
chercher quelqu'un/quelque chose	to look <u>for</u> sb/sth
demander quelqu'un/quelque chose	to ask <u>for</u> sb/sth
écouter quelqu'un/quelque chose	to listen <u>to</u> sb/sth
espérer quelque chose	to hope <u>for</u> sth
payer quelque chose	to pay <u>for</u> sth
regarder quelqu'un/quelque chose	to look <u>at</u> sb/sth

ⓘ Note that **attendre** does <u>NOT</u> mean *to attend* in English. It means *to wait for*. If you want to say that you attend something, use **assister à quelque chose**.

Je t'attends devant la gare.	I'll wait for you in front of the station.
Vous allez assister au concert ?	Are you going to attend the concert?

➤ **habiter** can be used with or without a preposition:

- **habiter** is mostly used <u>without a preposition</u> when you are talking about living in a house, an apartment, and so on

Nous habitons un petit appartement en ville.	We live in a small apartment in town.

- use **habiter** <u>with à</u> when you are talking about a town or city, and **au** (*singular*) or **aux** (*plural*) with the names of countries that are masculine in French

Nous habitons <u>à</u> Los Angeles.	We live in Los Angeles.
Nous habitons <u>aux</u> États-Unis.	We live in the United States.

- use **habiter** <u>with en</u> when you are talking about feminine countries

Nous habitons <u>en</u> Espagne.	We live in Spain.

Key points

✔ French prepositions after verbs are often not the ones that are used in English. French verbs often have a different construction from English verbs.

✔ French verbs are usually linked to their objects by **de**, **à**, or nothing at all.

✔ You can never leave out **à** in French in the way that you can leave out *to* in English constructions like *to give someone something*.

For further explanation of grammatical terms, please see pages viii-xii.

Prepositions after adjectives

➤ Just like verbs, some French adjectives can be linked to what follows by either **à** or **de**.

➤ An adjective followed by **de** or **à** can be followed by a noun, a pronoun, or an infinitive.

➤ Some adjectives that can be followed by **de** are used to say how you feel, that you are certain about something, or that it is necessary or important to do something. These are the most common:

certain	certain
content	happy
désolé	sorry
enchanté	delighted
heureux	happy
important	important
malheureux	unhappy
nécessaire	necessary
sûr	sure
triste	sad

Tu es <u>sûr de</u> pouvoir venir ?	Are you sure you can come?
<u>Enchanté de</u> faire votre connaissance.	Delighted to meet you.
Il est <u>nécessaire de</u> réserver.	You have to make a reservation.

Grammar Extra!

➤ Some adjectives, such as **facile** (meaning *easy*), **intéressant** (meaning *interesting*), or **impossible** (meaning *impossible*), can be followed by either **à** or **de**. **de** tends to be used when you are saying something that is usually true. **à** tends to be used when you are saying something about someone or something in particular.

Il est difficile <u>de</u> prendre une décision.	It's difficult to make a decision.
<u>Il</u> est difficile <u>à</u> connaître.	He's difficult to get to know.
<u>Son accent</u> est difficile <u>à</u> comprendre.	His accent is difficult to understand.

Conjunctions

> **What is a conjunction?**
> A **conjunction** is a word such as *and*, *but*, *or*, *so*, *if*, and *because*, that links two words or phrases of a similar type, or two parts of a sentence, for example, *Diane <u>and</u> I have been friends for years; I left <u>because</u> I was bored*.

et, mais, ou, parce que, and si

➤ **et**, **mais**, **ou**, **parce que**, and **si** are the most common conjunctions that you need to know in French.

- **et** and

toi <u>et</u> moi	you <u>and</u> me
Il pleut <u>et</u> il fait très froid.	It's raining <u>and</u> it's very cold.

- **mais** but

C'est cher <u>mais</u> de très bonne qualité.	It's expensive, <u>but</u> very good quality.

🛈 Note that **mais** is also commonly found in front of **oui** and **si**.

"Tu viens ce soir?" – "<u>Mais oui</u> !"	"Are you coming tonight?" – "Definitely!"
"Il n'a pas encore fini?" – "<u>Mais si</u> !"	"Hasn't he finished yet?" – "He certainly has!"

- **ou** or

Tu préfères le vert <u>ou</u> le bleu ?	Do you like the green one <u>or</u> the blue one?
Donne-moi ça <u>ou</u> je me fâche !	Give me that <u>or</u> I'll get angry!

> *Tip*
> Be careful not to confuse **ou** (meaning *or*) with **où** (meaning *where*).

- **parce que** because

Je ne peux pas sortir <u>parce que</u> j'ai encore du travail à faire.	I can't go out <u>because</u> I still have work to do.

> **Tip**
>
> **parce que** changes to **parce qu'** before a word beginning with a vowel, most words starting with **h**, and the French word **y**.
>
> | | |
> |---|---|
> | Il ne vient pas <u>parce qu'</u>il n'a pas de voiture. | He isn't coming <u>because</u> he doesn't have a car. |

- **si** if

Je me demande <u>si</u> elle ment.	I wonder <u>if</u> she's lying.
<u>Si</u> j'étais à ta place, je ne l'inviterais pas.	<u>If</u> I were you, I wouldn't invite him.

> **Tip**
>
> **si** changes to **s'** before **il** or **ils**.
>
> | | |
> |---|---|
> | <u>S'</u>il ne pleut pas, on mangera dehors. | <u>If</u> it doesn't rain, we'll eat outside. |

Some other common conjunctions

➤ Here are some other common French conjunctions:

- **car** because

Il faut prendre un bus pour y accéder <u>car</u> il est interdit d´y monter en voiture.	You need to take a bus to get there because cars are prohibited.

ⓘ Note that **car** is used in formal language or in writing. The normal way of saying *because* is **parce que**.

- **comme** since

<u>Comme</u> il pleut, je prends la voiture.	<u>Since</u> it's raining, I'm taking the car.

- **donc** so

J'ai raté le train, <u>donc</u> je serai en retard.	I missed the train, <u>so</u> I'll be late.

- **lorsque** when

J'allais composer ton numéro <u>lorsque</u> tu as appelé.	I was about to dial your number <u>when</u> you called.

- **quand** when

Je ne sors pas <u>quand</u> il pleut.	I don't go out <u>when</u> it rains.

ⓘ Note that when **quand** and **lorsque** are used to talk about something that will happen in the future, the French verb has to be in the <u>future tense</u> even though English uses a verb in the <u>present tense</u>.

Quand je <u>serai</u> riche, j'achèterai une belle maison.	When I'<u>m</u> rich, I'll buy a nice house.

⇨ *For more information on the **Present tense** and the **Future tense**, see pages 71 and 98.*

➤ French, like English, also has conjunctions which have more than one part. Here are the most common:

- **ne ... ni ... ni** neither ... nor

Je n'aime <u>ni</u> les lentilles <u>ni</u> les épinards.	I like <u>neither</u> lentils <u>nor</u> spinach.

ⓘ Note that the **ne** part of this expression goes just before the verb.

- **ou ... ou, ou bien ... ou bien** either ... or

<u>Ou</u> il est malade <u>ou</u> il ment.	<u>Either</u> he's sick <u>or</u> he's lying.
<u>Ou bien</u> il m'évite <u>ou bien</u> il ne me reconnaît pas.	<u>Either</u> he's avoiding me <u>or</u> else he doesn't recognize me.

The conjunction que

➤ When **que** is used to join two parts of a sentence, it means *that*.

Il dit qu'il m'aime.	He says <u>that</u> he loves me.
Elle sait que vous êtes là.	She knows <u>that</u> you're here.

> ### Tip
> In English you could say both *He says he loves me* and *He says <u>that</u> he loves me*, or *She knows you're here* and *She knows <u>that</u> you're here*. You can <u>NEVER</u> leave out **que** in French in the same way.

➤ **que** is also used when you are comparing two things or two people. In this case, it means *as* or *than*.

Ils n'y vont pas aussi souvent que nous.	They don't go as often <u>as</u> we do.
Les melons sont plus chers que les bananes.	Melons are more expensive <u>than</u> bananas.

⇨ *For more information on **Comparative adjectives**, see page 34.*

➤ Some words which give you information about when something happens, can also be conjunctions if you put **que** after them. **pendant que** (meaning *while*) is the most common of these.

Christian a téléphoné pendant que Chantal prenait son bain.	Christian called <u>while</u> Chantal was taking a bath.

🛈 Note that when **pendant que** (meaning *while*), **quand** (meaning *when*), and **lorsque** (meaning *when*) are used to talk about something that will happen in the future, the French verb has to be in the <u>future tense</u> even though English uses a verb in the <u>present tense</u>.

Pendant que je <u>serai</u> en France, j'irai les voir.	I'll go visit them while I'<u>m</u> in France.

⇨ *For more information on the **Present tense** and the **Future tense**, see pages 71 and 98.*

Grammar Extra!

que can replace another conjunction to avoid having to repeat it.

<u>Quand</u> **tu seras plus grand et que tu auras une maison à toi,...**	When you're older and you have a house of your own, ...
<u>Comme</u> **il pleut et que je n'ai pas de parapluie, ...**	Since it's raining and I don't have an umbrella, ...

Numbers

1	un (une)
2	deux
3	trois
4	quatre
5	cinq
6	six
7	sept
8	huit
9	neuf
10	dix
11	onze
12	douze
13	treize
14	quatorze
15	quinze
16	seize
17	dix-sept
18	dix-huit
19	dix-neuf
20	vingt
21	vingt et un (une)
22	vingt-deux
30	trente
40	quarante
50	cinquante
60	soixante
70	soixante-dix
71	soixante et onze
72	soixante-douze
80	quatre-vingts
81	quatre-vingt-un (-une)
90	quatre-vingt-dix
91	quatre-vingt-onze
100	cent
101	cent un (une)
300	trois cents
301	trois cent un (une)
1000	mille
2000	deux mille
1,000,000	un million

1st	premier (1er), première (1re)
2nd	deuxième (2e or 2ème) or second(e) ($2^{nd(e)}$)
3rd	troisième (3e or 3ème)
4th	quatrième (4e or 4ème)
5th	cinquième (5e or 5ème)
6th	sixième (6e or 6ème)
7th	septième (7e or 7ème)
8th	huitième (8e or 8ème)
9th	neuvième (9e or 9ème)
10th	dixième (10e or 10ème)
11th	onzième (11e or 11ème)
12th	douzième (12e or 12ème)
13th	treizième (13e or 13ème)
14th	quatorzième (14e or 14ème)
15th	quinzième (15e or 15ème)
16th	seizième (16e or 16ème)
17th	dix-septième (17e or 17ème)
18th	dix-huitième (18e or $18^{ème}v$)
19th	dix-neuvième (19e or 19ème)
20th	vingtième (20e or 20ème)
21st	vingt et unième (21e or 21ème)
22nd	vingt-deuxième (22e or 22ème)
30th	trentième (30e or 30ème)
100th	centième (100e or 100ème)
101st	cent unième (101e or 101ème)
1000th	millième (1000e or 1000ème)

1/2	un demi
1/3	un tiers
2/3	deux tiers
1/4	un quart
1/5	un cinquième
0.5	zéro virgule cinq (0,5)
3.4	trois virgule quatre (3,4)
10%	dix pour cent
100%	cent pour cent

EXEMPLES	EXAMPLES
Il habite au dix.	He lives at number ten.
à la page dix-neuf	on page nineteen
au chapitre sept	in chapter seven
Il habite au cinquième (étage).	He lives on the fifth floor.
Il est arrivé troisième.	He came in third.
échelle au vingt-cinq millième	a scale of one to twenty-five thousand

L'HEURE	THE TIME

Quelle heure est-il ? — What time is it?
Il est... — It's...
- **une heure** — one o'clock
- **une heure dix** — ten past one
- **une heure et quart** — a quarter after one
- **une heure et demie** — half past one
- **deux heures moins vingt** — twenty to two
- **deux heures moins le quart** — quarter to two

À quelle heure ? — At what time?
- **à minuit** — at midnight
- **à midi** — at noon, at midday
- **à une heure (de l'après-midi)** — at one o'clock (in the afternoon)
- **à huit heures (du soir)** — at eight o'clock (in the evening)
- **à 11h15** or **onze heures quinze** — at 11:15 or eleven fifteen
- **à 20h45** or **vingt heures quarante-cinq** — at 20:45 or twenty forty-five (8:45 p.m.)

LA DATE	THE DATE
LES JOURS DE LA SEMAINE	DAYS OF THE WEEK

- **lundi** — Monday
- **mardi** — Tuesday
- **mercredi** — Wednesday
- **jeudi** — Thursday
- **vendredi** — Friday
- **samedi** — Saturday
- **dimanche** — Sunday

Quand ? — When?
- **lundi** — on Monday
- **le lundi** — on Mondays
- **tous les lundis** — every Monday
- **mardi dernier** — last Tuesday
- **vendredi prochain** — next Friday
- **samedi en huit** — a week from Saturday
- **samedi en quinze** — two weeks from Saturday

ℹ️ Note that days of the week are <u>NOT</u> written with a capital letter in French.

LES MOIS	MONTHS OF THE YEAR
janvier	January
février	February
mars	March
avril	April
mai	May
juin	June
juillet	July
août	August
septembre	September
octobre	October
novembre	November
décembre	December

Quand ? / **When?**

en février	in February
le 1er décembre	on December 1st
le premier décembre	on December first
en 1998	in 1998
en mille neuf cent quatre-vingt-dix-huit	in nineteen ninety-eight

Quel jour sommes-nous ? / **What day is it?**
Nous sommes le… / **It's…**

lundi 26 février *or*	Monday, February 26 *or*
lundi vingt-six février	Monday, February twenty-sixth
dimanche 1er octobre *or*	Sunday, October 1st *or*
dimanche premier octobre	Sunday, October first

Note that months of the year are NOT written with a capital letter in French.

VOCABULAIRE

Quand ?
aujourd'hui
ce matin
cet après-midi
ce soir

Souvent ?
tous les jours
tous les deux jours
une fois par semaine
deux fois par semaine
une fois par mois

Ça s'est passé quand ?
le matin
le soir
hier
hier soir
avant-hier
il y a une semaine
il y a quinze jours
l'an dernier *or* l'année dernière

Ça va se passer quand ?
demain
demain matin
après-demain
dans deux jours
dans une semaine
dans quinze jours
le mois prochain
l'an prochain *or* l'année prochaine

USEFUL VOCABULARY

When?
today
this morning
this afternoon
this evening

How often?
every day
every other day
once a week
twice a week
once a month

When did it happen?
in the morning
in the evening
yesterday
yesterday evening
the day before yesterday
a week ago
two weeks ago
last year

When is it going to happen?
tomorrow
tomorrow morning
the day after tomorrow
in two days
in a week
in two weeks
next month
next year

General problems

➤ You can't always translate French into English and English into French word for word. While occasionally it is possible to do this, often it is not. For example:

- English <u>phrasal verbs</u> (verbs followed by a preposition or adverb), for example, *to run away*, *to fall down*, are often translated by <u>ONE</u> word in French.

continuer	to go on
tomber	to fall down
rendre	to give back

⇨ *For more information on **Verbs**, see pages 69–137.*

- Sentences which contain a verb and preposition in English might <u>NOT</u> contain a preposition in French.

payer quelque chose	to pay <u>for</u> something
regarder quelqu'un/quelque chose	to look <u>at</u> somebody/something
écouter quelqu'un/quelque chose	to listen <u>to</u> somebody/something

- Similarly, sentences which contain a verb and preposition in French might <u>NOT</u> contain a preposition in English.

obéir <u>à</u> quelqu'un/quelque chose	to obey somebody/something
changer <u>de</u> quelque chose	to change something
manquer <u>de</u> quelque chose	to lack something

- The same French preposition may be translated into English in different ways.

parler <u>de</u> quelque chose	to talk <u>about</u> something
sûr <u>de</u> quelque chose	sure <u>of</u> something
voler quelque chose <u>à</u> quelqu'un	to steal something <u>from</u> someone
croire <u>à</u> quelque chose	to believe <u>in</u> something

⇨ *For more information on **Prepositions**, see page 162.*

• A word which is singular in English may not be in French.

les bagages	luggage
ses cheveux	his/her hair

• Similarly, a word which is singular in French may not be in English.

un short	shorts
mon pantalon	my pants

➪ *For more information on **Nouns**, see page 1.*

• In English, you can use 's to show who or what something belongs to; in French, you have to use **de**.

la voiture de mon frère	my brother's car
la chambre des enfants	the children's bedroom

➪ *For more information on the preposition **de**, see page 166.*

Specific problems

1 -ing

➤ The -*ing* ending in English is translated in a number of different ways in French:

• *to be ...-ing* is translated by a verb consisting of one word.

Il **part** demain.	He's leaving tomorrow.
Je **lisais** un roman.	I was reading a book.

➪ *For more information on **Verbs**, see pages 69–137.*

i Note that when you are talking about somebody's or something's physical position, you use a past participle.

Elle est **assise** là-bas.	She's sitting over there.
Il était **couché** par terre.	He was lying on the ground.

➪ *For more information on the **Past participle**, see page 111.*

➤ -*ing* can also be translated by:

• an infinitive

J'aime **aller** au cinéma.	I like going to the movies.
Arrêtez de vous **disputer** !	Stop arguing!
Avant de **partir**...	Before leaving...

➪ *For more information on **Infinitives**, see page 133.*

● a present participle

Étant plus timide que moi, elle...   Being shyer than me, she...

⇨ *For more information on the **Present participle**, see page 125.*

● a noun

Le ski me maintient en forme.   Skiing keeps me in shape.

⇨ *For more information on **Nouns**, see page 1.*

2 to be

➤ The verb *to be* is generally translated by **être**.

Il est tard.   It's late.
Ce n'est pas possible !   It's not possible!

➤ When you are talking about the physical position of something, **se trouver** may be used.

Où se trouve la gare ?   Where's the station?

➤ In certain set phrases which describe how you are feeling or a state you are in, the verb **avoir** is used.

avoir chaud	to be warm
avoir froid	to be cold
avoir faim	to be hungry
avoir soif	to be thirsty
avoir peur	to be afraid
avoir tort	to be wrong
avoir raison	to be right

➤ When you are describing what the weather is like, use the verb **faire**.

Quel temps fait-il ?   What's the weather like?
Il fait beau.   It's lovely.
Il fait mauvais.   It's miserable.
Il fait du vent.   It's windy.

➤ When you are talking about someone's age, use the verb **avoir**.

Quel âge as-tu ?   How old are you?
J'ai quinze ans.   I'm fifteen.

➤ When talking about your health, use the verb **aller**.

Comment allez-vous ?   How are you?
Je vais très bien.   I'm very well.

3 it is, it's

➤ *it is* and *it's* are usually translated by **il est** or **elle est** when referring to a noun.

"Où est mon parapluie ?" – "**Il est** là, dans le coin."	"Where's my umbrella?" – "**It's** there, in the corner."
Descends la valise si **elle n'est** pas trop lourde.	Bring the suitcase down if **it is**n't too heavy.

➤ When you are talking about the time, use **il est**.

"Quelle heure **est-il** ?" – "**Il est** sept heures et demie."	"What time **is it**?" – "**It's** half past seven."

➤ When you are describing what the weather is like, use the verb **faire**.

Il **fait** beau.	It**'s** lovely.
Il **fait** mauvais.	It**'s** miserable.
Il **fait** du vent.	It**'s** windy.

➤ If you want to say, for example, *it is difficult to do something* or *it is easy to do something*, use **il est**.

Il est difficile de répondre à cette question.	**It is** difficult to answer this question.

➤ In ALL other phrases and constructions, use **c'est**.

C'est moi qui ne l'aime pas.	**It's** me who doesn't like him.
C'est Charles qui l'a dit.	**It's** Charles who said so.
C'est ici que je les ai achetés.	**It's** here that I bought them.
C'est parce que la poste est fermée que…	**It's** because the post office is closed that…

4 there is, there are

➤ Both *there is* and *there are* are translated by **il y a**.

Il y a quelqu'un à la porte.	**There is** someone at the door.
Il y a cinq livres sur la table.	**There are** five books on the table.

5 can, to be able

➤ If you want to talk about someone's physical ability to do something, use **pouvoir**.

Pouvez-vous faire dix kilomètres à pied ?	**Can** you walk ten kilometers?

➤ If you want to say that *you know how to do something*, use **savoir**.

> **Elle ne sait pas nager.**   She can't swim.

➤ When *can* is used with verbs to do with what you can see or hear, you do NOT use **pouvoir** in French.

> **Je ne vois rien.**   I can't see anything.
> **Il les entendait.**   He could hear them.

6 to

➤ The preposition *to* is generally translated by **à**.

> **Donne le livre à Patrick.**   Give the book to Patrick.

⇨ *For more information on the preposition à, see page 163.*

➤ When you are talking about the time, use **moins**.

> **dix heures moins cinq**   five to ten
> **à sept heures moins le quart**   at a quarter to seven

➤ If you want to say *(in order) to*, use **pour**.

> **Je l'ai fait pour vous aider.**   I did it to help you.
> **Il va en ville pour acheter un cadeau.**   He's going into town to buy a present.

The Alphabet

➤ The French alphabet is pronounced differently from the way it is pronounced in English. Use the list below to help you sound out the letters.

A, a	[ɑ]	(ah)	like "a" in "la"
B, b	[be]	(bay)	
C, c	[se]	(say)	
D, d	[de]	(day)	
E, e	[ə]	(uh)	like "e" in "le"
F, f	[ɛf]	(eff)	
G, g	[ʒe]	(jay)	
H, h	[aʃ]	(ash)	
I, i	[i]	(ee)	
J, j	[ʒi]	(jee)	
K, k	[ka]	(ka)	
L, l	[ɛl]	(ell)	
M, m	[ɛm]	(emm)	
N, n	[ɛn]	(enn)	
O, o	[o]	(oh)	
P, p	[pe]	(pay)	
Q, q	[ky]	(ku)	like "u" in "une"
R, r	[ɛr]	(air)	
S, s	[ɛs]	(ess)	
T, t	[te]	(tay)	
U, u	[y]	(u)	like "u" in "une"
V, v	[ve]	(vay)	
W, w	[dubləve]	(doobla-vay)	
X, x	[iks]	(eex)	
Y, y	[igrɛk]	(ee-grek)	
Z, z	[zɛd]	(zed)	

For further explanation of grammatical terms, please see pages viii-xii.

Main Index

Verb Tables

VERB TABLES

Introduction

The **Verb Tables** in the following section contain 115 tables of French verbs (some regular and some irregular) in alphabetical order. Each table shows you the following forms: **Present, Present Subjunctive, Perfect, Imperfect, Future, Conditional, Past Historic, Pluperfect, Imperative,** and the **Present** and **Past Participles**. For more information on these tenses and how they are formed you should look at the section on Verbs on pages 69–137.

In order to help you use the verbs shown in the **Verb Tables** correctly, there are also a number of example phrases at the bottom of each page to show the verb as it is used in context.

In French there are both **regular** (their forms follow the normal rules) and **irregular** verbs (their forms do not follow the normal rules). The regular verbs in these tables are:

donner (regular -er verb, page 274)
finir (regular -ir verb, page 304)
attendre (regular -re verb, page 226)

The irregular verbs are shown in full.

The **Verb Index** at the end of this section contains more than 2,000 verbs, each of which is cross-referred to one of the verbs given in the **Verb Tables**. The table shows the patterns that the verb listed in the index follows.

acheter (to buy)

PRESENT

j'	achète
tu	achètes
il/elle/on	achète
nous	achetons
vous	achetez
ils/elles	achètent

PRESENT SUBJUNCTIVE

j'	achète
tu	achètes
il/elle/on	achète
nous	achetions
vous	achetiez
ils/elles	achètent

PERFECT

j'	ai acheté
tu	as acheté
il/elle/on	a acheté
nous	avons acheté
vous	avez acheté
ils/elles	ont acheté

IMPERFECT

j'	achetais
tu	achetais
il/elle/on	achetait
nous	achetions
vous	achetiez
ils/elles	achetaient

PRESENT PARTICIPLE

achetant

PAST PARTICIPLE

acheté

EXAMPLE PHRASES

Nous n'**achetons** jamais de chips. We never buy chips.

Qu'est-ce que tu **as acheté** ? What did you buy?

Il faut que j'**achète** un cadeau pour son anniversaire. I must buy a present for his birthday.

Ses parents lui **achetaient** des bonbons. His parents bought him candy.

---

je/j' = I   **tu** = you   **il** = he/it   **elle** = she/it   **on** = we/one   **nous** = we   **vous** = you   **ils/elles** = they

acheter

FUTURE

j'	**achèterai**
tu	**achèteras**
il/elle/on	**achètera**
nous	**achèterons**
vous	**achèterez**
ils/elles	**achèteront**

CONDITIONAL

j'	**achèterais**
tu	**achèterais**
il/elle/on	**achèterait**
nous	**achèterions**
vous	**achèteriez**
ils/elles	**achèteraient**

PAST HISTORIC

j'	**achetai**
tu	**achetas**
il/elle/on	**acheta**
nous	**achetâmes**
vous	**achetâtes**
ils/elles	**achetèrent**

PLUPERFECT

j'	**avais acheté**
tu	**avais acheté**
il/elle/on	**avait acheté**
nous	**avions acheté**
vous	**aviez acheté**
ils/elles	**avaient acheté**

IMPERATIVE

achète / **achetons** / **achetez**

EXAMPLE PHRASES

J'**achèterai** des gâteaux à la pâtisserie. I'll buy some cakes at the bakery.

Elle **acheta** la robe rouge. She bought the red dress.

Si j'étais riche j'**achèterais** un voilier. If I were rich, I'd buy a yacht.

Il lui **avait acheté** une jolie robe, mais elle ne voulait pas la porter.
   He'd bought her a nice dress, but she didn't want to wear it.

N'**achète** rien pour moi. Don't buy anything for me.

je/j' = I **tu** = you **il** = he/it **elle** = she/it **on** = we/one **nous** = we **vous** = you **ils/elles** = they

acquérir (to acquire)

PRESENT

j'	acquiers
tu	acquiers
il/elle/on	acquiert
nous	acquérons
vous	acquérez
ils/elles	acquièrent

PRESENT SUBJUNCTIVE

j'	acquière
tu	acquières
il/elle/on	acquière
nous	acquérions
vous	acquériez
ils/elles	acquièrent

PERFECT

j'	ai acquis
tu	as acquis
il/elle/on	a acquis
nous	avons acquis
vous	avez acquis
ils/elles	ont acquis

IMPERFECT

j'	acquérais
tu	acquérais
il/elle/on	acquérait
nous	acquérions
vous	acquériez
ils/elles	acquéraient

PRESENT PARTICIPLE

acquérant

PAST PARTICIPLE

acquis

EXAMPLE PHRASES

Nous **acquérons** de nouvelles connaissances tous les jours. We acquire new knowledge every day.

Les mauvaises habitudes s'**acquièrent** facilement. One easily acquires bad habits.

Elle **a acquis** la nationalité française en 2003. She acquired French nationality in 2003.

Il faut qu'il **acquière** de l'expérience avant que nous puissions lui offrir un travail. He has to gain some experience before we can offer him a job.

je/j' = I   tu = you   il = he/it   elle = she/it   on = we/one   nous = we   vous = you   ils/elles = they

acquérir

FUTURE

j'	**acquerrai**
tu	**acquerras**
il/elle/on	**acquerra**
nous	**acquerrons**
vous	**acquerrez**
ils/elles	**acquerront**

CONDITIONAL

j'	**acquerrais**
tu	**acquerrais**
il/elle/on	**acquerrait**
nous	**acquerrions**
vous	**acquerriez**
ils/elles	**acquerraient**

PAST HISTORIC

j'	**acquis**
tu	**acquis**
il/elle/on	**acquit**
nous	**acquîmes**
vous	**acquîtes**
ils/elles	**acquirent**

PLUPERFECT

j'	**avais acquis**
tu	**avais acquis**
il/elle/on	**avait acquis**
nous	**avions acquis**
vous	**aviez acquis**
ils/elles	**avaient acquis**

IMPERATIVE

acquiers / acquérons / acquérez

EXAMPLE PHRASES

Elle **acquit** soudain la certitude qu'il lui avait toujours menti. She suddenly felt certain that he'd always lied to her.

Tu **acquerrais** un peu d'expérience si tu travaillais cet été. You'd gain some experience if you worked this summer.

Il **avait** mystérieusement **acquis** une superbe voiture de sport. He had mysteriously acquired a beautiful sportscar.

Le tableau **avait acquis** beaucoup de valeur. The painting had risen a lot in value.

je/j' = I **tu** = you **il** = he/it **elle** = she/it **on** = we/one **nous** = we **vous** = you **ils/elles** = they

aller (to go)

PRESENT

je **vais**
tu **vas**
il/elle/on **va**
nous **allons**
vous **allez**
ils/elles **vont**

PRESENT SUBJUNCTIVE

j' **aille**
tu **ailles**
il/elle/on **aille**
nous **allions**
vous **alliez**
ils/elles **aillent**

PERFECT

je **suis allé(e)**
tu **es allé(e)**
il/elle/on **est allé(e)**
nous **sommes allé(e)s**
vous **êtes allé(e)(s)**
ils/elles **sont allé(e)s**

IMPERFECT

j' **allais**
tu **allais**
il/elle/on **allait**
nous **allions**
vous **alliez**
ils/elles **allaient**

PRESENT PARTICIPLE
allant

PAST PARTICIPLE
allé

EXAMPLE PHRASES

Vous **allez** souvent au cinéma ? Do you often go to the movies?

Je **suis allé** à Londres. I went to London.

Est-ce que tu **es** déjà **allé** en Allemagne ? Have you ever been to Germany?

Il faut que j'**aille** la chercher à la gare. I have to go and get her at the train station.

J'**allais** tous les jours à l'école à pied. I would walk to school every day.

aller

FUTURE

j'	**irai**
tu	**iras**
il/elle/on	**ira**
nous	**irons**
vous	**irez**
ils/elles	**iront**

CONDITIONAL

j'	**irais**
tu	**irais**
il/elle/on	**irait**
nous	**irions**
vous	**iriez**
ils/elles	**iraient**

PAST HISTORIC

j'	**allai**
tu	**allas**
il/elle/on	**alla**
nous	**allâmes**
vous	**allâtes**
ils/elles	**allèrent**

PLUPERFECT

j'	**étais allé(e)**
tu	**étais allé(e)**
il/elle/on	**était allé(e)**
nous	**étions allé(e)s**
vous	**étiez allé(e)(s)**
ils/elles	**étaient allé(e)s**

IMPERATIVE

va / allons / allez

EXAMPLE PHRASES

J'**irai** en ville demain. I'll go into town tomorrow.

Ils **allèrent** la voir à l'hôpital. They went to see her at the hospital.

J'**irais** au théâtre avec toi s'il restait des places. I'd go to the theater with
   you if there were any tickets left.

Nous **étions allés** à New York en avion mais nous étions rentrés par le train.
   We'd flown to New York, but we'd come back by train.

Va voir s'ils sont arrivés. Go see if they have arrived.

---

je/j' = I **tu** = you **il** = he/it **elle** = she/it **on** = we/one **nous** = we **vous** = you **ils/elles** = they

s'amuser (to play; to enjoy oneself)

PRESENT

je	m'amuse
tu	t'amuses
il/elle/on	s'amuse
nous	nous amusons
vous	vous amusez
ils/elles	s'amusent

PRESENT SUBJUNCTIVE

je	m'amuse
tu	t'amuses
il/elle/on	s'amuse
nous	nous amusions
vous	vous amusiez
ils/elles	s'amusent

PERFECT

je	me suis amusé(e)
tu	t'es amusé(e)
il/elle/on	s'est amusé(e)
nous	nous sommes amusé(e)s
vous	vous êtes amusé(e)(s)
ils/elles	se sont amusé(e)s

IMPERFECT

je	m'amusais
tu	t'amusais
il/elle/on	s'amusait
nous	nous amusions
vous	vous amusiez
ils/elles	s'amusaient

PRESENT PARTICIPLE
s'amusant

PAST PARTICIPLE
amusé

EXAMPLE PHRASES

Les enfants **s'amusent** dehors. The children are playing outside.

On **s'est** bien **amusés** à cette soirée. We really enjoyed ourselves at that party.

J'ai peur que personne ne **s'amuse** cet après-midi. I'm scared nobody is enjoying themselves this afternoon.

Ils **s'amusaient** à sauter dans les flaques d'eau. They had fun jumping in the puddles.

je/j' = I   **tu** = you   **il** = he/it   **elle** = she/it   **on** = we/one   **nous** = we   **vous** = you   **ils/elles** = they

s'amuser

FUTURE

je	**m'amuserai**
tu	**t'amuseras**
il/elle/on	**s'amusera**
nous	**nous amuserons**
vous	**vous amuserez**
ils/elles	**s'amuseront**

CONDITIONAL

je	**m'amuserais**
tu	**t'amuserais**
il/elle/on	**s'amuserait**
nous	**nous amuserions**
vous	**vous amuseriez**
ils/elles	**s'amuseraient**

PAST HISTORIC

je	**m'amusai**
tu	**t'amusas**
il/elle/on	**s'amusa**
nous	**nous amusâmes**
vous	**vous amusâtes**
ils/elles	**s'amusèrent**

PLUPERFECT

je	**m'étais amusé(e)**
tu	**t'étais amusé(e)**
il/elle/on	**s'était amusé(e)**
nous	**nous étions amusé(e)s**
vous	**vous étiez amusé(e)(s)**
ils/elles	**s'étaient amusé(e)s**

IMPERATIVE

amuse-toi / amusons-nous / amusez-vous

EXAMPLE PHRASES

Je suis sûr qu'ils **s'amuseront** comme des fous. I'm sure they'll have a whale of a time.

Ils **s'amusèrent** à dessiner un monstre. They had fun drawing a monster.

Tu **t'amuserais** bien si tu venais avec nous. You'd have fun if you came with us.

Je **m'étais** bien **amusé** à leur mariage. I'd really enjoyed myself at their wedding.

Amuse-toi bien avec Florence. Have fun with Florence.

je/j' = I tu = you il = he/it elle = she/it on = we/one nous = we vous = you ils/elles = they

apercevoir (to notice)

PRESENT

j'	aperçois
tu	aperçois
il/elle/on	aperçoit
nous	apercevons
vous	apercevez
ils/elles	aperçoivent

PRESENT SUBJUNCTIVE

j'	aperçoive
tu	aperçoives
il/elle/on	aperçoive
nous	apercevions
vous	aperceviez
ils/elles	aperçoivent

PERFECT

j'	ai aperçu
tu	as aperçu
il/elle/on	a aperçu
nous	avons aperçu
vous	avez aperçu
ils/elles	ont aperçu

IMPERFECT

j'	apercevais
tu	apercevais
il/elle/on	apercevait
nous	apercevions
vous	aperceviez
ils/elles	apercevaient

PRESENT PARTICIPLE

apercevant

PAST PARTICIPLE

aperçu

EXAMPLE PHRASES

J'**aperçois** une lumière là-bas. I can see a light over there.

Je l'**ai aperçue** hier au marché. I saw her yesterday at the market.

Ils ont marché longtemps, jusqu'à ce qu'ils **aperçoivent** une maison.
They walked for a long time, until they saw a house.

Je les **apercevais** de temps en temps en allant travailler. I saw them from
time to time on my way to work.

je/j' = I   tu = you   il = he/it   elle = she/it   on = we/one   nous = we   vous = you   ils/elles = they

apercevoir

FUTURE

j'	apercevrai
tu	apercevras
il/elle/on	apercevra
nous	apercevrons
vous	apercevrez
ils/elles	apercevront

CONDITIONAL

j'	apercevrais
tu	apercevrais
il/elle/on	apercevrait
nous	apercevrions
vous	apercevriez
ils/elles	apercevraient

PAST HISTORIC

j'	aperçus
tu	aperçus
il/elle/on	aperçut
nous	aperçûmes
vous	aperçûtes
ils/elles	aperçurent

PLUPERFECT

j'	avais aperçu
tu	avais aperçu
il/elle/on	avait aperçu
nous	avions aperçu
vous	aviez aperçu
ils/elles	avaient aperçu

IMPERATIVE

not used

EXAMPLE PHRASES

Va jusqu'à l'arrêt du bus et tu **apercevras** le magasin au coin de la rue.
  Go up to the bus stop and you'll see the store on the street corner.
Ils **aperçurent** une silhouette au loin. **They saw a shadow in the distance.**
Il l'**avait aperçue** une ou deux fois chez les Duval il y avait très longtemps.
  He'd seen her once or twice at the Duvals' a long time before.
Je ne me souvenais pas de l'endroit où je l'**avais aperçu**. I couldn't remember
  where I'd seen him.

je/j' = I tu = you il = he/it elle = she/it on = we/one nous = we vous = you ils/elles = they

appeler (to call)

PRESENT

j'	**appelle**
tu	**appelles**
il/elle/on	**appelle**
nous	**appelons**
vous	**appelez**
ils/elles	**appellent**

PRESENT SUBJUNCTIVE

j'	**appelle**
tu	**appelles**
il/elle/on	**appelle**
nous	**appelions**
vous	**appeliez**
ils/elles	**appellent**

PERFECT

j'	**ai appelé**
tu	**as appelé**
il/elle/on	**a appelé**
nous	**avons appelé**
vous	**avez appelé**
ils/elles	**ont appelé**

IMPERFECT

j'	**appelais**
tu	**appelais**
il/elle/on	**appelait**
nous	**appelions**
vous	**appeliez**
ils/elles	**appelaient**

PRESENT PARTICIPLE

appelant

PAST PARTICIPLE

appelé

EXAMPLE PHRASES

Louise ! Descends : maman t'**appelle**. Louise! Go downstairs – Mom's calling you.

Comment tu t'**appelles** ? What's your name?

Elle **a appelé** le médecin. She called the doctor.

Il faut que je l'**appelle** après dîner. I have to call her after dinner.

Elle **appelait** souvent le soir. She often called in the evening.

je/j' = I   tu = you   il = he/it   elle = she/it   on = we/one   nous = we   vous = you   ils/elles = they

appeler

FUTURE

j'	**appellerai**
tu	**appelleras**
il/elle/on	**appellera**
nous	**appellerons**
vous	**appellerez**
ils/elles	**appelleront**

CONDITIONAL

j'	**appellerais**
tu	**appellerais**
il/elle/on	**appellerait**
nous	**appellerions**
vous	**appelleriez**
ils/elles	**appelleraient**

PAST HISTORIC

j'	**appelai**
tu	**appelas**
il/elle/on	**appela**
nous	**appelâmes**
vous	**appelâtes**
ils/elles	**appelèrent**

PLUPERFECT

j'	**avais appelé**
tu	**avais appelé**
il/elle/on	**avait appelé**
nous	**avions appelé**
vous	**aviez appelé**
ils/elles	**avaient appelé**

IMPERATIVE

appelle / appelons / appelez

EXAMPLE PHRASES

Je t'**appellerai** demain. I'll call you tomorrow.

On **appela** mon nom et je me levai. My name was called, and I stood up.

Je l'**appellerais** si j'étais sûr de ne pas le déranger. I'd call him if I was sure
not to disturb him.

Elle m'**avait appelé** mais je ne l'avais pas entendue. She had called me, but
I hadn't heard her.

Appelle-moi sur mon portable. Call me on my cell.

je/j' = I **tu** = you **il** = he/it **elle** = she/it **on** = we/one **nous** = we **vous** = you **ils/elles** = they

appuyer (to lean; to press)

PRESENT

j'	appuie
tu	appuies
il/elle/on	appuie
nous	appuyons
vous	appuyez
ils/elles	appuient

PRESENT SUBJUNCTIVE

j'	appuie
tu	appuies
il/elle/on	appuie
nous	appuyions
vous	appuyiez
ils/elles	appuient

PERFECT

j'	ai appuyé
tu	as appuyé
il/elle/on	a appuyé
nous	avons appuyé
vous	avez appuyé
ils/elles	ont appuyé

IMPERFECT

j'	appuyais
tu	appuyais
il/elle/on	appuyait
nous	appuyions
vous	appuyiez
ils/elles	appuyaient

PRESENT PARTICIPLE

appuyant

PAST PARTICIPLE

appuyé

EXAMPLE PHRASES

Elle **a appuyé** son vélo contre le mur. She leaned her bike against the wall.
Appuie sur le bouton rouge. Press the red button.
N'**appuie** pas trop fort. Don't press too hard.
Appuyez bien sur le couvercle. Press hard on the lid.
Il faut que tu **appuies** fort. You have to press hard.

appuyer

FUTURE

j'	appuierai
tu	appuieras
il/elle/on	appuiera
nous	appuierons
vous	appuierez
ils/elles	appuieront

CONDITIONAL

j'	appuierais
tu	appuierais
il/elle/on	appuierait
nous	appuierions
vous	appuieriez
ils/elles	appuieraient

PAST HISTORIC

j'	appuyai
tu	appuyas
il/elle/on	appuya
nous	appuyâmes
vous	appuyâtes
ils/elles	appuyèrent

PLUPERFECT

j'	avais appuyé
tu	avais appuyé
il/elle/on	avait appuyé
nous	avions appuyé
vous	aviez appuyé
ils/elles	avaient appuyé

IMPERATIVE

appuie / appuyons / appuyez

EXAMPLE PHRASES

J'**appuierai** trois fois sur la sonnette. **I'll press the bell three times.**

Il **appuya** longtemps mais la colle ne tenait pas. **He pressed for a long time, but the glue didn't hold.**

Il n'**appuierait** pas si fort si tu le laissais faire. **He wouldn't press so hard if you'd let him do it.**

Elle n'**avait** pas **appuyé** assez fort et la cloche n'avait pas sonné. **She hadn't pressed hard enough and the bell hadn't rung.**

arriver (to arrive)

PRESENT		PRESENT SUBJUNCTIVE	
j'	**arrive**	j'	**arrive**
tu	**arrives**	tu	**arrives**
il/elle/on	**arrive**	il/elle/on	**arrive**
nous	**arrivons**	nous	**arrivions**
vous	**arrivez**	vous	**arriviez**
ils/elles	**arrivent**	ils/elles	**arrivent**

PERFECT		IMPERFECT	
je	**suis arrivé(e)**	j'	**arrivais**
tu	**es arrivé(e)**	tu	**arrivais**
il/elle/on	**est arrivé(e)**	il/elle/on	**arrivait**
nous	**sommes arrivé(e)s**	nous	**arrivions**
vous	**êtes arrivé(e)(s)**	vous	**arriviez**
ils/elles	**sont arrivé(e)s**	ils/elles	**arrivaient**

PRESENT PARTICIPLE	PAST PARTICIPLE
arrivant	arrivé

EXAMPLE PHRASES

J'**arrive** à l'école à huit heures. I arrive at school at 8 o'clock.

Qu'est-ce qui **est arrivé** à Aurélie ? What happened to Aurélie?

Il faut que j'**arrive** à jouer cet air pour la leçon de demain. I'll have to be able to play this tune for tomorrow's lesson.

Il m'**arrivait** de dormir jusqu'à midi. I sometimes slept till noon.

je/j' = I   **tu** = you   **il** = he/it   **elle** = she/it   **on** = we/one   **nous** = we   **vous** = you   **ils/elles** = they

arriver

FUTURE

j'	**arriverai**
tu	**arriveras**
il/elle/on	**arrivera**
nous	**arriverons**
vous	**arriverez**
ils/elles	**arriveront**

CONDITIONAL

j'	**arriverais**
tu	**arriverais**
il/elle/on	**arriverait**
nous	**arriverions**
vous	**arriveriez**
ils/elles	**arriveraient**

PAST HISTORIC

j'	**arrivai**
tu	**arrivas**
il/elle/on	**arriva**
nous	**arrivâmes**
vous	**arrivâtes**
ils/elles	**arrivèrent**

PLUPERFECT

j'	**étais arrivé(e)**
tu	**étais arrivé(e)**
il/elle/on	**était arrivé(e)**
nous	**étions arrivé(e)s**
vous	**étiez arrivé(e)(s)**
ils/elles	**étaient arrivé(e)s**

IMPERATIVE
arrive / arrivons / arrivez

EXAMPLE PHRASES

Arriveras-tu à l'heure pour ton rendez-vous ? Will you be on time for your appointment?

La réunion était finie depuis longtemps quand il **arriva**. The meeting had finished long before he arrived.

Je n'**arriverais** jamais à faire tout ce travail sans ton aide. I would never be able to get all this work done without your help.

Le prof n'**était** pas encore **arrivé**. The teacher hadn't arrived yet.

N'**arrivez** pas en retard demain. Don't arrive late tomorrow.

je/j' = I **tu** = you **il** = he/it **elle** = she/it **on** = we/one **nous** = we **vous** = you **ils/elles** = they

s'asseoir (to sit down)

PRESENT

je	m'assieds/m'assois
tu	t'assieds/t'assois
il/elle/on	s'assied/s'assoit
nous	nous asseyons/nous assoyons
vous	vous asseyez/vous assoyez
ils/elles	s'asseyent/s'assoient

PRESENT SUBJUNCTIVE

je	m'asseye
tu	t'asseyes
il/elle/on	s'asseye
nous	nous asseyions
vous	vous asseyiez
ils/elles	s'asseyent

PERFECT

je	me suis assis(e)
tu	t'es assis(e)
il/elle/on	s'est assis(e)
nous	nous sommes assis(es)
vous	vous êtes assis(e(s))
ils/elles	se sont assis(es)

IMPERFECT

je	m'asseyais
tu	t'asseyais
il/elle/on	s'asseyait
nous	nous asseyions
vous	vous asseyiez
ils/elles	s'asseyaient

PRESENT PARTICIPLE

s'asseyant

PAST PARTICIPLE

assis

EXAMPLE PHRASES

Je peux **m'asseoir** ? May I sit down?

Je **me suis assise** sur un chewing-gum ! I've sat on chewing gum!

On **s'asseyait** toujours l'un à côté de l'autre. We would always sit next to each other.

s'asseoir

FUTURE

je	m'assiérai
tu	t'assiéras
il/elle/on	s'assiéra
nous	nous assiérons
vous	vous assiérez
ils/elles	s'assiéront

CONDITIONAL

je	m'assiérais
tu	t'assiérais
il/elle/on	s'assiérait
nous	nous assiérions
vous	vous assiériez
ils/elles	s'assiéraient

PAST HISTORIC

je	m'assis
tu	t'assis
il/elle/on	s'assit
nous	nous assîmes
vous	vous assîtes
ils/elles	s'assirent

PLUPERFECT

je	m'étais assis(e)
tu	t'étais assis(e)
il/elle/on	s'était assis(e)
nous	nous étions assis(es)
vous	vous étiez assis(e(s))
ils/elles	s'étaient assis(es)

IMPERATIVE

assieds-toi / asseyons-nous / asseyez-vous

EXAMPLE PHRASES

Je m'assiérai à côté de toi. I'll sit next to you.

Il s'assit en face de moi. He sat down across from me.

Je ne m'assiérais pas là si j'étais toi. I wouldn't sit there if I were you.

Elle ne s'était pas encore assise quand la fillette l'appela à nouveau.

   She hadn't even sat down when the little girl called her once again.

Assieds-toi, Nicole. Sit down, Nicole.

Asseyez-vous, les enfants. Sit down, children

je/j' = I   tu = you   il = he/it   elle = she/it   on = we/one   nous = we   vous = you   ils/elles = they

atteindre (to reach)

PRESENT

j'	**atteins**
tu	**atteins**
il/elle/on	**atteint**
nous	**atteignons**
vous	**atteignez**
ils/elles	**atteignent**

PRESENT SUBJUNCTIVE

j'	**atteigne**
tu	**atteignes**
il/elle/on	**atteigne**
nous	**atteignions**
vous	**atteigniez**
ils/elles	**atteignent**

PERFECT

j'	**ai atteint**
tu	**as atteint**
il/elle/on	**a atteint**
nous	**avons atteint**
vous	**avez atteint**
ils/elles	**ont atteint**

IMPERFECT

j'	**atteignais**
tu	**atteignais**
il/elle/on	**atteignait**
nous	**atteignions**
vous	**atteigniez**
ils/elles	**atteignaient**

PRESENT PARTICIPLE

atteignant

PAST PARTICIPLE

atteint

EXAMPLE PHRASES

Je n'arrive pas à **atteindre** ma valise. I can't reach my suitcase.

Cette Ferrari **atteint** une vitesse de 245 km/h. This Ferrari reaches a speed of 245km/h.

Ils **ont atteint** le sommet en quatre heures et demie. They reached the summit in four and a half hours.

Ils **atteignaient** Paris quand l'accident se produisit. They were nearing Paris when the accident happened.

je/j' = I **tu** = you **il** = he/it **elle** = she/it **on** = we/one **nous** = we **vous** = you **ils/elles** = they

atteindre

FUTURE

j'	atteindrai
tu	atteindras
il/elle/on	atteindra
nous	atteindrons
vous	atteindrez
ils/elles	atteindront

CONDITIONAL

j'	atteindrais
tu	atteindrais
il/elle/on	atteindrait
nous	atteindrions
vous	atteindriez
ils/elles	atteindraient

PAST HISTORIC

j'	atteignis
tu	atteignis
il/elle/on	atteignit
nous	atteignîmes
vous	atteignîtes
ils/elles	atteignirent

PLUPERFECT

j'	avais atteint
tu	avais atteint
il/elle/on	avait atteint
nous	avions atteint
vous	aviez atteint
ils/elles	avaient atteint

IMPERATIVE

atteins / atteignons / atteignez

EXAMPLE PHRASES

Nous **atteindrons** Rouen dans dix minutes. We'll reach Rouen in ten minutes.

Il **atteignit** sa destination en trois semaines. He reached his destination in three weeks.

Il se rendit compte qu'il n'**atteindrait** jamais son but. He realized that he would never reach his goal.

Le tableau **avait atteint** un prix exorbitant. The painting had reached a prohibitive price.

je/j' = I **tu** = you **il** = he/it **elle** = she/it **on** = we/one **nous** = we **vous** = you **ils/elles** = they

attendre (to wait)

PRESENT

j'	attends
tu	attends
il/elle/on	attend
nous	attendons
vous	attendez
ils/elles	attendent

PRESENT SUBJUNCTIVE

j'	attende
tu	attendes
il/elle/on	attende
nous	attendions
vous	attendiez
ils/elles	attendent

PERFECT

j'	ai attendu
tu	as attendu
il/elle/on	a attendu
nous	avons attendu
vous	avez attendu
ils/elles	ont attendu

IMPERFECT

j'	attendais
tu	attendais
il/elle/on	attendait
nous	attendions
vous	attendiez
ils/elles	attendaient

PRESENT PARTICIPLE

attendant

PAST PARTICIPLE

attendu

EXAMPLE PHRASES

Tu **attends** depuis longtemps ? Have you been waiting long?

Je l'**ai attendu** à la poste. I waited for him at the post office.

Elle veut que je l'**attende** dans le hall. She wants me to wait for her in the hall.

Elle **attendait** un bébé. She was expecting a baby.

attendre

FUTURE

j'	attendrai
tu	attendras
il/elle/on	attendra
nous	attendrons
vous	attendrez
ils/elles	attendront

CONDITIONAL

j'	attendrais
tu	attendrais
il/elle/on	attendrait
nous	attendrions
vous	attendriez
ils/elles	attendraient

PAST HISTORIC

j'	attendis
tu	attendis
il/elle/on	attendit
nous	attendîmes
vous	attendîtes
ils/elles	attendirent

PLUPERFECT

j'	avais attendu
tu	avais attendu
il/elle/on	avait attendu
nous	avions attendu
vous	aviez attendu
ils/elles	avaient attendu

IMPERATIVE

attends / attendons / attendez

EXAMPLE PHRASES

J'**attendrai** qu'il ne pleuve plus. I'll wait until it's stopped raining.

Nous **attendîmes** en silence. We waited in silence.

Je t'**attendrais** si tu n'étais pas si lente. I'd wait for you if you weren't so slow.

Elle m'**avait attendu** patiemment devant la poste. She had patiently waited for me in front of the post office.

Attends-moi ! Wait for me!

je/j' = I tu = you il = he/it elle = she/it on = we/one nous = we vous = you ils/elles = they

avoir (to have)

PRESENT

j'	**ai**
tu	**as**
il/elle/on	**a**
nous	**avons**
vous	**avez**
ils/elles	**ont**

PRESENT SUBJUNCTIVE

j'	**aie**
tu	**aies**
il/elle/on	**ait**
nous	**ayons**
vous	**ayez**
ils/elles	**aient**

PERFECT

j'	**ai eu**
tu	**as eu**
il/elle/on	**a eu**
nous	**avons eu**
vous	**avez eu**
ils/elles	**ont eu**

IMPERFECT

j'	**avais**
tu	**avais**
il/elle/on	**avait**
nous	**avions**
vous	**aviez**
ils/elles	**avaient**

PRESENT PARTICIPLE

ayant

PAST PARTICIPLE

eu

EXAMPLE PHRASES

Il **a** les yeux bleus. He's got blue eyes.

Quel âge **as**-tu ? How old are you?

Il y **a** beaucoup de monde. There are lots of people.

Il **a eu** un accident. He's had an accident.

J'**avais** faim. I was hungry.

---

je/j' = I   tu = you   il = he/it   elle = she/it   on = we/one   nous = we   vous = you   ils/elles = they

avoir

FUTURE

j'	aurai
tu	auras
il/elle/on	aura
nous	aurons
vous	aurez
ils/elles	auront

CONDITIONAL

j'	aurais
tu	aurais
il/elle/on	aurait
nous	aurions
vous	auriez
ils/elles	auraient

PAST HISTORIC

j'	eus
tu	eus
il/elle/on	eut
nous	eûmes
vous	eûtes
ils/elles	eurent

PLUPERFECT

j'	avais eu
tu	avais eu
il/elle/on	avait eu
nous	avions eu
vous	aviez eu
ils/elles	avaient eu

IMPERATIVE

aie / ayons / ayez

EXAMPLE PHRASES

Cloé **aura** cinq ans au mois d'août. **Cloé will be five in August.**

J'**eus** soudain l'idée de lui rendre visite. **I suddenly thought of paying him a visit.**

Je n'**aurais** pas tant mangé si j'avais su qu'il y avait un dessert. **I wouldn't have eaten so much if I'd known that there was a dessert.**

Paul **avait eu** mal au ventre toute la nuit. **Paul had had a bad stomach all night.**

je/j' = I   tu = you   il = he/it   elle = she/it   on = we/one   nous = we   vous = you   ils/elles = they

battre (to beat)

PRESENT

je	**bats**
tu	**bats**
il/elle/on	**bat**
nous	**battons**
vous	**battez**
ils/elles	**battent**

PRESENT SUBJUNCTIVE

je	**batte**
tu	**battes**
il/elle/on	**batte**
nous	**battions**
vous	**battiez**
ils/elles	**battent**

PERFECT

j'	**ai battu**
tu	**as battu**
il/elle/on	**a battu**
nous	**avons battu**
vous	**avez battu**
ils/elles	**ont battu**

IMPERFECT

je	**battais**
tu	**battais**
il/elle/on	**battait**
nous	**battions**
vous	**battiez**
ils/elles	**battaient**

PRESENT PARTICIPLE

battant

PAST PARTICIPLE

battu

EXAMPLE PHRASES

J'ai le cœur qui **bat vite** ! My heart's beating fast!

Arrêtez de vous **battre** ! Stop fighting!

On les **a battus** deux à un. We beat them two to one.

Elle le **battait** toujours au poker. She'd always beat him at poker.

---

je/j' = I   tu = you   il = he/it   elle = she/it   on = we/one   nous = we   vous = you   ils/elles = they

battre

FUTURE

je	**battrai**
tu	**battras**
il/elle/on	**battra**
nous	**battrons**
vous	**battrez**
ils/elles	**battront**

CONDITIONAL

je	**battrais**
tu	**battrais**
il/elle/on	**battrait**
nous	**battrions**
vous	**battriez**
ils/elles	**battraient**

PAST HISTORIC

je	**battis**
tu	**battis**
il/elle/on	**battit**
nous	**battîmes**
vous	**battîtes**
ils/elles	**battirent**

PLUPERFECT

j'	**avais battu**
tu	**avais battu**
il/elle/on	**avait battu**
nous	**avions battu**
vous	**aviez battu**
ils/elles	**avaient battu**

IMPERATIVE

bats / battons / battez

EXAMPLE PHRASES

Tu ne me **battras** jamais à la course. You'll never beat me at running.

Elle le **battit** au Scrabble®. She beat him at Scrabble®.

Ils se **battraient** tout le temps si je les laissais faire. They'd fight all the time if I let them.

Elle **avait battu** le record du monde du saut à la perche. She'd beaten the world record for the pole vault.

Bats les cartes, s'il te plaît. Shuffle the cards, please.

je/j' = I tu = you il = he/it elle = she/it on = we/one nous = we vous = you ils/elles = they

boire (to drink)

PRESENT

je	**bois**
tu	**bois**
il/elle/on	**boit**
nous	**buvons**
vous	**buvez**
ils/elles	**boivent**

PRESENT SUBJUNCTIVE

je	**boive**
tu	**boives**
il/elle/on	**boive**
nous	**buvions**
vous	**buviez**
ils/elles	**boivent**

PERFECT

j'	**ai bu**
tu	**as bu**
il/elle/on	**a bu**
nous	**avons bu**
vous	**avez bu**
ils/elles	**ont bu**

IMPERFECT

je	**buvais**
tu	**buvais**
il/elle/on	**buvait**
nous	**buvions**
vous	**buviez**
ils/elles	**buvaient**

PRESENT PARTICIPLE
buvant

PAST PARTICIPLE
bu

EXAMPLE PHRASES

Qu'est-ce que tu veux **boire** ? What would you like to drink?

Il ne **boit** jamais d'alcool. He never drinks alcohol.

J'**ai bu** un liter d'eau. I drank a liter of water.

Elle **buvait** un whisky tous les soirs. She had a whiskey every night.

boire

FUTURE

je	**boirai**
tu	**boiras**
il/elle/on	**boira**
nous	**boirons**
vous	**boirez**
ils/elles	**boiront**

CONDITIONAL

je	**boirais**
tu	**boirais**
il/elle/on	**boirait**
nous	**boirions**
vous	**boiriez**
ils/elles	**boiraient**

PAST HISTORIC

je	**bus**
tu	**bus**
il/elle/on	**but**
nous	**bûmes**
vous	**bûtes**
ils/elles	**burent**

PLUPERFECT

j'	**avais bu**
tu	**avais bu**
il/elle/on	**avait bu**
hous	**avions bu**
vous	**aviez bu**
ils/elles	**avaient bu**

IMPERATIVE

bois / buvons / buvez

EXAMPLE PHRASES

Que **boirez**-vous ? What will you have to drink?

Il **but** son jus d'orange d'un trait. He drank his orange juice in one gulp.

Je **boirais** bien un cognac. I'd really like a brandy.

On voyait qu'il **avait bu**. He was obviously drunk.

Bois ton café avant de partir. Drink your coffee before we leave.

je/j' = I **tu** = you **il** = he/it **elle** = she/it **on** = we/one **nous** = we **vous** = you **ils/elles** = they

bouillir (to boil)

PRESENT

je	**bous**
tu	**bous**
il/elle/on	**bout**
nous	**bouillons**
vous	**bouillez**
ils/elles	**bouillent**

PRESENT SUBJUNCTIVE

je	**bouille**
tu	**bouilles**
il/elle/on	**bouille**
nous	**bouillions**
vous	**bouilliez**
ils/elles	**bouillent**

PERFECT

j'	**ai bouilli**
tu	**as bouilli**
il/elle/on	**a bouilli**
nous	**avons bouilli**
vous	**avez bouilli**
ils/elles	**ont bouilli**

IMPERFECT

je	**bouillais**
tu	**bouillais**
il/elle/on	**bouillait**
nous	**bouillions**
vous	**bouilliez**
ils/elles	**bouillaient**

PRESENT PARTICIPLE

bouillant

PAST PARTICIPLE

bouilli

EXAMPLE PHRASES

Tu peux mettre de l'eau à **bouillir** ? Can you boil some water?

Faites **bouillir** pendant quelques minutes. Boil for a few minutes.

L'eau **bout**. The water's boiling.

La soupe **a bouilli** trop longtemps. The soup had boiled for too long.

Je **bouillais** d'impatience. I was bursting with impatience.

bouillir

FUTURE

je	**bouillirai**
tu	**bouilliras**
il/elle/on	**bouillira**
nous	**bouillirons**
vous	**bouillirez**
ils/elles	**bouilliront**

CONDITIONAL

je	**bouillirais**
tu	**bouillirais**
il/elle/on	**bouillirait**
nous	**bouillirions**
vous	**bouilliriez**
ils/elles	**bouilliraient**

PAST HISTORIC

je	**bouillis**
tu	**bouillis**
il/elle/on	**bouillit**
nous	**bouillîmes**
vous	**bouillîtes**
ils/elles	**bouillirent**

PLUPERFECT

j'	**avais bouilli**
tu	**avais bouilli**
il/elle/on	**avait bouilli**
nous	**avions bouilli**
vous	**aviez bouilli**
ils/elles	**avaient bouilli**

IMPERATIVE

bous / bouillons / bouillez

EXAMPLE PHRASES

Quand l'eau **bouillira**, la bouilloire sifflera. When the water boils, the kettle will whistle.

Le lait **bouillit** et déborda. The milk boiled over.

L'eau n'**avait** pas encore **bouilli**. The water hadn't boiled yet.

je/j' = I **tu** = you **il** = he/it **elle** = she/it **on** = we/one **nous** = we **vous** = you **ils/elles** = they

commencer (to start; to begin)

PRESENT

je	commence
tu	commences
il/elle/on	commence
nous	commençons
vous	commencez
ils/elles	commencent

PRESENT SUBJUNCTIVE

je	commence
tu	commences
il/elle/on	commence
nous	commencions
vous	commenciez
ils/elles	commencent

PERFECT

j'	ai commencé
tu	as commencé
il/elle/on	a commencé
nous	avons commencé
vous	avez commencé
ils/elles	ont commencé

IMPERFECT

je	commençais
tu	commençais
il/elle/on	commençait
nous	commencions
vous	commenciez
ils/elles	commençaient

PRESENT PARTICIPLE

commençant

PAST PARTICIPLE

commencé

EXAMPLE PHRASES

Les cours **commencent** à neuf heures. Classes start at nine o'clock.

Tu **as** déjà **commencé** a réviser pour tes examens ? Have you started studying for your exams?

Ne **commence** pas à m'embêter. Don't start annoying me.

J'aimerais que tu **commences** à faire les valises. I'd like you to start packing the suitcases.

Son attitude **commençait** à m'énerver. Her attitude had started to annoy me.

je/j' = I   **tu** = you   **il** = he/it   **elle** = she/it   **on** = we/one   **nous** = we   **vous** = you   **ils/elles** = they

commencer

FUTURE

je	commencerai
tu	commenceras
il/elle/on	commencera
nous	commencerons
vous	commencerez
ils/elles	commenceront

CONDITIONAL

je	commencerais
tu	commencerais
il/elle/on	commencerait
nous	commencerions
vous	commenceriez
ils/elles	commenceraient

PAST HISTORIC

je	commençai
tu	commenças
il/elle/on	commença
nous	commençâmes
vous	commençâtes
ils/elles	commencèrent

PLUPERFECT

j'	avais commencé
tu	avais commencé
il/elle/on	avait commencé
nous	avions commencé
vous	aviez commencé
ils/elles	avaient commencé

IMPERATIVE

commence / commençons / commencez

EXAMPLE PHRASES

Nous ne **commencerons** pas sans toi. We won't start without you.

C'est quand les nouveaux voisins arrivèrent que les ennuis **commencèrent**.
It was when the new neighbors arrived that the problems started.

Nous **commencerions** une partie de cartes si nous étions sûrs d'avoir le
temps de la finir. We'd start a game of cards if we were sure we'd have
time to finish it.

Il **avait commencé** à pleuvoir. It had started to rain.

je/j' = I tu = you il = he/it elle = she/it on = we/one nous = we vous = you ils/elles = they

conclure (to conclude)

PRESENT

je	conclus
tu	conclus
il/elle/on	conclut
nous	concluons
vous	concluez
ils/elles	concluent

PRESENT SUBJUNCTIVE

je	conclue
tu	conclues
il/elle/on	conclue
nous	concluions
vous	concluiez
ils/elles	concluent

PERFECT

j'	ai conclu
tu	as conclu
il/elle/on	a conclu
nous	avons conclu
vous	avez conclu
ils/elles	ont conclu

IMPERFECT

je	concluais
tu	concluais
il/elle/on	concluait
nous	concluions
vous	concluiez
ils/elles	concluaient

PRESENT PARTICIPLE

concluant

PAST PARTICIPLE

conclu

EXAMPLE PHRASES

J'en **conclus** qu'il ne m'a pas dit la vérité. I conclude from this that he didn't tell me the truth.

Ils **ont conclu** un marché. They concluded a deal.

Il en **a conclu** qu'il s'était trompé. He concluded that he had gotten it wrong.

Il faut que je **conclue** le marché aujourd'hui. I must conclude the deal today.

je/j' = I   tu = you   il = he/it   elle = she/it   on = we/one   nous = we   vous = you   ils/elles = they

conclure

FUTURE

je	conclurai
tu	concluras
il/elle/on	conclura
nous	conclurons
vous	conclurez
ils/elles	concluront

CONDITIONAL

je	conclurais
tu	conclurais
il/elle/on	conclurait
nous	conclurions
vous	concluriez
ils/elles	concluraient

PAST HISTORIC

je	conclus
tu	conclus
il/elle/on	conclut
nous	conclûmes
vous	conclûtes
ils/elles	conclurent

PLUPERFECT

j'	avais conclu
tu	avais conclu
il/elle/on	avait conclu
nous	avions conclu
vous	aviez conclu
ils/elles	avaient conclu

IMPERATIVE

conclus / concluons / concluez

EXAMPLE PHRASES

Je **conclurai** par ces mots... I will conclude with these words...

Elle en **conclut** qu'il était parti. She concluded that he had gone.

Nous n'**avions** encore rien **conclu** quand il est arrivé. We hadn't concluded anything when he arrived.

Ils **avaient conclu** la soirée par une partie de cartes. They had concluded the evening with a game of cards.

je/j' = I **tu** = you **il** = he/it **elle** = she/it **on** = we/one **nous** = we **vous** = you **ils/elles** = they

conduire (to drive)

PRESENT

je	conduis
tu	conduis
il/elle/on	conduit
nous	conduisons
vous	conduisez
ils/elles	conduisent

PRESENT SUBJUNCTIVE

je	conduise
tu	conduises
il/elle/on	conduise
nous	conduisions
vous	conduisiez
ils/elles	conduisent

PERFECT

j'	ai conduit
tu	as conduit
il/elle/on	a conduit
nous	avons conduit
vous	avez conduit
ils/elles	ont conduit

IMPERFECT

je	conduisais
tu	conduisais
il/elle/on	conduisait
nous	conduisions
vous	conduisiez
ils/elles	conduisaient

PRESENT PARTICIPLE

conduisant

PAST PARTICIPLE

conduit

EXAMPLE PHRASES

Elle **conduit** sa fille à l'école tous les matins. She drives her daughter to school every morning.

Cela fait longtemps que je n'**ai** pas **conduit**. I haven't driven for a long time.

J'aimerais que tu me **conduises** à la gare. I'd like you to drive me to the train station.

Il **conduisait** lentement quand l'accident est arrivé. He was driving slowly when the accident happened.

je/j' = I   tu = you   il = he/it   elle = she/it   on = we/one   nous = we   vous = you   ils/elles = they

conduire

FUTURE

je	**conduirai**
tu	**conduiras**
il/elle/on	**conduira**
nous	**conduirons**
vous	**conduirez**
ils/elles	**conduiront**

CONDITIONAL

je	**conduirais**
tu	**conduirais**
il/elle/on	**conduirait**
nous	**conduirions**
vous	**conduiriez**
ils/elles	**conduiraient**

PAST HISTORIC

je	**conduisis**
tu	**conduisis**
il/elle/on	**conduisit**
nous	**conduisîmes**
vous	**conduisîtes**
ils/elles	**conduisirent**

PLUPERFECT

j'	**avais conduit**
tu	**avais conduit**
il/elle/on	**avait conduit**
nous	**avions conduit**
vous	**aviez conduit**
ils/elles	**avaient conduit**

IMPERATIVE

conduis / conduisons / conduisez

EXAMPLE PHRASES

Je te **conduirai** chez le docteur. I'll drive you to the doctor.

Elle **conduisit** sans dire un mot. She drove without saying a word.

Je te **conduirais** en ville si j'avais le temps. I'd drive you into town if I had time.

Elle **avait conduit** toute la nuit et elle était épuisée. She'd driven all night, and she was exhausted.

Conduis prudemment. Drive carefully.

---

je/j' = I tu = you il = he/it elle = she/it on = we/one nous = we vous = you ils/elles = they

connaître (to know)

PRESENT

je	connais
tu	connais
il/elle/on	connaît
nous	connaissons
vous	connaissez
ils/elles	connaissent

PRESENT SUBJUNCTIVE

je	connaisse
tu	connaisses
il/elle/on	connaisse
nous	connaissions
vous	connaissiez
ils/elles	connaissent

PERFECT

j'	ai connu
tu	as connu
il/elle/on	a connu
nous	avons connu
vous	avez connu
ils/elles	ont connu

IMPERFECT

je	connaissais
tu	connaissais
il/elle/on	connaissait
nous	connaissions
vous	connaissiez
ils/elles	connaissaient

PRESENT PARTICIPLE

connaissant

PAST PARTICIPLE

connu

EXAMPLE PHRASES

Je ne **connais** pas du tout cette région. I don't know the area at all.

Vous **connaissez** M. Amiot ? Do you know Mr. Amiot?

Il n'**a** pas **connu** son grand-père. He never knew his grandfather.

Je **connaissais** bien sa mère. I knew his mother well.

connaître

FUTURE

je	connaîtrai
tu	connaîtras
il/elle/on	connaîtra
nous	connaîtrons
vous	connaîtrez
ils/elles	connaîtront

CONDITIONAL

je	connaîtrais
tu	connaîtrais
il/elle/on	connaîtrait
nous	connaîtrions
vous	connaîtriez
ils/elles	connaîtraient

PAST HISTORIC

je	connus
tu	connus
il/elle/on	connut
nous	connûmes
vous	connûtes
ils/elles	connurent

PLUPERFECT

j'	avais connu
tu	avais connu
il/elle/on	avait connu
nous	avions connu
vous	aviez connu
ils/elles	avaient connu

IMPERATIVE

connais / connaissons / connaissez

EXAMPLE PHRASES

Je ne la **connaîtrai** jamais bien. I'll never know her well.

Il **connut** d'abord Laura puis il rencontra Claire. First he got to know Laura, and then he met Claire.

Nous ne nous **connaîtrions** pas s'il ne nous avait pas présentés. We wouldn't know each other if he hadn't introduced us.

J'aurais gagné si j'**avais connu** la réponse à la dernière question. I would have won if I had known the answer to the last question.

Ils s'**étaient connus** à Rouen. They'd first met in Rouen.

je/j' = I tu = you il = he/it elle = she/it on = we/one nous = we vous = you ils/elles = they

continuer (to continue; to go on)

PRESENT

je	continue
tu	continues
il/elle/on	continue
nous	continuons
vous	continuez
ils/elles	continuent

PRESENT SUBJUNCTIVE

je	continue
tu	continues
il/elle/on	continue
nous	continuions
vous	continuiez
ils/elles	continuent

PERFECT

j'	ai continué
tu	as continué
il/elle/on	a continué
nous	avons continué
vous	avez continué
ils/elles	ont continué

IMPERFECT

je	continuais
tu	continuais
il/elle/on	continuait
nous	continuions
vous	continuiez
ils/elles	continuaient

PRESENT PARTICIPLE

continuant

PAST PARTICIPLE

continué

EXAMPLE PHRASES

Il **continue** de fumer malgré son asthme. He keeps on smoking despite his asthma.

Ils **ont continué** à regarder la télé sans me dire bonjour. They went on watching TV without saying hello to me.

Il faut que tu **continues** à réviser si tu veux réussir à ton examen. You'll have to keep studying if you want to do well in your exam.

La phrase **continuait** sur la page suivante. The sentence continued on the next page.

je/j' = I   tu = you   il = he/it   elle = she/it   on = we/one   nous = we   vous = you   ils/elles = they

continuer

FUTURE

je	**continuerai**
tu	**continueras**
il/elle/on	**continuera**
nous	**continuerons**
vous	**continuerez**
ils/elles	**continueront**

CONDITIONAL

je	**continuerais**
tu	**continuerais**
il/elle/on	**continuerait**
nous	**continuerions**
vous	**continueriez**
ils/elles	**continueraient**

PAST HISTORIC

je	**continuai**
tu	**continuas**
il/elle/on	**continua**
nous	**continuâmes**
vous	**continuâtes**
ils/elles	**continuèrent**

PLUPERFECT

j'	**avais continué**
tu	**avais continué**
il/elle/on	**avait continué**
nous	**avions continué**
vous	**aviez continué**
ils/elles	**avaient continué**

IMPERATIVE

continue / continuons / continuez

EXAMPLE PHRASES

Nous **continuerons** l'histoire demain. We'll continue the story tomorrow.

Ils **continuèrent** à la harceler toute la soirée. They went on harassing her all evening.

Je **continuerais** à regarder ce film si j'avais le temps. I'd keep watching this movie if I had time.

Ils **avaient continué** à lui rendre visite même après leur déménagement. They'd continued to visit her even after they had moved.

---

je/j' = I tu = you il = he/it elle = she/it on = we/one nous = we vous = you ils/elles = they

coudre (to sew)

PRESENT

je	couds
tu	couds
il/elle/on	coud
nous	cousons
vous	cousez
ils/elles	cousent

PRESENT SUBJUNCTIVE

je	couse
tu	couses
il/elle/on	couse
nous	cousions
vous	cousiez
ils/elles	cousent

PERFECT

j'	ai cousu
tu	as cousu
il/elle/on	a cousu
nous	avons cousu
vous	avez cousu
ils/elles	ont cousu

IMPERFECT

je	cousais
tu	cousais
il/elle/on	cousait
nous	cousions
vous	cousiez
ils/elles	cousaient

PRESENT PARTICIPLE

cousant

PAST PARTICIPLE

cousu

EXAMPLE PHRASES

Tu sais **coudre** ? Can you sew?

Ma mère **coud** beaucoup. My mom sews a lot.

J'**ai cousu** toute la soirée hier. I spent all evening yesterday sewing.

Elle **cousait** tous les soirs après dîner. She would sew every night after dinner.

coudre

FUTURE

je	**coudrai**
tu	**coudras**
il/elle/on	**coudra**
nous	**coudrons**
vous	**coudrez**
ils/elles	**coudront**

CONDITIONAL

je	**coudrais**
tu	**coudrais**
il/elle/on	**coudrait**
nous	**coudrions**
vous	**coudriez**
ils/elles	**coudraient**

PAST HISTORIC

je	**cousus**
tu	**cousus**
il/elle/on	**cousut**
nous	**cousûmes**
vous	**cousûtes**
ils/elles	**cousurent**

PLUPERFECT

j'	**avais cousu**
tu	**avais cousu**
il/elle/on	**avait cousu**
nous	**avions cousu**
vous	**aviez cousu**
ils/elles	**avaient cousu**

IMPERATIVE

couds / cousons / cousez

EXAMPLE PHRASES

Demain, je **coudrai** l'écusson sur ton sweat. **Tomorrow, I'll sew the badge on your sweatshirt.**

Elle **cousut** rapidement le bouton. **She quickly sewed the button on.**

Je **coudrais** l'ourlet si j'étais sûr de ce que je faisais. **I'd sew the hem if I knew what I was doing.**

Je n'**avais** pas bien **cousu** le bouton et je l'avais perdu. **I hadn't sewn the button on properly and I'd lost it.**

je/j' = I tu = you il = he/it elle = she/it on = we/one nous = we vous = you ils/elles = they

courir (to run)

PRESENT

je	**cours**
tu	**cours**
il/elle/on	**court**
nous	**courons**
vous	**courez**
ils/elles	**courent**

PRESENT SUBJUNCTIVE

je	**coure**
tu	**coures**
il/elle/on	**coure**
nous	**courions**
vous	**couriez**
ils/elles	**courent**

PERFECT

j'	**ai couru**
tu	**as couru**
il/elle/on	**a couru**
nous	**avons couru**
vous	**avez couru**
ils/elles	**ont couru**

IMPERFECT

je	**courais**
tu	**courais**
il/elle/on	**courait**
nous	**courions**
vous	**couriez**
ils/elles	**couraient**

PRESENT PARTICIPLE

courant

PAST PARTICIPLE

couru

EXAMPLE PHRASES

Je ne **cours** pas très vite. I can't run very fast.

J'**ai couru** jusqu'à l'école. I ran all the way to school.

Elle est sortie en **courant**. She ran out.

je/j' = I   **tu** = you   **il** = he/it   **elle** = she/it   **on** = we/one   **nous** = we   **vous** = you   **ils/elles** = they

courir

FUTURE

je	**courrai**
tu	**courras**
il/elle/on	**courra**
nous	**courrons**
vous	**courrez**
ils/elles	**courront**

CONDITIONAL

je	**courrais**
tu	**courrais**
il/elle/on	**courrait**
nous	**courrions**
vous	**courriez**
ils/elles	**courraient**

PAST HISTORIC

je	**courus**
tu	**courus**
il/elle/on	**courut**
nous	**courûmes**
vous	**courûtes**
ils/elles	**coururent**

PLUPERFECT

j'	**avais couru**
tu	**avais couru**
il/elle/on	**avait couru**
nous	**avions couru**
vous	**aviez couru**
ils/elles	**avaient couru**

IMPERATIVE

cours / **courons** / **courez**

EXAMPLE PHRASES

L'été prochain, nous **courrons** le marathon de New York. **Next summer, we'll run the New York marathon.**

Il **courut** après elle, mais elle était trop rapide. **He ran after her, but she was too fast.**

Je **courrais** bien plus vite si je n'étais pas fatigué. **I'd run much faster if I wasn't tired.**

J'étais essoufflé parce que j'**avais couru**. **I was out of breath because I'd been running.**

Ne **courez** pas dans le couloir. **Don't run in the corridor.**

je/j' = I **tu** = you **il** = he/it **elle** = she/it **on** = we/one **nous** = we **vous** = you **ils/elles** = they

craindre (to fear)

PRESENT

je	crains
tu	crains
il/elle/on	craint
nous	craignons
vous	craignez
ils/elles	craignent

PRESENT SUBJUNCTIVE

je	craigne
tu	craignes
il/elle/on	craigne
nous	craignions
vous	craigniez
ils/elles	craignent

PERFECT

j'	ai craint
tu	as craint
il/elle/on	a craint
nous	avons craint
vous	avez craint
ils/elles	ont craint

IMPERFECT

je	craignais
tu	craignais
il/elle/on	craignait
nous	craignions
vous	craigniez
ils/elles	craignaient

PRESENT PARTICIPLE

craignant

PAST PARTICIPLE

craint

EXAMPLE PHRASES

Tu n'as rien à **craindre**. You've got nothing to fear.

Je **crains** le pire. I fear the worst.

Il **craignait** qu'elle ne soit partie. He feared that she had gone.

---

craindre

FUTURE

je	**craindrai**
tu	**craindras**
il/elle/on	**craindra**
nous	**craindrons**
vous	**craindrez**
ils/elles	**craindront**

CONDITIONAL

je	**craindrais**
tu	**craindrais**
il/elle/on	**craindrait**
nous	**craindrions**
vous	**craindriez**
ils/elles	**craindraient**

PAST HISTORIC

je	**craignis**
tu	**craignis**
il/elle/on	**craignit**
nous	**craignîmes**
vous	**craignîtes**
ils/elles	**craignirent**

PLUPERFECT

j'	**avais craint**
tu	**avais craint**
il/elle/on	**avait craint**
nous	**avions craint**
vous	**aviez craint**
ils/elles	**avaient craint**

IMPERATIVE

crains / craignons / craignez

EXAMPLE PHRASES

Je **craignis** qu'il ne se vexe. I feared he might get upset.

Je ne le **craindrais** pas tant s'il n'était pas si irritable. I wouldn't fear him so much if he wasn't so irritable.

Si j'étais toi, je **craindrais** sa colère. If I were you, I'd fear his anger.

Elle **avait craint** sa colère, mais il n'avait rien dit. She had feared his anger, but he didn't say anything.

Ne **craignez** rien, ce chien n'est pas méchant. Don't be scared, this dog is harmless.

je/j' = I   tu = you   il = he/it   elle = she/it   on = we/one   nous = we   vous = you   ils/elles = they

créer (to create)

PRESENT		PRESENT SUBJUNCTIVE	
je	**crée**	je	**crée**
tu	**crées**	tu	**crées**
il/elle/on	**crée**	il/elle/on	**crée**
nous	**créons**	nous	**créions**
vous	**créez**	vous	**créiez**
ils/elles	**créent**	ils/elles	**créent**

PERFECT		IMPERFECT	
j'	**ai créé**	je	**créais**
tu	**as créé**	tu	**créais**
il/elle/on	**a créé**	il/elle/on	**créait**
nous	**avons créé**	nous	**créions**
vous	**avez créé**	vous	**créiez**
ils/elles	**ont créé**	ils/elles	**créaient**

PRESENT PARTICIPLE
créant

PAST PARTICIPLE
créé

EXAMPLE PHRASES

Ce virus **crée** des difficultés dans le monde entier. This virus is causing problems all over the world.

Il **a créé** une nouvelle recette. He's created a new recipe.

Nous **avons créé** ce parfum spécialement pour cette occasion. We've created this perfume specially for this occasion.

Elle **créait** souvent des disputes entre nous. She would often cause arguments between us.

je/j' = I   tu = you   il = he/it   elle = she/it   on = we/one   nous = we   vous = you   ils/elles = they

créer

FUTURE

je	**créerai**
tu	**créeras**
il/elle/on	**créera**
nous	**créerons**
vous	**créerez**
ils/elles	**créeront**

CONDITIONAL

je	**créerais**
tu	**créerais**
il/elle/on	**créerait**
nous	**créerions**
vous	**créeriez**
ils/elles	**créeraient**

PAST HISTORIC

je	**créai**
tu	**créas**
il/elle/on	**créa**
nous	**créâmes**
vous	**créâtes**
ils/elles	**créèrent**

PLUPERFECT

j'	**avais créé**
tu	**avais créé**
il/elle/on	**avait créé**
nous	**avions créé**
vous	**aviez créé**
ils/elles	**avaient créé**

IMPERATIVE

crée / créons / créez

EXAMPLE PHRASES

Le gouvernement **créera** deux mille emplois supplémentaires. The government will create an extra two thousand jobs.

Les licenciements **créèrent** des tensions dans l'entreprise. The layoffs created tensions in the company.

Elle **avait créé** une crème qui allait révolutionner l'industrie des produits cosmétiques. She had created a cream that was to revolutionize the cosmetics industry.

je/j' = I tu = you il = he/it elle = she/it on = we/one nous = we vous = you ils/elles = they

crier (to shout)

PRESENT

je	**crie**
tu	**cries**
il/elle/on	**crie**
nous	**crions**
vous	**criez**
ils/elles	**crient**

PRESENT SUBJUNCTIVE

je	**crie**
tu	**cries**
il/elle/on	**crie**
nous	**criions**
vous	**criiez**
ils/elles	**crient**

PERFECT

j'	**ai crié**
tu	**as crié**
il/elle/on	**a crié**
nous	**avons crié**
vous	**avez crié**
ils/elles	**ont crié**

IMPERFECT

je	**criais**
tu	**criais**
il/elle/on	**criait**
nous	**criions**
vous	**criiez**
ils/elles	**criaient**

PRESENT PARTICIPLE
criant

PAST PARTICIPLE
crié

EXAMPLE PHRASES

La maîtresse **crie** tout le temps après nous. The teacher's always shouting at us.

Elle **a crié** au secours. She cried for help.

Je ne veux pas que tu **cries** devant mes copines. I don't want you to shout in front of my friends.

Il **criait** toujours plus fort que moi. He would always shout louder than me.

crier

FUTURE

je **crierai**

tu **crieras**

il/elle/on **criera**

nous **crierons**

vous **crierez**

ils/elles **crieront**

CONDITIONAL

je **crierais**

tu **crierais**

il/elle/on **crierait**

nous **crierions**

vous **crieriez**

ils/elles **crieraient**

PAST HISTORIC

je **criai**

tu **crias**

il/elle/on **cria**

nous **criâmes**

vous **criâtes**

ils/elles **crièrent**

PLUPERFECT

j' **avais crié**

tu **avais crié**

il/elle/on **avait crié**

nous **avions crié**

vous **aviez crié**

ils/elles **avaient crié**

IMPERATIVE

crie / crions / criez

EXAMPLE PHRASES

Ton père ne **criera** pas si tu lui expliques ce qui s'est passé. **Your dad won't shout if you explain to him what happened.**

"Attention !", **cria**-t-il. **"Watch out!" he shouted.**

Elle **crierait** drôlement si tu lui tachais sa robe. **She would really shout if you stained her dress.**

Il n'**avait** pas **crié** comme ça depuis longtemps. **He hadn't shouted like that for a long time.**

Ne **crie** pas comme ça ! **Don't shout!**

je/j' = I   tu = you   il = he/it   elle = she/it   on = we/one   nous = we   vous = you   ils/elles = they

croire (to believe)

PRESENT

je	**crois**
tu	**crois**
il/elle/on	**croit**
nous	**croyons**
vous	**croyez**
ils/elles	**croient**

PRESENT SUBJUNCTIVE

je	**croie**
tu	**croies**
il/elle/on	**croie**
nous	**croyions**
vous	**croyiez**
ils/elles	**croient**

PERFECT

j'	**ai cru**
tu	**as cru**
il/elle/on	**a cru**
nous	**avons cru**
vous	**avez cru**
ils/elles	**ont cru**

IMPERFECT

je	**croyais**
tu	**croyais**
il/elle/on	**croyait**
nous	**croyions**
vous	**croyiez**
ils/elles	**croyaient**

PRESENT PARTICIPLE

croyant

PAST PARTICIPLE

cru

EXAMPLE PHRASES

Je ne te **crois** pas. I don't believe you.

J'**ai cru** que tu n'allais pas venir. I thought you weren't going to come.

Crois-moi, Mme Leblond est très stricte. Believe me, Mrs. Leblond is very strict.

Il faut que tu me **croies**. You have to believe me.

Elle **croyait** encore au père Noël. She still believed in Santa Claus.

croire

FUTURE
je	croirai
tu	croiras
il/elle/on	croira
nous	croirons
vous	croirez
ils/elles	croiront

CONDITIONAL
je	croirais
tu	croirais
il/elle/on	croirait
nous	croirions
vous	croiriez
ils/elles	croiraient

PAST HISTORIC
je	crus
tu	crus
il/elle/on	crut
nous	crûmes
vous	crûtes
ils/elles	crurent

PLUPERFECT
j'	avais cru
tu	avais cru
il/elle/on	avait cru
nous	avions cru
vous	aviez cru
ils/elles	avaient cru

IMPERATIVE
crois / croyons / croyez

EXAMPLE PHRASES

Elle ne me **croira** pas si je lui dis que j'ai gagné. She won't believe me if I tell her that I won.

Il **crut** que je me moquais de lui. He thought that I was making fun of him.

Elle te **croirait** peut-être si tu lui disais que tu as oublié ton maillot de bain. She might believe you if you tell her that you forgot your swimsuit.

Au début, il ne m'**avait** pas **cru**, mais plus tard il s'était rendu compte que c'était vrai. Initially he hadn't believed me, but later he had realized that it was true.

je/j' = I tu = you il = he/it elle = she/it on = we/one nous = we vous = you ils/elles = they

croître (to grow; to increase)

PRESENT

je	croîs
tu	croîs
il/elle/on	croît
nous	croissons
vous	croissez
ils/elles	croissent

PRESENT SUBJUNCTIVE

je	croisse
tu	croisses
il/elle/on	croisse
nous	croissions
vous	croissiez
ils/elles	croissent

PERFECT

j'	ai crû
tu	as crû
il/elle/on	a crû
nous	avons crû
vous	avez crû
ils/elles	ont crû

IMPERFECT

je	croissais
tu	croissais
il/elle/on	croissait
nous	croissions
vous	croissiez
ils/elles	croissaient

PRESENT PARTICIPLE

croissant

PAST PARTICIPLE

crû

EXAMPLE PHRASES

Les ventes **croissent** de 6 % par an. **Sales are growing by 6% per year.**

C'est une plante qui **croît** dans les pays chauds. **This plant grows in hot countries.**

Le nombre de gens qui partent travailler à l'étranger va **croissant**.
An increasing number of people go and work overseas.

---

je/j' = I   tu = you   il = he/it   elle = she/it   on = we/one   nous = we   vous = you   ils/elles = they

croître

FUTURE

je	croîtrai
tu	croîtras
il/elle/on	croîtra
nous	croîtrons
vous	croîtrez
ils/elles	croîtront

CONDITIONAL

je	croîtrais
tu	croîtrais
il/elle/on	croîtrait
nous	croîtrions
vous	croîtriez
ils/elles	croîtraient

PAST HISTORIC

je	crûs
tu	crûs
il/elle/on	crût
nous	crûmes
vous	crûtes
ils/elles	crûrent

PLUPERFECT

j'	avais crû
tu	avais crû
il/elle/on	avait crû
nous	avions crû
vous	aviez crû
ils/elles	avaient crû

IMPERATIVE

crois / croissons / croissez

EXAMPLE PHRASES

Les problèmes **crûrent** de jour en jour. Problems increased day after day.

Les dépenses **croîtraient** rapidement si on ne faisait pas attention.

Spending would increase rapidly if we weren't careful.

je/j' = I tu = you il = he/it elle = she/it on = we/one nous = we vous = you ils/elles = they

cueillir (to pick)

PRESENT

je	cueille
tu	cueilles
il/elle/on	cueille
nous	cueillons
vous	cueillez
ils/elles	cueillent

PRESENT SUBJUNCTIVE

je	cueille
tu	cueilles
il/elle/on	cueille
nous	cueillions
vous	cueilliez
ils/elles	cueillent

PERFECT

j'	ai cueilli
tu	as cueilli
il/elle/on	a cueilli
nous	avons cueilli
vous	avez cueilli
ils/elles	ont cueilli

IMPERFECT

je	cueillais
tu	cueillais
il/elle/on	cueillait
nous	cueillions
vous	cueilliez
ils/elles	cueillaient

PRESENT PARTICIPLE
cueillant

PAST PARTICIPLE
cueilli

EXAMPLE PHRASES

Il est interdit de **cueillir** des fleurs sauvages dans la montagne. It's forbidden to pick wild flowers in the mountains.

J'**ai cueilli** quelques fraises dans le jardin. I picked a few strawberries in the garden.

J'aimerais que tu me **cueilles** des mûres pour faire de la confiture. I'd like you to pick some blackberries for me to make jam.

je/j' = I   tu = you   il = he/it   elle = she/it   on = we/one   nous = we   vous = you   ils/elles = they

cueillir

FUTURE

je	cueillerai
tu	cueilleras
il/elle/on	cueillera
nous	cueillerons
vous	cueillerez
ils/elles	cueilleront

CONDITIONAL

je	cueillerais
tu	cueillerais
il/elle/on	cueillerait
nous	cueillerions
vous	cueilleriez
ils/elles	cueilleraient

PAST HISTORIC

je	cueillis
tu	cueillis
il/elle/on	cueillit
nous	cueillîmes
vous	cueillîtes
ils/elles	cueillirent

PLUPERFECT

j'	avais cueilli
tu	avais cueilli
il/elle/on	avait cueilli
nous	avions cueilli
vous	aviez cueilli
ils/elles	avaient cueilli

IMPERATIVE

cueille / cueillons / cueillez

EXAMPLE PHRASES

Je **cueillerai** des framboises à la ferme. **I'll pick some raspberries at the farm.**

Elle **cueillit** des fraises des bois. **She picked some wild strawberries.**

Je **cueillerais** toutes les fleurs de la terre entière pour toi. **I'd pick all the flowers in the whole wide world for you.**

Il lui **avait cueilli** un beau bouquet de fleurs. **He'd picked a beautiful bunch of flowers for her.**

Ne **cueille** pas les fleurs dans le parc. **Don't pick the flowers in the park.**

je/j' = I tu = you il = he/it elle = she/it on = we/one nous = we vous = you ils/elles = they

cuire (to cook)

PRESENT		PRESENT SUBJUNCTIVE	
je	**cuis**	je	**cuise**
tu	**cuis**	tu	**cuises**
il/elle/on	**cuit**	il/elle/on	**cuise**
nous	**cuisons**	nous	**cuisions**
vous	**cuisez**	vous	**cuisiez**
ils/elles	**cuisent**	ils/elles	**cuisent**

PERFECT		IMPERFECT	
j'	**ai cuit**	je	**cuisais**
tu	**as cuit**	tu	**cuisais**
il/elle/on	**a cuit**	il/elle/on	**cuisait**
nous	**avons cuit**	nous	**cuisions**
vous	**avez cuit**	vous	**cuisiez**
ils/elles	**ont cuit**	ils/elles	**cuisaient**

PRESENT PARTICIPLE
cuisant

PAST PARTICIPLE
cuit

EXAMPLE PHRASES

Ce gâteau prend environ une heure à **cuire**. This cake takes about an hour
   to bake.

En général, je **cuis** les légumes à la vapeur. I usually steam vegetables.

Je les **ai cuits** au beurre. I cooked them in butter.

Mon père **cuisait** toujours la viande au barbecue. My dad always barbecued
   meat.

---

je/j' = I   **tu** = you   **il** = he/it   **elle** = she/it   **on** = we/one   **nous** = we   **vous** = you   **ils/elles** = they

cuire

FUTURE

je	cuirai
tu	cuiras
il/elle/on	cuira
nous	cuirons
vous	cuirez
ils/elles	cuiront

CONDITIONAL

je	cuirais
tu	cuirais
il/elle/on	cuirait
nous	cuirions
vous	cuiriez
ils/elles	cuiraient

PAST HISTORIC

je	cuisis
tu	cuisis
il/elle/on	cuisit
nous	cuisîmes
vous	cuisîtes
ils/elles	cuisirent

PLUPERFECT

j'	avais cuit
tu	avais cuit
il/elle/on	avait cuit
nous	avions cuit
vous	aviez cuit
ils/elles	avaient cuit

IMPERATIVE

cuis / cuisons / cuisez

EXAMPLE PHRASES

Nous **cuirons** les côtelettes sur le gril. We'll grill the chops.

Elle **cuisit** l'omelette et la servit. She cooked the omelet and served it.

Je **cuirais** les crêpes plus longtemps si je n'avais pas peur de les faire brûler.
  I'd cook the pancakes longer if I wasn't scared of burning them.

Elle **avait cuit** le poisson au four. She'd baked the fish in the oven.

je/j' = I   tu = you   il = he/it   elle = she/it   on = we/one   nous = we   vous = you   ils/elles = they

se débrouiller (to manage)

PRESENT

je	**me débrouille**
tu	**te débrouilles**
il/elle/on	**se débrouille**
nous	**nous débrouillons**
vous	**vous débrouillez**
ils/elles	**se débrouillent**

PRESENT SUBJUNCTIVE

je	**me débrouille**
tu	**te débrouilles**
il/elle/on	**se débrouille**
nous	**nous débrouillions**
vous	**vous débrouilliez**
ils/elles	**se débrouillent**

PERFECT

je	**me suis débrouillé(e)**
tu	**t'es débrouillé(e)**
il/elle/on	**s'est débrouillé(e)**
nous	**nous sommes débrouillé(e)s**
vous	**vous êtes débrouillé(e)(s)**
ils/elles	**se sont débrouillé(e)s**

IMPERFECT

je	**me débrouillais**
tu	**te débrouillais**
il/elle/on	**se débrouillait**
nous	**nous débrouillions**
vous	**vous débrouilliez**
ils/elles	**se débrouillaient**

PRESENT PARTICIPLE

se débrouillant

PAST PARTICIPLE

débrouillé

EXAMPLE PHRASES

Elle **se débrouille** bien à l'école. She gets along well at school.

C'était difficile, mais je ne **me suis** pas trop mal **débrouillé**. It was difficult, but I managed OK.

Débrouille-toi tout seul. Sort things out for yourself.

Débrouillez-vous pour arriver à l'heure. Make sure you're on time.

Je **me débrouillais** mieux en français qu'en maths. I did better in French than in math.

---

je/j' = I   tu = you   il = he/it   elle = she/it   on = we/one   nous = we   vous = you   ils/elles = they

se débrouiller

FUTURE

je	me débrouillerai
tu	te débrouilleras
il/elle/on	se débrouillera
nous	nous débrouillerons
vous	vous débrouillerez
ils/elles	se débrouilleront

CONDITIONAL

je	me débrouillerais
tu	te débrouillerais
il/elle/on	se débrouillerait
nous	nous débrouillerions
vous	vous débrouilleriez
ils/elles	se débrouilleraient

PAST HISTORIC

je	me débrouillai
tu	te débrouillas
il/elle/on	se débrouilla
nous	nous débrouillâmes
vous	vous débrouillâtes
ils/elles	se débrouillèrent

PLUPERFECT

je	m'étais débrouillé(e)
tu	t'étais débrouillé(e)
il/elle/on	s'était débrouillé(e)
nous	nous étions débrouillé(e)s
vous	vous étiez débrouillé(e)(s)
ils/elles	s'étaient débrouillé(e)s

IMPERATIVE

débrouille-toi / débrouillons-nous / débrouillez-vous

EXAMPLE PHRASES

Nous **nous débrouillerons** bien sans toi. We'll manage fine without you.

Il **se débrouilla** tant bien que mal pour préparer le dîner. He just about managed to prepare dinner.

Il **se débrouillerait** bien tout seul s'il était obligé. He would manage fine by himself if he had to.

Comme mes parents étaient partis, je **m'étais débrouillée** toute seule. As my parents were away, I had managed by myself.

je/j' = I   tu = you   il = he/it   elle = she/it   on = we/one   nous = we   vous = you   ils/elles = they

descendre (to go down)

PRESENT

je	descends
tu	descends
il/elle/on	descend
nous	descendons
vous	descendez
ils/elles	descendent

PRESENT SUBJUNCTIVE

je	descende
tu	descendes
il/elle/on	descende
nous	descendions
vous	descendiez
ils/elles	descendent

PERFECT

je	suis descendu(e)
tu	es descendu(e)
il/elle/on	est descendu(e)
nous	sommes descendu(e)s
vous	êtes descendu(e)(s)
ils/elles	sont descendu(e)s

IMPERFECT

je	descendais
tu	descendais
il/elle/on	descendait
nous	descendions
vous	descendiez
ils/elles	descendaient

PRESENT PARTICIPLE

descendant

PAST PARTICIPLE

descendu

EXAMPLE PHRASES

Vous pouvez **descendre** ma valise, s'il vous plaît ? Could you get my suitcase down, please?

Reste en bas : je **descends** ! Stay downstairs – I'm coming down!

Nous **sommes descendus** à la station Trocadéro. We got off at Trocadéro.

Descendez la rue jusqu'au rond-point. Go down the street to the traffic circle.

Il faut que je **descende** chercher quelque chose à la cave. I have to go down to the basement to get something.

je/j' = I   tu = you   il = he/it   elle = she/it   on = we/one   nous = we   vous = you   ils/elles = they

descendre

FUTURE

je	descendrai
tu	descendras
il/elle/on	descendra
nous	descendrons
vous	descendrez
ils/elles	descendront

CONDITIONAL

je	descendrais
tu	descendrais
il/elle/on	descendrait
nous	descendrions
vous	descendriez
ils/elles	descendraient

PAST HISTORIC

je	descendis
tu	descendis
il/elle/on	descendit
nous	descendîmes
vous	descendîtes
ils/elles	descendirent

PLUPERFECT

j'	étais descendu(e)
tu	étais descendu(e)
il/elle/on	était descendu(e)
nous	étions descendu(e)s
vous	étiez descendu(e)(s)
ils/elles	étaient descendu(e)s

IMPERATIVE

descends / descendons / descendez

EXAMPLE PHRASES

Nous **descendrons** dans le Midi au mois de juillet. We'll go down to the south of France in July.

Il **descendit** les escaliers en courant. He ran down the stairs.

Si j'étais toi, je ne **descendrais** pas l'escalier si vite. I wouldn't rush down the stairs if I were you.

Ils **étaient descendus** regarder la télé quand les plombs ont sauté. They had gone down to watch TV when the fuses blew

je/j' = I   tu = you   il = he/it   elle = she/it   on = we/one   nous = we   vous = you   ils/elles = they

devenir (to become)

PRESENT

je	**deviens**
tu	**deviens**
il/elle/on	**devient**
nous	**devenons**
vous	**devenez**
ils/elles	**deviennent**

PRESENT SUBJUNCTIVE

je	**devienne**
tu	**deviennes**
il/elle/on	**devienne**
nous	**devenions**
vous	**deveniez**
ils/elles	**deviennent**

PERFECT

je	**suis devenu(e)**
tu	**es devenu(e)**
il/elle/on	**est devenu(e)**
nous	**sommes devenu(e)s**
vous	**êtes devenu(e)(s)**
ils/elles	**sont devenu(e)s**

IMPERFECT

je	**devenais**
tu	**devenais**
il/elle/on	**devenait**
nous	**devenions**
vous	**deveniez**
ils/elles	**devenaient**

PRESENT PARTICIPLE
devenant

PAST PARTICIPLE
devenu

EXAMPLE PHRASES

Ça **devient** de plus en plus difficile. It's becoming more and more difficult.

Il **est devenu** médecin. He became a doctor.

Qu'est-ce qu'elle **est devenue** ? What has become of her?

Il ne faut pas que ça **devienne** une corvée. It mustn't become a chore.

Elle **devenait** de plus en plus exigeante. She was becoming more and more demanding.

je/j' = I   tu = you   il = he/it   elle = she/it   on = we/one   nous = we   vous = you   ils/elles = they

devenir

FUTURE

je	**deviendrai**
tu	**deviendras**
il/elle/on	**deviendra**
nous	**deviendrons**
vous	**deviendrez**
ils/elles	**deviendront**

CONDITIONAL

je	**deviendrais**
tu	**deviendrais**
il/elle/on	**deviendrait**
nous	**deviendrions**
vous	**deviendriez**
ils/elles	**deviendraient**

PAST HISTORIC

je	**devins**
tu	**devins**
il/elle/on	**devint**
nous	**devînmes**
vous	**devîntes**
ils/elles	**devinrent**

PLUPERFECT

j'	**étais devenu(e)**
tu	**étais devenu(e)**
il/elle/on	**était devenu(e)**
nous	**étions devenu(e)s**
vous	**étiez devenu(e)(s)**
ils/elles	**étaient devenu(e)s**

IMPERATIVE

deviens / devenons / devenez

EXAMPLE PHRASES

J'espère qu'elle ne **deviendra** pas comme sa mère. I hope that she won't become like her mother.

Elle **devint** la première femme à traverser l'Atlantique en avion. She became the first woman to fly across the Atlantic.

Si on les nourrissait trop, les poissons rouges **deviendraient** énormes. If we overfed them, the goldfish would become enormous.

Je me demandais ce qu'ils **étaient devenus**. I wondered what had become of them.

je/j' = I tu = you il = he/it elle = she/it on = we/one nous = we vous = you ils/elles = they

devoir (to have to; to owe)

PRESENT

je	**dois**
tu	**dois**
il/elle/on	**doit**
nous	**devons**
vous	**devez**
ils/elles	**doivent**

PRESENT SUBJUNCTIVE

je	**doive**
tu	**doives**
il/elle/on	**doive**
nous	**devions**
vous	**deviez**
ils/elles	**doivent**

PERFECT

j'	**ai dû**
tu	**as dû**
il/elle/on	**a dû**
nous	**avons dû**
vous	**avez dû**
ils/elles	**ont dû**

IMPERFECT

je	**devais**
tu	**devais**
il/elle/on	**devait**
nous	**devions**
vous	**deviez**
ils/elles	**devaient**

PRESENT PARTICIPLE

devant

PAST PARTICIPLE

dû (NB: due, dus, dues)

EXAMPLE PHRASES

Je **dois** aller faire les courses ce matin. I have to do the shopping this morning.

À quelle heure est-ce que tu **dois** partir ? What time do you have to leave?

J'**ai dû** partir avant la fin du film. I had to leave before the end of the movie.

Il **a dû** changer d'avis. He must have changed his mind.

Il **devait** prendre le train pour aller travailler. He had to go to work by train.

---

je/j' = I   tu = you   il = he/it   elle = she/it   on = we/one   nous = we   vous = you   ils/elles = they

devoir

FUTURE

je	devrai
tu	devras
il/elle/on	devra
nous	devrons
vous	devrez
ils/elles	devront

CONDITIONAL

je	devrais
tu	devrais
il/elle/on	devrait
nous	devrions
vous	devriez
ils/elles	devraient

PAST HISTORIC

je	dus
tu	dus
il/elle/on	dut
nous	dûmes
vous	dûtes
ils/elles	durent

PLUPERFECT

j'	avais dû
tu	avais dû
il/elle/on	avait dû
nous	avions dû
vous	aviez dû
ils/elles	avaient dû

IMPERATIVE

dois / devons / devez

EXAMPLE PHRASES

Ils **devront** finir leurs devoirs avant de venir. They'll have to finish their
homework before they come.

Elle **dut** lui annoncer elle-même la mauvaise nouvelle. She had to tell him
the bad news herself.

Tu ne **devrais** pas les déranger tout le temps comme ça. You shouldn't
disturb them all the time like that.

Comme il était malade, il **avait dû** arrêter de fumer. Since he was sick, he'd
had to stop smoking.

je/j' = I tu = you il = he/it elle = she/it on = we/one nous = we vous = you ils/elles = they

dire (to say; to tell)

PRESENT

je	**dis**
tu	**dis**
il/elle/on	**dit**
nous	**disons**
vous	**dites**
ils/elles	**disent**

PRESENT SUBJUNCTIVE

je	**dise**
tu	**dises**
il/elle/on	**dise**
nous	**disions**
vous	**disiez**
ils/elles	**disent**

PERFECT

j'	**ai dit**
tu	**as dit**
il/elle/on	**a dit**
nous	**avons dit**
vous	**avez dit**
ils/elles	**ont dit**

IMPERFECT

je	**disais**
tu	**disais**
il/elle/on	**disait**
nous	**disions**
vous	**disiez**
ils/elles	**disaient**

PRESENT PARTICIPLE

disant

PAST PARTICIPLE

dit

EXAMPLE PHRASES

Qu'est-ce qu'elle **dit** ? What is she saying?

Comment ça se **dit** en anglais ? How do you say that in English?

"Bonjour !", a-t-il **dit**. "Hello!" he said.

Ils m'**ont dit** que le film était nul. They told me that the movie was a load of trash.

dire

FUTURE

je	**dirai**
tu	**diras**
il/elle/on	**dira**
nous	**dirons**
vous	**direz**
ils/elles	**diront**

CONDITIONAL

je	**dirais**
tu	**dirais**
il/elle/on	**dirait**
nous	**dirions**
vous	**diriez**
ils/elles	**diraient**

PAST HISTORIC

je	**dis**
tu	**dis**
il/elle/on	**dit**
nous	**dîmes**
vous	**dîtes**
ils/elles	**dirent**

PLUPERFECT

j'	**avais dit**
tu	**avais dit**
il/elle/on	**avait dit**
nous	**avions dit**
vous	**aviez dit**
ils/elles	**avaient dit**

IMPERATIVE

dis / disons / dites

EXAMPLE PHRASES

Je lui **dirai** de venir à midi. I'll tell him to come at noon.

"Viens ici !", **dit**-il. Mais le chien refusait de bouger. "Come here!" he said.
  But the dog refused to move.

On **dirait** qu'il va neiger. It looks like snow.

On ne m'**avait** pas **dit** que tu serais là. I hadn't been told that you'd be there.

Ne **dis** pas de bêtises. Don't talk nonsense.

je/j' = I **tu** = you **il** = he/it **elle** = she/it **on** = we/one **nous** = we **vous** = you **ils/elles** = they

donner (to give)

PRESENT		PRESENT SUBJUNCTIVE	
je	donne	je	donne
tu	donnes	tu	donnes
il/elle/on	donne	il/elle/on	donne
nous	donnons	nous	donnions
vous	donnez	vous	donniez
ils/elles	donnent	ils/elles	donnent

PERFECT		IMPERFECT	
j'	ai donné	je	donnais
tu	as donné	tu	donnais
il/elle/on	a donné	il/elle/on	donnait
nous	avons donné	nous	donnions
vous	avez donné	vous	donniez
ils/elles	ont donné	ils/elles	donnaient

PRESENT PARTICIPLE
donnant

PAST PARTICIPLE
donné

EXAMPLE PHRASES

L'appartement **donne** sur la place. The apartment overlooks the square.

Est-ce que je t'**ai donné** mon adresse ? Did I give you my address?

Il faut que tu me **donnes** plus de détails. You must give me more details.

Je **donnais** des sucres aux chevaux. I'd give sugar lumps to the horses.

donner

FUTURE

je	**donnerai**
tu	**donneras**
il/elle/on	**donnera**
nous	**donnerons**
vous	**donnerez**
ils/elles	**donneront**

CONDITIONAL

je	**donnerais**
tu	**donnerais**
il/elle/on	**donnerait**
nous	**donnerions**
vous	**donneriez**
ils/elles	**donneraient**

PAST HISTORIC

je	**donnai**
tu	**donnas**
il/elle/on	**donna**
nous	**donnâmes**
vous	**donnâtes**
ils/elles	**donnèrent**

PLUPERFECT

j'	**avais donné**
tu	**avais donné**
il/elle/on	**avait donné**
nous	**avions donné**
vous	**aviez donné**
ils/elles	**avaient donné**

IMPERATIVE

donne / donnons / donnez

EXAMPLE PHRASES

Je te **donnerai** un ticket de métro. I'll give you a subway ticket.

Il lui **donna** un vieux livre. He gave him an old book.

Je lui **donnerais** des nouvelles si j'avais son adresse. I'd give her some news if I had her address.

Je lui **avais donné** mon numéro de téléphone mais il a dû le perdre. I had given him my phone number, but he must have lost it.

Donne-moi la main. Give me your hand.

je/j' = I tu = you il = he/it elle = she/it on = we/one nous = we vous = you ils/elles = they

dormir (to sleep)

PRESENT

je	**dors**
tu	**dors**
il/elle/on	**dort**
nous	**dormons**
vous	**dormez**
ils/elles	**dorment**

PRESENT SUBJUNCTIVE

je	**dorme**
tu	**dormes**
il/elle/on	**dorme**
nous	**dormions**
vous	**dormiez**
ils/elles	**dorment**

PERFECT

j'	**ai dormi**
tu	**as dormi**
il/elle/on	**a dormi**
nous	**avons dormi**
vous	**avez dormi**
ils/elles	**ont dormi**

IMPERFECT

je	**dormais**
tu	**dormais**
il/elle/on	**dormait**
nous	**dormions**
vous	**dormiez**
ils/elles	**dormaient**

PRESENT PARTICIPLE
dormant

PAST PARTICIPLE
dormi

EXAMPLE PHRASES

Nous **dormons** dans la même chambre. We sleep in the same bedroom.

Tu **as** bien **dormi** ? Did you sleep well?

Elle m'a fait une tisane pour que je **dorme** bien. She made me a herbal tea so I would sleep well.

À 9 heures, il **dormait** déjà. He was already asleep by nine.

dormir

FUTURE

je	**dormirai**
tu	**dormiras**
il/elle/on	**dormira**
nous	**dormirons**
vous	**dormirez**
ils/elles	**dormiront**

CONDITIONAL

je	**dormirais**
tu	**dormirais**
il/elle/on	**dormirait**
nous	**dormirions**
vous	**dormiriez**
ils/elles	**dormiraient**

PAST HISTORIC

je	**dormis**
tu	**dormis**
il/elle/on	**dormit**
nous	**dormîmes**
vous	**dormîtes**
ils/elles	**dormirent**

PLUPERFECT

j'	**avais dormi**
tu	**avais dormi**
il/elle/on	**avait dormi**
nous	**avions dormi**
vous	**aviez dormi**
ils/elles	**avaient dormi**

IMPERATIVE

dors / dormons / dormez

EXAMPLE PHRASES

Ce soir, nous **dormirons** sous la tente. Tonight, we'll sleep in the tent.

Il était si fatigué qu'il **dormit** toute la journée. He was so tired that he slept all day.

Il **dormirait** mieux s'il buvait moins de café. He'd sleep better if he didn't drink so much coffee.

J'étais épuisé car je n'**avais** pas **dormi** de la nuit. I was exhausted, as I hadn't slept all night.

Dors bien. Sleep well.

je/j' = I **tu** = you **il** = he/it **elle** = she/it **on** = we/one **nous** = we **vous** = you **ils/elles** = they

écrire (to write)

PRESENT

j'	**écris**
tu	**écris**
il/elle/on	**écrit**
nous	**écrivons**
vous	**écrivez**
ils/elles	**écrivent**

PRESENT SUBJUNCTIVE

j'	**écrive**
tu	**écrives**
il/elle/on	**écrive**
nous	**écrivions**
vous	**écriviez**
ils/elles	**écrivent**

PERFECT

j'	**ai écrit**
tu	**as écrit**
il/elle/on	**a écrit**
nous	**avons écrit**
vous	**avez écrit**
ils/elles	**ont écrit**

IMPERFECT

j'	**écrivais**
tu	**écrivais**
il/elle/on	**écrivait**
nous	**écrivions**
vous	**écriviez**
ils/elles	**écrivaient**

PRESENT PARTICIPLE

écrivant

PAST PARTICIPLE

écrit

EXAMPLE PHRASES

Elle **écrit** des romans. She writes novels.

Tu **as écrit** à ta correspondante récemment ? Have you written to your pen pal recently?

Écrivez votre nom en haut de la feuille. Write your name at the top of the page.

Elle aimerait que tu **écrives** plus souvent. She'd like you to write more often.

Il ne nous **écrivait** jamais quand il était en France. He never wrote to us when he was in France.

je/j' = I **tu** = you **il** = he/it **elle** = she/it **on** = we/one **nous** = we **vous** = you **ils/elles** = they

écrire

FUTURE

j'	**écrirai**
tu	**écriras**
il/elle/on	**écrira**
nous	**écrirons**
vous	**écrirez**
ils/elles	**écriront**

CONDITIONAL

j'	**écrirais**
tu	**écrirais**
il/elle/on	**écrirait**
nous	**écririons**
vous	**écririez**
ils/elles	**écriraient**

PAST HISTORIC

j'	**écrivis**
tu	**écrivis**
il/elle/on	**écrivit**
nous	**écrivîmes**
vous	**écrivîtes**
ils/elles	**écrivirent**

PLUPERFECT

j'	**avais écrit**
tu	**avais écrit**
il/elle/on	**avait écrit**
nous	**avions écrit**
vous	**aviez écrit**
ils/elles	**avaient écrit**

IMPERATIVE

écris / écrivons / écrivez

EXAMPLE PHRASES

Demain, j'**écrirai** une lettre au directeur. **Tomorrow, I'll write a letter to the principal.**

Il **écrivit** un poème à la lueur de la bougie. **He wrote a poem by candlelight.**

J'**écrirais** plus souvent si j'avais le temps. **I'd write more often if I had the time.**

Comme il n'**avait** encore rien **écrit** sur sa feuille, il se fit disputer par la maîtresse **As he hadn't written anything on his paper yet, he was told off by the teacher.**

je/j' = I tu = you il = he/it elle = she/it on = we/one nous = we vous = you ils/elles = they

émouvoir (to move)

PRESENT

j'	**émeus**
tu	**émeus**
il/elle/on	**émeut**
nous	**émouvons**
vous	**émouvez**
ils/elles	**émeuvent**

PRESENT SUBJUNCTIVE

j'	**émeuve**
tu	**émeuves**
il/elle/on	**émeuve**
nous	**émeuvions**
vous	**émeuviez**
ils/elles	**émeuvent**

PERFECT

j'	**ai ému**
tu	**as ému**
il/elle/on	**a ému**
nous	**avons ému**
vous	**avez ému**
ils/elles	**ont ému**

IMPERFECT

j'	**émouvais**
tu	**émouvais**
il/elle/on	**émouvait**
nous	**émouvions**
vous	**émouviez**
ils/elles	**émouvaient**

PRESENT PARTICIPLE

émouvant

PAST PARTICIPLE

ému

EXAMPLE PHRASES

Cette histoire m'**émeut** toujours beaucoup. This story always moves me to tears.

Sa fausse gentillesse ne m'**émeut** pas. I won't be moved by his fake kindness.

Ce film nous **a émus**. This movie moved us.

Cela m'**émouvait** toujours de les voir se quitter à la fin de l'été. It always moved me to see them part at the end of the summer.

je/j' = I   **tu** = you   **il** = he/it   **elle** = she/it   **on** = we/one   **nous** = we   **vous** = you   **ils/elles** = they

émouvoir

FUTURE

j'	**émouvrai**
tu	**émouvras**
il/elle/on	**émouvra**
nous	**émouvrons**
vous	**émouvrez**
ils/elles	**émouvront**

CONDITIONAL

j'	**émouvrais**
tu	**émouvrais**
il/elle/on	**émouvrait**
nous	**émouvrions**
vous	**émouvriez**
ils/elles	**émouvraient**

PAST HISTORIC

j'	**émus**
tu	**émus**
il/elle/on	**émut**
nous	**émûmes**
vous	**émûtes**
ils/elles	**émurent**

PLUPERFECT

j'	**avais ému**
tu	**avais ému**
il/elle/on	**avait ému**
nous	**avions ému**
vous	**aviez ému**
ils/elles	**avaient ému**

IMPERATIVE

émeus / émouvons / émouvez

EXAMPLE PHRASES

Sa franchise l'**émut** vraiment. His frankness really moved her.

Sa lettre l'**avait** beaucoup **émue**. She had been deeply moved by his letter.

s'ennuyer (to be bored)

PRESENT

je	**m'ennuie**
tu	**t'ennuies**
il/elle/on	**s'ennuie**
nous	**nous ennuyons**
vous	**vous ennuyez**
ils/elles	**s'ennuient**

PRESENT SUBJUNCTIVE

je	**m'ennuie**
tu	**t'ennuies**
il/elle/on	**s'ennuie**
nous	**nous ennuyions**
vous	**vous ennuyiez**
ils/elles	**s'ennuient**

PERFECT

je	**me suis ennuyé(e)**
tu	**t'es ennuyé(e)**
Il/elle/on	**s'est ennuyé(e)**
nous	**nous sommes ennuyé(e)s**
vous	**vous êtes ennuyé(e)(s)**
ils/elles	**se sont ennuyé(e)s**

IMPERFECT

je	**m'ennuyais**
tu	**t'ennuyais**
il/elle/on	**s'ennuyait**
nous	**nous ennuyions**
vous	**vous ennuyiez**
ils/elles	**s'ennuyaient**

PRESENT PARTICIPLE

s'ennuyant

PAST PARTICIPLE

ennuyé

EXAMPLE PHRASES

Elle **s'ennuie** un peu à l'école. She's a little bored at school.

Je **me suis ennuyé** quand tu étais partie. I got bored when you were away.

Ne **t'ennuie** pas trop cet après-midi. Don't get too bored this afternoon.

Je ne voudrais pas qu'elle **s'ennuie** avec moi. I wouldn't want her to get
bored with me.

On ne **s'ennuyait** jamais avec lui. We never got bored with him.

je/j' = I   tu = you   il = he/it   elle = she/it   on = we/one   nous = we   vous = you   ils/elles = they

s'ennuyer

FUTURE

je	**m'ennuierai**
tu	**t'ennuieras**
il/elle/on	**s'ennuiera**
nous	**nous ennuierons**
vous	**vous ennuierez**
ils/elles	**s'ennuieront**

CONDITIONAL

je	**m'ennuierais**
tu	**t'ennuierais**
il/elle/on	**s'ennuierait**
nous	**nous ennuierions**
vous	**vous ennuieriez**
ils/elles	**s'ennuieraient**

PAST HISTORIC

je	**m'ennuyai**
tu	**t'ennuyas**
il/elle/on	**s'ennuya**
nous	**nous ennuyâmes**
vous	**vous ennuyâtes**
ils/elles	**s'ennuyèrent**

PLUPERFECT

je	**m'étais ennuyé(e)**
tu	**t'étais ennuyé(e)**
il/elle/on	**s'était ennuyé(e)**
nous	**nous étions ennuyé(e)s**
vous	**vous étiez ennuyé(e)(s)**
ils/elles	**s'étaient ennuyé(e)s**

IMPERATIVE

ennuie-toi / ennuyons-nous / ennuyez-vous

EXAMPLE PHRASES

Il **s'ennuiera** sûrement quand ses copains seront partis. He'll probably be
bored when his friends are away.

Elle **s'ennuya** un peu. She got a little bored.

Tu ne **t'ennuierais** pas tant si tu allais jouer avec les autres. You wouldn't
be so bored if you went to play with the others.

Il **s'était ennuyé** pendant les vacances et il était content de retrouver ses
copains. He'd gotten bored during the holidays, and he was happy to be
with his friends again.

je/j' = I tu = you il = he/it elle = she/it on = we/one nous = we vous = you ils/elles = they

entendre (to hear)

PRESENT	**PRESENT SUBJUNCTIVE**

	PRESENT		PRESENT SUBJUNCTIVE
j'	entends	j'	entende
tu	entends	tu	entendes
il/elle/on	entend	il/elle/on	entende
nous	entendons	nous	entendions
vous	entendez	vous	entendiez
ils/elles	entendent	ils/elles	entendent

	PERFECT		IMPERFECT
j'	ai entendu	j'	entendais
tu	as entendu	tu	entendais
il/elle/on	a entendu	il/elle/on	entendait
nous	avons entendu	nous	entendions
vous	avez entendu	vous	entendiez
ils/elles	ont entendu	ils/elles	entendaient

PRESENT PARTICIPLE
entendant

PAST PARTICIPLE
entendu

EXAMPLE PHRASES

Il n'**entend** pas bien. He can't hear very well.

Tu **as entendu** ce que je t'ai dit ? Did you hear what I said to you?

Il ne faut pas qu'elle nous **entende**. She mustn't hear us.

Elle n'**entendait** jamais le réveil sonner. She never heard the alarm clock ring.

je/j' = I   **tu** = you   **il** = he/it   **elle** = she/it   **on** = we/one   **nous** = we   **vous** = you   **ils/elles** = they

entendre

FUTURE

j'	**entendrai**
tu	**entendras**
il/elle/on	**entendra**
nous	**entendrons**
vous	**entendrez**
ils/elles	**entendront**

CONDITIONAL

j'	**entendrais**
tu	**entendrais**
il/elle/on	**entendrait**
nous	**entendrions**
vous	**entendriez**
ils/elles	**entendraient**

PAST HISTORIC

j'	**entendis**
tu	**entendis**
il/elle/on	**entendit**
nous	**entendîmes**
vous	**entendîtes**
ils/elles	**entendirent**

PLUPERFECT

j'	**avais entendu**
tu	**avais entendu**
il/elle/on	**avait entendu**
nous	**avions entendu**
vous	**aviez entendu**
ils/elles	**avaient entendu**

IMPERATIVE

entends / entendons / entendez

EXAMPLE PHRASES

Tu les **entendras** sûrement rentrer. You'll probably hear them come back.

Elle **entendit** les oiseaux chanter. She heard the birds singing.

On **entendrait** moins les voisins si les murs étaient plus épais. We'd hear the neighbors less if the walls were thicker.

Il ne les **avait** pas **entendus** arriver. He hadn't heard them arrive.

je/j' = I **tu** = you **il** = he/it **elle** = she/it **on** = we/one **nous** = we **vous** = you **ils/elles** = they

entrer (to come in; to go in)

PRESENT

j'	entre
tu	entres
il/elle/on	entre
nous	entrons
vous	entrez
ils/elles	entrent

PRESENT SUBJUNCTIVE

j'	entre
tu	entres
il/elle/on	entre
nous	entrions
vous	entriez
ils/elles	entrent

PERFECT

je	suis entré(e)
tu	es entré(e)
il/elle/on	est entré(e)
nous	sommes entré(e)s
vous	êtes entré(e)(s)
ils/elles	sont entré(e)s

IMPERFECT

j'	entrais
tu	entrais
il/elle/on	entrait
nous	entrions
vous	entriez
ils/elles	entraient

PRESENT PARTICIPLE

entrant

PAST PARTICIPLE

entré

EXAMPLE PHRASES

Je peux **entrer** ? Can I come in?

Ils **sont** tous **entrés** dans la maison. They all went inside the house.

Entrez par la porte de derrière. Come in by the back door.

Essuie-toi les pieds en **entrant**. Wipe your feet as you come in.

entrer

FUTURE

j'	**entrerai**
tu	**entreras**
il/elle/on	**entrera**
nous	**entrerons**
vous	**entrerez**
ils/elles	**entreront**

CONDITIONAL

j'	**entrerais**
tu	**entrerais**
il/elle/on	**entrerait**
nous	**entrerions**
vous	**entreriez**
ils/elles	**entreraient**

PAST HISTORIC

j'	**entrai**
tu	**entras**
il/elle/on	**entra**
nous	**entrâmes**
vous	**entrâtes**
ils/elles	**entrèrent**

PLUPERFECT

j'	**étais entré(e)**
tu	**étais entré(e)**
il/elle/on	**était entré(e)**
nous	**étions entré(e)s**
vous	**étiez entré(e)(s)**
ils/elles	**étaient entré(e)s**

IMPERATIVE

entre / entrons / entrez

EXAMPLE PHRASES

Elle **entrera** en sixième à la rentrée. She'll start high school after the summer.

Comme personne ne répondit, il poussa la porte et **entra**. As nobody answered, he pushed the door and went in.

Je n'**entrerais** pas sans frapper si j'étais toi. I wouldn't go in without knocking if I were you.

Comme j'avais perdu les clés, j'**étais entré** par la fenêtre. Since I'd lost the keys, I'd gone in through the window.

je/j' = I tu = you il = he/it elle = she/it on = we/one nous = we vous = you ils/elles = they

envoyer (to send)

PRESENT

j'	envoie
tu	envoies
il/elle/on	envoie
nous	envoyons
vous	envoyez
ils/elles	envoient

PRESENT SUBJUNCTIVE

j'	envoie
tu	envoies
il/elle/on	envoie
nous	envoyions
vous	envoyiez
ils/elles	envoient

PERFECT

j'	ai envoyé
tu	as envoyé
il/elle/on	a envoyé
nous	avons envoyé
vous	avez envoyé
ils/elles	ont envoyé

IMPERFECT

j'	envoyais
tu	envoyais
il/elle/on	envoyait
nous	envoyions
vous	envoyiez
ils/elles	envoyaient

PRESENT PARTICIPLE

envoyant

PAST PARTICIPLE

envoyé

EXAMPLE PHRASES

Ma cousine nous **envoie** toujours des cadeaux pour Noël. My cousin always sends us presents for Christmas.

J'**ai envoyé** une carte postale à ma tante. I sent my aunt a postcard.

Il faut que j'**envoie** ce paquet demain. I must send this package out tomorrow.

Elle m'**envoyait** toujours une carte pour mon anniversaire. She would always send me a card for my birthday.

---

je/j' = I   tu = you   il = he/it   elle = she/it   on = we/one   nous = we   vous = you   ils/elles = they

envoyer

FUTURE

j'	enverrai
tu	enverras
il/elle/on	enverra
nous	enverrons
vous	enverrez
ils/elles	enverront

CONDITIONAL

j'	enverrais
tu	enverrais
il/elle/on	enverrait
nous	enverrions
vous	enverriez
ils/elles	enverraient

PAST HISTORIC

j'	envoyai
tu	envoyas
il/elle/on	envoya
nous	envoyâmes
vous	envoyâtes
ils/elles	envoyèrent

PLUPERFECT

j'	avais envoyé
tu	avais envoyé
il/elle/on	avait envoyé
nous	avions envoyé
vous	aviez envoyé
ils/elles	avaient envoyé

IMPERATIVE

envoie / envoyons / envoyez

EXAMPLE PHRASES

J'**enverrai** Julie te chercher à l'aéroport. I'll send Julie to pick you up at the airport.

Sa mère l'**envoya** chercher du pain. His mother sent him to get some bread.

Je lui **enverrais** un cadeau si j'étais sûr de lui faire plaisir. I'd send her a present if I thought it would make her happy.

Je ne lui **avais** pas **envoyé** mes vœux et elle était très vexée. I hadn't sent her a Christmas card, and she was very upset.

Envoie-moi un e-mail. Send me an email.

je/j' = I **tu** = you **il** = he/it **elle** = she/it **on** = we/one **nous** = we **vous** = you **ils/elles** = they

espérer (to hope)

PRESENT

j'	espère
tu	espères
il/elle/on	espère
nous	espérons
vous	espérez
ils/elles	espèrent

PRESENT SUBJUNCTIVE

j'	espère
tu	espères
il/elle/on	espère
nous	espérions
vous	espériez
ils/elles	espèrent

PERFECT

j'	ai espéré
tu	as espéré
il/elle/on	a espéré
nous	avons espéré
vous	avez espéré
ils/elles	ont espéré

IMPERFECT

j'	espérais
tu	espérais
il/elle/on	espérait
nous	espérions
vous	espériez
ils/elles	espéraient

PRESENT PARTICIPLE

espérant

PAST PARTICIPLE

espéré

EXAMPLE PHRASES

J'**espère** que tu vas bien. I hope you're well.

Tu penses réussir tes examens ? – J'**espère** bien ! Do you think you'll pass your exams? – I hope so!

Il **espérait** pouvoir venir. He was hoping he'd be able to come.

Elle **espérait** qu'il n'était pas déjà parti. She was hoping that he hadn't already left.

je/j' = I   tu = you   il = he/it   elle = she/it   on = we/one   nous = we   vous = you   ils/elles = they

espérer

FUTURE

j'	espérerai
tu	espéreras
il/elle/on	espérera
nous	espérerons
vous	espérerez
ils/elles	espéreront

CONDITIONAL

j'	espérerais
tu	espérerais
il/elle/on	espérerait
nous	espérerions
vous	espéreriez
ils/elles	espéreraient

PAST HISTORIC

j'	espérai
tu	espéras
il/elle/on	espéra
nous	espérâmes
vous	espérâtes
ils/elles	espérèrent

PLUPERFECT

j'	avais espéré
tu	avais espéré
il/elle/on	avait espéré
nous	avions espéré
vous	aviez espéré
ils/elles	avaient espéré

IMPERATIVE

espère / espérons / espérez

EXAMPLE PHRASES

Il **espéra** qu'ils se reverraient bientôt. **He hoped that they would see each other again soon.**

Si j'étais toi, je n'**espérerais** pas trop qu'il vienne : tu risques d'être déçu.
If I were you, I wouldn't put too much hope in his coming – you could be disappointed.

J'**avais espéré** que tu pourrais venir. **I had hoped that you would be able to come.**

je/j' = I tu = you il = he/it elle = she/it on = we/one nous = we vous = you ils/elles = they

essayer (to try)

PRESENT

j'	essaie
tu	essaies
il/elle/on	essaie
nous	essayons
vous	essayez
ils/elles	essaient

PRESENT SUBJUNCTIVE

j'	essaie
tu	essaies
il/elle/on	essaie
nous	essayions
vous	essayiez
ils/elles	essaient

PERFECT

j'	ai essayé
tu	as essayé
il/elle/on	a essayé
nous	avons essayé
vous	avez essayé
ils/elles	ont essayé

IMPERFECT

j'	essayais
tu	essayais
il/elle/on	essayait
nous	essayions
vous	essayiez
ils/elles	essayaient

PRESENT PARTICIPLE

essayant

PAST PARTICIPLE

essayé

EXAMPLE PHRASES

Elle adorait **essayer** mes vêtements. She loved trying on my clothes.

J'**ai essayé** de t'appeler hier soir. I tried to call you last night.

Essaie de ne pas t'énerver. Try not to get all worked up.

Il faut que j'**essaie** cette nouvelle recette. I must try this new recipe.

Il **essayait** de la comprendre, mais il n'y arrivait pas. He tried to understand her, but he couldn't.

je/j' = I **tu** = you **il** = he/it **elle** = she/it **on** = we/one **nous** = we **vous** = you **ils/elles** = they

essayer

FUTURE

j'	essaierai
tu	essaieras
il/elle/on	essaiera
nous	essaierons
vous	essaierez
ils/elles	essaieront

CONDITIONAL

j'	essaierais
tu	essaierais
il/elle/on	essaierait
nous	essaierions
vous	essaieriez
ils/elles	essaieraient

PAST HISTORIC

j'	essayai
tu	essayas
il/elle/on	essaya
nous	essayâmes
vous	essayâtes
ils/elles	essayèrent

PLUPERFECT

j'	avais essayé
tu	avais essayé
il/elle/on	avait essayé
nous	avions essayé
vous	aviez essayé
ils/elles	avaient essayé

IMPERATIVE

essaie / essayons / essayez

EXAMPLE PHRASES

J'**essaierai** d'aller le voir après le travail demain. **I'll try to go and see him after work tomorrow.**

Ils **essayèrent** de la rattraper. **They tried to catch up with her.**

Je n'**essaierais** pas de lui parler tout de suite si j'étais toi. **I wouldn't try to speak to her right now if I were you.**

Elle **avait essayé** la robe, mais elle ne lui allait pas. **She'd tried on the dress, but it didn't fit her.**

je/j' = I tu = you il = he/it elle = she/it on = we/one nous = we vous = you ils/elles = they

éteindre (to turn off)

PRESENT

j'	**éteins**
tu	**éteins**
il/elle/on	**éteint**
nous	**éteignons**
vous	**éteignez**
ils/elles	**éteignent**

PRESENT SUBJUNCTIVE

j'	**éteigne**
tu	**éteignes**
il/elle/on	**éteigne**
nous	**éteignions**
vous	**éteigniez**
ils/elles	**éteignent**

PERFECT

j'	**ai éteint**
tu	**as éteint**
il/elle/on	**a éteint**
nous	**avons éteint**
vous	**avez éteint**
ils/elles	**ont éteint**

IMPERFECT

j'	**éteignais**
tu	**éteignais**
il/elle/on	**éteignait**
nous	**éteignions**
vous	**éteigniez**
ils/elles	**éteignaient**

PRESENT PARTICIPLE

éteignant

PAST PARTICIPLE

éteint

EXAMPLE PHRASES

N'oubliez pas d'**éteindre** la lumière en sortant. Don't forget to turn off
the light when you leave.

Elle n'**éteint** jamais la lumière dans sa chambre. She never turns off her
bedroom light.

Tu **as éteint** la lumière dans la salle de bain ? Have you turned off the
bathroom light?

Karine, **éteins** la télé, s'il te plaît. Turn off the TV please, Karine.

---

je/j' = I   **tu** = you   **il** = he/it   **elle** = she/it   **on** = we/one   **nous** = we   **vous** = you   **ils/elles** = they

éteindre

FUTURE

j'	**éteindrai**
tu	**éteindras**
il/elle/on	**éteindra**
nous	**éteindrons**
vous	**éteindrez**
ils/elles	**éteindront**

CONDITIONAL

j'	**éteindrais**
tu	**éteindrais**
il/elle/on	**éteindrait**
nous	**éteindrions**
vous	**éteindriez**
ils/elles	**éteindraient**

PAST HISTORIC

j'	**éteignis**
tu	**éteignis**
il/elle/on	**éteignit**
nous	**éteignîmes**
vous	**éteignîtes**
ils/elles	**éteignirent**

PLUPERFECT

j'	**avais éteint**
tu	**avais éteint**
il/elle/on	**avait éteint**
nous	**avions éteint**
vous	**aviez éteint**
ils/elles	**avaient éteint**

IMPERATIVE

éteins / éteignons / éteignez

EXAMPLE PHRASES

J'**éteindrai** tout avant de partir. I'll turn everything off before I leave.

Elle **éteignit** la lumière et s'endormit. She turned off the light and fell asleep.

Il **éteindrait** sa cigarette s'il savait que la fumée te dérange. He'd put out his cigarette if he knew that the smoke bothers you.

Il **avait éteint** son portable en entrant dans le cinéma. He'd turned off his cell on the way into the movie.

je/j' = I **tu** = you **il** = he/it **elle** = she/it **on** = we/one **nous** = we **vous** = you **ils/elles** = they

être (to be)

PRESENT

je **suis**

tu **es**

il/elle/on **est**

nous **sommes**

vous **êtes**

ils/elles **sont**

PRESENT SUBJUNCTIVE

je **sois**

tu **sois**

il/elle/on **soit**

nous **soyons**

vous **soyez**

ils/elles **soient**

PERFECT

j' **ai été**

tu **as été**

il/elle/on **a été**

nous **avons été**

vous **avez été**

ils/elles **ont été**

IMPERFECT

j' **étais**

tu **étais**

il/elle/on **était**

nous **étions**

vous **étiez**

ils/elles **étaient**

PRESENT PARTICIPLE

étant

PAST PARTICIPLE

été

EXAMPLE PHRASES

Quelle heure **est**-il ? – Il **est** dix heures. What time is it? – It's ten o'clock.

Ils ne **sont** pas encore arrivés. They haven't arrived yet.

Sois courageux. Be brave.

Je veux que vous **soyez** particulièrement sages aujourd'hui. I want you to behave particularly well today.

Il **était** professeur de maths dans mon lycée. He was a math teacher in my school.

---

je/j' = I **tu** = you **il** = he/it **elle** = she/it **on** = we/one **nous** = we **vous** = you **ils/elles** = they

être

FUTURE

je	**serai**
tu	**seras**
il/elle/on	**sera**
nous	**serons**
vous	**serez**
ils/elles	**seront**

CONDITIONAL

je	**serais**
tu	**serais**
il/elle/on	**serait**
nous	**serions**
vous	**seriez**
ils/elles	**seraient**

PAST HISTORIC

je	**fus**
tu	**fus**
il/elle/on	**fut**
nous	**fûmes**
vous	**fûtes**
ils/elles	**furent**

PLUPERFECT

j'	**avais été**
tu	**avais été**
il/elle/on	**avait été**
nous	**avions été**
vous	**aviez été**
ils/elles	**avaient été**

IMPERATIVE

sois / soyons / soyez

EXAMPLE PHRASES

Je **serai** chez moi à partir de midi. I'll be at home from noon onwards.

Il **fut** tellement vexé qu'il ne lui parla pas de la soirée. He was so upset that he didn't speak to her all evening.

Nous **serions** contents de vous voir si vous aviez le temps de passer. We'd be happy to see you if you had time to drop by.

Nous étions punis parce que nous n'**avions** pas **été** sages. We were punished because we hadn't been good.

je/j' = I tu = you il = he/it elle = she/it on = we/one nous = we vous = you ils/elles = they

faillir (faire qch to almost do sth)

PRESENT

je	faillis
tu	faillis
il/elle/on	faillit
nous	faillissons
vous	faillissez
ils/elles	faillissent

PRESENT SUBJUNCTIVE

je	faillisse
tu	faillisses
il/elle/on	faillisse
nous	faillissions
vous	faillissiez
ils/elles	faillissent

PERFECT

j'	ai failli
tu	as failli
il/elle/on	a failli
nous	avons failli
vous	avez failli
ils/elles	ont failli

IMPERFECT

je	faillissais
tu	faillissais
il/elle/on	faillissait
nous	faillissions
vous	faillissiez
ils/elles	faillissaient

PRESENT PARTICIPLE

faillissant

PAST PARTICIPLE

failli

EXAMPLE PHRASES

J'**ai failli** tomber. I nearly fell.

Il **a failli** s'énerver. He almost got angry.

Nous **avons failli** rater notre train. We almost missed our train.

Ils **ont failli** ne pas venir. They almost didn't come.

---

je/j' = I   tu = you   il = he/it   elle = she/it   on = we/one   nous = we   vous = you   ils/elles = they

faillir

FUTURE

je	**faillirai**
tu	**failliras**
il/elle/on	**faillira**
nous	**faillirons**
vous	**faillirez**
ils/elles	**failliront**

CONDITIONAL

je	**faillirais**
tu	**faillirais**
il/elle/on	**faillirait**
nous	**faillirions**
vous	**failliriez**
ils/elles	**failliraient**

PAST HISTORIC

je	**faillis**
tu	**faillis**
il/elle/on	**faillit**
nous	**faillîmes**
vous	**faillîtes**
ils/elles	**faillirent**

PLUPERFECT

j'	**avais failli**
tu	**avais failli**
il/elle/on	**avait failli**
nous	**avions failli**
vous	**aviez failli**
ils/elles	**avaient failli**

IMPERATIVE

not used

EXAMPLE PHRASES

Il **faillit** s'en aller sans dire au revoir. He almost left without saying goodbye.

Elle **faillit** pleurer quand ils lui annoncèrent la nouvelle. She almost cried when they told her the news.

Nous **avions failli** nous perdre en venant vous voir ce jour-là. We had almost gotten lost on our way to see you that day.

Ils **avaient failli** se battre, mais la cloche avait sonné au bon moment. They had almost had a fight, but the bell had rung at the right time.

je/j' = I   tu = you   il = he/it   elle = she/it   on = we/one   nous = we   vous = you   ils/elles = they

faire (to do; to make)

PRESENT

je	**fais**
tu	**fais**
il/elle/on	**fait**
nous	**faisons**
vous	**faites**
ils/elles	**font**

PRESENT SUBJUNCTIVE

je	**fasse**
tu	**fasses·**
il/elle/on	**fasse**
nous	**fassions**
vous	**fassiez**
ils/elles	**fassent**

PERFECT

j'	**ai fait**
tu	**as fait**
il/elle/on	**a fait**
nous	**avons fait**
vous	**avez fait**
ils/elles	**ont fait**

IMPERFECT

je	**faisais**
tu	**faisais**
il/elle/on	**faisait**
nous	**faisions**
vous	**faisiez**
ils/elles	**faisaient**

PRESENT PARTICIPLE

faisant

PAST PARTICIPLE

fait

EXAMPLE PHRASES

Qu'est-ce que tu **fais** ? What are you doing?

Qu'est-ce qu'il **a fait** ? What has he done?

Il s'**est fait** couper les cheveux. He's had his hair cut.

J'aimerais que tu **fasses** la vaisselle plus souvent. I'd like you to wash the dishes more often.

Il ne **faisait** jamais son lit. He would never make his bed.

---

je/j' = I   tu = you   il = he/it   elle = she/it   on = we/one   nous = we   vous = you   ils/elles = they

faire

FUTURE

je	**ferai**
tu	**feras**
il/elle/on	**fera**
nous	**ferons**
vous	**ferez**
ils/elles	**feront**

CONDITIONAL

je	**ferais**
tu	**ferais**
il/elle/on	**ferait**
nous	**ferions**
vous	**feriez**
ils/elles	**feraient**

PAST HISTORIC

je	**fis**
tu	**fis**
il/elle/on	**fit**
nous	**fîmes**
vous	**fîtes**
ils/elles	**firent**

PLUPERFECT

j'	**avais fait**
tu	**avais fait**
il/elle/on	**avait fait**
nous	**avions fait**
vous	**aviez fait**
ils/elles	**avaient fait**

IMPERATIVE

fais / faisons / faites

EXAMPLE PHRASES

Demain, nous **ferons** une promenade sur la plage. Tomorrow, we'll go for
a walk on the beach.

Il **fit** semblant de ne pas comprendre. He pretended not to understand.

Si je gagnais à la loterie, je **ferais** le tour du monde. If I won the lottery,
I would take a trip around the world.

Elle **avait fait** un gâteau. She'd made a cake.

Ne **fais** pas l'idiot. Don't behave like an idiot.

je/j' = I **tu** = you **il** = he/it **elle** = she/it **on** = we/one **nous** = we **vous** = you **ils/elles** = they

falloir (to be necessary)

PRESENT

il **faut**

PRESENT SUBJUNCTIVE

il **faille**

PERFECT

il **a fallu**

IMPERFECT

il **fallait**

PRESENT PARTICIPLE

not used

PAST PARTICIPLE

fallu

EXAMPLE PHRASES

Il **faut** se dépêcher ! We have to hurry up!

Il ne **faut** pas paniquer. Let's not panic.

Il **a fallu** que je lui prête ma voiture. I had to lend her my car.

Il me **fallait** de l'argent. I needed money.

falloir

FUTURE

il **faudra**

CONDITIONAL

il **faudrait**

PAST HISTORIC

il **fallut**

PLUPERFECT

il **avait fallu**

IMPERATIVE

not used

EXAMPLE PHRASES

Il **faudra** que tu sois là à 8 heures. You'll have to be there at 8 o'clock.

Il **fallut** qu'ils partent de très bonne heure. They had to leave very early.

Il **faudrait** t'arrêter de fumer. You should stop smoking.

Il **avait fallu** nettoyer toute la maison. We'd had to clean the whole house.

---

je/j' = I **tu** = you **il** = he/it **elle** = she/it **on** = we/one **nous** = we **vous** = you **ils/elles** = they

finir (to finish)

PRESENT

je	**finis**
tu	**finis**
il/elle/on	**finit**
nous	**finissons**
vous	**finissez**
ils/elles	**finissent**

PRESENT SUBJUNCTIVE

je	**finisse**
tu	**finisses**
il/elle/on	**finisse**
nous	**finissions**
vous	**finissiez**
ils/elles	**finissent**

PERFECT

j'	**ai fini**
tu	**as fini**
il/elle/on	**a fini**
nous	**avons fini**
vous	**avez fini**
ils/elles	**ont fini**

IMPERFECT

je	**finissais**
tu	**finissais**
il/elle/on	**finissait**
nous	**finissions**
vous	**finissiez**
ils/elles	**finissaient**

PRESENT PARTICIPLE

finissant

PAST PARTICIPLE

fini

EXAMPLE PHRASES

Je **finis** mes cours à 17h. I finish my classes at 5 pm.

J'**ai fini** ! I've finished!

Il faut que je **finisse** mon livre avant de commencer celui-là. I have to finish my book before I start that one.

Elle **finissait** toujours en retard. She'd always finish late.

finir

FUTURE

je	**finirai**
tu	**finiras**
il/elle/on	**finira**
nous	**finirons**
vous	**finirez**
ils/elles	**finiront**

CONDITIONAL

je	**finirais**
tu	**finirais**
il/elle/on	**finirait**
nous	**finirions**
vous	**finiriez**
ils/elles	**finiraient**

PAST HISTORIC

je	**finis**
tu	**finis**
il/elle/on	**finit**
nous	**finîmes**
vous	**finîtes**
ils/elles	**finirent**

PLUPERFECT

j'	**avais fini**
tu	**avais fini**
il/elle/on	**avait fini**
nous	**avions fini**
vous	**aviez fini**
ils/elles	**avaient fini**

IMPERATIVE

finis / finissons / finissez

EXAMPLE PHRASES

Je **finirai** mes devoirs demain. **I'll finish my homework tomorrow.**

Il **finit** son dîner et alla se coucher. **He finished his dinner and went to bed.**

Si on l'ignorait, elle **finirait** par comprendre. **If we ignored her, she'd eventually understand.**

Elle n'**avait** pas **fini** de manger quand nous sommes arrivés. **She hadn't finished eating when we arrived.**

Finis ta soupe ! **Finish your soup!**

je/j' = I   **tu** = you   **il** = he/it   **elle** = she/it   **on** = we/one   **nous** = we   **vous** = you   **ils/elles** = they

fuir (to flee; to leak)

PRESENT

je	**fuis**
tu	**fuis**
il/elle/on	**fuit**
nous	**fuyons**
vous	**fuyez**
ils/elles	**fuient**

PRESENT SUBJUNCTIVE

je	**fuie**
tu	**fuies**
il/elle/on	**fuie**
nous	**fuyions**
vous	**fuyiez**
ils/elles	**fuient**

PERFECT

j'	**ai fui**
tu	**as fui**
il/elle/on	**a fui**
nous	**avons fui**
vous	**avez fui**
ils/elles	**ont fui**

IMPERFECT

je	**fuyais**
tu	**fuyais**
il/elle/on	**fuyait**
nous	**fuyions**
vous	**fuyiez**
ils/elles	**fuyaient**

PRESENT PARTICIPLE
fuyant

PAST PARTICIPLE
fui

EXAMPLE PHRASES

J'ai un stylo qui **fuit**. My pen leaks.

Ils **ont fui** leur pays. They fled their country.

Il ne faut pas que tu le **fuies** comme ça. You mustn't run away from him like that.

Le robinet **fuyait**. The faucet was dripping.

fuir

FUTURE

je	**fuirai**
tu	**fuiras**
il/elle/on	**fuira**
nous	**fuirons**
vous	**fuirez**
ils/elles	**fuiront**

CONDITIONAL

je	**fuirais**
tu	**fuirais**
il/elle/on	**fuirait**
nous	**fuirions**
vous	**fuiriez**
ils/elles	**fuiraient**

PAST HISTORIC

je	**fuis**
tu	**fuis**
il/elle/on	**fuit**
nous	**fuîmes**
vous	**fuîtes**
ils/elles	**fuirent**

PLUPERFECT

j'	**avais fui**
tu	**avais fui**
il/elle/on	**avait fui**
nous	**avions fui**
vous	**aviez fui**
ils/elles	**avaient fui**

IMPERATIVE

fuis / fuyons / fuyez

EXAMPLE PHRASES

Il **fuira** toujours les responsabilités. He will always run away from responsibilities.

Beaucoup de gens **fuirent** vers le sud. A lot of people fled south.

La machine à laver **fuirait** si on la remplissait trop. The washing machine would leak if we overloaded it.

Ils **avaient fui** leur village et s'étaient réfugiés dans les montagnes. They had fled from their village and had taken refuge in the mountains.

je/j' = I **tu** = you **il** = he/it **elle** = she/it **on** = we/one **nous** = we **vous** = you **ils/elles** = they

haïr (to hate)

PRESENT

je	hais
tu	hais
il/elle/on	hait
nous	haïssons
vous	haïssez
ils/elles	haïssent

PRESENT SUBJUNCTIVE

je	haïsse
tu	haïsses
il/elle/on	haïsse
nous	haïssions
vous	haïssiez
ils/elles	haïssent

PERFECT

j'	ai haï
tu	as haï
il/elle/on	a haï
nous	avons haï
vous	avez haï
ils/elles	ont haï

IMPERFECT

je	haïssais
tu	haïssais
il/elle/on	haïssait
nous	haïssions
vous	haïssiez
ils/elles	haïssaient

PRESENT PARTICIPLE

haïssant

PAST PARTICIPLE

haï

EXAMPLE PHRASES

Je te **hais** ! I hate you!

Ils se **haïssent**. They hate each other.

Il ne faut pas que tu le **haïsses** pour ça. You mustn't hate him for that.

Elle **haïssait** tout le monde. She hated everyone.

haïr

FUTURE

je	**haïrai**
tu	**haïras**
il/elle/on	**haïra**
nous	**haïrons**
vous	**haïrez**
ils/elles	**haïront**

CONDITIONAL

je	**haïrais**
tu	**haïrais**
il/elle/on	**haïrait**
nous	**haïrions**
vous	**haïriez**
ils/elles	**haïraient**

PAST HISTORIC

je	**haïs**
tu	**haïs**
il/elle/on	**haït**
nous	**haïmes**
vous	**haïtes**
ils/elles	**haïrent**

PLUPERFECT

j'	**avais haï**
tu	**avais haï**
il/elle/on	**avait haï**
nous	**avions haï**
vous	**aviez haï**
ils/elles	**avaient haï**

IMPERATIVE

hais / haïssons / haïssez

EXAMPLE PHRASES

Je la **haïrai** toujours. I'll always hate her.

Elle le **haït** pour ce qu'il venait de dire. She hated him for what he'd just said.

Elle me **haïrait** si je n'allais pas voir ses parents avec elle. She'd hate me if I didn't go to see her parents with her.

Elle m'**avait haï** durant toutes ces années et maintenant nous étions les meilleures amies du monde. She had hated me all these years, and now we were the best of friends.

je/j' = I tu = you il = he/it elle = she/it on = we/one nous = we vous = you ils/elles = they

s'inquiéter (to worry)

PRESENT
je **m'inquiète**
tu **t'inquiètes**
il/elle/on **s'inquiète**
nous **nous inquiétons**
vous **vous inquiétez**
ils/elles **s'inquiètent**

PRESENT SUBJUNCTIVE
je **m'inquiète**
tu **t'inquiètes**
il/elle/on **s'inquiète**
nous **nous inquiétions**
vous **vous inquiétiez**
ils/elles **s'inquiètent**

PERFECT
je **me suis inquiété(e)**
tu **t'es inquiété(e)**
il/elle/on **s'est inquiété(e)**
nous **nous sommes inquiété(e)s**
vous **vous êtes inquiété(e)(s)**
ils/elles **se sont inquiété(e)s**

IMPERFECT
je **m'inquiétais**
tu **t'inquiétais**
il/elle/on **s'inquiétait**
nous **nous inquiétions**
vous **vous inquiétiez**
ils/elles **s'inquiétaient**

PRESENT PARTICIPLE
s'inquiétant

PAST PARTICIPLE
inquiété

EXAMPLE PHRASES
Elle **s'inquiète** toujours si je suis en retard. She always worries if I'm late.
Comme je savais où tu étais, je ne **me suis** pas **inquiétée**. As I knew where you were, I didn't worry.
Je ne veux pas qu'ils **s'inquiètent**. I don't want them to worry.
Ça **m'inquiétait** un peu que tu ne nous aies pas téléphoné. I was a little worried that you hadn't called us.

s'inquiéter

FUTURE

je	m'inquiéterai
tu	t'inquiéteras
il/elle/on	s'inquiétera
nous	nous inquiéterons
vous	vous inquiéterez
ils/elles	s'inquiéteront

CONDITIONAL

je	m'inquiéterais
tu	t'inquiéterais
il/elle/on	s'inquiéterait
nous	nous inquiéterions
vous	vous inquiéteriez
ils/elles	s'inquiéteraient

PAST HISTORIC

je	m'inquiétai
tu	t'inquiétas
il/elle/on	s'inquiéta
nous	nous inquiétâmes
vous	vous inquiétâtes
ils/elles	s'inquiétèrent

PLUPERFECT

je	m'étais inquiété(e)
tu	t'étais inquiété(e)
il/elle/on	s'était inquiété(e)
nous	nous étions inquiété(e)s
vous	vous étiez inquiété(e)(s)
ils/elles	s'étaient inquiété(e)s

IMPERATIVE

inquiète-toi / inquiétons-nous / inquiétez-vous

EXAMPLE PHRASES

Mes parents **s'inquiéteront** si j'y vais toute seule. **My parents will worry if I go there on my own.**

Il **s'inquiéta** pour elle. **He worried about her.**

Je **m'inquiéterais** moins si tu n'étais pas si loin. **I'd worry less if you weren't so far away.**

Comme ils savaient qu'elle était avec Vincent, ils ne **s'étaient** pas **inquiétés**. **As they knew that she was with Vincent, they hadn't worried.**

Ne **t'inquiète** pas, je ne rentrerai pas tard. **Don't worry, I won't be late coming home.**

je/j' = I   tu = you   il = he/it   elle = she/it   on = we/one   nous = we   vous = you   ils/elles = they

interdire (to forbid)

PRESENT

j'	interdis
tu	interdis
il/elle/on	interdit
nous	interdisons
vous	interdisez
ils/elles	interdisent

PRESENT SUBJUNCTIVE

j'	interdise
tu	interdises
il/elle/on	interdise
nous	interdisions
vous	interdisiez
ils/elles	interdisent

PERFECT

j'	ai interdit
tu	as interdit
il/elle/on	a interdit
nous	avons interdit
vous	avez interdit
ils/elles	ont interdit

IMPERFECT

j'	interdisais
tu	interdisais
il/elle/on	interdisait
nous	interdisions
vous	interdisiez
ils/elles	interdisaient

PRESENT PARTICIPLE

interdisant

PAST PARTICIPLE

interdit

EXAMPLE PHRASES

Je t'**interdis** de toucher à ça. I forbid you to touch this.

Ses parents lui **ont interdit** de sortir. His parents have forbidden him to go out.

Interdisons-leur de regarder la télé ce week-end. Let's ban them from watching TV over the weekend.

Elle nous **interdisait** de jouer avec lui. She forbade us to play with him.

interdire

FUTURE

j'	**interdirai**
tu	**interdiras**
il/elle/on	**interdira**
nous	**interdirons**
vous	**interdirez**
ils/elles	**interdiront**

CONDITIONAL

j'	**interdirais**
tu	**interdirais**
il/elle/on	**interdirait**
nous	**interdirions**
vous	**interdiriez**
ils/elles	**interdiraient**

PAST HISTORIC

j'	**interdis**
tu	**interdis**
il/elle/on	**interdit**
nous	**interdîmes**
vous	**interdîtes**
ils/elles	**interdirent**

PLUPERFECT

j'	**avais interdit**
tu	**avais interdit**
il/elle/on	**avait interdit**
nous	**avions interdit**
vous	**aviez interdit**
ils/elles	**avaient interdit**

IMPERATIVE

interdis / interdisons / interdisez

EXAMPLE PHRASES

Si vous n'êtes pas raisonnables, je vous **interdirai** de sortir du jardin. **If you're not sensible, I'll forbid you to leave the yard.**

À partir de ce jour, ils nous **interdirent** de la voir. **From that day on, they forbade us to see her.**

Si ma fille me parlait comme ça, je lui **interdirais** de sortir avec ses copines. **If my daughter spoke to me like that, I'd keep her from going out with her friends.**

Elle nous **avait interdit** de lui en parler. **She had forbidden us to tell him about it.**

je/j' = I tu = you il = he/it elle = she/it on = we/one nous = we vous = you ils/elles = they

jeter (to throw)

PRESENT

je	**jette**
tu	**jettes**
il/elle/on	**jette**
nous	**jetons**
vous	**jetez**
ils/elles	**jettent**

PRESENT SUBJUNCTIVE

je	**jette**
tu	**jettes**
il/elle/on	**jette**
nous	**jetions**
vous	**jetiez**
ils/elles	**jettent**

PERFECT

j'	**ai jeté**
tu	**as jeté**
il/elle/on	**a jeté**
nous	**avons jeté**
vous	**avez jeté**
ils/elles	**ont jeté**

IMPERFECT

je	**jetais**
tu	**jetais**
il/elle/on	**jetait**
nous	**jetions**
vous	**jetiez**
ils/elles	**jetaient**

PRESENT PARTICIPLE

jetant

PAST PARTICIPLE

jeté

EXAMPLE PHRASES

Ils ne **jettent** jamais rien. **They never throw anything away.**

Elle **a jeté** son chewing-gum par la fenêtre. **She threw her chewing gum out of the window.**

Ne **jette** pas de papiers par terre. **Don't throw litter on the ground.**

Il faut qu'on **jette** tous ces vieux jouets cassés. **We'll have to throw away all these old broken toys.**

Il **jetait** toujours ses vêtements par terre. **He'd always throw his clothes on the floor.**

je/j' = I tu = you il = he/it elle = she/it on = we/one nous = we vous = you ils/elles = they

jeter

FUTURE

je	**jetterai**
tu	**jetteras**
il/elle/on	**jettera**
nous	**jetterons**
vous	**jetterez**
ils/elles	**jetteront**

CONDITIONAL

je	**jetterais**
tu	**jetterais**
il/elle/on	**jetterait**
nous	**jetterions**
vous	**jetteriez**
ils/elles	**jetteraient**

PAST HISTORIC

je	**jetai**
tu	**jetas**
il/elle/on	**jeta**
nous	**jetâmes**
vous	**jetâtes**
ils/elles	**jetèrent**

PLUPERFECT

j'	**avais jeté**
tu	**avais jeté**
il/elle/on	**avait jeté**
nous	**avions jeté**
vous	**aviez jeté**
ils/elles	**avaient jeté**

IMPERATIVE

jette / jetons / jetez

EXAMPLE PHRASES

Je **jetterai** tout ça à la poubelle. **I'll throw all this in the garbage can.**

Il **jeta** sa veste sur la chaise et répondit au téléphone. **He threw his jacket on the chair and answered the phone.**

Je **jetterais** bien tous ces vieux magazines. **I'd really like to throw all these old magazines away.**

Elle jurait qu'elle n'**avait** rien **jeté**. **She swore she hadn't thrown anything away.**

je/j' = I tu = you il = he/it elle = she/it on = we/one nous = we vous = you ils/elles = they

joindre (to join)

PRESENT

je	**joins**
tu	**joins**
il/elle/on	**joint**
nous	**joignons**
vous	**joignez**
ils/elles	**joignent**

PRESENT SUBJUNCTIVE

je	**joigne**
tu	**joignes**
il/elle/on	**joigne**
nous	**joignions**
vous	**joigniez**
ils/elles	**joignent**

PERFECT

j'	**ai joint**
tu	**as joint**
il/elle/on	**a joint**
nous	**avons joint**
vous	**avez joint**
ils/elles	**ont joint**

IMPERFECT

je	**joignais**
tu	**joignais**
il/elle/on	**joignait**
nous	**joignions**
vous	**joigniez**
ils/elles	**joignaient**

PRESENT PARTICIPLE

joignant

PAST PARTICIPLE

joint

EXAMPLE PHRASES

Où est-ce qu'on peut te **joindre** ce week-end ? Where can we contact you this weekend?

Il n'est pas facile à **joindre**. He's not easy to reach.

Je vous **ai joint** un plan de la ville. I have enclosed a map of the town.

je/j' = I   **tu** = you   **il** = he/it   **elle** = she/it   **on** = we/one   **nous** = we   **vous** = you   **ils/elles** = they

joindre

FUTURE

je	**joindrai**
tu	**joindras**
il/elle/on	**joindra**
nous	**joindrons**
vous	**joindrez**
ils/elles	**joindront**

CONDITIONAL

je	**joindrais**
tu	**joindrais**
il/elle/on	**joindrait**
nous	**joindrions**
vous	**joindriez**
ils/elles	**joindraient**

PAST HISTORIC

je	**joignis**
tu	**joignis**
il/elle/on	**joignit**
nous	**joignîmes**
vous	**joignîtes**
ils/elles	**joignirent**

PLUPERFECT

j'	**avais joint**
tu	**avais joint**
il/elle/on	**avait joint**
nous	**avions joint**
vous	**aviez joint**
ils/elles	**avaient joint**

IMPERATIVE

joins / joignons / joignez

EXAMPLE PHRASES

Il **joignit** les mains et se mit à prier. He put his hands together and started to pray.

On **avait joint** les deux tables. We'd put the two tables together.

Nous **avions joint** nos efforts. It had been a joint effort.

je/j' = I **tu** = you **il** = he/it **elle** = she/it **on** = we/one **nous** = we **vous** = you **ils/elles** = they

lever (to lift)

PRESENT

je	**lève**
tu	**lèves**
il/elle/on	**lève**
nous	**levons**
vous	**levez**
ils/elles	**lèvent**

PRESENT SUBJUNCTIVE

je	**lève**
tu	**lèves**
il/elle/on	**lève**
nous	**levions**
vous	**leviez**
ils/elles	**lèvent**

PERFECT

j'	**ai levé**
tu	**as levé**
il/elle/on	**a levé**
nous	**avons levé**
vous	**avez levé**
ils/elles	**ont levé**

IMPERFECT

je	**levais**
tu	**levais**
il/elle/on	**levait**
nous	**levions**
vous	**leviez**
ils/elles	**levaient**

PRESENT PARTICIPLE

levant

PAST PARTICIPLE

levé

EXAMPLE PHRASES

Je me **lève** tous les matins à sept heures. I get up at seven every day.

Elle **a levé** la main pour répondre à la question. She put her hand up to answer the question.

Levons notre verre à ta réussite. Let's raise our glasses to your success.

lever

FUTURE

je	**lèverai**
tu	**lèveras**
il/elle/on	**lèvera**
nous	**lèverons**
vous	**lèverez**
ils/elles	**lèveront**

CONDITIONAL

je	**lèverais**
tu	**lèverais**
il/elle/on	**lèverait**
nous	**lèverions**
vous	**lèveriez**
ils/elles	**lèveraient**

PAST HISTORIC

je	**levai**
tu	**levas**
il/elle/on	**leva**
nous	**levâmes**
vous	**levâtes**
ils/elles	**levèrent**

PLUPERFECT

j'	**avais levé**
tu	**avais levé**
il/elle/on	**avait levé**
nous	**avions levé**
vous	**aviez levé**
ils/elles	**avaient levé**

IMPERATIVE

lève / **levons** / **levez**

EXAMPLE PHRASES

Je ne **lèverai** pas le petit doigt pour l'aider. **I won't lift a finger to help him.**

Elle **leva** les yeux et vit qu'il était en train de tricher. **She looked up and saw that he was cheating.**

Si mon père était encore là, il **lèverait** les bras au ciel. **If my dad were still here, he'd throw his arms up in despair.**

Levez le doigt ! **Raise your hand!**

je/j' = I   tu = you   il = he/it   elle = she/it   on = we/one   nous = we   vous = you   ils/elles = they

lire (to read)

PRESENT

je	lis
tu	lis
il/elle/on	lit
nous	lisons
vous	lisez
ils/elles	lisent

PRESENT SUBJUNCTIVE

je	lise
tu	lises
il/elle/on	lise
nous	lisions
vous	lisiez
ils/elles	lisent

PERFECT

j'	ai lu
tu	as lu
il/elle/on	a lu
nous	avons lu
vous	avez lu
ils/elles	ont lu

IMPERFECT

je	lisais
tu	lisais
Il/elle/on	lisait
nous	lisions
vous	lisiez
ils/elles	lisaient

PRESENT PARTICIPLE

lisant

PAST PARTICIPLE

lu

EXAMPLE PHRASES

Il **lit** beaucoup. He reads a lot.
Vous **avez lu** "Madame Bovary" ? Have you read "Madame Bovary?"
J'aimerais que tu **lises** ce livre. I'd like you to read this book.
Elle lui **lisait** une histoire. She was reading him a story.

lire

FUTURE

je	**lirai**
tu	**liras**
il/elle/on	**lira**
nous	**lirons**
vous	**lirez**
ils/elles	**liront**

CONDITIONAL

je	**lirais**
tu	**lirais**
il/elle/on	**lirait**
nous	**lirions**
vous	**liriez**
ils/elles	**liraient**

PAST HISTORIC

je	**lus**
tu	**lus**
il/elle/on	**lut**
nous	**lûmes**
vous	**lûtes**
ils/elles	**lurent**

PLUPERFECT

j'	**avais lu**
tu	**avais lu**
il/elle/on	**avait lu**
nous	**avions lu**
vous	**aviez lu**
ils/elles	**avaient lu**

IMPERATIVE

lis / lisons / lisez

EXAMPLE PHRASES

Je le **lirai** dans l'avion. I'll read it on the plane.

Il **lut** la lettre à haute voix. He read the letter aloud.

Je **lirais** plus si j'avais le temps. I'd read more if I had time.

La maîtresse s'aperçut qu'il n'**avait** pas **lu** le livre. The teacher realized that he hadn't read the book.

Lisez bien les instructions. Read the instructions carefully.

je/j' = I **tu** = you **il** = he/it **elle** = she/it **on** = we/one **nous** = we **vous** = you **ils/elles** = they

manger (to eat)

PRESENT

je	mange
tu	manges
il/elle/on	mange
nous	mangeons
vous	mangez
ils/elles	mangent

PRESENT SUBJUNCTIVE

je	mange
tu	manges
il/elle/on	mange
nous	mangions
vous	mangiez
ils/elles	mangent

PERFECT

j'	ai mangé
tu	as mangé
il/elle/on	a mangé
nous	avons mangé
vous	avez mangé
ils/elles	ont mangé

IMPERFECT

je	mangeais
tu	mangeais
il/elle/on	mangeait
nous	mangions
vous	mangiez
ils/elles	mangeaient

PRESENT PARTICIPLE

mangeant

PAST PARTICIPLE

mangé

EXAMPLE PHRASES

Nous ne **mangeons** pas souvent ensemble. We don't often eat together.

Tu **as** assez **mangé** ? Have you had enough to eat?

Il faut que je **mange** avant de partir. I have to eat before I leave.

Ils **mangeaient** en regardant la télé. They were eating while watching TV.

---

je/j' = I   tu = you   il = he/it   elle = she/it   on = we/one   nous = we   vous = you   ils/elles = they

manger

FUTURE

je	mangerai
tu	mangeras
il/elle/on	mangera
nous	mangerons
vous	mangerez
ils/elles	mangeront

CONDITIONAL

je	mangerais
tu	mangerais
il/elle/on	mangerait
nous	mangerions
vous	mangeriez
ils/elles	mangeraient

PAST HISTORIC

je	mangeai
tu	mangeas
il/elle/on	mangea
nous	mangeâmes
vous	mangeâtes
ils/elles	mangèrent

PLUPERFECT

j'	avais mangé
tu	avais mangé
il/elle/on	avait mangé
nous	avions mangé
vous	aviez mangé
ils/elles	avaient mangé

IMPERATIVE

mange / mangeons / mangez

EXAMPLE PHRASES

Je **mangerai** plus tard. I'll eat later on.

Il **mangea** rapidement et retourna travailler. He ate quickly and went back to work.

Je **mangerais** bien le reste si je n'avais pas peur de grossir. I'd gladly eat the rest if I wasn't afraid of putting on weight.

Comme ils **avaient** bien **mangé** le midi, ils ont tenu jusqu'au soir. As they had had a good lunch, they kept going until dinner time.

Mange ta soupe. Eat your soup.

je/j' = I tu = you il = he/it elle = she/it on = we/one nous = we vous = you ils/elles = they

maudire (to curse)

PRESENT

je	maudis
tu	maudis
il/elle/on	maudit
nous	maudissons
vous	maudissez
ils/elles	maudissent

PRESENT SUBJUNCTIVE

je	maudisse
tu	maudisses
il/elle/on	maudisse
nous	maudissions
vous	maudissiez
ils/elles	maudissent

PERFECT

j'	ai maudit
tu	as maudit
il/elle/on	a maudit
nous	avons maudit
vous	avez maudit
ils/elles	ont maudit

IMPERFECT

je	maudissais
tu	maudissais
il/elle/on	maudissait
nous	maudissions
vous	maudissiez
ils/elles	maudissaient

PRESENT PARTICIPLE
maudissant

PAST PARTICIPLE
maudit

EXAMPLE PHRASES

Ils **maudissent** leurs ennemis. They curse their enemies.

Je **maudis** le jour où je l'ai rencontrée. I curse the day I met her.

Elle me **maudissait** en nettoyant mon manteau couvert de boue. She cursed me as she was cleaning my muddy coat.

Ce **maudit** stylo ne marche pas ! This blasted pen doesn't work!

maudire

FUTURE

je	**maudirai**
tu	**maudiras**
il/elle/on	**maudira**
nous	**maudirons**
vous	**maudirez**
ils/elles	**maudiront**

CONDITIONAL

je	**maudirais**
tu	**maudirais**
il/elle/on	**maudirait**
nous	**maudirions**
vous	**maudiriez**
ils/elles	**maudiraient**

PAST HISTORIC

je	**maudis**
tu	**maudis**
il/elle/on	**maudit**
nous	**maudîmes**
vous	**maudîtes**
ils/elles	**maudirent**

PLUPERFECT

j'	**avais maudit**
tu	**avais maudit**
il/elle/on	**avait maudit**
nous	**avions maudit**
vous	**aviez maudit**
ils/elles	**avaient maudit**

IMPERATIVE

maudis / maudissons / maudissez

EXAMPLE PHRASES

Je les **maudirai** jusqu'à ma mort. I'll curse them till the day I die.

Il la **maudit** pour sa stupidité. He cursed her for her stupidity.

Je te **maudirais** si tu arrivais en retard. I'd curse you if you arrived late.

Nous les **avions maudits** de nous avoir laissés les attendre sous la pluie.
We had cursed them for making us wait for them in the rain.

je/j' = I   tu = you   il = he/it   elle = she/it   on = we/one   nous = we   vous = you   ils/elles = they

mentir (to lie)

PRESENT

je	**mens**
tu	**mens**
il/elle/on	**ment**
nous	**mentons**
vous	**mentez**
ils/elles	**mentent**

PRESENT SUBJUNCTIVE

je	**mente**
tu	**mentes**
il/elle/on	**mente**
nous	**mentions**
vous	**mentiez**
ils/elles	**mentent**

PERFECT

j'	**ai menti**
tu	**as menti**
il/elle/on	**a menti**
nous	**avons menti**
vous	**avez menti**
ils/elles	**ont menti**

IMPERFECT

je	**mentais**
tu	**mentais**
il/elle/on	**mentait**
nous	**mentions**
vous	**mentiez**
ils/elles	**mentaient**

PRESENT PARTICIPLE

mentant

PAST PARTICIPLE

menti

EXAMPLE PHRASES

Je ne **mens** jamais. I never lie.

Il lui **a menti**. He lied to her.

Je ne veux pas que tu me **mentes**. I don't want you to lie to me.

Elle savait qu'il **mentait**. She knew that he was lying.

---

je/j' = I   tu = you   il = he/it   elle = she/it   on = we/one   nous = we   vous = you   ils/elles = they

mentir

FUTURE

je	mentirai
tu	mentiras
il/elle/on	mentira
nous	mentirons
vous	mentirez
ils/elles	mentiront

CONDITIONAL

je	mentirais
tu	mentirais
il/elle/on	mentirait
nous	mentirions
vous	mentiriez
ils/elles	mentiraient

PAST HISTORIC

je	mentis
tu	mentis
il/elle/on	mentit
nous	mentîmes
vous	mentîtes
ils/elles	mentirent

PLUPERFECT

j'	avais menti
tu	avais menti
il/elle/on	avait menti
nous	avions menti
vous	aviez menti
ils/elles	avaient menti

IMPERATIVE

mens / mentons / mentez

EXAMPLE PHRASES

Je **mentirai** s'il le faut. I'll lie if I have to.

Il **mentit** pour qu'on le laisse tranquille. He lied so that he'd be left alone.

Elle ne **mentirait** pas si tu ne lui faisais pas aussi peur. She wouldn't lie if you didn't frighten her so much.

Il **avait menti** pour ne pas la contrarier. He had lied in order not to upset her.

Ne **mens** pas, s'il te plaît. Please don't lie.

je/j' = I tu = you il = he/it elle = she/it on = we/one nous = we vous = you ils/elles = they

mettre (to put)

PRESENT

je	**mets**
tu	**mets**
il/elle/on	**met**
nous	**mettons**
vous	**mettez**
ils/elles	**mettent**

PRESENT SUBJUNCTIVE

je	**mette**
tu	**mettes**
il/elle/on	**mette**
nous	**mettions**
vous	**mettiez**
ils/elles	**mettent**

PERFECT

j'	**ai mis**
tu	**as mis**
il/elle/on	**a mis**
nous	**avons mis**
vous	**avez mis**
ils/elles	**ont mis**

IMPERFECT

je	**mettais**
tu	**mettais**
il/elle/on	**mettait**
nous	**mettions**
vous	**mettiez**
ils/elles	**mettaient**

PRESENT PARTICIPLE

mettant

PAST PARTICIPLE

mis

EXAMPLE PHRASES

Il **met** du gel dans ses cheveux. He puts gel in his hair.

Où est-ce que tu **as mis** les clés ? Where have you put the keys?

Il faut que je **mette** le gâteau au four. I have to put the cake in the oven.

Elle **mettait** toujours des heures à s'habiller. She would always take hours
to get dressed.

---

je/j' = I   tu = you   il = he/it   elle = she/it   on = we/one   nous = we   vous = you   ils/elles = they

mettre

FUTURE

je	**mettrai**
tu	**mettras**
il/elle/on	**mettra**
nous	**mettrons**
vous	**mettrez**
ils/elles	**mettront**

CONDITIONAL

je	**mettrais**
tu	**mettrais**
il/elle/on	**mettrait**
nous	**mettrions**
vous	**mettriez**
ils/elles	**mettraient**

PAST HISTORIC

je	**mis**
tu	**mis**
il/elle/on	**mit**
nous	**mîmes**
vous	**mîtes**
ils/elles	**mirent**

PLUPERFECT

j'	**avais mis**
tu	**avais mis**
il/elle/on	**avait mis**
nous	**avions mis**
vous	**aviez mis**
ils/elles	**avaient mis**

IMPERATIVE

mets / mettons / mettez

EXAMPLE PHRASES

Je **mettrai** ma robe rose demain. I'll wear my pink dress tomorrow.

Elle **mit** la bouilloire à chauffer. She put the kettle on.

Je **mettrais** une robe si tu en mettais une aussi. I'd put on a dress if you'd put one on too.

J'**avais mis** le livre sur la table. I had put the book on the table.

Mets ton manteau ! Put your coat on!

je/j' = I   tu = you   il = he/it   elle = she/it   on = we/one   nous = we   vous = you   ils/elles = they

monter (to go up; to take up)

PRESENT		**PRESENT SUBJUNCTIVE**	
je	monte	je	monte
tu	montes	tu	montes
il/elle/on	monte	il/elle/on	monte
nous	montons	nous	montions
vous	montez	vous	montiez
ils/elles	montent	ils/elles	montent

PERFECT		**IMPERFECT**	
je	suis monté(e)	je	montais
tu	es monté(e)	tu	montais
il/elle/on	est monté(e)	il/elle/on	montait
nous	sommes monté(e)s	nous	montions
vous	êtes monté(e)(s)	vous	montiez
ils/elles	sont monté(e)s	ils/elles	montaient

PRESENT PARTICIPLE	**PAST PARTICIPLE**
montant	monté

In the perfect and the pluperfect, use the auxiliary "avoir" when there is a direct object.

EXAMPLE PHRASES

Je **monte** ces escaliers cent fois par jour. I go up these stairs a hundred times a day.

Hier, je **suis montée** à cheval pour la première fois. Yesterday, I went horseback riding for the first time.

Il s'est tordu la cheville en **montant** à une échelle. He twisted his ankle going up a ladder.

---

je/j' = I   **tu** = you   **il** = he/it   **elle** = she/it   **on** = we/one   **nous** = we   **vous** = you   **ils/elles** = they

monter

FUTURE

je	**monterai**
tu	**monteras**
il/elle/on	**montera**
nous	**monterons**
vous	**monterez**
ils/elles	**monteront**

CONDITIONAL

je	**monterais**
tu	**monterais**
il/elle/on	**monterait**
nous	**monterions**
vous	**monteriez**
ils/elles	**monteraient**

PAST HISTORIC

je	**montai**
tu	**montas**
il/elle/on	**monta**
nous	**montâmes**
vous	**montâtes**
ils/elles	**montèrent**

PLUPERFECT

j'	**étais monté(e)**
tu	**étais monté(e)**
il/elle/on	**était monté(e)**
nous	**étions monté(e)s**
vous	**étiez monté(e)(s)**
ils/elles	**étaient monté(e)s**

IMPERATIVE

monte / montons / montez

EXAMPLE PHRASES

Je **monterai** lui dire bonsoir dans cinq minutes. I'll go up to say goodnight to her in five minutes.

Il **monta** les escaliers en courant et sonna à la porte. He ran up the stairs and rang the bell.

Je **monterais** en haut de la tour si je n'avais pas tant le vertige. I'd go up the tower if I wasn't so scared of heights.

Comme elle était malade, je lui **avais monté** son dîner. As she was ill, I had taken her dinner up to her.

Monte dans la voiture, je t'y emmène. Get into the car; I'll take you there.

je/j' = I   tu = you   il = he/it   elle = she/it   on = we/one   nous = we   vous = you   ils/elles = they

mordre (to bite)

PRESENT

je	mords
tu	mords
il/elle/on	mord
nous	mordons
vous	mordez
ils/elles	mordent

PRESENT SUBJUNCTIVE

je	morde
tu	mordes
il/elle/on	morde
nous	mordions
vous	mordiez
ils/elles	mordent

PERFECT

j'	ai mordu
tu	as mordu
il/elle/on	a mordu
nous	avons mordu
vous	avez mordu
ils/elles	ont mordu

IMPERFECT

je	mordais
tu	mordais
il/elle/on	mordait
nous	mordions
vous	mordiez
ils/elles	mordaient

PRESENT PARTICIPLE

mordant

PAST PARTICIPLE

mordu

EXAMPLE PHRASES

Il ne va pas te **mordre** ! He won't bite you!

Attention, il **mord** ! Watch out, he bites!

Le chien m'**a mordue**. The dog bit me.

Je me **suis mordu** la langue. I bit my tongue.

mordre

FUTURE

je	**mordrai**
tu	**mordras**
il/elle/on	**mordra**
nous	**mordrons**
vous	**mordrez**
ils/elles	**mordront**

CONDITIONAL

je	**mordrais**
tu	**mordrais**
il/elle/on	**mordrait**
nous	**mordrions**
vous	**mordriez**
ils/elles	**mordraient**

PAST HISTORIC

je	**mordis**
tu	**mordis**
il/elle/on	**mordit**
nous	**mordîmes**
vous	**mordîtes**
ils/elles	**mordirent**

PLUPERFECT

j'	**avais mordu**
tu	**avais mordu**
il/elle/on	**avait mordu**
nous	**avions mordu**
vous	**aviez mordu**
ils/elles	**avaient mordu**

IMPERATIVE

mords / mordons / mordez

EXAMPLE PHRASES

Il ne te **mordra** pas. He won't bite you.

Elle lui **mordit** le doigt et partit se cacher. She bit his finger and ran off to hide.

Il ne **mordrait** jamais personne. He would never bite anybody.

Le chien l'**avait mordu** au mollet. The dog had bitten him on the shin.

je/j' = I **tu** = you **il** = he/it **elle** = she/it **on** = we/one **nous** = we **vous** = you **ils/elles** = they

moudre (to grind)

PRESENT

je	**mouds**
tu	**mouds**
il/elle/on	**moud**
nous	**moulons**
vous	**moulez**
ils/elles	**moulent**

PRESENT SUBJUNCTIVE

je	**moule**
tu	**moules**
il/elle/on	**moule**
nous	**moulions**
vous	**mouliez**
ils/elles	**moulent**

PERFECT

j'	**ai moulu**
tu	**as moulu**
il/elle/on	**a moulu**
nous	**avons moulu**
vous	**avez moulu**
ils/elles	**ont moulu**

IMPERFECT

je	**moulais**
tu	**moulais**
il/elle/on	**moulait**
nous	**moulions**
vous	**mouliez**
ils/elles	**moulaient**

PRESENT PARTICIPLE
moulant

PAST PARTICIPLE
moulu

EXAMPLE PHRASES

"Qui va m'aider à **moudre** ce grain ?", demanda la petite poule rousse.
"Who will help me to grind this grain?" asked the little red hen.

Il **moud** toujours son café lui-même. He always grinds his coffee himself.

J'**ai moulu** du café pour demain matin. I've ground some coffee for
tomorrow morning.

Le meunier **moulait** le blé à la meule. The miller ground the wheat with
the millstone.

je/j' = I   **tu** = you   **il** = he/it   **elle** = she/it   **on** = we/one   **nous** = we   **vous** = you   **ils/elles** = they

moudre

FUTURE

je	**moudrai**
tu	**moudras**
il/elle/on	**moudra**
nous	**moudrons**
vous	**moudrez**
ils/elles	**moudront**

CONDITIONAL

je	**moudrais**
tu	**moudrais**
il/elle/on	**moudrait**
nous	**moudrions**
vous	**moudriez**
ils/elles	**moudraient**

PAST HISTORIC

je	**moulus**
tu	**moulus**
il/elle/on	**moulut**
nous	**moulûmes**
vous	**moulûtes**
ils/elles	**moulurent**

PLUPERFECT

j'	**avais moulu**
tu	**avais moulu**
il/elle/on	**avait moulu**
nous	**avions moulu**
vous	**aviez moulu**
ils/elles	**avaient moulu**

IMPERATIVE

mouds / moulons / moulez

EXAMPLE PHRASES

Je **moudrai** du café tout à l'heure. I'll grind some coffee in a moment.

Elle **moulut** un peu de poivre sur le rôti. She ground some pepper over the roast.

Si j'avais le temps je **moudrais** mon café moi-même. If I had time, I'd grind my coffee myself.

Il mesura le café qu'il **avait moulu**. He measured the coffee that he'd ground.

je/j' = I tu = you il = he/it elle = she/it on = we/one nous = we vous = you ils/elles = they

mourir (to die)

PRESENT

je	**meurs**
tu	**meurs**
il/elle/on	**meurt**
nous	**mourons**
vous	**mourez**
ils/elles	**meurent**

PRESENT SUBJUNCTIVE

je	**meure**
tu	**meures**
il/elle/on	**meure**
nous	**mourions**
vous	**mouriez**
ils/elles	**meurent**

PERFECT

je	**suis mort(e)**
tu	**es mort(e)**
il/elle/on	**est mort(e)**
nous	**sommes mort(e)s**
vous	**êtes mort(e)(s)**
ils/elles	**sont mort(e)s**

IMPERFECT

je	**mourais**
tu	**mourais**
il/elle/on	**mourait**
nous	**mourions**
vous	**mouriez**
ils/elles	**mouraient**

PRESENT PARTICIPLE

mourant

PAST PARTICIPLE

mort

EXAMPLE PHRASES

On **meurt** de froid ici ! We're freezing to death here!

Elle **est morte** en 2008. She died in 2008.

Ils **sont morts**. They're dead.

Je ne veux pas qu'il **meure**. I don't want him to die.

Nous **mourions** de froid. We were freezing to death.

mourir

FUTURE

je	**mourrai**
tu	**mourras**
il/elle/on	**mourra**
nous	**mourrons**
vous	**mourrez**
ils/elles	**mourront**

CONDITIONAL

je	**mourrais**
tu	**mourrais**
il/elle/on	**mourrait**
nous	**mourrions**
vous	**mourriez**
ils/elles	**mourraient**

PAST HISTORIC

je	**mourus**
tu	**mourus**
il/elle/on	**mourut**
nous	**mourûmes**
vous	**mourûtes**
ils/elles	**moururent**

PLUPERFECT

j'	**étais mort(e)**
tu	**étais mort(e)**
il/elle/on	**était mort(e)**
nous	**étions mort(e)s**
vous	**étiez mort(e)(s)**
ils/elles	**étaient mort(e)s**

IMPERATIVE

meurs / **mourons** / **mourez**

EXAMPLE PHRASES

Si tu t'en vas, j'en **mourrai** de chagrin. If you go, I'll die of sorrow.

Il **mourut** quelques heures plus tard. He died a few hours later.

Je **mourrais** de honte si tu le lui disais. I'd die of shame if you told him about it.

Nous **étions morts** de peur. We were scared to death.

je/j' = I **tu** = you **il** = he/it **elle** = she/it **on** = we/one **nous** = we **vous** = you **ils/elles** = they

naître (to be born)

PRESENT

je	**nais**
tu	**nais**
il/elle/on	**naît**
nous	**naissons**
vous	**naissez**
ils/elles	**naissent**

PRESENT SUBJUNCTIVE

je	**naisse**
tu	**naisses**
il/elle/on	**naisse**
nous	**naissions**
vous	**naissiez**
ils/elles	**naissent**

PERFECT

je	**suis né(e)**
tu	**es né(e)**
il/elle/on	**est né(e)**
nous	**sommes né(e)s**
vous	**êtes né(e)(s)**
ils/elles	**sont né(e)s**

IMPERFECT

je	**naissais**
tu	**naissais**
il/elle/on	**naissait**
nous	**naissions**
vous	**naissiez**
ils/elles	**naissaient**

PRESENT PARTICIPLE

naissant

PAST PARTICIPLE

né

EXAMPLE PHRASES

Il a l'air innocent comme l'agneau qui vient de **naître**. He looks as innocent as a newborn lamb.

Quand est-ce que tu **es né** ? When were you born?

Je **suis née** le 12 février. I was born on February 12.

Je ne **suis** pas **né** de la dernière pluie. I wasn't born yesterday.

je/j' = I **tu** = you **il** = he/it **elle** = she/it **on** = we/one **nous** = we **vous** = you **ils/elles** = they

naître

FUTURE

je	naîtrai
tu	naîtras
il/elle/on	naîtra
nous	naîtrons
vous	naîtrez
ils/elles	naîtront

CONDITIONAL

je	naîtrais
tu	naîtrais
il/elle/on	naîtrait
nous	naîtrions
vous	naîtriez
ils/elles	naîtraient

PAST HISTORIC

je	naquis
tu	naquis
il/elle/on	naquit
nous	naquîmes
vous	naquîtes
ils/elles	naquirent

PLUPERFECT

j'	étais né(e)
tu	étais né(e)
il/elle/on	était né(e)
nous	étions né(e)s
vous	étiez né(e)(s)
ils/elles	étaient né(é)s

IMPERATIVE

nais / naissons / naissez

EXAMPLE PHRASES

Le bébé de Delphine **naîtra** en mars. Delphine is going to have a baby in March.

Il **naquit** le 5 juillet 2001. He was born on July 5 2001.

Ses enfants n'**étaient** pas **nés** aux États-Unis. Her children weren't born in the USA.

je/j' = I tu = you il = he/it elle = she/it on = we/one nous = we vous = you ils/elles = they

nettoyer (to clean)

PRESENT

je	nettoie
tu	nettoies
il/elle/on	nettoie
nous	nettoyons
vous	nettoyez
ils/elles	nettoient

PRESENT SUBJUNCTIVE

je	nettoie
tu	nettoies
il/elle/on	nettoie
nous	nettoyions
vous	nettoyiez
ils/elles	nettoient

PERFECT

j'	ai nettoyé
tu	as nettoyé
il/elle/on	a nettoyé
nous	avons nettoyé
vous	avez nettoyé
ils/elles	ont nettoyé

IMPERFECT

je	nettoyais
tu	nettoyais
il/elle/on	nettoyait
nous	nettoyions
vous	nettoyiez
ils/elles	nettoyaient

PRESENT PARTICIPLE

nettoyant

PAST PARTICIPLE

nettoyé

EXAMPLE PHRASES

Je ne **nettoie** pas souvent mes lunettes. I don't clean my glasses very often.

Richard **a nettoyé** tout l'appartement. Richard has cleaned the whole apartment.

J'aimerais que vous **nettoyiez** ta chambre. I'd like you to clean your room.

Elle **nettoyait** le sol en écoutant la radio. She was cleaning the floor while listening to the radio.

nettoyer

FUTURE

je	nettoierai
tu	nettoieras
il/elle/on	nettoiera
nous	nettoierons
vous	nettoierez
ils/elles	nettoieront

CONDITIONAL

je	nettoierais
tu	nettoierais
il/elle/on	nettoierait
nous	nettoierions
vous	nettoieriez
ils/elles	nettoieraient

PAST HISTORIC

je	nettoyai
tu	nettoyas
il/elle/on	nettoya
nous	nettoyâmes
vous	nettoyâtes
ils/elles	nettoyèrent

PLUPERFECT

j'	avais nettoyé
tu	avais nettoyé
il/elle/on	avait nettoyé
nous	avions nettoyé
vous	aviez nettoyé
ils/elles	avaient nettoyé

IMPERATIVE

nettoie / nettoyons / nettoyez

EXAMPLE PHRASES

Je **nettoierai** tout ça ce soir. I'll clean everything this evening.

Elle **nettoya** le miroir et s'y regarda longuement. She cleaned the mirror and looked at herself for a long time.

Il **nettoierait** sa chambre tout seul si je l'encourageais à le faire. He'd clean his bedroom himself if I encouraged him to do it.

Quand je suis rentrée, ils **avaient** tout **nettoyé**. When I got back, they'd cleaned everything up.

Nettoie tes chaussures avant de les ranger. Clean your shoes before putting them away.

je/j' = I tu = you il = he/it elle = she/it on = we/one nous = we vous = you ils/elles = they

obéir (to obey)

PRESENT

j'	obéis
tu	obéis
il/elle/on	obéit
nous	obéissons
vous	obéissez
ils/elles	obéissent

PRESENT SUBJUNCTIVE

j'	obéisse
tu	obéisses
il/elle/on	obéisse
nous	obéissions
vous	obéissiez
ils/elles	obéissent

PERFECT

j'	ai obéi
tu	as obéi
il/elle/on	a obéi
nous	avons obéi
vous	avez obéi
ils/elles	ont obéi

IMPERFECT

j'	obéissais
tu	obéissais
il/elle/on	obéissait
nous	obéissions
vous	obéissiez
ils/elles	obéissaient

PRESENT PARTICIPLE
obéissant

PAST PARTICIPLE
obéi

EXAMPLE PHRASES

Je n'**obéis** pas toujours à mes parents. I don't always obey my parents.

J'aimerais que tu **obéisses** quand je te demande de faire quelque chose.
I'd like you to obey when I ask you to do something.

Mon chien n'**obéissait** jamais. My dog never obeyed commands.

obéir

FUTURE

j'	obéirai
tu	obéiras
il/elle/on	obéira
nous	obéirons
vous	obéirez
ils/elles	obéiront

CONDITIONAL

j'	obéirais
tu	obéirais
il/elle/on	obéirait
nous	obéirions
vous	obéiriez
ils/elles	obéiraient

PAST HISTORIC

j'	obéis
tu	obéis
il/elle/on	obéit
nous	obéîmes
vous	obéîtes
ils/elles	obéirent

PLUPERFECT

j'	avais obéi
tu	avais obéi
il/elle/on	avait obéi
nous	avions obéi
vous	aviez obéi
ils/elles	avaient obéi

IMPERATIVE

obéis / obéissons / obéissez

EXAMPLE PHRASES

Il n'**obéira** jamais si tu lui parles comme ça. **He'll never obey if you speak to him like that.**

Ils **obéirent** sans se plaindre. **They obeyed without complaining.**

Ils ne lui **obéiraient** pas s'ils ne l'aimaient pas. **They wouldn't obey her if they didn't like her.**

Comme elle n'avait pas le choix, elle **avait obéi** à ses ordres. **As she didn't have any choice, she'd obeyed his orders.**

je/j' = I tu = you il = he/it elle = she/it on = we/one nous = we vous = you ils/elles = they

offrir (to offer)

PRESENT

j'	**offre**
tu	**offres**
il/elle/on	**offre**
nous	**offrons**
vous	**offrez**
ils/elles	**offrent** ·

PRESENT SUBJUNCTIVE

j'	**offre**
tu	**offres**
il/elle/on	**offre**
nous	**offrions**
vous	**offriez**
ils/elles	**offrent**

PERFECT

j'	**ai offert**
tu	**as offert**
il/elle/on	**a offert**
nous	**avons offert**
vous	**avez offert**
ils/elles	**ont offert**

IMPERFECT

j'	**offrais**
tu	**offrais**
il/elle/on	**offrait**
nous	**offrions**
vous	**offriez**
ils/elles	**offraient**

PRESENT PARTICIPLE

offrant

PAST PARTICIPLE

offert

EXAMPLE PHRASES

Viens, je t'**offre** à boire. Come on, I'll buy you a drink.

Paul m'**a offert** du parfum pour mon anniversaire. Paul gave me some perfume for my birthday.

Offre-lui des fleurs. Give her some flowers.

Il **offrait** souvent de me raccompagner. He would often offer me a ride back.

je/j' = I   tu = you   il = he/it   elle = she/it   on = we/one   nous = we   vous = you   ils/elles = they

offrir

FUTURE

j'	**offrirai**
tu	**offriras**
il/elle/on	**offrira**
nous	**offrirons**
vous	**offrirez**
ils/elles	**offriront**

CONDITIONAL

j'	**offrirais**
tu	**offrirais**
il/elle/on	**offrirait**
nous	**offririons**
vous	**offririez**
ils/elles	**offriraient**

PAST HISTORIC

j'	**offris**
tu	**offris**
il/elle/on	**offrit**
nous	**offrîmes**
vous	**offrîtes**
ils/elles	**offrirent**

PLUPERFECT

j'	**avais offert**
tu	**avais offert**
il/elle/on	**avait offert**
nous	**avions offert**
vous	**aviez offert**
ils/elles	**avaient offert**

IMPERATIVE

offre / offrons / offrez

EXAMPLE PHRASES

Je lui **offrirai** une voiture pour ses 21 ans. **I'll buy her a car for her 21st birthday.**

Il lui **offrit** de l'aider. **He offered to help her.**

S'il était plus aimable, je lui **offrirais** de l'aider. **If he were more pleasant, I'd offer to help him.**

On lui **avait offert** un poste de secrétaire. **They had offered her a secretarial post.**

je/j' = I **tu** = you **il** = he/it **elle** = she/it **on** = we/one **nous** = we **vous** = you **ils/elles** = they

ouvrir (to open)

PRESENT		PRESENT SUBJUNCTIVE	
j'	**ouvre**	j'	**ouvre**
tu	**ouvres**	tu	**ouvres**
il/elle/on	**ouvre**	il/elle/on	**ouvre**
nous	**ouvrons**	nous	**ouvrions**
vous	**ouvrez**	vous	**ouvriez**
ils/elles	**ouvrent**	ils/elles	**ouvrent**

PERFECT		IMPERFECT	
j'	**ai ouvert**	j'	**ouvrais**
tu	**as ouvert**	tu	**ouvrais**
il/elle/on	**a ouvert**	il/elle/on	**ouvrait**
nous	**avons ouvert**	nous	**ouvrions**
vous	**avez ouvert**	vous	**ouvriez**
ils/elles	**ont ouvert**	ils/elles	**ouvraient**

PRESENT PARTICIPLE

ouvrant

PAST PARTICIPLE

ouvert

EXAMPLE PHRASES

Est-ce que tu pourrais **ouvrir** la fenêtre ? Could you open the window?

Elle **a ouvert** la porte. She opened the door.

La porte s'**est ouverte**. The door opened.

Je me suis coupé en **ouvrant** une boîte de conserve. I cut myself opening a can.

je/j' = I   tu = you   il = he/it   elle = she/it   on = we/one   nous = we   vous = you   ils/elles = they

ouvrir

FUTURE

j'	**ouvrirai**
tu	**ouvriras**
il/elle/on	**ouvrira**
nous	**ouvrirons**
vous	**ouvrirez**
ils/elles	**ouvriront**

CONDITIONAL

j'	**ouvrirais**
tu	**ouvrirais**
il/elle/on	**ouvrirait**
nous	**ouvririons**
vous	**ouvririez**
ils/elles	**ouvriraient**

PAST HISTORIC

j'	**ouvris**
tu	**ouvris**
il/elle/on	**ouvrit**
nous	**ouvrîmes**
vous	**ouvrîtes**
ils/elles	**ouvrirent**

PLUPERFECT

j'	**avais ouvert**
tu	**avais ouvert**
il/elle/on	**avait ouvert**
nous	**avions ouvert**
vous	**aviez ouvert**
ils/elles	**avaient ouvert**

IMPERATIVE

ouvre / ouvrons / ouvrez

EXAMPLE PHRASES

J'**ouvrirai** la fenêtre tout à l'heure. **I'll open the window in a moment.**

Elle **ouvrit** les yeux et lui sourit. **She opened her eyes and smiled at him.**

J'**ouvrirais** la fenêtre s'il ne faisait pas si froid. **I would open the window if it weren't so cold.**

Ils **avaient ouvert** tous leurs cadeaux de Noël. **They had opened all their Christmas presents.**

Ouvre la porte, s'il te plaît. **Open the door, please.**

Ouvrez vos livres à la page 10. **Open your books to page 10.**

je/j' = I   tu = you   il = he/it   elle = she/it   on = we/one   nous = we   vous = you   ils/elles = they

paraître (to appear)

PRESENT

je	**parais**
tu	**parais**
il/elle/on	**paraît**
nous	**paraissons**
vous	**paraissez**
ils/elles	**paraissent**

PRESENT SUBJUNCTIVE

je	**paraisse**
tu	**paraisses**
il/elle/on	**paraisse**
nous	**paraissions**
vous	**paraissiez**
ils/elles	**paraissent**

PERFECT

j'	**ai paru**
tu	**as paru**
il/elle/on	**a paru**
nous	**avons paru**
vous	**avez paru**
ils/elles	**ont paru**

IMPERFECT

je	**paraissais**
tu	**paraissais**
il/elle/on	**paraissait**
nous	**paraissions**
vous	**paraissiez**
ils/elles	**paraissaient**

PRESENT PARTICIPLE

paraissant

PAST PARTICIPLE

paru

EXAMPLE PHRASES

Gisèle **paraît** plus jeune que son âge. Gisèle doesn't look her age.

Il **paraît** qu'il fait chaud toute l'année là-bas. Apparently it's hot all year round over there.

Il m'**a paru** angoissé. I thought he looked stressed.

Elle **paraissait** fatiguée. She seemed tired.

paraître

FUTURE

je	**paraîtrai**
tu	**paraîtras**
il/elle/on	**paraîtra**
nous	**paraîtrons**
vous	**paraîtrez**
ils/elles	**paraîtront**

CONDITIONAL

je	**paraîtrais**
tu	**paraîtrais**
il/elle/on	**paraîtrait**
nous	**paraîtrions**
vous	**paraîtriez**
ils/elles	**paraîtraient**

PAST HISTORIC

je	**parus**
tu	**parus**
il/elle/on	**parut**
nous	**parûmes**
vous	**parûtes**
ils/elles	**parurent**

PLUPERFECT

j'	**avais paru**
tu	**avais paru**
il/elle/on	**avait paru**
nous	**avions paru**
vous	**aviez paru**
ils/elles	**avaient paru**

IMPERATIVE

parais / paraissons / paraissez

EXAMPLE PHRASES

Cet article **paraîtra** le mois prochain. This article will come out next month.

Il **parut** gêné. He looked embarrassed.

Cela **paraîtrait** étrange si je venais sans mon mari. It would look strange if I came without my husband.

Il **avait paru** pressé de partir. He had seemed in a hurry to leave.

je/j' = I **tu** = you **il** = he/it **elle** = she/it **on** = we/one **nous** = we **vous** = you **ils/elles** = they

partir (to go; to leave)

PRESENT

je	**pars**
tu	**pars**
il/elle/on	**part**
nous	**partons**
vous	**partez**
ils/elles	**partent**

PRESENT SUBJUNCTIVE

je	**parte**
tu	**partes**
il/elle/on	**parte**
nous	**partions**
vous	**partiez**
ils/elles	**partent**

PERFECT

je	**suis parti(e)**
tu	**es parti(e)**
il/elle/on	**est parti(e)**
nous	**sommes parti(e)s**
vous	**êtes parti(e)(s)**
ils/elles	**sont parti(e)s**

IMPERFECT

je	**partais**
tu	**partais**
il/elle/on	**partait**
nous	**partions**
vous	**partiez**
ils/elles	**partaient**

PRESENT PARTICIPLE

partant

PAST PARTICIPLE

parti

EXAMPLE PHRASES

On **part** en vacances le 15 août. We're going on vacation on August 15.

Elle **est partie** tôt ce matin. She left early this morning.

Il faut qu'on **parte** de bonne heure. We have to leave early.

Il **partait** à huit heures tous les matins. He left at eight o'clock every morning.

---

je/j' = I   tu = you   il = he/it   elle = she/it   on = we/one   nous = we   vous = you   ils/elles = they

partir

FUTURE

je	partirai
tu	partiras
il/elle/on	partira
nous	partirons
vous	partirez
ils/elles	partiront

CONDITIONAL

je	partirais
tu	partirais
il/elle/on	partirait
nous	partirions
vous	partiriez
ils/elles	partiraient

PAST HISTORIC

je	partis
tu	partis
il/elle/on	partit
nous	partîmes
vous	partîtes
ils/elles	partirent

PLUPERFECT

j'	étais parti(e)
tu	étais parti(e)
il/elle/on	était parti(e)
nous	étions parti(e)s
vous	étiez parti(e)(s)
ils/elles	étaient parti(e)s

IMPERATIVE

pars / partons / partez

EXAMPLE PHRASES

Nous **partirons** demain. We'll leave tomorrow.

Il **partit** sans rien dire. He left without saying a word.

Je ne **partirais** pas sans dire au revoir. I wouldn't leave without saying goodbye.

Quand je suis arrivée, ils **étaient** déjà **partis**. When I arrived, they had already left.

Ne **partez** pas sans moi ! Don't leave without me!

je/j' = I tu = you il = he/it elle = she/it on = we/one nous = we vous = you ils/elles = they

passer (to pass)

PRESENT

je	passe
tu	passes
il/elle/on	passe
nous	passons
vous	passez
ils/elles	passent

PRESENT SUBJUNCTIVE

je	passe
tu	passes
il/elle/on	passe
nous	passions
vous	passiez
ils/elles	passent

PERFECT

je	suis passé(e)
tu	es passé(e)
il/elle/on	est passé(e)
nous	sommes passé(e)s
vous	êtes passé(e)(s)
ils/elles	sont passé(e)s

IMPERFECT

je	passais
tu	passais
il/elle/on	passait
nous	passions
vous	passiez
ils/elles	passaient

PRESENT PARTICIPLE

passant

PAST PARTICIPLE

passé

In the perfect and the pluperfect, use the auxiliary "avoir" when there is a direct object.

EXAMPLE PHRASES

Je vais **passer** les vacances chez mes grands-parents. I'm going to spend my vacation at my grandparents' house.

L'histoire se **passe** au Mexique. The story takes place in Mexico.

Il **a passé** son examen en juin. He took his exam in June.

Elle **est passée** me dire bonjour. She came by to say hello.

Ils **passaient** leur temps à regarder la télé. They spent their time watching TV.

passer

FUTURE

je	passerai
tu	passeras
il/elle/on	passera
nous	passerons
vous	passerez
ils/elles	passeront

CONDITIONAL

je	passerais
tu	passerais
il/elle/on	passerait
nous	passerions
vous	passeriez
ils/elles	passeraient

PAST HISTORIC

je	passai
tu	passas
il/elle/on	passa
nous	passâmes
vous	passâtes
ils/elles	passèrent

PLUPERFECT

j'	étais passé(e)
tu	étais passé(e)
il/elle/on	était passé(e)
nous	étions passé(e)s
vous	étiez passé(e)(s)
ils/elles	étaient passé(e)s

IMPERATIVE

passe / passons / passez

EXAMPLE PHRASES

Je **passerai** te voir ce soir. I'll come to see you tonight.

Elle **passa** la soirée à emballer les cadeaux de Noël. She spent the evening wrapping the Christmas presents.

Ils **passeraient** plus de temps à jouer dehors s'il faisait moins mauvais. They'd spend more time playing outside if the weather weren't so bad.

Les mois **avaient passé**. Months had passed.

Passe-moi le pain, s'il te plaît. Pass me the bread, please.

je/j' = I tu = you il = he/it elle = she/it on = we/one nous = we vous = you ils/elles = they

payer (to pay)

PRESENT

je	**paye**
tu	**payes**
il/elle/on	**paye**
nous	**payons**
vous	**payez**
ils/elles	**payent**

PRESENT SUBJUNCTIVE

je	**paye**
tu	**payes**
il/elle/on	**paye**
nous	**payions**
vous	**payiez**
ils/elles	**payent**

PERFECT

j'	**ai payé**
tu	**as payé**
il/elle/on	**a payé**
nous	**avons payé**
vous	**avez payé**
ils/elles	**ont payé**

IMPERFECT

je	**payais**
tu	**payais**
il/elle/on	**payait**
nous	**payions**
vous	**payiez**
ils/elles	**payaient**

PRESENT PARTICIPLE

payant

PAST PARTICIPLE

payé

EXAMPLE PHRASES

Les étudiants **payent** moitié prix. Students pay half price.

Tu l'**as payé** combien ? How much did you pay for it?

Il faut que je **paye** l'électricien. I have to pay the electrician.

Il ne **payait** jamais son loyer. He never paid his rent.

payer

FUTURE

je	payerai
tu	payeras
il/elle/on	payera
nous	payerons
vous	payerez
ils/elles	payeront

CONDITIONAL

je	payerais
tu	payerais
il/elle/on	payerait
nous	payerions
vous	payeriez
ils/elles	payeraient

PAST HISTORIC

je	payai
tu	payas
il/elle/on	paya
nous	payâmes
vous	payâtes
ils/elles	payèrent

PLUPERFECT

j'	avais payé
tu	avais payé
il/elle/on	avait payé
nous	avions payé
vous	aviez payé
ils/elles	avaient payé

IMPERATIVE

paye / payons / payez

EXAMPLE PHRASES

Je vous **payerai** demain. I'll pay you tomorrow.

Il **paya** la note et partit. He paid the bill and left.

Je lui ai dit que je le **payerais** le prochaine fois. I told him that I would pay him the next time.

Sa patronne ne l'**avait** pas **payée** depuis deux mois. Her boss hadn't paid her for the last two months.

je/j' = I tu = you il = he/it elle = she/it on = we/one nous = we vous = you ils/elles = they

peindre (to paint)

PRESENT

je	**peins**
tu	**peins**
il/elle/on	**peint**
nous	**peignons**
vous	**peignez**
ils/elles	**peignent**

PRESENT SUBJUNCTIVE

je	**peigne**
tu	**peignes**
il/elle/on	**peigne**
nous	**peignions**
vous	**peigniez**
ils/elles	**peignent**

PERFECT

j'	**ai peint**
tu	**as peint**
il/elle/on	**a peint**
nous	**avons peint**
vous	**avez peint**
ils/elles	**ont peint**

IMPERFECT

je	**peignais**
tu	**peignais**
il/elle/on	**peignait**
nous	**peignions**
vous	**peigniez**
ils/elles	**peignaient**

PRESENT PARTICIPLE

peignant

PAST PARTICIPLE

peint

EXAMPLE PHRASES

Il ne **peint** plus depuis son opération. He hasn't painted since his operation.

On **a peint** l'entrée en bleu clair. We painted the hall light blue.

Ce tableau **a été peint** en 1913. This picture was painted in 1913.

Il **peignait** toujours des paysages. He always painted landscapes.

je/j' = I   **tu** = you   **il** = he/it   **elle** = she/it   **on** = we/one   **nous** = we   **vous** = you   **ils/elles** = they

peindre

FUTURE

je	**peindrai**
tu	**peindras**
il/elle/on	**peindra**
nous	**peindrons**
vous	**peindrez**
ils/elles	**peindront**

CONDITIONAL

je	**peindrais**
tu	**peindrais**
il/elle/on	**peindrait**
nous	**peindrions**
vous	**peindriez**
ils/elles	**peindraient**

PAST HISTORIC

je	**peignis**
tu	**peignis**
il/elle/on	**peignit**
nous	**peignîmes**
vous	**peignîtes**
ils/elles	**peignirent**

PLUPERFECT

j'	**avais peint**
tu	**avais peint**
il/elle/on	**avait peint**
nous	**avions peint**
vous	**aviez peint**
ils/elles	**avaient peint**

IMPERATIVE

peins / peignons / peignez

EXAMPLE PHRASES

Je **peindrai** le plafond demain. I'll paint the ceiling tomorrow.

Il **peignit** les volets en rose. He painted the shutters pink.

Si j'étais toi, je **peindrais** les murs avant de poser le carrelage. If I were you, I would paint the walls before laying the tiles.

Elle n'**avait peint** que la moitié de la pièce. She'd only painted half of the room.

je/j' = I   tu = you   il = he/it   elle = she/it   on = we/one   nous = we   vous = you   ils/elles = they

perdre (to lose)

PRESENT

je	**perds**
tu	**perds**
il/elle/on	**perd**
nous	**perdons**
vous	**perdez**
ils/elles	**perdent**

PRESENT SUBJUNCTIVE

je	**perde**
tu	**perdes**
il/elle/on	**perde**
nous	**perdions**
vous	**perdiez**
ils/elles	**perdent**

PERFECT

j'	**ai perdu**
tu	**as perdu**
il/elle/on	**a perdu**
nous	**avons perdu**
vous	**avez perdu**
ils/elles	**ont perdu**

IMPERFECT

je	**perdais**
tu	**perdais**
il/elle/on	**perdait**
nous	**perdions**
vous	**perdiez**
ils/elles	**perdaient**

PRESENT PARTICIPLE

perdant

PAST PARTICIPLE

perdu

EXAMPLE PHRASES

Si tu te **perds**, appelle-moi. Call me if you get lost.

L'Italie **a perdu** un à zéro. Italy lost one to nothing.

J'**ai perdu** mon porte-monnaie dans le métro. I lost my wallet on the subway.

Il ne faut pas que je **perde** son adresse. I mustn't lose his address.

Il **perdait** toujours ses affaires. He was always losing his things.

---

je/j' = I   **tu** = you   **il** = he/it   **elle** = she/it   **on** = we/one   **nous** = we   **vous** = you   **ils/elles** = they

perdre

FUTURE

je	**perdrai**
tu	**perdras**
il/elle/on	**perdra**
nous	**perdrons**
vous	**perdrez**
ils/elles	**perdront**

CONDITIONAL

je	**perdrais**
tu	**perdrais**
il/elle/on	**perdrait**
nous	**perdrions**
vous	**perdriez**
ils/elles	**perdraient**

PAST HISTORIC

je	**perdis**
tu	**perdis**
il/elle/on	**perdit**
nous	**perdîmes**
vous	**perdîtes**
ils/elles	**perdirent**

PLUPERFECT

j'	**avais perdu**
tu	**avais perdu**
il/elle/on	**avait perdu**
nous	**avions perdu**
vous	**aviez perdu**
ils/elles	**avaient perdu**

IMPERATIVE

perds / perdons / perdez

EXAMPLE PHRASES

Je **perdrai** forcément contre lui. I'll obviously lose against him.

Il **perdit** patience et se mit à crier. He lost his patience and began to shout.

Tu ne **perdrais** pas tes affaires si tu faisais plus attention. You wouldn't lose your things if you were more careful.

Elle **avait perdu** la mémoire depuis son accident. She had lost her memory after her accident.

Ne **perds** pas encore tes gants. Don't lose your gloves again.

je/j' = I tu = you il = he/it elle = she/it on = we/one nous = we vous = you ils/elles = they

plaire (to please)

PRESENT

je	**plais**
tu	**plais**
il/elle/on	**plaît**
nous	**plaisons**
vous	**plaisez**
ils/elles	**plaisent**

PRESENT SUBJUNCTIVE

je	**plaise**
tu	**plaises**
il/elle/on	**plaise**
nous	**plaisions**
vous	**plaisiez**
ils/elles	**plaisent**

PERFECT

j'	**ai plu**
tu	**as plu**
il/elle/on	**a plu**
nous	**avons plu**
vous	**avez plu**
ils/elles	**ont plu**

IMPERFECT

je	**plaisais**
tu	**plaisais**
il/elle/on	**plaisait**
nous	**plaisions**
vous	**plaisiez**
ils/elles	**plaisaient**

PRESENT PARTICIPLE

plaisant

PAST PARTICIPLE

plu

EXAMPLE PHRASES

Le menu ne me **plaît** pas. I don't like the menu.

s'il te **plaît** please

s'il vous **plaît** please

Ça t'**a plu**, le film ? Did you like the movie?

La robe noire me **plaisait** beaucoup. I really liked the black dress.

je/j' = I tu = you il = he/it elle = she/it on = we/one nous = we vous = you ils/elles = they

plaire

FUTURE

je	**plairai**
tu	**plairas**
il/elle/on	**plaira**
nous	**plairons**
vous	**plairez**
ils/elles	**plairont**

CONDITIONAL

je	**plairais**
tu	**plairais**
il/elle/on	**plairait**
nous	**plairions**
vous	**plairiez**
ils/elles	**plairaient**

PAST HISTORIC

je	**plus**
tu	**plus**
il/elle/on	**plut**
nous	**plûmes**
vous	**plûtes**
ils/elles	**plurent**

PLUPERFECT

j'	**avais plu**
tu	**avais plu**
il/elle/on	**avait plu**
nous	**avions plu**
vous	**aviez plu**
ils/elles	**avaient plu**

IMPERATIVE

plais / plaisons / plaisez

EXAMPLE PHRASES

Ce film ne lui **plaira** pas. He won't like this movie.

Elle lui **plut** immédiatement. He liked her right away.

Ça te **plairait** d'aller à la mer ? Would you like to go to the seaside?

Cette remarque ne lui **avait** pas **plu**. He hadn't liked that remark.

pleuvoir (to rain)

PRESENT

   il **pleut**

PRESENT SUBJUNCTIVE

   il **pleuve**

PERFECT

   il **a plu**

IMPERFECT

   il **pleuvait**

PRESENT PARTICIPLE

pleuvant

PAST PARTICIPLE

plu

EXAMPLE PHRASES

Il **pleut** beaucoup à Seattle. It rains a lot in Seattle.

Il **a plu** toute la journée. It rained all day long.

J'ai peur qu'il **pleuve** cet après-midi. I'm afraid it might rain this afternoon.

Il **pleuvait** tellement qu'ils décidèrent de rester chez eux. It rained so much that they decided to stay at home.

pleuvoir

FUTURE

il **pleuvra**

CONDITIONAL

il **pleuvrait**

PAST HISTORIC

il **plut**

PLUPERFECT

il **avait plu**

IMPERATIVE

not used

EXAMPLE PHRASES

J'espère qu'il ne **pleuvra** pas demain. I hope it won't rain tomorrow.

Il **plut** pendant quarante jours et quarante nuits. It rained for forty days and forty nights.

Il **pleuvrait** probablement si je ne prenais pas mon parapluie. It would probably rain if I didn't take my umbrella.

Il n'**avait** pas **plu** de tout l'été. It hadn't rained all summer.

je/j' = I tu = you il = he/it elle = she/it on = we/one nous = we vous = you ils/elles = they

pouvoir (to be able)

PRESENT

je	**peux**
tu	**peux**
il/elle/on	**peut**
nous	**pouvons**
vous	**pouvez**
ils/elles	**peuvent**

PRESENT SUBJUNCTIVE

je	**puisse**
tu	**puisses**
il/elle/on	**puisse**
nous	**puissions**
vous	**puissiez**
ils/elles	**puissent**

PERFECT

j'	**ai pu**
tu	**as pu**
il/elle/on	**a pu**
nous	**avons pu**
vous	**avez pu**
ils/elles	**ont pu**

IMPERFECT

je	**pouvais**
tu	**pouvais**
il/elle/on	**pouvait**
nous	**pouvions**
vous	**pouviez**
ils/elles	**pouvaient**

PRESENT PARTICIPLE

pouvant

PAST PARTICIPLE

pu

EXAMPLE PHRASES

Je **peux** vous aider ? Can I help you?

J'ai fait tout ce que j'**ai pu**. I did all I could.

Nous avons changé la date du baptême de Clara pour que tu **puisses** venir.

We've changed the date of Clara's baptism so that you're able to come.

Elle ne **pouvait** pas s'empêcher de rire. She couldn't help laughing.

je/j' = I   tu = you   il = he/it   elle = she/it   on = we/one   nous = we   vous = you   ils/elles = they

pouvoir

FUTURE

je	**pourrai**
tu	**pourras**
il/elle/on	**pourra**
nous	**pourrons**
vous	**pourrez**
ils/elles	**pourront**

CONDITIONAL

je	**pourrais**
tu	**pourrais**
il/elle/on	**pourrait**
nous	**pourrions**
vous	**pourriez**
ils/elles	**pourraient**

PAST HISTORIC

je	**pus**
tu	**pus**
il/elle/on	**put**
nous	**pûmes**
vous	**pûtes**
ils/elles	**purent**

PLUPERFECT

j'	**avais pu**
tu	**avais pu**
il/elle/on	**avait pu**
nous	**avions pu**
vous	**aviez pu**
ils/elles	**avaient pu**

IMPERATIVE

not used

EXAMPLE PHRASES

Je ne **pourrai** pas venir samedi. **I won't be able to come Saturday.**

Il ne **put** se souvenir de son nom. **He couldn't remember her name.**

Je **pourrais** te prêter ma robe si tu voulais. **I could lend you my dress if you like.**

Il n'**avait** pas **pu** les rejoindre. **He hadn't been able to join them.**

je/j' = I tu = you il = he/it elle = she/it on = we/one nous = we vous = you ils/elles = they

prendre (to take)

PRESENT

je	prends
tu	prends
il/elle/on	prend
nous	prenons
vous	prenez
ils/elles	prennent

PRESENT SUBJUNCTIVE

je	prenne
tu	prennes
il/elle/on	prenne
nous	prenions
vous	preniez
ils/elles	prennent

PERFECT

j'	ai pris
tu	as pris
il/elle/on	a pris
nous	avons pris
vous	avez pris
ils/elles	ont pris

IMPERFECT

je	prenais
tu	prenais
il/elle/on	prenait
nous	prenions
vous	preniez
ils/elles	prenaient

PRESENT PARTICIPLE

prenant

PAST PARTICIPLE

pris

EXAMPLE PHRASES

N'oublie pas de **prendre** ton passeport. Don't forget to take your passport.

Pour qui est-ce qu'il se **prend** ? Who does he think he is?

J'**ai pris** plein de photos. I took lots of pictures.

Il faut que je **prenne** mes affaires de gym. I have to take my gym stuff.

Il **prenait** le bus à huit heures le matin. He got the bus at eight in the
   morning.

---

je/j' = I   tu = you   il = he/it   elle = she/it   on = we/one   nous = we   vous = you   ils/elles = they

prendre

FUTURE

je	prendrai
tu	prendras
il/elle/on	prendra
nous	prendrons
vous	prendrez
ils/elles	prendront

CONDITIONAL

je	prendrais
tu	prendrais
il/elle/on	prendrait
nous	prendrions
vous	prendriez
ils/elles	prendraient

PAST HISTORIC

je	pris
tu	pris
il/elle/on	prit
nous	prîmes
vous	prîtes
ils/elles	prirent

PLUPERFECT

j'	avais pris
tu	avais pris
il/elle/on	avait pris
nous	avions pris
vous	aviez pris
ils/elles	avaient pris

IMPERATIVE

prends / prenons / prenez

EXAMPLE PHRASES

Il **prendra** le train de 8h20. He'll take the 8:20 train.

Elle **prit** son sac et partit. She took her bag and left.

Si j'habitais ici, je **prendrais** le bus pour aller travailler. If I lived here, I'd take the bus to work.

Il n'**avait** jamais **pris** l'avion. He'd never traveled by plane.

Prends ton appareil photo. Take your camera.

je/j' = I **tu** = you **il** = he/it **elle** = she/it **on** = we/one **nous** = we **vous** = you **ils/elles** = they

protéger (to protect)

PRESENT

je	protège
tu	protèges
il/elle/on	protège
nous	protégeons
vous	protégez
ils/elles	protègent

PRESENT SUBJUNCTIVE

je	protège
tu	protèges
il/elle/on	protège
nous	protégions
vous	protégiez
ils/elles	protègent

PERFECT

j'	ai protégé
tu	as protégé
il/elle/on	a protégé
nous	avons protégé
vous	avez protégé
ils/elles	ont protégé

IMPERFECT

je	protégeais
tu	protégeais
il/elle/on	protégeait
nous	protégions
vous	protégiez
ils/elles	protégeaient

PRESENT PARTICIPLE

protégeant

PAST PARTICIPLE

protégé

EXAMPLE PHRASES

Ne crains rien, je te **protège**. Don't be scared; I'm looking after you.

Le champ **est protégé** du vent par la colline. The field is sheltered from the wind by the hill.

Je voudrais une tente qui **protège** bien contre le froid. I'd like a tent that protects you from the cold.

Il me **protégeait** contre tous ceux qui m'embêtaient. He protected me from all those who annoyed me.

---

je/j' = I   tu = you   il = he/it   elle = she/it   on = we/one   nous = we   vous = you   ils/elles = they

protéger

FUTURE

je	**protégerai**
tu	**protégeras**
il/elle/on	**protégera**
nous	**protégerons**
vous	**protégerez**
ils/elles	**protégeront**

CONDITIONAL

je	**protégerais**
tu	**protégerais**
il/elle/on	**protégerait**
nous	**protégerions**
vous	**protégeriez**
ils/elles	**protégeraient**

PAST HISTORIC

je	**protégeai**
tu	**protégeas**
il/elle/on	**protégea**
nous	**protégeâmes**
vous	**protégeâtes**
ils/elles	**protégèrent**

PLUPERFECT

j'	**avais protégé**
tu	**avais protégé**
il/elle/on	**avait protégé**
nous	**avions protégé**
vous	**aviez protégé**
ils/elles	**avaient protégé**

IMPERATIVE

protège / protégeons / protégez

EXAMPLE PHRASES

Ce manteau te **protégera** bien du froid. This coat will protect you from the cold.

Il se **protégea** le visage avec ses mains. He protected his face with his hands.

Cette crème te **protégerait** mieux les mains. This cream would protect your hands better.

Il **avait** toujours **protégé** sa petite sœur à l'école. He'd always protected his little sister at school.

Protège ton livre de la pluie. Protect your book from the rain.

je/j' = I tu = you il = he/it elle = she/it on = we/one nous = we vous = you ils/elles = they

recevoir (to receive)

PRESENT		PRESENT SUBJUNCTIVE	
je	**reçois**	je	**reçoive**
tu	**reçois**	tu	**reçoives**
il/elle/on	**reçoit**	il/elle/on	**reçoive**
nous	**recevons**	nous	**recevions**
vous	**recevez**	vous	**receviez**
ils/elles	**reçoivent**	ils/elles	**reçoivent**

PERFECT		IMPERFECT	
j'	**ai reçu**	je	**recevais**
tu	**as reçu**	tu	**recevais**
il/elle/on	**a reçu**	il/elle/on	**recevait**
nous	**avons reçu**	nous	**recevions**
vous	**avez reçu**	vous	**receviez**
ils/elles	**ont reçu**	ils/elles	**recevaient**

PRESENT PARTICIPLE
recevant

PAST PARTICIPLE
reçu

EXAMPLE PHRASES

Je ne **reçois** jamais de courrier. I never get any mail.

Elle **a reçu** une lettre de Charlotte. She received a letter from Charlotte.

J'attendais que tu **reçoives** l'invitation pour t'emmener choisir un cadeau.
I was waiting for you to get the invitation before I took you to choose
a present.

Il **recevait** d'étranges messages. He was getting strange messages.

---

je/j' = I   tu = you   il = he/it   elle = she/it   on = we/one   nous = we   vous = you   ils/elles = they

recevoir

FUTURE

je	**recevrai**
tu	**recevras**
il/elle/on	**recevra**
nous	**recevrons**
vous	**recevrez**
ils/elles	**recevront**

CONDITIONAL

je	**recevrais**
tu	**recevrais**
il/elle/on	**recevrait**
nous	**recevrions**
vous	**recevriez**
ils/elles	**recevraient**

PAST HISTORIC

je	**reçus**
tu	**reçus**
il/elle/on	**reçut**
nous	**reçûmes**
vous	**reçûtes**
ils/elles	**reçurent**

PLUPERFECT

j'	**avais reçu**
tu	**avais reçu**
il/elle/on	**avait reçu**
nous	**avions reçu**
vous	**aviez reçu**
ils/elles	**avaient reçu**

IMPERATIVE

reçois / recevons / recevez

EXAMPLE PHRASES

Elle **recevra** une réponse la semaine prochaine. **She'll get an answer next week.**

Il **reçut** une lettre anonyme. **He received an anonymous letter.**

Tu ne **recevrais** pas autant de monde si ta maison n'était pas aussi grande. **You wouldn't entertain so many people if your house weren't so big.**

Cela faisait une semaine qu'il n'**avait** pas **reçu** de courrier. **He hadn't gotten any mail for a week.**

Recevez, Monsieur, mes salutations. **Yours sincerely.**

je/j' = I tu = you il = he/it elle = she/it on = we/one nous = we vous = you ils/elles = they

réfléchir (to think)

PRESENT

je	**réfléchis**
tu	**réfléchis**
il/elle/on	**réfléchit**
nous	**réfléchissons**
vous	**réfléchissez**
ils/elles	**réfléchissent**

PRESENT SUBJUNCTIVE

je	**réfléchisse**
tu	**réfléchisses**
il/elle/on	**réfléchisse**
nous	**réfléchissions**
vous	**réfléchissiez**
ils/elles	**réfléchissent**

PERFECT

j'	**ai réfléchi**
tu	**as réfléchi**
il/elle/on	**a réfléchi**
nous	**avons réfléchi**
vous	**avez réfléchi**
ils/elles	**ont réfléchi**

IMPERFECT

je	**réfléchissais**
tu	**réfléchissais**
il/elle/on	**réfléchissait**
nous	**réfléchissions**
vous	**réfléchissiez**
ils/elles	**réfléchissaient**

PRESENT PARTICIPLE

réfléchissant

PAST PARTICIPLE

réfléchi

EXAMPLE PHRASES

Il est en train de **réfléchir**. He's thinking.

Je vais **réfléchir** à ta proposition. I'll think about your suggestion.

Il faut que j'y **réfléchisse**. I'll have to think about it.

réfléchir

FUTURE

je	**réfléchirai**
tu	**réfléchiras**
il/elle/on	**réfléchira**
nous	**réfléchirons**
vous	**réfléchirez**
ils/elles	**réfléchiront**

CONDITIONAL

je	**réfléchirais**
tu	**réfléchirais**
il/elle/on	**réfléchirait**
nous	**réfléchirions**
vous	**réfléchiriez**
ils/elles	**réfléchiraient**

PAST HISTORIC

je	**réfléchis**
tu	**réfléchis**
il/elle/on	**réfléchit**
nous	**réfléchîmes**
vous	**réfléchîtes**
ils/elles	**réfléchirent**

PLUPERFECT

j'	**avais réfléchi**
tu	**avais réfléchi**
il/elle/on	**avait réfléchi**
nous	**avions réfléchi**
vous	**aviez réfléchi**
ils/elles	**avaient réfléchi**

IMPERATIVE

réfléchis / réfléchissons / réfléchissez

EXAMPLE PHRASES

J'y **réfléchirai** et nous en reparlerons lors de notre prochaine réunion. I'll think about it and we'll talk about it at our next meeting.

Il **réfléchit** longuement avant de parler. He thought for a long time before he spoke.

Si j'étais toi, j'y **réfléchirais** encore un peu. If I were you, I'd give it more thought.

Ils **avaient** bien **réfléchi** et ils avaient décidé de vendre la maison. They had thought it over, and they had decided to sell the house.

Réfléchissez avant de répondre. Think before answering.

je/j' = I tu = you il = he/it elle = she/it on = we/one nous = we vous = you ils/elles = they

rentrer (to go back; to go in)

PRESENT

je	rentre
tu	rentres
il/elle/on	rentre
nous	rentrons
vous	rentrez
ils/elles	rentrent

PRESENT SUBJUNCTIVE

je	rentre
tu	rentres
il/elle/on	rentre
nous	rentrions
vous	rentriez
ils/elles	rentrent

PERFECT

je	suis rentré(e)
tu	es rentré(e)
il/elle/on	est rentré(e)
nous	sommes rentré(e)s
vous	êtes rentré(e)(s)
ils/elles	sont rentré(e)s

IMPERFECT

je	rentrais
tu	rentrais
il/elle/on	rentrait
nous	rentrions
vous	rentriez
ils/elles	rentraient

PRESENT PARTICIPLE

rentrant

PAST PARTICIPLE

rentré

In the perfect and the pluperfect, use the auxiliary "avoir" when there is a direct object.

EXAMPLE PHRASES

Je **rentre** déjeuner à midi. I go home for lunch.

À quelle heure est-ce qu'elle **est rentrée** ? What time did she get in?

Il faut que je **rentre** de bonne heure aujourd'hui. I have to go home early today.

Il ne **rentrait** jamais avant neuf heures le soir. He never came home before nine in the evening.

rentrer

FUTURE

je	**rentrerai**
tu	**rentreras**
il/elle/on	**rentrera**
nous	**rentrerons**
vous	**rentrerez**
ils/elles	**rentreront**

CONDITIONAL

je	**rentrerais**
tu	**rentrerais**
il/elle/on	**rentrerait**
nous	**rentrerions**
vous	**rentreriez**
ils/elles	**rentreraient**

PAST HISTORIC

je	**rentrai**
tu	**rentras**
il/elle/on	**rentra**
nous	**rentrâmes**
vous	**rentrâtes**
ils/elles	**rentrèrent**

PLUPERFECT

j'	**étais rentré(e)**
tu	**étais rentré(e)**
il/elle/on	**était rentré(e)**
nous	**étions rentré(e)s**
vous	**étiez rentré(e)(s)**
ils/elles	**étaient rentré(e)s**

IMPERATIVE

rentre / rentrons / rentrez

EXAMPLE PHRASES

Nous ne **rentrerons** pas tard. **We won't come home late.**

Il **rentra** chez lui en courant. **He ran all the way home.**

Si je n'avais pas peur de me perdre, je **rentrerais** sans toi. **If I weren't afraid I'd get lost, I'd go home without you.**

Ils **étaient rentrés** dans le magasin. **They'd gone into the store.**

Il **avait** déjà **rentré** la voiture dans le garage. **He'd already put the car into the garage.**

Ne **rentre** pas trop tard. **Don't come home too late.**

je/j' = I tu = you il = he/it elle = she/it on = we/one nous = we vous = you ils/elles = they

répondre (to answer)

PRESENT

je	**réponds**
tu	**réponds**
il/elle/on	**répond**
nous	**répondons**
vous	**répondez**
ils/elles	**répondent**

PRESENT SUBJUNCTIVE

je	**réponde**
tu	**répondes**
il/elle/on	**réponde**
nous	**répondions**
vous	**répondiez**
ils/elles	**répondent**

PERFECT

j'	**ai répondu**
tu	**as répondu**
il/elle/on	**a répondu**
nous	**avons répondu**
vous	**avez répondu**
ils/elles	**ont répondu**

IMPERFECT

je	**répondais**
tu	**répondais**
il/elle/on	**répondait**
nous	**répondions**
vous	**répondiez**
ils/elles	**répondaient**

PRESENT PARTICIPLE

répondant

PAST PARTICIPLE

répondu

EXAMPLE PHRASES

Ça ne **répond** pas. There's no answer.

C'est elle qui **a répondu** au téléphone. She answered the phone.

J'attendais que tu **répondes** à ma lettre. I was waiting for you to reply to my letter.

Il ne **répondait** jamais au téléphone le soir. He never answered the phone in the evening.

répondre

FUTURE

je	**répondrai**
tu	**répondras**
il/elle/on	**répondra**
nous	**répondrons**
vous	**répondrez**
ils/elles	**répondront**

CONDITIONAL

je	**répondrais**
tu	**répondrais**
il/elle/on	**répondrait**
nous	**répondrions**
vous	**répondriez**
ils/elles	**répondraient**

PAST HISTORIC

je	**répondis**
tu	**répondis**
il/elle/on	**répondit**
nous	**répondîmes**
vous	**répondîtes**
ils/elles	**répondirent**

PLUPERFECT

j'	**avais répondu**
tu	**avais répondu**
il/elle/on	**avait répondu**
nous	**avions répondu**
vous	**aviez répondu**
ils/elles	**avaient répondu**

IMPERATIVE

réponds / répondons / répondez

EXAMPLE PHRASES

Je **répondrai** à son message ce soir. I'll reply to his message this evening.

"Je ne sais pas," **répondit**-elle. "I don't know," she answered.

Il ne te **répondrait** pas comme ça si tu étais plus stricte. He wouldn't answer back like that if you were stricter.

Je n'**avais** pas encore **répondu** à son invitation. I hadn't replied to her invitation yet.

Lisez le texte et **répondez** aux questions. Read the text and answer the questions.

je/j' = I **tu** = you **il** = he/it **elle** = she/it **on** = we/one **nous** = we **vous** = you **ils/elles** = they

résoudre (to solve; to resolve)

PRESENT

je	**résous**
tu	**résous**
il/elle/on	**résout**
nous	**résolvons**
vous	**résolvez**
ils/elles	**résolvent**

PRESENT SUBJUNCTIVE

je	**résolve**
tu	**résolves**
il/elle/on	**résolve**
nous	**résolvions**
vous	**résolviez**
ils/elles	**résolvent**

PERFECT

j'	**ai résolu**
tu	**as résolu**
il/elle/on	**a résolu**
nous	**avons résolu**
vous	**avez résolu**
ils/elles	**ont résolu**

IMPERFECT

je	**résolvais**
tu	**résolvais**
il/elle/on	**résolvait**
nous	**résolvions**
vous	**résolviez**
ils/elles	**résolvaient**

PRESENT PARTICIPLE

résolvant

PAST PARTICIPLE

résolu

EXAMPLE PHRASES

C'est un problème qui sera difficile à **résoudre**. This problem will be difficult to solve.

La violence ne **résout** rien. Violence doesn't solve anything.

J'**ai résolu** le problème. I've solved the problem.

J'aimerais que vous **résolviez** la question aujourd'hui. I'd like you to resolve the matter today.

---

résoudre

FUTURE

je	**résoudrai**
tu	**résoudras**
il/elle/on	**résoudra**
nous	**résoudrons**
vous	**résoudrez**
ils/elles	**résoudront**

CONDITIONAL

je	**résoudrais**
tu	**résoudrais**
il/elle/on	**résoudrait**
nous	**résoudrions**
vous	**résoudriez**
ils/elles	**résoudraient**

PAST HISTORIC

je	**résolus**
tu	**résolus**
il/elle/on	**résolut**
nous	**résolûmes**
vous	**résolûtes**
ils/elles	**résolurent**

PLUPERFECT

j'	**avais résolu**
tu	**avais résolu**
il/elle/on	**avait résolu**
nous	**avions résolu**
vous	**aviez résolu**
ils/elles	**avaient résolu**

IMPERATIVE

résous / résolvons / résolvez

EXAMPLE PHRASES

Son refus de s'excuser ne **résoudra** pas la querelle. His refusal to apologize won't resolve the quarrel.

Il **résolut** l'énigme en quelques minutes. He solved the riddle in a few minutes.

C'est un problème qui se **résoudrait** rapidement s'il n'y avait pas déjà d'autres problèmes. This problem could be solved quickly if there weren't already other problems.

À la fin de la réunion, nous **avions résolu** la question. By the end of the meeting, we had resolved the matter.

je/j' = I tu = you il = he/it elle = she/it on = we/one nous = we vous = you ils/elles = they

rester (to stay)

PRESENT

je	**reste**
tu	**restes**
il/elle/on	**reste**
nous	**restons**
vous	**restez**
ils/elles	**restent**

PRESENT SUBJUNCTIVE

je	**reste**
tu	**restes**
il/elle/on	**reste**
nous	**restions**
vous	**restiez**
ils/elles	**restent**

PERFECT

je	**suis resté(e)**
tu	**es resté(e)**
il/elle/on	**est resté(e)**
nous	**sommes resté(e)s**
vous	**êtes resté(e)(s)**
ils/elles	**sont resté(e)s**

IMPERFECT

je	**restais**
tu	**restais**
il/elle/on	**restait**
nous	**restions**
vous	**restiez**
ils/elles	**restaient**

PRESENT PARTICIPLE

restant

PAST PARTICIPLE

resté

EXAMPLE PHRASES

Cet été, je **reste** au Québec. I'm staying in Quebec this summer.

Ils ne **sont** pas **restés** très longtemps. They didn't stay very long.

Elle aimerait que Marianne **reste** dormir ce soir. She'd like Marianne to sleep over tonight.

Il leur **restait** encore un peu d'argent. They still had some money left.

je/j' = I   tu = you   il = he/it   elle = she/it   on = we/one   nous = we   vous = you   ils/elles = they

rester

FUTURE

je	**resterai**
tu	**resteras**
il/elle/on	**restera**
nous	**resterons**
vous	**resterez**
ils/elles	**resteront**

CONDITIONAL

je	**resterais**
tu	**resterais**
il/elle/on	**resterait**
nous	**resterions**
vous	**resteriez**
ils/elles	**resteraient**

PAST HISTORIC

je	**restai**
tu	**restas**
il/elle/on	**resta**
nous	**restâmes**
vous	**restâtes**
ils/elles	**restèrent**

PLUPERFECT

j'	**étais resté(e)**
tu	**étais resté(e)**
il/elle/on	**était resté(e)**
nous	**étions resté(e)s**
vous	**étiez resté(e)(s)**
ils/elles	**étaient resté(e)s**

IMPERATIVE

reste / restons / restez

EXAMPLE PHRASES

Si tu finis les biscuits il n'en **restera** plus pour ce soir. If you finish the cookies, there won't be any left for tonight.

Il **resta** dans sa chambre toute la soirée. He stayed in his bedroom all evening.

Si c'était à moi de choisir, je **resterais** à la maison. If it were my choice, I'd stay home.

Nous **étions restés** à la maison pour regarder le match de football. We'd stayed home to watch the football match.

Reste ici ! Stay here!

je/j' = I **tu** = you **il** = he/it **elle** = she/it **on** = we/one **nous** = we **vous** = you **ils/elles** = they

retourner (to return; to turn)

PRESENT

je	**retourne**
tu	**retournes**
il/elle/on	**retourne**
nous	**retournons**
vous	**retournez**
ils/elles	**retournent**

PRESENT SUBJUNCTIVE

je	**retourne**
tu	**retournes**
il/elle/on	**retourne**
nous	**retournions**
vous	**retourniez**
ils/elles	**retournent**

PERFECT

je	**suis retourné(e)**
tu	**es retourné(e)**
il/elle/on	**est retourné(e)**
nous	**sommes retourné(e)s**
vous	**êtes retourné(e)(s)**
ils/elles	**sont retourné(e)s**

IMPERFECT

je	**retournais**
tu	**retournais**
il/elle/on	**retournait**
nous	**retournions**
vous	**retourniez**
ils/elles	**retournaient**

PRESENT PARTICIPLE

retournant

PAST PARTICIPLE

retourné

In the perfect and the pluperfect, use the auxiliary "avoir" when there is a direct object.

EXAMPLE PHRASES

J'aimerais bien **retourner** en Italie un jour. **I'd like to go back to Italy one day.**

Cet été, nous **retournons** en Grèce. **We're going back to Greece this summer.**

Est-ce que tu **es retournée** à Londres ? **Have you ever been back to London?**

Il va falloir que je **retourne** voir le film. **I'll have to go back to see the movie.**

Elle **retournait** rarement dans son pays natal. **She rarely went back to her native country.**

retourner

FUTURE

je	**retournerai**
tu	**retourneras**
il/elle/on	**retournera**
nous	**retournerons**
vous	**retournerez**
ils/elles	**retourneront**

CONDITIONAL

je	**retournerais**
tu	**retournerais**
il/elle/on	**retournerait**
nous	**retournerions**
vous	**retourneriez**
ils/elles	**retourneraient**

PAST HISTORIC

je	**retournai**
tu	**retournas**
il/elle/on	**retourna**
nous	**retournâmes**
vous	**retournâtes**
ils/elles	**retournèrent**

PLUPERFECT

j'	**étais retourné(e)**
tu	**étais retourné(e)**
il/elle/on	**était retourné(e)**
nous	**étions retourné(e)s**
vous	**étiez retourné(e)(s)**
ils/elles	**étaient retourné(e)s**

IMPERATIVE

retourne / retournons / retournez

EXAMPLE PHRASES

Je ne **retournerai** jamais les voir. I'll never go back to see them.

Elle déjeuna rapidement et **retourna** travailler. She had a quick lunch and
went back to work.

Il disait qu'il ne **retournerait** jamais vivre avec elle. He said that he would
never go back to live with her.

Elle **avait retourné** la carte pour vérifier. She had turned the card over to
check

Zoë, **retourne**-toi ! Turn around, Zoë!

je/j' = I   tu = you   il = he/it   elle = she/it   on = we/one   nous = we   vous = you   ils/elles = they

réussir (to be successful)

PRESENT

je	**réussis**
tu	**réussis**
il/elle/on	**réussit**
nous	**réussissons**
vous	**réussissez**
ils/elles	**réussissent**

PRESENT SUBJUNCTIVE

je	**réussisse**
tu	**réussisses**
il/elle/on	**réussisse**
nous	**réussissions**
vous	**réussissiez**
ils/elles	**réussissent**

PERFECT

j'	**ai réussi**
tu	**as réussi**
il/elle/on	**a réussi**
nous	**avons réussi**
vous	**avez réussi**
ils/elles	**ont réussi**

IMPERFECT

je	**réussissais**
tu	**réussissais**
il/elle/on	**réussissait**
nous	**réussissions**
vous	**réussissiez**
ils/elles	**réussissaient**

PRESENT PARTICIPLE

réussissant

PAST PARTICIPLE

réussi

EXAMPLE PHRASES

Il faut se battre pour **réussir** dans la vie. You have to fight to be successful in life.

Tous ses enfants **ont** très bien **réussi**. All her children are very successful.

J'aimerais qu'il **réussisse** à son permis de conduire. I'd like him to pass his driving test.

Elle **réussissait** toujours à me faire rire quand j'étais triste. She always managed to make me laugh when I was sad.

---

je/j' = I   tu = you   il = he/it   elle = she/it   on = we/one   nous = we   vous = you   ils/elles = they

réussir

FUTURE

je	**réussirai**
tu	**réussiras**
il/elle/on	**réussira**
nous	**réussirons**
vous	**réussirez**
ils/elles	**réussiront**

CONDITIONAL

je	**réussirais**
tu	**réussirais**
il/elle/on	**réussirait**
nous	**réussirions**
vous	**réussiriez**
ils/elles	**réussiraient**

PAST HISTORIC

je	**réussis**
tu	**réussis**
il/elle/on	**réussit**
nous	**réussîmes**
vous	**réussîtes**
ils/elles	**réussirent**

PLUPERFECT

j'	**avais réussi**
tu	**avais réussi**
il/elle/on	**avait réussi**
nous	**avions réussi**
vous	**aviez réussi**
ils/elles	**avaient réussi**

IMPERATIVE

réussis / réussissons / réussissez

EXAMPLE PHRASES

Je suis sûr que tu **réussiras** à ton examen. I'm sure you'll pass your exam.

Finalement, elle **réussit** à le convaincre. She eventually managed to convince him.

Je **réussirais** peut-être mes gâteaux si j'avais un four qui marchait. My cakes might turn out OK if I had an oven that worked.

Elle **avait réussi** à battre le record du monde. She had succeeded in beating the world record.

je/j' = I tu = you il = he/it elle = she/it on = we/one nous = we vous = you ils/elles = they

se réveiller (to wake up)

	PRESENT		**PRESENT SUBJUNCTIVE**
je	me réveille	je	me réveille
tu	te réveilles	tu	te réveilles
il/elle/on	se réveille	il/elle/on	se réveille
nous	nous réveillons	nous	nous réveillions
vous	vous réveillez	vous	vous réveilliez
ils/elles	se réveillent	ils/elles	se réveillent

	PERFECT		**IMPERFECT**
je	me suis réveillé(e)	je	me réveillais
tu	t'es réveillé(e)	tu	te réveillais
il/elle/on	s'est réveillé(e)	il/elle/on	se réveillait
nous	nous sommes réveillé(e)s	nous	nous réveillions
vous	vous êtes réveillé(e)(s)	vous	vous réveilliez
ils/elles	se sont réveillé(e)s	ils/elles	se réveillaient

PRESENT PARTICIPLE
se réveillant

PAST PARTICIPLE
réveillé

EXAMPLE PHRASES

Je **me réveille** à sept heures tous les matins. **I wake up at seven every morning.**

Il **s'est réveillé** en retard. **He overslept.**

Il faut que je **me réveille** à cinq heures demain matin. **I have to get up at five tomorrow morning.**

Elle **se réveillait** toujours avant moi. **She always woke up before me.**

je/j' = I   tu = you   il = he/it   elle = she/it   on = we/one   nous = we   vous = you   ils/elles = they

se réveiller

FUTURE

je	me réveillerai
tu	te réveilleras
il/elle/on	se réveillera
nous	nous réveillerons
vous	vous réveillerez
ils/elles	se réveilleront

CONDITIONAL

je	me réveillerais
tu	te réveillerais
il/elle/on	se réveillerait
nous	nous réveillerions
vous	vous réveilleriez
ils/elles	se réveilleraient

PAST HISTORIC

je	me réveillai
tu	te réveillas
il/elle/on	se réveilla
nous	nous reveillâmes
vous	vous réveillâtes
ils/elles	se réveillèrent

PLUPERFECT

je	m'étais réveillé(e)
tu	t'étais réveillé(e)
il/elle/on	s'était réveillé(e)
nous	nous étions réveillé(e)s
vous	vous étiez réveillé(e)(s)
ils/elles	s'étaient réveillé(e)s

IMPERATIVE

réveille-toi / réveillons-nous / réveillez-vous

EXAMPLE PHRASES

Louise ne **se réveillera** probablement pas avant neuf heures. **Louise probably won't wake up before nine.**

Elle **se réveilla** en sursaut. **She woke up with a start.**

Je ne **me réveillerais** pas sans mon réveil. **I wouldn't wake up without my alarm clock.**

Elle ne **s'était** pas **réveillée** quand je l'avais appelée. **She hadn't woken up when I called her.**

Réveille-toi : il est huit heures ! **Wake up - it's eight!**

je/j' = I   tu = you   il = he/it   elle = she/it   on = we/one   nous = we   vous = you   ils/elles = they

revenir (to come back)

PRESENT

je	reviens
tu	reviens
il/elle/on	revient
nous	revenons
vous	revenez
ils/elles	reviennent

PRESENT SUBJUNCTIVE

je	revienne
tu	reviennes
il/elle/on	revienne
nous	revenions
vous	reveniez
ils/elles	reviennent

PERFECT

je	suis revenu(e)
tu	es revenu(e)
il/elle/on	est revenu(e)
nous	sommes revenu(e)s
vous	êtes revenu(e)(s)
ils/elles	sont revenu(e)s

IMPERFECT

je	revenais
tu	revenais
il/elle/on	revenait
nous	revenions
vous	reveniez
ils/elles	revenaient

PRESENT PARTICIPLE

revenant

PAST PARTICIPLE

revenu

EXAMPLE PHRASES

Je **reviens** dans cinq minutes ! I'll be back in five minutes!

Ça me **revient** ! It's coming back to me now!

Mon chat n'**est** toujours pas **revenu**. My cat still hasn't come back.

J'aimerais qu'il **revienne** me voir. I'd like him to come back to see me.

Son chien se promenait souvent loin de chez lui mais il **revenait** toujours.
His dog often wandered far away from his house, but he'd always come back.

je/j' = I   tu = you   il = he/it   elle = she/it   on = we/one   nous = we   vous = you   ils/elles = they

revenir

FUTURE

je	**reviendrai**
tu	**reviendras**
il/elle/on	**reviendra**
nous	**reviendrons**
vous	**reviendrez**
ils/elles	**reviendront**

CONDITIONAL

je	**reviendrais**
tu	**reviendrais**
il/elle/on	**reviendrait**
nous	**reviendrions**
vous	**reviendriez**
ils/elles	**reviendraient**

PAST HISTORIC

je	**revins**
tu	**revins**
il/elle/on	**revint**
nous	**revînmes**
vous	**revîntes**
ils/elles	**revinrent**

PLUPERFECT

j'	**étais revenu(e)**
tu	**étais revenu(e)**
il/elle/on	**était revenu(e)**
nous	**étions revenu(e)s**
vous	**étiez revenu(e)(s)**
ils/elles	**étaient revenu(e)s**

IMPERATIVE

reviens / revenons / revenez

EXAMPLE PHRASES

Je ne **reviendrai** jamais ici. I'll never come back here.

Il **revint** nous voir le lendemain. He came back to see us the next day.

Elle ne **reviendrait** pas si elle avait le choix. She wouldn't come back if she had the choice.

Ils **étaient revenus** le soir même avec leur fille. They had come back that same evening with their daughter.

Philippe ! **Reviens** immédiatement ! Philippe! Come back immediately!

je/j' = I tu = you il = he/it elle = she/it on = we/one nous = we vous = you ils/elles = they

rire (to laugh)

PRESENT

je	**ris**
tu	**ris**
il/elle/on	**rit**
nous	**rions**
vous	**riez**
ils/elles	**rient**

PRESENT SUBJUNCTIVE

je	**rie**
tu	**ries**
il/elle/on	**rie**
nous	**riions**
vous	**riiez**
ils/elles	**rient**

PERFECT

j'	**ai ri**
tu	**as ri**
il/elle/on	**a ri**
nous	**avons ri**
vous	**avez ri**
ils/elles	**ont ri**

IMPERFECT

je	**riais**
tu	**riais**
il/elle/on	**riait**
nous	**riions**
vous	**riiez**
ils/elles	**riaient**

PRESENT PARTICIPLE

riant

PAST PARTICIPLE

ri

EXAMPLE PHRASES

C'était juste pour **rire**. It was only for a laugh.

Elle **rit** toujours de mes plaisanteries. She always laughs at my jokes.

On **a** bien **ri**. We had a good laugh.

Je n'aime pas qu'on **rie** derrière mon dos. I don't like it when people laugh behind my back.

je/j' = I   tu = you   il = he/it   elle = she/it   on = we/one   nous = we   vous = you   ils/elles = they

rire

FUTURE

je	rirai
tu	riras
il/elle/on	rira
nous	rirons
vous	rirez
ils/elles	riront

CONDITIONAL

je	rirais
tu	rirais
il/elle/on	rirait
nous	ririons
vous	ririez
ils/elles	riraient

PAST HISTORIC

je	ris
tu	ris
il/elle/on	rit
nous	rîmes
vous	rîtes
ils/elles	rirent

PLUPERFECT

j'	avais ri
tu	avais ri
il/elle/on	avait ri
nous	avions ri
vous	aviez ri
ils/elles	avaient ri

IMPERATIVE

ris / rions / riez

EXAMPLE PHRASES

Tu ne **riras** pas tant quand ce sera ton tour. You won't be laughing so much
when it's your turn.

Elle **rit** quand il lui raconta l'histoire. She laughed when he told her the
story.

Il ne **rirait** pas s'il savait où tu es allé. He wouldn't be laughing if he knew
where you've been.

Ils **avaient ri** quand elle leur avait raconté ce qui s'était passé. They had
laughed when she had told them what had happened.

Ne **ris** pas, ce n'est pas drôle ! Don't laugh, it's not funny!

je/j' = I **tu** = you **il** = he/it **elle** = she/it **on** = we/one **nous** = we **vous** = you **ils/elles** = they

rompre (to break; to split up)

PRESENT

je	romps
tu	romps
il/elle/on	rompt
nous	rompons
vous	rompez
ils/elles	rompent

PRESENT SUBJUNCTIVE

je	rompe
tu	rompes
il/elle/on	rompe
nous	rompions
vous	rompiez
ils/elles	rompent

PERFECT

j'	ai rompu
tu	as rompu
il/elle/on	a rompu
nous	avons rompu
vous	avez rompu
ils/elles	ont rompu

IMPERFECT

je	rompais
tu	rompais
il/elle/on	rompait
nous	rompions
vous	rompiez
ils/elles	rompaient

PRESENT PARTICIPLE

rompant

PAST PARTICIPLE

rompu

EXAMPLE PHRASES

Elle **a rompu** le silence. She broke the silence.

Paul et Jo **ont rompu**. Paul and Jo have split up.

Ils ont tiré sur la corde jusqu'à ce qu'elle **rompe**. They pulled on the rope until it broke.

rompre

FUTURE

je	**romprai**
tu	**rompras**
il/elle/on	**rompra**
nous	**romprons**
vous	**romprez**
ils/elles	**rompront**

CONDITIONAL

je	**romprais**
tu	**romprais**
il/elle/on	**romprait**
nous	**romprions**
vous	**rompriez**
ils/elles	**rompraient**

PAST HISTORIC

je	**rompis**
tu	**rompis**
il/elle/on	**rompit**
nous	**rompîmes**
vous	**rompîtes**
ils/elles	**rompirent**

PLUPERFECT

j'	**avais rompu**
tu	**avais rompu**
il/elle/on	**avait rompu**
nous	**avions rompu**
vous	**aviez rompu**
ils/elles	**avaient rompu**

IMPERATIVE

romps / rompons / rompez

EXAMPLE PHRASES

Il **rompit** le silence en entrant. He broke the silence when he came in.

Le charme **était rompu**. The spell was broken.

Il **avait** déjà **rompu** avec Alice quand il a rencontré Christine. He'd already split up with Alice when he met Christine.

---

je/j' = I tu = you il = he/it elle = she/it on = we/one nous = we vous = you ils/elles = they

savoir (to know)

PRESENT

je	**sais**
tu	**sais**
il/elle/on	**sait**
nous	**savons**
vous	**savez**
ils/elles	**savent**

PRESENT SUBJUNCTIVE

je	**sache**
tu	**saches**
il/elle/on	**sache**
nous	**sachions**
vous	**sachiez**
ils/elles	**sachent**

PERFECT

j'	**ai su**
tu	**as su**
il/elle/on	**a su**
nous	**avons su**
vous	**avez su**
ils/elles	**ont su**

IMPERFECT

je	**savais**
tu	**savais**
il/elle/on	**savait**
nous	**savions**
vous	**saviez**
ils/elles	**savaient**

PRESENT PARTICIPLE

sachant

PAST PARTICIPLE

su

EXAMPLE PHRASES

Tu **sais** ce que tu vas faire l'année prochaine ? Do you know what you're going to do next year?

Je ne **sais** pas. I don't know.

Elle ne **sait** pas nager. She can't swim.

Je voulais qu'il le **sache**. I wanted him to know about it.

Tu **savais** que son père était enseignant ? Did you know that her father was a teacher?

---

je/j' = I   **tu** = you   **il** = he/it   **elle** = she/it   **on** = we/one   **nous** = we   **vous** = you   **ils/elles** = they

savoir

FUTURE

je	**saurai**
tu	**sauras**
il/elle/on	**saura**
nous	**saurons**
vous	**saurez**
ils/elles	**sauront**

CONDITIONAL

je	**saurais**
tu	**saurais**
il/elle/on	**saurait**
nous	**saurions**
vous	**sauriez**
ils/elles	**sauraient**

PAST HISTORIC

je	**sus**
tu	**sus**
il/elle/on	**sut**
nous	**sûmes**
vous	**sûtes**
ils/elles	**surent**

PLUPERFECT

j'	**avais su**
tu	**avais su**
il/elle/on	**avait su**
nous	**avions su**
vous	**aviez su**
ils/elles	**avaient su**

IMPERATIVE

sache / sachons / sachez

EXAMPLE PHRASES

Elle ne **saura** pas où on est. She won't know where we are.

Il ne le **sut** que beaucoup plus tard. He only knew about it a lot later.

Tous ces enfants **sauraient** lire si on leur apprenait. All these children would be able to read if they were taught.

Ils ne l'**avaient su** que beaucoup plus tard. They hadn't known about it until a lot later.

je/j' = I tu = you il = he/it elle = she/it on = we/one nous = we vous = you ils/elles = they

sentir (to smell; to feel)

PRESENT

je	**sens**
tu	**sens**
il/elle/on	**sent**
nous	**sentons**
vous	**sentez**
ils/elles	**sentent**

PRESENT SUBJUNCTIVE

je	**sente**
tu	**sentes**
il/elle/on	**sente**
nous	**sentions**
vous	**sentiez**
ils/elles	**sentent**

PERFECT

j'	**ai senti**
tu	**as senti**
il/elle/on	**a senti**
nous	**avons senti**
vous	**avez senti**
ils/elles	**ont senti**

IMPERFECT

je	**sentais**
tu	**sentais**
il/elle/on	**sentait**
nous	**sentions**
vous	**sentiez**
ils/elles	**sentaient**

PRESENT PARTICIPLE

sentant

PAST PARTICIPLE

senti

EXAMPLE PHRASES

Ça **sent** bon ici. It smells nice in here.

Elle ne se **sent** pas bien. She's not feeling well.

Je n'**ai** rien **senti**. I didn't feel a thing.

Ça **sentait** mauvais. It smelled bad.

---

sentir

FUTURE

je	sentirai
tu	sentiras
il/elle/on	sentira
nous	sentirons
vous	sentirez
ils/elles	sentiront

CONDITIONAL

je	sentirais
tu	sentirais
il/elle/on	sentirait
nous	sentirions
vous	sentiriez
ils/elles	sentiraient

PAST HISTORIC

je	sentis
tu	sentis
il/elle/on	sentit
nous	sentîmes
vous	sentîtes
ils/elles	sentirent

PLUPERFECT

j'	avais senti
tu	avais senti
il/elle/on	avait senti
nous	avions senti
vous	aviez senti
ils/elles	avaient senti

IMPERATIVE

sens / sentons / sentez

EXAMPLE PHRASES

Ne vous inquiétez pas : vous ne **sentirez** rien. Don't worry – you won't feel a thing.

Il **sentit** que ce n'était pas le bon moment. He felt that it wasn't the right time.

Elle se **sentirait** mieux si elle se reposait. She'd feel better if she rested.

Il n'**avait** rien **senti** pendant l'opération. He hadn't felt a thing during the operation.

Sens ces fleurs. Smell these flowers.

je/j' = I **tu** = you **il** = he/it **elle** = she/it **on** = we/one **nous** = we **vous** = you **ils/elles** = they

servir (to serve; to be of use to)

PRESENT

je	**sers**
tu	**sers**
il/elle/on	**sert**
nous	**servons**
vous	**servez**
ils/elles	**servent**

PRESENT SUBJUNCTIVE

je	**serve**
tu	**serves**
il/elle/on	**serve**
nous	**servions**
vous	**serviez**
ils/elles	**servent**

PERFECT

j'	**ai servi**
tu	**as servi**
il/elle/on	**a servi**
nous	**avons servi**
vous	**avez servi**
ils/elles	**ont servi**

IMPERFECT

je	**servais**
tu	**servais**
il/elle/on	**servait**
nous	**servions**
vous	**serviez**
ils/elles	**servaient**

PRESENT PARTICIPLE
servant

PAST PARTICIPLE
servi

EXAMPLE PHRASES

On vous **sert** ? Are you being helped?

Ça **sert** à quoi ce bouton ? What is this button for?

Il faut que je **serve** la soupe. I have to serve the soup.

Ça ne **servait** à rien de le supplier. It was no use begging him.

je/j' = I   tu = you   il = he/it   elle = she/it   on = we/one   nous = we   vous = you   ils/elles = they

servir

FUTURE

je	**servirai**
tu	**serviras**
il/elle/on	**servira**
nous	**servirons**
vous	**servirez**
ils/elles	**serviront**

CONDITIONAL

je	**servirais**
tu	**servirais**
il/elle/on	**servirait**
nous	**servirions**
vous	**serviriez**
ils/elles	**serviraient**

PAST HISTORIC

je	**servis**
tu	**servis**
il/elle/on	**servit**
nous	**servîmes**
vous	**servîtes**
ils/elles	**servirent**

PLUPERFECT

j'	**avais servi**
tu	**avais servi**
il/elle/on	**avait servi**
nous	**avions servi**
vous	**aviez servi**
ils/elles	**avaient servi**

IMPERATIVE

sers / servons / servez

EXAMPLE PHRASES

Ces boîtes te **serviront** quand tu déménageras. You'll find these boxes useful when you move.

Elle leur **servit** des profiteroles en dessert. She served them profiteroles for dessert.

Ça ne **servirait** à rien d'y aller maintenant. It would serve no purpose to go there now.

Cette valise n'**avait** pas **servi** depuis dix ans. This suitcase hadn't been used for ten years.

Servez-vous. Help yourself.

je/j' = I **tu** = you **il** = he/it **elle** = she/it **on** = we/one **nous** = we **vous** = you **ils/elles** = they

sortir (to go out; to take out)

PRESENT

je	**sors**
tu	**sors**
il/elle/on	**sort**
nous	**sortons**
vous	**sortez**
ils/elles	**sortent**

PRESENT SUBJUNCTIVE

je	**sorte**
tu	**sortes**
il/elle/on	**sorte**
nous	**sortions**
vous	**sortiez**
ils/elles	**sortent**

PERFECT

je	**suis sorti(e)**
tu	**es sorti(e)**
il/elle/on	**est sorti(e)**
nous	**sommes sorti(e)s**
vous	**êtes sorti(e)(s)**
ils/elles	**sont sorti(e)s**

IMPERFECT

je	**sortais**
tu	**sortais**
il/elle/on	**sortait**
nous	**sortions**
vous	**sortiez**
ils/elles	**sortaient**

PRESENT PARTICIPLE

sortant

PAST PARTICIPLE

sorti

In the perfect and the imperfect, use the auxiliary "avoir" when there is a direct object.

EXAMPLE PHRASES

Aurélie **sort** avec Bruno. **Aurélie is going out with Bruno.**

Je ne **suis** pas **sortie** ce week-end. **I didn't go out this weekend.**

Je n'**ai** pas **sorti** le chien parce qu'il pleuvait. **I didn't take the dog out for a walk because it was raining.**

Je ne veux pas que tu **sortes** habillée comme ça. **I don't want you to go out dressed like that.**

Il **sortait** quand c'est arrivé. **He was going out when it happened.**

sortir

FUTURE

je	sortirai
tu	sortiras
il/elle/on	sortira
nous	sortirons
vous	sortirez
ils/elles	sortiront

CONDITIONAL

je	sortirais
tu	sortirais
il/elle/on	sortirait
nous	sortirions
vous	sortiriez
ils/elles	sortiraient

PAST HISTORIC

je	sortis
tu	sortis
il/elle/on	sortit
nous	sortîmes
vous	sortîtes
ils/elles	sortirent

PLUPERFECT

j'	étais sorti(e)
tu	étais sorti(e)
il/elle/on	était sorti(e)
nous	étions sorti(e)s
vous	étiez sorti(e)(s)
ils/elles	étaient sorti(e)s

IMPERATIVE

sors / sortons / sortez

EXAMPLE PHRASES

Je **sortirai** la poubelle en partant. I'll take out the trash on my way out.

Il **sortit** une photo de sa poche. He took a photo out of his pocket.

Elle ne **sortirait** jamais de chez elle si son mari ne l'y obligeait pas.
   She'd never leave her house if her husband didn't force her.

Elle **était sortie** de l'hôpital la veille. She had come out of the hospital the
   day before.

Sortez en silence. Go out quietly.

je/j' = I tu = you il = he/it elle = she/it on = we/one nous = we vous = you ils/elles = they

souffrir (to be in pain)

je/j' = I   tu = you   il = he/it   elle = she/it   on = we/one   nous = we   vous = you   ils/elles = they

PRESENT

je	**souffre**
tu	**souffres**
il/elle/on	**souffre**
nous	**souffrons**
vous	**souffrez**
ils/elles	**souffrent**

PRESENT SUBJUNCTIVE

je	**souffre**
tu	**souffres**
il/elle/on	**souffre**
nous	**souffrions**
vous	**souffriez**
ils/elles	**souffrent**

PERFECT

j'	**ai souffert**
tu	**as souffert**
il/elle/on	**a souffert**
nous	**avons souffert**
vous	**avez souffert**
ils/elles	**ont souffert**

IMPERFECT

je	**souffrais**
tu	**souffrais**
il/elle/on	**souffrait**
nous	**souffrions**
vous	**souffriez**
ils/elles	**souffraient**

PRESENT PARTICIPLE

souffrant

PAST PARTICIPLE

souffert

EXAMPLE PHRASES

Il **souffre** beaucoup. He's in a lot of pain.

Elle **a** beaucoup **souffert** quand il l'a quittée. She suffered a lot when he left her.

J'ai peur qu'il ne **souffre**. I'm scared he might be suffering.

Il **souffrait** de ne plus la voir. It pained him not to see her any more.

---

souffrir

FUTURE

je	**souffrirai**
tu	**souffriras**
il/elle/on	**souffrira**
nous	**souffrirons**
vous	**souffrirez**
ils/elles	**souffriront**

CONDITIONAL

je	**souffrirais**
tu	**souffrirais**
il/elle/on	**souffrirait**
nous	**souffririons**
vous	**souffririez**
ils/elles	**souffriraient**

PAST HISTORIC

je	**souffris**
tu	**souffris**
il/elle/on	**souffrit**
nous	**souffrîmes**
vous	**souffrîtes**
ils/elles	**souffrirent**

PLUPERFECT

j'	**avais souffert**
tu	**avais souffert**
il/elle/on	**avait souffert**
nous	**avions souffert**
vous	**aviez souffert**
ils/elles	**avaient souffert**

IMPERATIVE

souffre / souffrons / souffrez

EXAMPLE PHRASES

Je te promets que tu ne **souffriras** pas trop. I promise that you won't be in too much pain.

Ils **souffrirent** en silence. They suffered in silence.

Elle ne **souffrirait** pas tant si elle prenait son médicament. She wouldn't suffer so much if she took her medicine.

Elle **avait** beaucoup **souffert** durant son enfance. She had suffered a lot during her childhood.

Souffre en silence. Suffer in silence.

je/j' = I **tu** = you **il** = he/it **elle** = she/it **on** = we/one **nous** = we **vous** = you **ils/elles** = they

se souvenir (to remember)

PRESENT

je	**me souviens**
tu	**te souviens**
il/elle/on	**se souvient**
nous	**nous souvenons**
vous	**vous souvenez**
ils/elles	**se souviennent**

PRESENT SUBJUNCTIVE

je	**me souvienne**
tu	**te souviennes**
il/elle/on	**se souvienne**
nous	**nous souvenions**
vous	**vous souveniez**
ils/elles	**se souviennent**

PERFECT

je	**me suis souvenu(e)**
tu	**t'es souvenu(e)**
il/elle/on	**s'est souvenu(e)**
nous	**nous sommes souvenu(e)s**
vous	**vous êtes souvenu(e)(s)**
ils/elles	**se sont souvenu(e)s**

IMPERFECT

je	**me souvenais**
tu	**te souvenais**
il/elle/on	**se souvenait**
nous	**nous souvenions**
vous	**vous souveniez**
ils/elles	**se souvenaient**

PRESENT PARTICIPLE

se souvenant

PAST PARTICIPLE

souvenu

EXAMPLE PHRASES

Je ne **me souviens** pas de son adresse. I can't remember his address.

Te souviens-tu du jour où Pierre s'est cassé le bras ? Do you remember the day when Pierre broke his arm?

Je ne crois pas qu'elle **s'en souvienne**. I don't think that she remembers it.

Il ne **se souvenait** pas où il avait mis ses clés. He couldn't remember where he'd put his keys.

---

je/j' = I   tu = you   il = he/it   elle = she/it   on = we/one   nous = we   vous = you   ils/elles = they

se souvenir

FUTURE

je	**me souviendrai**
tu	**te souviendras**
il/elle/on	**se souviendra**
nous	**nous souviendrons**
vous	**vous souviendrez**
ils/elles	**se souviendront**

CONDITIONAL

je	**me souviendrais**
tu	**te souviendrais**
il/elle/on	**se souviendrait**
nous	**nous souviendrions**
vous	**vous souviendriez**
ils/elles	**se souviendraient**

PAST HISTORIC

je	**me souvins**
tu	**te souvins**
il/elle/on	**se souvint**
nous	**nous souvînmes**
vous	**vous souvîntes**
ils/elles	**se souvinrent**

PLUPERFECT

je	**m'étais souvenu(e)**
tu	**t'étais souvenu(e)**
il/elle/on	**s'était souvenu(e)**
nous	**nous étions souvenu(e)s**
vous	**vous étiez souvenu(e)(s)**
ils/elles	**s'étaient souvenu(e)s**

IMPERATIVE

souviens-toi / souvenons-nous / souvenez-vous

EXAMPLE PHRASES

Fais-lui une liste, sinon il ne **se souviendra** pas de ce qu'il doit acheter.
  Make him a list, otherwise he won't remember what he has to buy.
Elle **se souvint** qu'elle leur avait promis une surprise. She remembered that
  she'd promised them a surprise.
Si je ne prenais pas de notes, je ne **me souviendrais** pas de mes cours.
  If I didn't take notes, I wouldn't remember my lessons.
Il **s'était souvenu** un peu tard de son anniversaire. He had remembered her
  birthday a little late.
Souviens-toi : il neigeait ce jour-là. Remember – it was snowing that day.

je/j' = I **tu** = you **il** = he/it **elle** = she/it **on** = we/one **nous** = we **vous** = you **ils/elles** = they

suffire (to be enough)

PRESENT

je	**suffis**
tu	**suffis**
il/elle/on	**suffit**
nous	**suffisons**
vous	**suffisez**
ils/elles	**suffisent**

PRESENT SUBJUNCTIVE

je	**suffise**
tu	**suffises**
il/elle/on	**suffise**
nous	**suffisions**
vous	**suffisiez**
ils/elles	**suffisent**

PERFECT

j'	**ai suffi**
tu	**as suffi**
il/elle/on	**a suffi**
nous	**avons suffi**
vous	**avez suffi**
ils/elles	**ont suffi**

IMPERFECT

je	**suffisais**
tu	**suffisais**
il/elle/on	**suffisait**
nous	**suffisions**
vous	**suffisiez**
ils/elles	**suffisaient**

PRESENT PARTICIPLE

suffisant

PAST PARTICIPLE

suffi

EXAMPLE PHRASES

Ça **suffit** ! That's enough!

Ses jouets lui **suffisent**. His toys are enough for him.

Une séance avec le chiropracteur **a suffi** pour me soulager. One session with the chiropractor was enough to ease the pain.

Il **suffisait** de me le demander. You only had to ask.

suffire

FUTURE

je	**suffirai**
tu	**suffiras**
il/elle/on	**suffira**
nous	**suffirons**
vous	**suffirez**
ils/elles	**suffiront**

CONDITIONAL

je	**suffirais**
tu	**suffirais**
il/elle/on	**suffirait**
nous	**suffirions**
vous	**suffiriez**
ils/elles	**suffiraient**

PAST HISTORIC

je	**suffis**
tu	**suffis**
il/elle/on	**suffit**
nous	**suffîmes**
vous	**suffîtes**
ils/elles	**suffirent**

PLUPERFECT

j'	**avais suffi**
tu	**avais suffi**
il/elle/on	**avait suffi**
nous	**avions suffi**
vous	**aviez suffi**
ils/elles	**avaient suffi**

IMPERATIVE

suffis / suffisons / suffisez

EXAMPLE PHRASES

Ça te **suffira**, dix euros ? **Will ten euros be enough?**

Sa promesse lui **suffit** : il lui faisait confiance. **Her promise was enough for him – he trusted her.**

Il **suffirait** de se dépêcher un peu pour le rattraper. **We'd only have to hurry a little to catch up with him.**

Il nous **avait suffi** d'aller à la bibliothèque municipale pour trouver le livre. **We only had to go to the community library to find the book.**

je/j' = I   tu = you   il = he/it   elle = she/it   on = we/one   nous = we   vous = you   ils/elles = they

suivre (to follow)

PRESENT

je	**suis**
tu	**suis**
il/elle/on	**suit**
nous	**suivons**
vous	**suivez**
ils/elles	**suivent**

PRESENT SUBJUNCTIVE

je	**suive**
tu	**suives**
il/elle/on	**suive**
nous	**suivions**
vous	**suiviez**
ils/elles	**suivent**

PERFECT

j'	**ai suivi**
tu	**as suivi**
il/elle/on	**a suivi**
nous	**avons suivi**
vous	**avez suivi**
ils/elles	**ont suivi**

IMPERFECT

je	**suivais**
tu	**suivais**
il/elle/on	**suivait**
nous	**suivions**
vous	**suiviez**
ils/elles	**suivaient**

PRESENT PARTICIPLE

suivant

PAST PARTICIPLE

suivi

EXAMPLE PHRASES

Elle n'arrive pas à **suivre** en maths. She can't keep up in math.

Mon chat me **suit** partout dans la maison. My cat follows me all around the house.

Il **a suivi** un cours d'allemand pendant six mois. He took a German course for six months.

Je n'aime pas qu'il me **suive** partout comme un petit chien. I don't like him following me everywhere like a dog.

Ils nous **suivaient** à vélo. They were cycling behind us.

je/j' = I   **tu** = you   **il** = he/it   **elle** = she/it   **on** = we/one   **nous** = we   **vous** = you   **ils/elles** = they

suivre

FUTURE

je	**suivrai**
tu	**suivras**
il/elle/on	**suivra**
nous	**suivrons**
vous	**suivrez**
ils/elles	**suivront**

CONDITIONAL

je	**suivrais**
tu	**suivrais**
il/elle/on	**suivrait**
nous	**suivrions**
vous	**suivriez**
ils/elles	**suivraient**

PAST HISTORIC

je	**suivis**
tu	**suivis**
il/elle/on	**suivit**
nous	**suivîmes**
vous	**suivîtes**
ils/elles	**suivirent**

PLUPERFECT

j'	**avais suivi**
tu	**avais suivi**
il/elle/on	**avait suivi**
nous	**avions suivi**
vous	**aviez suivi**
ils/elles	**avaient suivi**

IMPERATIVE

suis / suivons / suivez

EXAMPLE PHRASES

Je vous **suivrai** de loin. I'll follow you at a distance.

Elle le **suivit** dans son bureau. She followed him into his office.

Il lui dit qu'il la **suivrait** en voiture. He told her that he would follow her in his car.

Je n'**avais** pas bien **suivi** les derniers événements. I hadn't really been following the latest events.

Suivez-moi. Follow me.

je/j' = I **tu** = you **il** = he/it **elle** = she/it **on** = we/one **nous** = we **vous** = you **ils/elles** = they

se taire (to stop talking)

PRESENT

je	**me tais**
tu	**te tais**
il/elle/on	**se tait**
nous	**nous taisons**
vous	**vous taisez**
ils/elles	**se taisent**

PRESENT SUBJUNCTIVE

je	**me taise**
tu	**te taises**
il/elle/on	**se taise**
nous	**nous taisions**
vous	**vous taisiez**
ils/elles	**se taisent**

PERFECT

je	**me suis tu(e)**
tu	**t'es tu(e)**
il/elle/on	**s'est tu(e)**
nous	**nous sommes tu(e)s**
vous	**vous êtes tu(e)(s)**
ils/elles	**se sont tu(e)s**

IMPERFECT

je	**me taisais**
tu	**te taisais**
il/elle/on	**se taisait**
nous	**nous taisions**
vous	**vous taisiez**
ils/elles	**se taisaient**

PRESENT PARTICIPLE

se taisant

PAST PARTICIPLE

tu

EXAMPLE PHRASES

Je préfère **me taire** quand ils se disputent. I prefer to keep quiet when they argue.

Il **s'est tu**. He stopped talking.

se taire

FUTURE

je	**me tairai**
tu	**te tairas**
il/elle/on	**se taira**
nous	**nous tairons**
vous	**vous tairez**
ils/elles	**se tairont**

CONDITIONAL

je	**me tairais**
tu	**te tairais**
il/elle/on	**se tairait**
nous	**nous tairions**
vous	**vous tairiez**
ils/elles	**se tairaient**

PAST HISTORIC

je	**me tus**
tu	**te tus**
il/elle/on	**se tut**
nous	**nous tûmes**
vous	**vous tûtes**
ils/elles	**se turent**

PLUPERFECT

je	**m'étais tu(e)**
tu	**t'étais tu(e)**
il/elle/on	**s'était tu(e)**
nous	**nous étions tu(e)s**
vous	**vous étiez tu(e)(s)**
ils/elles	**s'étaient tu(e)s**

IMPERATIVE

tais-toi / taisons-nous / taisez-vous

EXAMPLE PHRASES

Je **me tairai** si tu me laisses finir ma phrase. **I'll stop talking if you let me finish my sentence.**

Elle **se tut**. **She stopped talking.**

Je **me tairais** si j'étais sûr que tu n'allais pas inventer un mensonge. **I'd stop talking if I were sure that you wouldn't invent some lie.**

Il **s'était tu** et tout resta silencieux pendant quelques minutes. **He had stopped talking and for a few minutes all was silent.**

Sophie, **tais-toi** ! **Be quiet, Sophie!**

Taisez-vous ! **Be quiet!**

je/j' = I   tu = you   il = he/it   elle = she/it   on = we/one   nous = we   vous = you   ils/elles = they

tenir (to hold)

PRESENT

je	**tiens**
tu	**tiens**
il/elle/on	**tient**
nous	**tenons**
vous	**tenez**
ils/elles	**tiennent**

PRESENT SUBJUNCTIVE

je	**tienne**
tu	**tiennes**
il/elle/on	**tienne**
nous	**tenions**
vous	**teniez**
ils/elles	**tiennent**

PERFECT

j'	**ai tenu**
tu	**as tenu**
il/elle/on	**a tenu**
nous	**avons tenu**
vous	**avez tenu**
ils/elles	**ont tenu**

IMPERFECT

je	**tenais**
tu	**tenais**
il/elle/on	**tenait**
nous	**tenions**
vous	**teniez**
ils/elles	**tenaient**

PRESENT PARTICIPLE

tenant

PAST PARTICIPLE

tenu

EXAMPLE PHRASES

Il **tient** de son père. He takes after his father.

Tiens-moi la main. Hold my hand.

Tiens, prends mon stylo. Here, take my pen.

Tiens-toi droit ! Sit up straight!

Elle **tenait** beaucoup à son chat. She was really attached to her cat.

je/j' = I   tu = you   il = he/it   elle = she/it   on = we/one   nous = we   vous = you   ils/elles = they

tenir

FUTURE

je	tiendrai
tu	tiendras
il/elle/on	tiendra
nous	tiendrons
vous	tiendrez
ils/elles	tiendront

CONDITIONAL

je	tiendrais
tu	tiendrais
il/elle/on	tiendrait
nous	tiendrions
vous	tiendriez
ils/elles	tiendraient

PAST HISTORIC

je	tins
tu	tins
il/elle/on	tint
nous	tînmes
vous	tîntes
ils/elles	tinrent

PLUPERFECT

j'	avais tenu
tu	avais tenu
il/elle/on	avait tenu
nous	avions tenu
vous	aviez tenu
ils/elles	avaient tenu

IMPERATIVE

tiens / tenons / tenez

EXAMPLE PHRASES

Vous ne pourrez pas tomber car je vous **tiendrai** le bras. There's no chance
  of your falling as I'll be holding your arm.

Il **tint** sa promesse. He kept his promise.

Il ne me **tiendrait** pas la main s'il voyait un de ses copains. He wouldn't hold
  my hand if he saw one of his friends.

Elle **avait tenu** à y aller. She insisted on going.

je/j' = I **tu** = you **il** = he/it **elle** = she/it **on** = we/one **nous** = we **vous** = you **ils/elles** = they

tomber (to fall)

PRESENT

je	**tombe**
tu	**tombes**
il/elle/on	**tombe**
nous	**tombons**
vous	**tombez**
ils/elles	**tombent**

PRESENT SUBJUNCTIVE

je	**tombe**
tu	**tombes**
il/elle/on	**tombe**
nous	**tombions**
vous	**tombiez**
ils/elles	**tombent**

PERFECT

je	**suis tombé(e)**
tu	**es tombé(e)**
il/elle/on	**est tombé(e)**
nous	**sommes tombé(e)s**
vous	**êtes tombé(e)(s)**
ils/elles	**sont tombé(e)s**

IMPERFECT

je	**tombais**
tu	**tombais**
il/elle/on	**tombait**
nous	**tombions**
vous	**tombiez**
ils/elles	**tombaient**

PRESENT PARTICIPLE

tombant

PAST PARTICIPLE

tombé

EXAMPLE PHRASES

Attention, tu vas **tomber** ! Be careful, you'll fall!

Ça **tombe** bien. That's lucky.

Nicole **est tombée** de son cheval. Nicole fell off her horse.

Il **tombait** de sommeil. He was asleep on his feet.

Elle s'est fait mal en **tombant** dans l'escalier. She hurt herself falling down the stairs.

je/j' = I   tu = you   il = he/it   elle = she/it   on = we/one   nous = we   vous = you   ils/elles = they

tomber

FUTURE

je	**tomberai**
tu	**tomberas**
il/elle/on	**tombera**
nous	**tomberons**
vous	**tomberez**
ils/elles	**tomberont**

CONDITIONAL

je	**tomberais**
tu	**tomberais**
il/elle/on	**tomberait**
nous	**tomberions**
vous	**tomberiez**
ils/elles	**tomberaient**

PAST HISTORIC

je	**tombai**
tu	**tombas**
il/elle/on	**tomba**
nous	**tombâmes**
vous	**tombâtes**
ils/elles	**tombèrent**

PLUPERFECT

j'	**étais tombé(e)**
tu	**étais tombé(e)**
il/elle/on	**était tombé(e)**
nous	**étions tombé(e)s**
vous	**étiez tombé(e)(s)**
ils/elles	**étaient tombé(e)s**

IMPERATIVE

tombe / **tombons** / **tombez**

EXAMPLE PHRASES

J'espère qu'il ne **tombera** pas de son cheval. I hope he won't fall off his horse.

La tasse **tomba** par terre et se cassa. The cup fell on the floor and broke.

Tu ne **tomberais** pas si souvent si tu regardais où tu marches. You wouldn't fall so often if you watched where you were going.

Il **était** mal **tombé** et s'était cassé le bras. He'd fallen awkwardly and had broken his arm.

je/j' = I   tu = you   il = he/it   elle = she/it   on = we/one   nous = we   vous = you   ils/elles = they

traire (to milk)

PRESENT

je	**trais**
tu	**trais**
il/elle/on	**trait**
nous	**trayons**
vous	**trayez**
ils/elles	**traient**

PRESENT SUBJUNCTIVE

je	**traie**
tu	**traies**
il/elle/on	**traie**
nous	**trayions**
vous	**trayiez**
ils/elles	**traient**

PERFECT

j'	**ai trait**
tu	**as trait**
il/elle/on	**a trait**
nous	**avons trait**
vous	**avez trait**
ils/elles	**ont trait**

IMPERFECT

je	**trayais**
tu	**trayais**
il/elle/on	**trayait**
nous	**trayions**
vous	**trayiez**
ils/elles	**trayaient**

PRESENT PARTICIPLE
trayant

PAST PARTICIPLE
trait

EXAMPLE PHRASES

À la ferme, on a appris à **traire** les vaches. We learned to milk cows on the farm.

Elle **trait** les vaches à six heures du matin. She milks the cows at six am.

Nous **avons trait** les vaches. We milked the cows.

Il faut qu'elle **traie** les vaches de bonne heure tous les matins. She has to milk the cows early every morning.

On **trayait** les vaches avant d'aller à l'école. We milked the cows before going to school.

je/j' = I tu = you il = he/it elle = she/it on = we/one nous = we vous = you ils/elles = they

traire

FUTURE

je	**trairai**
tu	**trairas**
il/elle/on	**traira**
nous	**trairons**
vous	**trairez**
ils/elles	**trairont**

CONDITIONAL

je	**trairais**
tu	**trairais**
il/elle/on	**trairait**
nous	**trairions**
vous	**trairiez**
ils/elles	**trairaient**

PAST HISTORIC

not used

PLUPERFECT

j'	**avais trait**
tu	**avais trait**
il/elle/on	**avait trait**
nous	**avions trait**
vous	**aviez trait**
ils/elles	**avaient trait**

IMPERATIVE

trais / trayons / trayez

EXAMPLE PHRASES

Je **trairai** les vaches pour toi quand tu seras parti. I'll milk the cows for you when you're away.

Je **trairais** les brebis si je savais comment faire. I'd milk the ewes if I knew how.

Cela faisait longtemps qu'elle n'**avait** pas **trait** une vache. She hadn't milked a cow for a long time.

je/j' = I   tu = you   il = he/it   elle = she/it   on = we/one   nous = we   vous = you   ils/elles = they

vaincre (to defeat)

PRESENT

je	vaincs
tu	vaincs
il/elle/on	vainc
nous	vainquons
vous	vainquez
ils/elles	vainquent

PRESENT SUBJUNCTIVE

je	vainque
tu	vainques
il/elle/on	vainque
nous	vainquions
vous	vainquiez
ils/elles	vainquent

PERFECT

j'	ai vaincu
tu	as vaincu
il/elle/on	a vaincu
nous	avons vaincu
vous	avez vaincu
ils/elles	ont vaincu

IMPERFECT

je	vainquais
tu	vainquais
il/elle/on	vainquait
nous	vainquions
vous	vainquiez
ils/elles	vainquaient

PRESENT PARTICIPLE

vainquant

PAST PARTICIPLE

vaincu

EXAMPLE PHRASES

Il a réussi à **vaincre** sa timidité. **He managed to overcome his shyness.**

L'armée **a été vaincue**. **The army was defeated.**

La France **a vaincu** la Corée trois buts à deux. **France beat Korea three goals to two.**

vaincre

FUTURE

je	vaincrai
tu	vaincras
il/elle/on	vaincra
nous	vaincrons
vous	vaincrez
ils/elles	vaincront

CONDITIONAL

je	vaincrais
tu	vaincrais
il/elle/on	vaincrait
nous	vaincrions
vous	vaincriez
ils/elles	vaincraient

PAST HISTORIC

je	vainquis
tu	vainquis
il/elle/on	vainquit
nous	vainquîmes
vous	vainquîtes
ils/elles	vainquirent

PLUPERFECT

j'	avais vaincu
tu	avais vaincu
il/elle/on	avait vaincu
nous	avions vaincu
vous	aviez vaincu
ils/elles	avaient vaincu

IMPERATIVE

vaincs / vainquons / vainquez

EXAMPLE PHRASES

Tu ne **vaincras** pas ta peur en restant dans ta chambre. You won't overcome
   your fear if you stay in your bedroom.

Ils **vainquirent** l'armée ennemie après une bataille acharnée. They defeated
   the enemy army after a fierce battle.

Elle **avait** déjà **vaincu** cette adversaire. She'd already beaten this opponent.

---

je/j' = I   tu = you   il = he/it   elle = she/it   on = we/one   nous = we   vous = you   ils/elles = they

valoir (to be worth)

PRESENT

je	**vaux**
tu	**vaux**
il/elle/on	**vaut**
nous	**valons**
vous	**valez**
ils/elles	**valent**

PRESENT SUBJUNCTIVE

je	**vaille**
tu	**vailles**
il/elle/on	**vaille**
nous	**valions**
vous	**valiez**
ils/elles	**vaillent**

PERFECT

j'	**ai valu**
tu	**as valu**
il/elle/on	**a valu**
nous	**avons valu**
vous	**avez valu**
ils/elles	**ont valu**

IMPERFECT

je	**valais**
tu	**valais**
il/elle/on	**valait**
nous	**valions**
vous	**valiez**
ils/elles	**valaient**

PRESENT PARTICIPLE

valant

PAST PARTICIPLE

valu

EXAMPLE PHRASES

Ça **vaut** combien ? How much is it worth?

Ça ne **vaut** pas la peine de s'inquiéter. It's not worth worrying about.

Cette voiture **vaut** très cher. That car's worth a lot of money.

Il **valait** mieux ne pas y penser. It was best not to think about it.

valoir

FUTURE

je	**vaudrai**
tu	**vaudras**
il/elle/on	**vaudra**
nous	**vaudrons**
vous	**vaudrez**
ils/elles	**vaudront**

CONDITIONAL

je	**vaudrais**
tu	**vaudrais**
il/elle/on	**vaudrait**
nous	**vaudrions**
vous	**vaudriez**
ils/elles	**vaudraient**

PAST HISTORIC

je	**valus**
tu	**valus**
il/elle/on	**valut**
nous	**valûmes**
vous	**valûtes**
ils/elles	**valurent**

PLUPERFECT

j'	**avais valu**
tu	**avais valu**
il/elle/on	**avait valu**
nous	**avions valu**
vous	**aviez valu**
ils/elles	**avaient valu**

IMPERATIVE

vaux / valons / valez

EXAMPLE PHRASES

Ça **vaudra** sûrement la peine d'y aller. It will probably be worth going.

Ça **vaudrait** la peine d'essayer. It would be worth a try.

Il **vaudrait** mieux que tu demandes la permission. You'd better ask for permission.

Son insolence lui **avait valu** une punition. His insolence had earned him a punishment.

je/j' = I tu = you il = he/it elle = she/it on = we/one nous = we vous = you ils/elles = they

vendre (to sell)

PRESENT

je	**vends**
tu	**vends**
il/elle/on	**vend**
nous	**vendons**
vous	**vendez**
ils/elles	**vendent**

PRESENT SUBJUNCTIVE

je	**vende**
tu	**vendes**
il/elle/on	**vende**
nous	**vendions**
vous	**vendiez**
ils/elles	**vendent**

PERFECT

j'	**ai vendu**
tu	**as vendu**
il/elle/on	**a vendu**
nous	**avons vendu**
vous	**avez vendu**
ils/elles	**ont vendu**

IMPERFECT

je	**vendais**
tu	**vendais**
il/elle/on	**vendait**
nous	**vendions**
vous	**vendiez**
ils/elles	**vendaient**

PRESENT PARTICIPLE

vendant

PAST PARTICIPLE

vendu

EXAMPLE PHRASES

Elle voudrait **vendre** sa voiture. She would like to sell her car.

Est-ce que vous **vendez** des piles ? Do you sell batteries?

Il m'**a vendu** son vélo pour cinquante euros. He sold me his bike for fifty euros.

Il **vendait** des glaces sur la plage. He sold ice cream on the beach.

vendre

FUTURE

je	**vendrai**
tu	**vendras**
il/elle/on	**vendra**
nous	**vendrons**
vous	**vendrez**
ils/elles	**vendront**

CONDITIONAL

je	**vendrais**
tu	**vendrais**
il/elle/on	**vendrait**
nous	**vendrions**
vous	**vendriez**
ils/elles	**vendraient**

PAST HISTORIC

je	**vendis**
tu	**vendis**
il/elle/on	**vendit**
nous	**vendîmes**
vous	**vendîtes**
ils/elles	**vendirent**

PLUPERFECT

j'	**avais vendu**
tu	**avais vendu**
il/elle/on	**avait vendu**
nous	**avions vendu**
vous	**aviez vendu**
ils/elles	**avaient vendu**

IMPERATIVE

vends / vendons / vendez

EXAMPLE PHRASES

Tu ne **vendras** rien à ce prix-là. **You'll never sell anything at that price.**

Elle **vendit** son appartement et partit vivre en Provence. **She sold her apartment and went to live in Provence.**

Je ne **vendrais** pas ce piano pour tout l'or du monde. **I wouldn't sell this piano for all the gold in the world.**

Il **avait** déjà **vendu** sa maison. **He'd already sold his house.**

venir (to come)

PRESENT

je	**viens**
tu	**viens**
il/elle/on	**vient**
nous	**venons**
vous	**venez**
ils/elles	**viennent**

PRESENT SUBJUNCTIVE

je	**vienne**
tu	**viennes**
il/elle/on	**vienne**
nous	**venions**
vous	**veniez**
ils/elles	**viennent**

PERFECT

je	**suis venu(e)**
tu	**es venu(e)**
il/elle/on	**est venu(e)**
nous	**sommes venu(e)s**
vous	**êtes venu(e)(s)**
ils/elles	**sont venu(e)s**

IMPERFECT

je	**venais**
tu	**venais**
il/elle/on	**venait**
nous	**venions**
vous	**veniez**
ils/elles	**venaient**

PRESENT PARTICIPLE

venant

PAST PARTICIPLE

venu

EXAMPLE PHRASES

Fatou et Malik **viennent** du Sénégal. Fatou and Malik come from Senegal.

Ils **sont venus** la voir ce matin. They came to see her this morning.

Elle aimerait que tu **viennes** à son mariage. She'd like you to come to her wedding.

Je **venais** de finir mes devoirs quand ils sont arrivés. I'd just finished my homework when they arrived.

je/j' = I   tu = you   il = he/it   elle = she/it   on = we/one   nous = we   vous = you   ils/elles = they

venir

FUTURE

je	**viendrai**
tu	**viendras**
il/elle/on	**viendra**
nous	**viendrons**
vous	**viendrez**
ils/elles	**viendront**

CONDITIONAL

je	**viendrais**
tu	**viendrais**
il/elle/on	**viendrait**
nous	**viendrions**
vous	**viendriez**
ils/elles	**viendraient**

PAST HISTORIC

je	**vins**
tu	**vins**
il/elle/on	**vint**
nous	**vînmes**
vous	**vîntes**
ils/elles	**vinrent**

PLUPERFECT

j'	**étais venu(e)**
tu	**étais venu(e)**
il/elle/on	**était venu(e)**
nous	**étions venu(e)s**
vous	**étiez venu(e)(s)**
ils/elles	**étaient venu(e)s**

IMPERATIVE

viens / venons / venez

EXAMPLE PHRASES

Elle ne **viendra** pas cette année. She won't be coming this year.

Il **vint** nous voir après la messe. He came to see us after mass.

Elle **viendrait** avec nous si elle n'avait pas tant de travail. She'd come with us if she didn't have so much work.

Ils **étaient venus** nous annoncer leurs fiançailles. They had come to tell us that they had gotten engaged.

Viens avec moi ! Come with me!

---

je/j' = I tu = you il = he/it elle = she/it on = we/one nous = we vous = you ils/elles = they

vêtir (to dress)

PRESENT

je	**vêts**
tu	**vêts**
il/elle/on	**vêt**
nous	**vêtons**
vous	**vêtez**
ils/elles	**vêtent**

PRESENT SUBJUNCTIVE

je	**vête**
tu	**vêtes**
il/elle/on	**vête**
nous	**vêtions**
vous	**vêtiez**
ils/elles	**vêtent**

PERFECT

j'	**ai vêtu**
tu	**as vêtu**
il/elle/on	**a vêtu**
nous	**avons vêtu**
vous	**avez vêtu**
ils/elles	**ont vêtu**

IMPERFECT

je	**vêtais**
tu	**vêtais**
il/elle/on	**vêtait**
nous	**vêtions**
vous	**vêtiez**
ils/elles	**vêtaient**

PRESENT PARTICIPLE

vêtant

PAST PARTICIPLE

vêtu

EXAMPLE PHRASES

Il faut se lever, se laver et se **vêtir** en dix minutes. You have to get up, get washed, and get dressed in ten minutes.

Vous n'**êtes** pas **vêtus** suffisamment chaudement pour aller jouer dehors. You're not dressed warmly enough to go and play outside.

Tu **es** bizarrement **vêtu** aujourd'hui ! You are strangely dressed today!

Nous vîmes une mariée tout de blanc **vêtue**. We saw a bride dressed all in white.

je/j' = I   tu = you   il = he/it   elle = she/it   on = we/one   nous = we   vous = you   ils/elles = they

vêtir

FUTURE

je	**vêtirai**
tu	**vêtiras**
il/elle/on	**vêtira**
nous	**vêtirons**
vous	**vêtirez**
ils/elles	**vêtiront**

CONDITIONAL

je	**vêtirais**
tu	**vêtirais**
il/elle/on	**vêtirait**
nous	**vêtirions**
vous	**vêtiriez**
ils/elles	**vêtiraient**

PAST HISTORIC

je	**vêtis**
tu	**vêtis**
il/elle/on	**vêtit**
nous	**vêtîmes**
vous	**vêtîtes**
ils/elles	**vêtirent**

PLUPERFECT

j'	**avais vêtu**
tu	**avais vêtu**
il/elle/on	**avait vêtu**
nous	**avions vêtu**
vous	**aviez vêtu**
ils/elles	**avaient vêtu**

IMPERATIVE

vêts / vêtons / vêtez

EXAMPLE PHRASES

Il **était vêtu** d'un pantalon et d'un pull. He was wearing slacks and a sweater.

Nous **étions** chaudement **vêtus**. We were warmly dressed.

Il **était** toujours bien **vêtu**. He was always well dressed.

Ils n'**étaient** pas **vêtus** de façon adéquate pour aller marcher dans les montagnes. They weren't properly dressed for hiking in the mountains.

je/j' = I **tu** = you **il** = he/it **elle** = she/it **on** = we/one **nous** = we **vous** = you **ils/elles** = they

vivre (to live)

PRESENT

je	**vis**
tu	**vis**
il/elle/on	**vit**
nous	**vivons**
vous	**vivez**
ils/elles	**vivent**

PRESENT SUBJUNCTIVE

je	**vive**
tu	**vives**
il/elle/on	**vive**
nous	**vivions**
vous	**viviez**
ils/elles	**vivent**

PERFECT

j'	**ai vécu**
tu	**as vécu**
il/elle/on	**a vécu**
nous	**avons vécu**
vous	**avez vécu**
ils/elles	**ont vécu**

IMPERFECT

je	**vivais**
tu	**vivais**
il/elle/on	**vivait**
nous	**vivions**
vous	**viviez**
ils/elles	**vivaient**

PRESENT PARTICIPLE

vivant

PAST PARTICIPLE

vécu

EXAMPLE PHRASES

Et ton grand-père ? Il **vit** encore ? What about your grandfather? Is he still alive?

Les gorilles **vivent** surtout dans la forêt. Gorillas mostly live in the forest.

Il **a vécu** dix ans à Lyon. He lived in Lyons for ten years.

Cela ne faisait pas longtemps qu'ils **vivaient** ensemble. They hadn't lived together for long.

---

je/j' = I   tu = you   il = he/it   elle = she/it   on = we/one   nous = we   vous = you   ils/elles = they

vivre

FUTURE

je	**vivrai**
tu	**vivras**
il/elle/on	**vivra**
nous	**vivrons**
vous	**vivrez**
ils/elles	**vivront**

CONDITIONAL

je	**vivrais**
tu	**vivrais**
il/elle/on	**vivrait**
nous	**vivrions**
vous	**vivriez**
ils/elles	**vivraient**

PAST HISTORIC

je	**vécus**
tu	**vécus**
il/elle/on	**vécut**
nous	**vécûmes**
vous	**vécûtes**
ils/elles	**vécurent**

PLUPERFECT

j'	**avais vécu**
tu	**avais vécu**
il/elle/on	**avait vécu**
nous	**avions vécu**
vous	**aviez vécu**
ils/elles	**avaient vécu**

IMPERATIVE

vis / vivons / vivez

EXAMPLE PHRASES

Vivras-tu avec ta sœur quand tu feras tes études à Paris ? **Will you live with your sister when you're studying in Paris?**

Elle **vécut** d'abord en Espagne, puis en Italie. **She lived in Spain first and then in Italy.**

S'ils n'avaient pas d'enfants, ils ne **vivraient** plus ensemble depuis longtemps. **If they didn't have children, they would have stopped living together long ago.**

Ils n'**avaient** jamais **vécu** à la campagne. **They'd never lived in the countryside.**

---

je/j' = I **tu** = you **il** = he/it **elle** = she/it **on** = we/one **nous** = we **vous** = you **ils/elles** = they

voir (to see)

PRESENT

je	**vois**
tu	**vois**
il/elle/on	**voit**
nous	**voyons**
vous	**voyez**
ils/elles	**voient**

PRESENT SUBJUNCTIVE

je	**voie**
tu	**voies**
il/elle/on	**voie**
nous	**voyions**
vous	**voyiez**
ils/elles	**voient**

PERFECT

j'	**ai vu**
tu	**as vu**
il/elle/on	**a vu**
nous	**avons vu**
vous	**avez vu**
ils/elles	**ont vu**

IMPERFECT

je	**voyais**
tu	**voyais**
il/elle/on	**voyait**
nous	**voyions**
vous	**voyiez**
ils/elles	**voyaient**

PRESENT PARTICIPLE
voyant

PAST PARTICIPLE
vu

EXAMPLE PHRASES

Venez me **voir** quand vous serez à Paris. Come and see me when you're in Paris.

Est-ce que cette tache se **voit** ? Does that stain show?

Est-ce que tu l'**as vu** ? Have you seen him?

Il ne **voyait** rien sans ses lunettes. He couldn't see anything without his glasses.

voir

FUTURE

je	**verrai**
tu	**verras**
il/elle/on	**verra**
nous	**verrons**
vous	**verrez**
ils/elles	**verront**

CONDITIONAL

je	**verrais**
tu	**verrais**
il/elle/on	**verrait**
nous	**verrions**
vous	**verriez**
ils/elles	**verraient**

PAST HISTORIC

je	**vis**
tu	**vis**
il/elle/on	**vit**
nous	**vîmes**
vous	**vîtes**
ils/elles	**virent**

PLUPERFECT

j'	**avais vu**
tu	**avais vu**
il/elle/on	**avait vu**
nous	**avions vu**
vous	**aviez vu**
ils/elles	**avaient vu**

IMPERATIVE

vois / voyons / voyez

EXAMPLE PHRASES

Tu **verras** que je ne t'ai pas menti. You'll see that I didn't lie to you.

Il la **vit** arriver de loin. He saw her arrive from a long way off.

Il savait qu'il ne la **verrait** pas avant le lendemain. He knew that he wouldn't see her until the next day.

Ils ne l'**avaient** pas **vue** depuis son accident. They hadn't seen her since her accident.

je/j' = I **tu** = you **il** = he/it **elle** = she/it **on** = we/one **nous** = we **vous** = you **ils/elles** = they

vouloir (to want)

PRESENT

je	**veux**
tu	**veux**
il/elle/on	**veut**
nous	**voulons**
vous	**voulez**
ils/elles	**veulent**

PRESENT SUBJUNCTIVE

je	**veuille**
tu	**veuilles**
il/elle/on	**veuille**
nous	**voulions**
vous	**vouliez**
ils/elles	**veuillent**

PERFECT

j'	**ai voulu**
tu	**as voulu**
il/elle/on	**a voulu**
nous	**avons voulu**
vous	**avez voulu**
ils/elles	**ont voulu**

IMPERFECT

je	**voulais**
tu	**voulais**
il/elle/on	**voulait**
nous	**voulions**
vous	**vouliez**
ils/elles	**voulaient**

PRESENT PARTICIPLE

voulant

PAST PARTICIPLE

voulu

EXAMPLE PHRASES

Elle **veut** un vélo pour Noël. She wants a bike for Christmas.

Veux-tu que je t'aide ? Do you want me to help you?

Il n'**a** pas **voulu** te déranger. He didn't want to disturb you.

Ils **voulaient** aller au cinéma. They wanted to go to the movies.

je/j' = I   tu = you   il = he/it   elle = she/it   on = we/one   nous = we   vous = you   ils/elles = they

vouloir

FUTURE

je	**voudrai**
tu	**voudras**
il/elle/on	**voudra**
nous	**voudrons**
vous	**voudrez**
ils/elles	**voudront**

CONDITIONAL

je	**voudrais**
tu	**voudrais**
il/elle/on	**voudrait**
nous	**voudrions**
vous	**voudriez**
ils/elles	**voudraient**

PAST HISTORIC

je	**voulus**
tu	**voulus**
il/elle/on	**voulut**
nous	**voulûmes**
vous	**voulûtes**
ils/elles	**voulurent**

PLUPERFECT

j'	**avais voulu**
tu	**avais voulu**
il/elle/on	**avait voulu**
nous	**avions voulu**
vous	**aviez voulu**
ils/elles	**avaient voulu**

IMPERATIVE

veuille / veuillons / veuillez

EXAMPLE PHRASES

Ils ne **voudront** pas partir trop tard. **They won't want to leave too late.**

Elle ne **voulut** pas les inquiéter. **She didn't want to worry them.**

Tu **voudrais** une tasse de thé ? **Would you like a cup of tea?**

Il n'**avait** pas **voulu** partir sans lui dire au revoir. **He hadn't wanted to leave without saying goodbye to her.**

je/j' = I tu = you il = he/it elle = she/it on = we/one nous = we vous = you ils/elles = they

se vouvoyer (to address each other as "vous")

PRESENT

on	se vouvoie
nous	nous vouvoyons
vous	vous vouvoyez
ils/elles	se vouvoient

PRESENT SUBJUNCTIVE

on	se vouvoie
nous	nous vouvoyions
vous	vous vouvoyiez
ils/elles	se vouvoient

PERFECT

on	s'est vouvoyé
nous	nous sommes vouvoyé(e)s
vous	vous êtes vouvoyé(e)s
ils/elles	se sont vouvoyé(e)s

IMPERFECT

on	se vouvoyait
nous	nous vouvoyions
vous	vous vouvoyiez
ils/elles	se vouvoyaient

PRESENT PARTICIPLE

se vouvoyant

PAST PARTICIPLE

vouvoyé

EXAMPLE PHRASES

Avec Hélène, on **se vouvoie** encore. Hélène and I are still addressing each other as "vous."

Vous **vous êtes** toujours **vouvoyés** avec Michel ? Have you and Michel always addressed each other as "vous?"

Je préférerais qu'on **se vouvoie**. I'd rather we addressed each other as "vous."

Ils ne **se vouvoyaient** plus. They weren't addressing each other as "vous" anymore.

je/j' = I   tu = you   il = he/it   elle = she/it   on = we/one   nous = we   vous = you   ils/elles = they

se vouvoyer

FUTURE

on	**se vouvoiera**
nous	**nous vouvoierons**
vous	**vous vouvoierez**
ils/elles	**se vouvoieront**

CONDITIONAL

on	**se vouvoierait**
nous	**nous vouvoierions**
vous	**vous vouvoieriez**
ils/elles	**se vouvoieraient**

PAST HISTORIC

on	**se vouvoya**
nous	**nous vouvoyâmes**
vous	**vous vouvoyâtes**
ils/elles	**se vouvoyèrent**

PLUPERFECT

on	**s'était vouvoyé**
nous	**nous étions vouvoyé(e)s**
vous	**vous étiez vouvoyé(e)s**
ils/elles	**s'étaient vouvoyé(e)s**

IMPERATIVE

not used

EXAMPLE PHRASES

Je te parie qu'ils **se vouvoieront**. I bet they'll address each other as "vous."

Ils **se vouvoyèrent** les premiers jours. They addressed each other as "vous" for the first few days.

On **se vouvoierait** encore si je n'avais rien dit. We'd still be addressing each other as "vous" if I hadn't said anything.

Nous **nous étions vouvoyés** au début. We'd addressed each other as "vous" at the beginning.

je/j' = I tu = you il = he/it elle = she/it on = we/one nous = we vous = you ils/elles = they

How to use the Verb Index

The verbs in bold are the model verbs which you will find in the Verb Tables. All the other verbs follow one of these patterns, so the number next to each verb indicates which pattern fits this particular verb. For example, aider (*to help*) follows the same pattern as donner (number 274 in the verb tables). All the verbs are in alphabetical order. For reflexive verbs like s'asseoir (*to sit down*) or se taire (*to stop talking*), look under asseoir or taire, not under s' or se.

Superior numbers (¹, ² etc) refer you to notes on page 446. These notes explain any differences between the verbs and their model.

With the exception of reflexive verbs which *always* take être, all verbs have the same auxiliary (être or avoir) as their model verb. There are a few exceptions which are indicated by a superior number ¹ or ². An asterisk (*) means that the verb takes avoir when it is used with a direct object, and être when it isn't. For more information on verbs that take either avoir or être, see pages 113–116.

abaisser	274	accoter	274	advenir³	424	alerter	274
abandonner	274	accoucher	274	aérer	290	alimenter	274
abattre	230	accouder (s')	274	affaiblir	304	allécher	290
abêtir	304	accourir⁵	248	affairer (s')	274	alléger	368
abîmer	274	accoutumer	274	affaisser (s')	274	alléguer	290
abolir	304	accrocher	274	affamer	274	aller	210
abonder	274	accroître⁶	258	affermir	304	allier	254
abonner	274	accroupir (s')	304	afficher	274	allonger (s')	322
aborder	274	accueillir	260	affirmer	274	allumer	274
aboutir	304	accumuler	274	affliger	322	altérer	290
aboyer	340	accuser	274	affoler	274	alterner	274
abréger	368	acharner (s')	274	affranchir	304	alunir	304
abreuver	274	acheminer	274	affréter	290	amaigrir	304
abriter	274	acheter	206	affronter	274	ambitionner	274
abrutir	304	achever	318	agacer	236	améliorer	274
absenter (s')	274	acquérir	208	agenouiller (s')	274	aménager	322
absorber	274	acquitter	274	aggraver	274	amener	318
absoudre⁴	378	actionner	274	agir	304	ameuter	274
abstenir (s')	412	activer	274	agiter	274	amincir	304
abstraire	416	adapter	274	agrandir	304	amoindrir	304
abuser	274	additionner	274	agréer	252	amollir	304
accabler	274	adhérer	290	ahurir	304	amonceler	216
accaparer	274	adjoindre	316	aider	274	amorcer	236
accéder	290	admettre	328	aigrir	304	amplifier	254
accélérer	290	admirer	274	aiguiser	274	amputer	274
accentuer	274	adopter	274	aimanter	274	amuser (s')	212
accepter	274	adorer	274	aimer	274	analyser	274
accompagner	274	adosser	274	ajouter	274	anéantir	304
accomplir	304	adoucir	304	ajuster	274	angoisser	274
accorder	274	adresser	274	alarmer	274	animer	274

Notes

1. Auxiliary = avoir.

2. Auxiliary = être.

3. Only infinitive and 3rd persons of each tense used.

4. Past participle: absous, absoute.

5. Conjugated with either avoir or être.

6. No circumflex on: j'accrois, tu accrois, and accru.

7. Hardly used except in the infinitive and the 3rd persons of the present, future, and conditional.

8. Past participle: circoncis.

9. Past participle: confit.

10. No circumflex on: je décrois, tu décrois, and décru.

11. When demeurer means *to live*, the auxiliary is avoir; when it means *to remain*, the auxiliary is être.

12. Past participle: dissous, dissoute.

13. Present participle: faillant; past participle: failli; future: je faillirai, *etc*; conditional: je faillirais, *etc*. NB: J'ai failli tomber = I nearly fell.

14. When fleurir means *to prosper*, the present participle is florissant, and the imperfect is florissait.

15. Past participle: frit; used mainly in the present tense singular and in compound tenses.

16. Past participle: inclus.

17. Past participle: mû, mue, mus, mues.

18. Past participle: nui.

19. In questions, je peux can be replaced by je puis: Puis-je vous aider ? May I help you?

20. Subjunctive: je prévale, *etc*.

21. Future: je prévoirai, *etc*; conditional: je prévoirais, *etc*.

22. Used only in the infinitive, present and past participles, and compound tenses.

23. Past participle: relui.

24. No past participle, no compound tenses.

Vocabulary

contents

This vocabulary section is divided into 50 topics, arranged in alphabetical order. This thematic approach enables you to learn related words and phrases together, so that you can become confident in using particular vocabulary in context.

Vocabulary within each topic is divided into nouns and useful phrases which are aimed at helping you to express yourself in idiomatic French. Vocabulary within each topic is graded to help you prioritize your learning. Essential words include the basic words you will need to be able to communicate effectively; important words help expand your knowledge; and useful words provide additional vocabulary which will enable you to express yourself more fully.

Nouns are grouped by gender: masculine ("le") nouns are given on the left-hand page, and feminine ("la") nouns on the right-hand page, enabling you to memorize words according to their gender. In addition, all feminine forms of adjectives are shown, as are irregular plurals and plurals of compound nouns.

At the end of the section you will find a list of supplementary vocabulary, grouped according to part of speech – adjective, verb, noun, and so on. This is vocabulary which you will come across in many everyday situations.

Finally, there is an English index which lists all the essential and important nouns given under the topic headings for quick reference.

ABBREVIATIONS

adj	adjective
adv	adverb
conj	conjunction
f	feminine
inv	invariable
m	masculine
m+f	masculine and feminine form
n	noun
pl	plural
prep	preposition
qch	quelque chose
qn	quelqu'un
sb	somebody
sth	something
subj	subjunctive

The swung dash ~ is used to indicate the basic elements of the compound, and appropriate endings are then added.

PHONETICS

i	as in	vie, lit
e	as in	blé, jouer
ɛ	as in	merci, très
a	as in	patte, plat
ɑ	as in	bas, gras
ɔ	as in	mort, donner
o	as in	mot, gauche
u	as in	genou, roue
y	as in	rue, tu
ø	as in	peu, deux
œ	as in	peur, meuble
ə	as in	le, premier
ɛ̃	as in	matin, plein
ɑ̃	as in	sans, vent
ɔ̃	as in	bon, ombre
œ̃	as in	brun, lundi
j	as in	yeux, pied
ɥ	as in	lui, huile
ɲ	as in	agneau, vigne
ŋ	as in	English -ing
ʃ	as in	chat, tache
ʒ	as in	je, gens
ʀ	as in	rue, venir

A colon : precedes words beginning with an aspirate h
(le :hibou as opposed to l'hippopotame).

ESSENTIAL WORDS *(masculine)*

un	**aéroport**	airport
un	**aller-retour**	round-trip ticket
un	**aller simple**	one-way ticket
un	**avion**	plane
les	**bagages**	luggage
les	**bagages à main**	carry-on luggage
le	**billet (d'avion)**	(plane) ticket
le	**bureau de renseignements**	information desk
le	**départ**	departure
le	**douanier**	customs officer
le	**duty-free**	duty-free (shop)
	l'**horaire**	timetable
le	**numéro**	number
le	**passager**	passenger
le	**passeport**	passport
le	**prix du billet**	fare
les	**renseignements**	information
le	**retard**	delay
le	**sac**	bag
le	**taxi**	taxi
le	**touriste**	tourist
le	**vol**	flight
le	**voyage**	trip
le	**voyageur**	traveler

USEFUL PHRASES

voyager par avion **to travel by plane**

retenir une place d'avion **to book a plane ticket**

"par avion" **"by airmail"**

enregistrer ses bagages **to check in one's luggage**

j'ai manqué la correspondance **I missed my connection**

l'avion a décollé/a atterri **the plane has taken off/has landed**

le tableau des arrivées/des départs **the arrivals/departures board**

le vol numéro 776 en provenance de Nice/à destination de Nice **flight number 776 from Nice/to Nice**

ESSENTIAL WORDS *(feminine)*

une	agence de voyages	travel agency
une	annulation	cancelation
une	arrivée	arrival
la	carte d'identité	ID card
la	carte d'embarquement	boarding card
la	correspondance	connection
la	douane	customs
une	entrée	entrance
une	hôtesse de l'air	flight attendant
la	location de voitures	car rental
la	passagère	passenger
la	porte d'embarquement	departure gate
la	réduction	discount
la	réservation	reservation
la	sortie	exit
la	sortie de secours	emergency exit
les	toilettes	restroom
la	touriste	tourist
la	valise	suitcase

USEFUL PHRASES

récupérer ses bagages to pick up one's baggage
"livraison des bagages" "baggage claim"
passer la douane to go through customs
j'ai quelque chose à déclarer I have something to declare
je n'ai rien à déclarer I have nothing to declare
fouiller les bagages to search the bags
voyager en classe affaires/économique to travel business/
  economy class

IMPORTANT WORDS *(masculine)*

un	accident d'avion	plane crash
le	billet électronique	e-ticket
le	chariot	luggage cart
un	escalier roulant	escalator
un	hélicoptère	helicopter
le	mal de l'air	airsickness
le	pilote	pilot
le	plan	map

USEFUL WORDS *(masculine)*

un	aiguilleur du ciel	air-traffic controller
un	atterrissage	landing
un	avion à réaction	jet plane
un	avion gros porteur	jumbo jet
le	contrôle de sécurité	security check
le	décollage	take-off
les	droits de douane	customs duty
	l'embarquement	boarding
un	équipage	crew
un	espace bébés	baby change facility
le	hublot	window
le	mur du son	sound barrier
le	parachute	parachute
le	portique de détection	metal detector
le	réacteur	jet engine
le	siège	seat
le	steward	steward
le	tapis roulant	moving walkway; luggage carousel
le	trou d'air	air pocket

USEFUL PHRASES

à bord **on board**
horaire prévu d'arrivée/de départ **estimated time of arrival/departure**
"attachez vos ceintures" **"fasten your seat belts"**
nous survolons Londres **we are flying over London**
j'ai le mal de l'air **I am feeling airsick**
détourner un avion **to hijack a plane**

IMPORTANT WORDS *(feminine)*

la	ceinture de sécurité	seat belt
la	destination	destination
la	durée	length, duration
une	horloge	clock
la	salle d'embarquement	departure lounge
la	vitesse	speed

USEFUL WORDS *(feminine)*

une	aérogare	terminal
une	aile	wing
	l'altitude	altitude
la	boîte noire	black box
la	boutique hors taxes	duty-free shop
les	commandes	controls
une	escale	stopover
une	étiquette	label
la	:hauteur	height
une	hélice	propeller
la	compagnie aérienne	airline
la	piste	runway
la	soute	baggage hold
la	tour de contrôle	control tower
la	turbulence	turbulence

USEFUL PHRASES

"vol AB251 pour Paris : embarquement immédiat, porte 51"
  "flight AB251 to Paris now boarding at gate 51"
nous avons fait escale à New York we stopped over in New York
un atterrissage forcé an emergency landing
un atterrissage en catastrophe a crash landing
des cigarettes hors taxes duty-free cigarettes

ESSENTIAL WORDS (*masculine*)

un	**agneau**	lamb
un	**animal** (*pl* animaux)	animal
le	**bœuf** [bœf] (*pl* ~s [bø])	ox
le	**chat**	cat
le	**chaton**	kitten
le	**cheval** (*pl* chevaux)	horse
le	**chien**	dog
le	**chiot**	puppy
le	**cochon**	pig
un	**éléphant**	elephant
le	**:hamster**	hamster
le	**jardin zoologique**	zoo
le	**lapin**	rabbit
le	**lion**	lion
le	**mouton**	sheep
un	**oiseau** (*pl* -x)	bird
le	**poisson**	fish
le	**poulain**	foal
le	**tigre**	tiger
le	**veau**	calf
le	**zoo**	zoo

USEFUL PHRASES

j'aime les chats, je déteste les serpents, je préfère les souris
  I like cats, I hate snakes, I prefer mice
nous avons 12 animaux chez nous we have 12 pets (in our house)
nous n'avons pas d'animaux chez nous we have no pets (in our house)
les animaux sauvages wild animals
les animaux domestiques pets; livestock
mettre un animal en cage to put an animal in a cage
libérer un animal to set an animal free

ESSENTIAL WORDS *(feminine)*

la **chatte**	cat *(female)*
la **chienne**	dog *(female)*
la **fourrure**	fur
la **souris**	mouse
la **tortue**	tortoise
la **vache**	cow

IMPORTANT WORDS *(feminine)*

| la **cage** | cage |
| la **queue** [kø] | tail |

USEFUL PHRASES

le chien aboie the dog barks; il grogne it growls
le chat miaule the cat meows; il ronronne it purrs
j'aime faire du cheval *or* monter à cheval I like horseback riding
à cheval on horseback
"attention, chien méchant" "beware of the dog"
"chiens interdits" "no dogs allowed"
"bas les pattes !" *(to dog)* "down, boy!"
les droits des animaux animal rights

USEFUL WORDS (*masculine*)

un	**âne**	donkey
le	**bouc**	billy goat
le	**cerf** [sɛʀ]	stag
le	**chameau** (*pl* -x)	camel
le	**cochon d'Inde**	guinea pig
le	**crapaud**	toad
le	**crocodile**	crocodile
un	**écureuil**	squirrel
le	**:hérisson**	hedgehog
un	**hippopotame**	hippopotamus
le	**kangourou**	kangaroo
le	**lièvre**	hare
le	**loup**	wolf
le	**mulet**	mule
le	**museau** (*pl* -x)	snout
un	**ours** [uʀs]	bear
un	**ours blanc**	polar bear
le	**phoque**	seal
le	**piège**	trap
le	**poil**	coat, hair
le	**poney**	pony
le	**porc** [pɔʀ]	pig
le	**renard**	fox
le	**requin**	shark
le	**rhinocéros**	rhinocéros
le	**sabot**	hoof
le	**serpent**	snake
le	**singe**	monkey
le	**taureau** (*pl* -x)	bull
le	**zèbre**	zebra

USEFUL WORDS *(feminine)*

une	animalerie	pet store
la	baleine	whale
la	bosse	hump *(of camel)*
la	carapace	shell *(of tortoise)*
la	chauve-souris *(pl ~s~)*	bat
la	chèvre	goat
la	corne	horn
la	crinière	mane
la	défense	tusk
la	dinde	turkey
la	fourrure	fur
la	girafe	giraffe
la	grenouille	frog
la	griffe	claw
la	gueule	mouth *(of dog, cat, lion etc)*
la	jument	mare
la	lionne	lioness
la	mule	mule
la	patte	paw
la	poche	pouch *(of kangaroo)*
la	ramure	antlers
les	rayures	stripes *(of zebra)*
la	taupe	mole
la	tigresse	tigress
la	trompe	trunk *(of elephant)*

ESSENTIAL WORDS *(masculine)*

le	casque	helmet
le	cyclisme	cycling
le	cycliste	cyclist
le	frein	brake
le	pneu	tire
le	Tour de France	Tour de France cycle race
le	vélo	bike
le	vélo tout terrain	mountain bike
le	VTT	mountain bike

USEFUL WORDS *(masculine)*

un	antivol	padlock
le	catadioptre	reflector
le	dérailleur	derailleur
le	garde-boue *(pl inv)*	fender
le	guidon	handlebars
le	moyeu *(pl -x)*	hub
le	pare-boue *(pl inv)*	mudguard
le	phare	front light
le	porte-bagages *(pl inv)*	luggage rack
le	rayon	spoke
le	réflecteur	reflector
le	sommet	top *(of hill)*

USEFUL PHRASES

aller à bicyclette, aller en vélo to go by bike
je suis venu(e) en vélo I came by bike
faire du cyclisme, faire du vélo to cycle
rouler to travel
à toute vitesse at full speed
changer de vitesse to change gears
s'arrêter to stop
freiner brusquement to brake sharply

ESSENTIAL WORDS *(feminine)*

| la **bicyclette** | bicycle |
| la **lampe** | light |

IMPORTANT WORDS *(feminine)*

la **crevaison**	flat tire
la **roue**	wheel
la **vitesse**	speed; gear

USEFUL WORDS *(feminine)*

la **barre**	crossbar
la **chaîne**	chain
la **côte**	slope
la **descente**	descent
la **dynamo**	generator
la **montée**	climb
la **pédale**	pedal
la **pente**	slope
la **piste cyclable**	bike path
la **pompe**	pump
la **sacoche**	saddlebag
la **selle**	saddle
la **sonnette**	bell
la **trousse pour crevaisons**	tire repair kit
la **valve**	valve

USEFUL PHRASES

faire une promenade à *or* en vélo to go for a bike ride
avoir un pneu crevé to have a flat tire
réparer un pneu crevé patch a flat tire
la roue avant/arrière the front/back wheel
gonfler les pneus to inflate the tires
brillant(e), reluisant(e) shiny
rouillé(e) rusty
fluorescent(e) fluorescent

ESSENTIAL WORDS *(masculine)*

le	canard	duck
le	ciel	sky
le	coq	rooster
le	dindon	turkey
un	oiseau *(pl* -x)	bird
le	perroquet	parrot

USEFUL WORDS *(masculine)*

un	aigle	eagle
le	bec	beak
le	choucas	jackdaw *(European bird related to the crow)*
le	coq de bruyère	grouse
le	corbeau *(pl* -x)	raven
le	coucou	cuckoo
le	cygne [siɲ]	swan
un	étourneau *(pl* -x)	starling
le	faisan	pheasant
le	faucon	falcon
le	:hibou *(pl* -x)	owl
le	martin-pêcheur *(pl* ~s~s)	kingfisher
le	merle	blackbird
le	moineau *(pl* -x)	sparrow
le	nid	nest
un	œuf	egg
le	paon [pã]	peacock
le	pic	woodpecker
le	pigeon	pigeon
le	pingouin	penguin
le	rapace	raptor
le	roitelet	wren
le	rossignol	nightingale
le	serin	canary
le	vautour	vulture

ESSENTIAL WORDS *(feminine)*

une	**oie**	goose
la	**perruche**	parakeet
la	**poule**	hen

USEFUL WORDS *(feminine)*

une	**aile**	wing
une	**alouette**	lark
une	**autruche**	ostrich
la	**cage**	cage
la	**caille**	quail
la	**cigogne**	stork
la	**colombe**	dove
la	**corneille**	crow
la	**grive**	thrush
la	**grouse**	grouse
une	**hirondelle**	swallow
la	**mésange bleue**	bluetit (*blue European titmouse*)
la	**mouette**	seagull
la	**perdrix** [pɛʀdʀi]	partridge
la	**pie**	magpie
la	**plume**	feather

USEFUL PHRASES

voler **to fly**
s'envoler **to fly away**
faire son nid **to build a nest**
siffler **to whistle**
chanter **to sing**
on les met en cage **people put them in cages**
migrer **to migrate**
pondre un œuf **to lay an egg**
un oiseau migrateur **a migratory bird**

ESSENTIAL WORDS *(masculine)*

le	**bras**	arm
les	**cheveux**	hair
le	**cœur**	heart
le	**corps** [kɔʀ]	body
le	**doigt**	finger
le	**dos**	back
	l'**estomac** [ɛstɔma]	stomach
le	**genou** (pl -x)	knee
le	**nez**	nose
un	**œil** (pl yeux)	eye
le	**pied**	foot
le	**ventre**	belly
le	**visage**	face
les	**yeux**	eyes

IMPORTANT WORDS *(masculine)*

le	**cou**	neck
le	**front**	forehead
le	**menton**	chin
le	**pouce**	thumb
le	**sang**	blood
le	**sourcil** [suʀsi]	eyebrow

USEFUL PHRASES
debout standing
assis(e) sitting
couché(e) lying
je vais me faire couper les cheveux I am going to have my hair cut

ESSENTIAL WORDS *(feminine)*

la	**bouche**	mouth
la	**dent**	tooth
la	**gorge**	throat
la	**jambe**	leg
la	**main**	hand
une	**oreille**	ear
la	**tête**	head

IMPORTANT WORDS *(feminine)*

la	**cheville**	ankle
une	**épaule**	shoulder
la	**figure**	face
la	**joue**	cheek
la	**langue**	tongue
la	**peau**	skin
la	**poitrine**	chest, bust
la	**voix**	voice

USEFUL PHRASES

grand(e) tall, big
petit(e) small, short
gros(se) fat
maigre skinny
mince slim
joli(e) pretty
laid(e) ugly
mignon(ne) cute

USEFUL WORDS *(masculine)*

le	cerveau	brain
le	cil [sil]	eyelash
le	coude	elbow
le	derrière	behind, buttocks
les	doigts de pied	toes
le	foie	liver
le	geste	gesture
le	gros orteil	the big toe
un	index	index finger
le	mollet	calf (*of leg*)
le	muscle	muscle
un	ongle	nail
un	orteil	toe
un	os [ɔs] (*pl* [o])	bone
le	poignet	wrist
le	poing	fist
le	poumon	lung
le	rein	kidney
le	sein	breast
le	squelette	skeleton
le	talon	heel
le	teint	complexion
le	trait	feature

USEFUL PHRASES

se moucher to blow one's nose
se couper les ongles to cut one's nails
se faire couper les cheveux to have one's hair cut
hausser les épaules to shrug one's shoulders
faire oui/non de la tête to nod/shake one's head
voir to see; entendre to hear; se sentir to feel
sentir to smell; toucher to touch; goûter to taste
serrer la main à qn to shake hands with sb
faire bonjour/au revoir de la main à qn to wave hello/goodbye to sb
montrer qch du doigt to point at sth

USEFUL WORDS *(feminine)*

une	**artère**	artery
la	**chair**	flesh
la	**colonne vertébrale**	spine
la	**côte**	rib
la	**cuisse**	thigh
la	**:hanche**	hip
la	**lèvre**	lip
la	**mâchoire**	jaw
la	**nuque**	nape of the neck
la	**paupière**	eyelid
la	**plante du pied**	sole of the foot
la	**prunelle**	pupil *(of the eye)*
la	**taille**	waist; size
la	**tempe**	temple
la	**veine**	vein

USEFUL PHRASES

tour de hanches hip measurement
tour de taille waist measurement
tour de poitrine chest measurement
sourd(e) deaf
aveugle blind
muet(te) dumb
handicapé(e) handicapped
handicapé(e) mental(e) mentally handicapped
il est plus grand que toi he is taller than you
elle a beaucoup grandi she has grown a lot
je me trouve trop gros I think I am overweight
elle a grossi/maigri she has put on/lost weight
elle fait 1,47 mètres she is 1.47 meters tall
il pèse 40 kilos he weighs 40 kilos

SEASONS

le **printemps**	spring
l'**été** *(m)*	summer
l'**automne** *(m)*	fall
l'**hiver** *(m)*	winter

MONTHS

janvier	January	**juillet**	July
février	February	**août**	August
mars	March	**septembre**	September
avril	April	**octobre**	October
mai	May	**novembre**	November
juin	June	**décembre**	December

DAYS OF THE WEEK

lundi	Monday
mardi	Tuesday
mercredi	Wednesday
jeudi	Thursday
vendredi	Friday
samedi	Saturday
dimanche	Sunday

USEFUL PHRASES

au printemps in spring
en été/automne/hiver in summer/the fall/winter
en mai in May
le 10 juillet 2011 on July 10 2011
nous sommes le 3 décembre it's December 3
le samedi, je vais à la piscine on Saturdays I go to the swimming pool
samedi je suis allé à la piscine on Saturday I went to the swimming pool
samedi prochain/dernier next/last Saturday
le samedi précédent/suivant the previous/following Saturday

CALENDAR

le	**calendrier**	calendar
le	**jour**	day
la	**saison**	season
la	**semaine**	week
le	**mois**	month
les	**jours de la semaine**	days of the week
le	**jour férié**	national holiday

USEFUL PHRASES

le premier avril **April Fools' Day**

le premier mai **May Day**

le quatorze juillet **Bastille Day** (*French national holiday*)

le dimanche de Pâques **Easter Sunday**

le lundi de Pâques **Easter Monday** (*the day after Easter*)

mercredi des Cendres **Ash Wednesday**

vendredi saint **Good Friday**

le jour de l'An **New Year's Day**

le réveillon du jour de l'An **New Year's Eve dinner** *or* **party**

le jour J **D-Day**

l'Avent (*m*) **Advent**

le Carême **Lent**

la Marseillaise **the Marseillaise** (*French national anthem*)

Noël (*m*) **Christmas**

à Noël **at Christmas**

le jour de Noël **Christmas Day**

la veille de Noël, la nuit de Noël **Christmas Eve**

Pâques (*fpl*) **Easter**

le jour de Pâques **Easter Day**

la Pâque juive **Passover**

le poisson d'avril **April fool's trick**

le Ramadan **Ramadan**

la Saint-Sylvestre **New Year's Eve**

la Saint-Valentin **Valentine's Day**

la Toussaint **All Saints' Day** (*November 1*)

ESSENTIAL WORDS (*masculine*)

un	**anniversaire**	birthday
un	**anniversaire de mariage**	wedding anniversary
le	**cadeau** (*pl* -x)	gift, present
le	**divorce**	divorce
le	**mariage**	marriage, wedding
le	**rendez-vous** (*pl inv*)	appointment, date

IMPORTANT WORDS (*masculine*)

le	**festival**	festival
le	**feu d'artifice**	firework; firework display
le	**feu de joie**	bonfire

USEFUL WORDS (*masculine*)

le	**baptême**	baptism
le	**cimetière**	cemetery
le	**décès**	death
le	**défilé**	procession; march
un	**enterrement**	funeral
le	**faire-part (de mariage)** (*pl inv*)	wedding invitation
le	**témoin**	witness

USEFUL PHRASES

fêter son anniversaire to celebrate one's birthday
ma sœur est née en 1995 my sister was born in 1995
elle vient d'avoir 17 ans she's just turned 17
il m'a offert ce cadeau he gave me this gift
je te l'offre ! I'm giving it to you!
je vous remercie thank you
divorcer to get divorced
se marier to get married
se fiancer (avec qn) to get engaged (to sb)
mon père est mort il y a deux ans my father died two years ago
enterrer, ensevelir to bury

ESSENTIAL WORDS *(feminine)*

la	**date**	date
la	**fête**	saint's day; festival; holiday; party

IMPORTANT WORDS *(feminine)*

les	**festivités**	festivities
la	**fête foraine**	carnival
les	**fiançailles**	engagement
la	**foire**	fair
la	**mort**	death
la	**naissance**	birth

USEFUL WORDS *(feminine)*

la	**carte de vœux**	greeting card
la	**cérémonie**	ceremony
la	**demoiselle d'honneur**	bridesmaid
les	**étrennes**	New Year's gift
la	**fête folklorique**	folk festival
la	**lune de miel**	honeymoon
les	**noces**	wedding
la	**retraite**	retirement

USEFUL PHRASES

les noces d'argent/d'or/de diamant silver/golden/diamond wedding anniversary
souhaiter la bonne année à qn to wish sb a happy New Year
faire une fête to have a party
inviter ses amis to invite one's friends
choisir un cadeau to choose a gift
joyeux Noël ! Merry Christmas!
bon anniversaire ! happy birthday!
tous mes vœux best wishes

ESSENTIAL WORDS *(masculine)*

le	bloc sanitaire	washrooms
le	campeur	camper *(male)*
le	camping	camping; campsite
le	canif	penknife
le	couteau *(pl -x)*	knife
un	emplacement	site
le	feu de camp	campfire
le	gardien	warden
le	gaz	gas *(propane or butane)*
le	lavabo	washbasin
le	lit de camp	cot
le	mobile home	trailer
le	supplément	extra charge
le	terrain de camping	campsite
le	véhicule	vehicle
les	WC	toilets

IMPORTANT WORDS *(masculine)*

le	barbecue	barbecue
le	matelas pneumatique	air mattress
un	ouvre-boîtes	can opener
le	réchaud	stove
le	règlement	rules
le	sac à dos	backpack
le	sac de couchage	sleeping bag
le	tire-bouchon *(pl ~s)*	corkscrew

USEFUL PHRASES

faire du camping to go camping
camper to camp
bien aménagé(e) well equipped
faire un feu to build a fire

ESSENTIAL WORDS *(feminine)*

une	allumette	match
une	assiette	plate
la	boîte	can; box
les	boîtes de conserve	canned food
la	campeuse	camper *(female)*
la	caravane	camping trailer
la	chaise longue	deckchair
la	cuiller, la cuillère	spoon
la	douche	shower
	l'eau non potable	nonpotable water
	l'eau potable	drinking water
la	fourchette	fork
la	glace	mirror
la	lampe électrique	flashlight
la	lampe de poche	pocket flashlight
la	machine à laver	washing machine
la	nuit	night
la	piscine	swimming pool
la	poubelle	garbage can
la	salle	room; hall
la	table	table
la	tente	tent
les	toilettes	toilets

IMPORTANT WORDS *(feminine)*

les	installations sanitaires	washing facilities
la	laverie	coin laundry
la	lessive	laundry detergent; laundry
	l'ombre	shade; shadow
la	prise de courant	electrical outlet
la	salle de jeux	game room

USEFUL PHRASES

dresser *or* monter une tente to pitch a tent
griller des saucisses to grill some sausages

ESSENTIAL WORDS *(masculine)*

un	agent (de police)	policeman, police officer
un	agriculteur	farmer
un	artisan	artisan, craftsman
le	boulot	job
le	bureau *(pl* -x)	office
le	caissier	cashier, salesclerk
le	chauffeur de taxi	taxi driver
le	conseiller d'orientation	career counselor
le	designer web	web designer
un	électricien	electrician
un	employé	employee
un	employeur	employer
un	enseignant	teacher
le	facteur	letter carrier
le	garagiste	mechanic; garage owner
un	infirmier	(male) nurse
un	informaticien	computer scientist
le	mécanicien	mechanic; engineer; train engineer
le	médecin *(m+f)*	doctor
le	métier	trade, business
le	mineur	miner
le	patron	boss
le	pharmacien	pharmacist
le	pompier	firefighter
le	professeur	teacher
le	rédacteur	editor
le	salaire	wages
le	soldat	soldier
le	travail	work
le	vendeur	salesclerk

USEFUL PHRASES

intéressant(e)/peu intéressant(e) interesting/not very interesting
il est facteur he is a letter carrier
il/elle est médecin he/she is a doctor
travailler to work
devenir to become

ESSENTIAL WORDS *(feminine)*

une	**agricultrice**	farmer
une	**ambition**	ambition
une	**artisane**	artisan, craftswoman
la	**banque**	bank
la	**caissière**	cashier, salesclerk
la	**conseillère d'orientation**	career counselor
la	**dactylo**	typist
une	**employée**	employee
une	**enseignante**	teacher
la	**factrice**	letter carrier
une	**hôtesse de l'air**	flight attendant
une	**industrie**	industry
une	**infirmière**	nurse
une	**informaticienne**	computer scientist
la	**patronne**	boss
la	**professeur**	teacher
la	**profession**	profession
la	**réceptionniste**	receptionist
la	**rédactrice**	editor
la	**retraite**	retirement
la	**secrétaire**	secretary
une	**usine**	factory
la	**vedette** *(m+f)*	star
la	**vendeuse**	salesclerk
la	**vie**	life
la	**vie active**	working life

USEFUL PHRASES

travailler pour gagner sa vie **to work for one's living**
mon ambition est d'être juge **it is my ambition to be a judge**
que faites-vous dans la vie ? **what is your job?**
postuler à un emploi **to apply for a job**

IMPORTANT WORDS *(masculine)*

un	apprentissage	apprenticeship
	l'avenir	future
le	CDD	short-term contract, temporary contract
le	CDI	permanent contract
le	chef	boss
le	chômage	unemployment
le	chômeur	unemployed person
le	coiffeur	hairdresser
le	collègue	colleague
le	commerçant	storekeeper
le	commerce	business
le	concierge	caretaker
le	contrat	contract
le	décorateur	decorator
un	emploi	job
un	entretien (d'embauche)	(job) interview
le	gérant	manager
un	homme d'affaires	businessman
un	intérimaire	temp
le	marché du travail	job market
un	opticien	optician
un	ouvrier	worker
le	peintre	painter
le	pilote	pilot
le	plombier	plumber
le	président	president; chairman
le	salarié	hourly worker
le	sapeur-pompier (*pl* ~s~s)	firefighter
le	syndicat	labor union

USEFUL PHRASES

être au chômage **to be unemployed**
licencier qn **to fire sb**
l'emploi saisonnier **seasonal work**
"offres d'emplois" **"help wanted"**
être syndiqué **to be in a union**
gagner 150 euros par semaine **to earn 150 euros a week**

IMPORTANT WORDS *(feminine)*

les	**affaires**	business
une	**agence d'intérim**	temp agency
	l'**ANPE**	job center
une	**augmentation**	raise
la	**candidature**	application
la	**carrière**	career
la	**coiffeuse**	hairdresser
la	**collègue**	colleague
la	**concierge**	caretaker
la	**cuisinière**	cook
une	**entrevue**	interview
la	**femme d'affaires**	businesswoman
la	**femme de ménage**	cleaner
la	**gérante**	manager
la	**grève**	strike
une	**intérimaire**	temp
la	**lettre de motivation**	cover letter
une	**ouvrière**	worker
la	**peintre**	painter
la	**politique**	politics
la	**présidente**	president; chairwoman
la	**salariée**	hourly worker
la	**situation**	job; situation

USEFUL PHRASES

une augmentation de salaire **a pay raise**
se mettre en grève **to go on strike**
faire la grève **to be on strike**
travailler à plein temps/à mi-temps **to work full-time/part-time**
faire des heures supplémentaires **to work overtime**
la réduction du temps de travail **cutback in working hours**

USEFUL WORDS (*masculine*)

un	animateur	leader, organizer
un	architecte	architect
un	artiste	artist
un	avocat	trial lawyer, attorney
un	avoué	lawyer
le	cadre	executive
le	chercheur	researcher
le	chirurgien	surgeon
le	comptable	accountant
le	couturier	fashion designer
le	député	legislator
un	écrivain	writer
le	fonctionnaire	civil servant
un	horaire	schedule
un	ingénieur	engineer
un	interprète	interpreter
le	journaliste	journalist
le	juge	judge
le	maçon	mason
le	mannequin (*m+f*)	model (*person*)
le	marin	sailor; seaman
le	menuisier	carpenter
le	notaire	notary public
le	personnel	staff
le	photographe	photographer
le	président-directeur général, le PDG	chairman and managing director
le	prêtre	priest
le	représentant	rep
le	stage en entreprise	work placement
le	stage de formation	training course
le	traducteur	translator
le	vétérinaire (*m+f*)	vet
le	vigneron	wine grower
le	VRP	sales rep

USEFUL WORDS *(feminine)*

	l'administration	administration
une	animatrice	leader, organizer
une	artiste	artist
une	avocate	lawyer
la	comptable	accountant
la	couturière	dressmaker
une	entreprise	business
la	femme-agent	policewoman, police officer
la	femme au foyer	housewife
la	fonctionnaire	civil servant
la	formation	training
la	formation continue	in-house training
la	grève du zèle	work-to-rule
la	grève perlée	work slowdown
une	indemnité de chômage	unemployment benefit
une	indemnité de licenciement	severance payment
une	interprète	interpreter
la	journaliste	journalist
	l'orientation professionnelle	careers guidance
la	religieuse	nun
la	représentante	rep
la	société	company
la	speakerine [spikʀin]	announcer
la	sténo-dactylo	shorthand typist
la	traductrice	translator

USEFUL PHRASES

un emploi temporaire/permanent a temporary/permanent job
être engagé(e) to be taken on, to be hired
être renvoyé(e) to be dismissed
mettre qn à la porte to fire sb
un emploi à mi-temps a part-time job
chercher du travail to look for work
faire un stage de formation to go on a training course
pointer to clock in *or* out
avoir un horaire flexible to work flextime

ESSENTIAL WORDS *(masculine)*

un	**agent** (de police)	policeman, police officer
	l'**auto-stop**	hitchhiking
un	**auto-stoppeur** (*pl* ~s)	hitchhiker
le	**bouchon**	traffic jam
le	**camion**	truck
le	**carrefour**	intersection, crossroads
le	**chauffeur** (*m+f*)	driver; chauffeur
le	**conducteur**	driver
le	**cycliste**	cyclist
le	**diesel**	diesel
le	**feu rouge**	traffic lights, red light
les	**feux**	traffic lights
le	**frein**	brake
le	**garage**	garage
le	**garagiste**	mechanic; garage owner
le	**gas-oil**	diesel (oil)
le	**kilomètre**	kilometer
le	**litre**	liter
le	**mécanicien**	mechanic
le	**numéro**	number
le	**parking**	parking lot
le	**péage**	toll
le	**permis de conduire**	driver's license
le	**piéton**	pedestrian
le	**plan** (de la ville)	street map
le	**pneu**	tire
le	**radar**	radar
le	**voyage**	journey

USEFUL PHRASES

faire de l'auto-stop **to hitchhike**
s'arrêter au feu rouge **to stop at the red light**
freiner brusquement **to brake sharply**
100 kilomètres à l'heure **100 kilometers an hour**
crever, avoir un pneu crevé **to have a flat tire**
as-tu ton permis ? **do you have a driver's license?**

ESSENTIAL WORDS (feminine)

une	**auto**	car
une	**automobile**	car
une	**autoroute**	freeway, highway
une	**autoroute à péage**	tollway
une	**auto-stoppeuse** (pl ~s)	hitchhiker
la	**caravane**	camping trailer
la	**carte grise**	auto registration
la	**carte routière**	road map
la	**carte verte**	certificate of insurance
la	**conductrice**	driver
la	**déviation**	detour
la	**direction**	direction
la	**direction assistée**	power steering
la	**distance**	distance
	l'**eau**	water
	l'**essence**	gasoline
	l'**essence sans plomb**	unleaded gas
	l'**huile**	oil
la	**police**	police
la	**route**	road
la	**route nationale**	main road
la	**station-service** (pl ~s)	gas station
la	**voiture**	car

USEFUL PHRASES

on va faire une promenade en voiture **we're going for a drive (in the car)**
le plein, s'il vous plaît **fill her up, please!**
prenez la route de Lyon **take the road to Lyons**
c'est un voyage de 3 heures **it's a 3-hour drive**
bonne route ! **have a good trip!**
allez, en route ! **let's go!**
en route nous avons vu ... **on the way we saw ...**
doubler or dépasser une voiture **to pass a car**
se garer **to park (the car)**
réparer **to fix**

IMPORTANT WORDS (*masculine*)

un	accident (de la route)	(road) accident
un	alcootest	Breathalyzer® test
un	automobiliste	motorist
le	camionneur	truck driver
le	carburant	gas
le	code de la route	highway code
le	coffre	trunk
le	contrôle technique	vehicle inspection
le(s)	dommage(s)	damage
un	embouteillage	traffic jam
	l'embrayage	clutch
le	klaxon	horn
le	lavage	(car) wash
le	moteur	engine
les	papiers	official papers
le	phare	headlight
le	pompiste	gas station attendant
le	rond-point (*pl* ~s~s)	traffic circle
le	sens unique	one-way street
le	stationnement	parking
le	tableau de bord	dashboard

USEFUL PHRASES

d'abord on met le moteur en marche first you switch on the engine
le moteur démarre the engine starts up
la voiture démarre the car moves off
on roule we're driving along
accélérer to accelerate
continuer to continue
ralentir to slow down
s'arrêter to stop
stationner to park; to be parked
couper le moteur to switch off the engine
il y a eu un accident there's been an accident
vos papiers, s'il vous plaît may I see your papers, please?

IMPORTANT WORDS *(feminine)*

une	amende	fine
une	assurance	insurance
une	auto-école *(pl ~s)*	driving school
une	automobiliste	motorist
la	batterie	battery
la	carrosserie	bodywork
la	ceinture de sécurité	seat belt
la	circulation	traffic
la	collision	collision
la	crevaison	flat tire
la	frontière	border
la	marque	make *(of car)*
la	panne	breakdown
la	pièce de rechange	spare part
la	police d'assurance	insurance policy
la	pompe à essence	gas pump
la	portière	(car) door
la	priorité	right of way
la	roue	tire
la	roue de secours	spare tire
la	vitesse	speed; gear
la	voiture de dépannage	tow truck
la	zone bleue	restricted parking zone

USEFUL PHRASES

être en panne d'essence to run out of gas
aux heures d'affluence at rush hour
il a eu 150 euros d'amende he got a 150-euro fine
êtes-vous assuré(e) ? are you insured?
n'oubliez pas de mettre vos ceintures don't forget to put on your seat belts
à la frontière at the border
être *or* tomber en panne to break down
je suis tombé(e) en panne sèche I've run out of gas
la roue avant/arrière the front/back wheel

USEFUL WORDS *(masculine)*

un	accélérateur	accelerator
un	apprenti conducteur	student driver
un	arrêt d'urgence	emergency stop
le	blessé	casualty
le	capot	hood
le	carburateur	carburetor
le	clignotant	turn signal
le	compteur de vitesse	speedometer
le	contractuel	traffic policeman
le	démarreur	starter
le	détour	detour
un	essuie-glace *(pl inv)*	windshield wiper
le	lavage auto	car wash
le	moniteur d'auto-école	driving instructor
le	motard	motorcycle policeman; motorcyclist
le	panneau *(pl* -x)	road sign
le	parcmètre	parking meter
le	pare-brise *(pl inv)*	windshield
le	pare-chocs *(pl inv)*	bumper
le	périphérique	ring road
le	pot catalytique	catalytic converter
le	PV	fine
le	rétroviseur	rearview mirror
le	routier	long-distance truck driver
le	starter	choke
le	système de navigation GPS	satellite navigation system, GPS
le	virage	bend
le	volant	steering wheel

USEFUL PHRASES

l'accident a fait 6 blessés/morts 6 people were injured/killed in the accident

il faut faire un détour **we have to make a detour**

une contravention pour excès de vitesse **a fine for speeding**

dresser un PV à un conducteur **to ticket a driver**

USEFUL WORDS *(feminine)*

une	agglomération	built-up area
une	aire de services	service area
une	aire de stationnement	lay-by
une	apprentie conductrice	student driver
une	auto-école	driving school
la	bande d'arrêt d'urgence	hard shoulder
la	bande médiane	median strip
la	boîte de vitesses	gearbox
la	bretelle de raccordement	on-ramp; off-ramp
la	conduite accompagnée	*driving as a learner accompanied by an experienced driver*
la	consommation d'essence	gas consumption
la	contractuelle	traffic policeman
la	contravention	traffic offense
la	dépanneuse	tow truck
la	file	lane
la	galerie	roof rack
la	leçon de conduite	driving lesson
la	limitation de vitesse	speed limit
la	pédale	pedal
la	plaque d'immatriculation *or* minéralogique	license plate
la	pression	pressure
la	remorque	trailer
la	routière	long-distance truck driver
la	voie	way, road; lane *(on road)*
la	voie de raccordement	on-ramp; off-ramp

USEFUL PHRASES

"priorité à droite" "give way to the right"
"serrez à droite" "keep to the right"
"accès interdit" "no entry"
"stationnement interdit" "no parking"
"travaux" "roadwork"

ESSENTIAL WORDS *(masculine)*

un	anorak	anorak, parka
le	bouton	button
le	caleçon	boxer shorts
le	chapeau *(pl* -x)	hat
le	col	collar
le	collant	tights, pantyhose
le	complet	suit
le	costume	suit *(for man)*; costume
un	imper(méable)	raincoat
le	jean [dʒin]	jeans
le	maillot (de bain)	swimming trunks *or* swimsuit
le	manteau *(pl* -x)	coat
le	mouchoir	handkerchief
le	pantalon	pants, trousers
le	parapluie	umbrella
le	pardessus	overcoat
le	pull-over, le pull [pyl(ɔvœʀ)]	sweater, jersey
le	pyjama	pajamas
le	sac	bag, purse
le	slip de bain	swimming trunks
le	slip	underpants
le	soulier	shoe
les	sous-vêtements	underwear
le	T-shirt, le tee-shirt	T-shirt
les	vêtements	clothes

IMPORTANT WORDS *(masculine)*

le	blouson	jacket
le	chemisier	blouse
le	gant	glove
le	sac à main	purse
le	short [ʃɔʀt]	shorts
le	tricot	pullover
un	uniforme	uniform
le	veston	jacket *(for man)*

ESSENTIAL WORDS *(feminine)*

la	capuche	hood
la	chaussette	sock
la	chaussure	shoe
la	chemise	shirt
la	chemise de nuit	nightshirt
la	cravate	tie
la	culotte	panties
la	jupe	skirt
la	mode	fashion
la	parka	parka
la	pointure	(shoe) size
la	robe	dress
la	sandale	sandal
la	taille	size; waist
la	veste	jacket

IMPORTANT WORDS *(feminine)*

la	botte	boot
la	ceinture	belt
la	pantoufle	slipper
la	poche	pocket

USEFUL PHRASES

le matin je m'habille in the morning I get dressed
le soir je me déshabille in the evening I get undressed
porter to wear
mettre to put on
quand je rentre du lycée je me change when I get home from school I
   change clothes
à la mode fashionable
démodé(e) old-fashioned
cela fait très chic that's very chic
cela vous va bien that suits you
quelle est votre taille ? what size do you take?
quelle est votre pointure ? what shoe size do you take?
je chausse du 38 I take size 38 in shoes

USEFUL WORDS *(masculine)*

les	accessoires	accessories
les	bas	stockings
les	baskets	sneakers, running shoes
le	béret	beret
le	bermuda	Bermuda shorts
le	bleu de travail	overalls
le	bonnet	(knit) hat
le	chandail	(heavy) sweater
le	chapeau *(pl* -x*)* melon	bowler hat
le	collant	tights, pantyhose
le	débardeur	tank top
le	défilé	fashion show
le	foulard	scarf
le	gilet de corps	undershirt
le	gilet	vest
les	hauts talons	high heels
le	jupon	petticoat
les	lacets	(shoe)laces
le	linge	washing
le	nettoyage à sec	dry cleaning
le	nœud papillon	bow tie
le	pantacourt	three-quarter length pants
le	polo	polo shirt
le	ruban	ribbon
le	sac à bandoulière	shoulder bag
le	soutien-gorge *(pl* ~s~*)*	bra
le	survêtement	tracksuit
le	sweat [swɛt]	sweatshirt
le	sweat à capuche	hooded top
le	tablier	apron
le	tailleur	woman's suit
les	talons aiguilles	stiletto heels
le	tricot de corps	undershirt

USEFUL WORDS *(feminine)*

la	**boutonnière**	buttonhole
les	**bretelles**	suspenders
la	**cabine d'essayage**	fitting room
la	**canne**	cane, walking stick
la	**casquette**	cap
la	**doudoune**	down jacket
une	**écharpe**	scarf
une	**espadrille**	espadrille
la	**fermeture éclair**	zipper
la	**:haute couture**	haute couture
la	**jupe-culotte** *(pl ~s~s)*	culottes
la	**manche**	sleeve
la	**polaire**	fleece
la	**robe de chambre**	bathrobe
la	**robe de mariée**	wedding dress
la	**robe du soir**	evening dress *(for woman)*
la	**salopette**	(bib) overalls
la	**tong**	flip flop

USEFUL PHRASES

long(ue) **long**
court(e) **short**
une robe à manches courtes/longues **a short-sleeved/long-sleeved dress**
serré(e) **tight**
ample **loose**
une jupe serrée **a tight skirt**
rayé(e) **striped**
à carreaux **checkered**
à pois **polka-dotted**
les vêtements sport **casual clothes**
en tenue de soirée **in evening dress**
à la mode **fashionable**
branché(e) **trendy**
démodé(e) **old-fashioned**

beige	beige
blanc (blanche)	white
bleu(e)	blue
bordeaux	maroon
brun(e)	brown
doré(e)	golden
fauve	fawn
gris(e)	gray
jaune	yellow
marron	brown
mauve	mauve
noir(e)	black
orange, orangé(e)	orange
rose	pink
rouge	red
turquoise	turquoise
vert(e)	green
violet (violette)	violet, purple
bleu clair	pale blue
bleu foncé	dark blue
rouge vif	bright red
bleu ciel	sky blue
bleu marine	navy blue
bleu roi	royal blue

USEFUL PHRASES

la couleur color
de quelle couleur sont tes yeux/tes cheveux ? what color are your eyes/
  is your hair?
le bleu te va bien blue suits you; the blue one suits you
peindre qch en bleu to paint sth blue
des chaussures bleues blue shoes
des chaussures bleu clair light blue shoes
elle a les yeux verts she has green eyes
changer de couleur to change color
la Maison Blanche the White House
un Blanc a white man
une Blanche a white woman
un Noir a black man
une Noire a black woman
blanc comme neige as white as snow
Blanche-Neige Snow White
un steak bleu a very rare steak, an underdone steak
le Petit Chaperon rouge Little Red Riding Hood
rougir to turn red
rougir de honte to blush with shame
pâle comme un linge as white as a sheet
tout(e) bronzé(e) as brown as a berry
il était couvert de bleus he was black and blue
un œil poché, un œil au beurre noir a black eye

ESSENTIAL WORDS *(masculine)*

un	ordinateur	computer
le	PC	PC, personal computer
le	programme	program
le	programmeur	programmer

USEFUL WORDS *(masculine)*

le	CD-ROM	CD-ROM
le	clavier	keyboard
le	correcteur orthographique	spellchecker
le	courriel	email
le	courrier électronique	email
le	curseur	cursor
le	disque dur	hard disk
le	document	document
un	écran	screen
le	fichier	file
le	graveur de DVD	DVD writer
le	haut débit	broadband
un	internaute	internet user
l'	Internet	internet
le	jeu vidéo	computer game
le	lecteur de disquettes	disk drive
le	logiciel	software
le	matériel	hardware
le	menu	menu
le	modem	modem
le	moniteur	monitor
le	navigateur	browser
un	octet	byte
le	pirate	hacker
le	portable	laptop
le	réseau	network
le	serveur	server
le	système d'exploitation	operating system
le	tableur	spreadsheet (program)
le	traitement de texte	word processor
le	virus	virus
le	Web	Web
le	wifi	Wi-Fi

ESSENTIAL WORDS *(feminine)*

une **imprimante**	printer
l'**informatique**	computer science; computer studies
la **souris**	mouse

USEFUL WORDS *(feminine)*

une **adresse électronique**	email address
une **application**	program
la **base de données**	database
la **cartouche d'encre**	ink cartridge
la **clé USB**	USB key
la **corbeille**	recycle bin
la **disquette**	floppy disk
les **données**	data
la **fenêtre**	window
la **fonction**	function
une **icône**	icon
une **interface**	interface
une **internaute**	internet user
la **manette**	joystick
la **mémoire**	memory
la **mémoire morte**	ROM, Read-Only Memory
la **mémoire vive**	RAM, random-access memory
la **page d'accueil**	home page
la **sauvegarde**	back-up
la **Toile**	Web
la **touche**	key
la **webcam**	webcam

USEFUL PHRASES

taper to key
copier to copy
effacer to delete
sauvegarder to save
imprimer to print
formater to format
surfer sur Internet to surf the internet
télécharger un fichier to download a file

COUNTRIES

ESSENTIAL WORDS *(masculine)*

le **Canada**	Canada
les **États-Unis**	United States
le **pays**	country
le **Royaume-Uni**	United Kingdom
les **USA**	USA

USEFUL WORDS *(masculine)*

l'**Hexagone**	France
le **Japon**	Japan
le **Maroc**	Morocco
le **Pakistan**	Pakistan
les **Pays-Bas**	Netherlands
le **pays de Galles**	Wales
le **tiers-monde**	Third World

USEFUL PHRASES

mon pays natal my native country
la capitale de la France the capital of France
de quel pays venez-vous ? what country do you come from?
je viens des États-Unis/du Canada I come from the United States/
 from Canada
je suis né(e) en Écosse I was born in Scotland
je vais aux Pays-Bas I'm going to the Netherlands
je reviens du Canada I have just come back from Canada
les pays en voie de développement the developing countries

ESSENTIAL WORDS (*feminine*)

	l'Afrique	Africa
	l'Amérique	America
	l'Amérique du Sud	South America
	l'Angleterre	England
	l'Asie	Asia
la	Belgique	Belgium
	l'Europe	Europe
la	France	France
la	Grande-Bretagne	Great Britain
la	Suisse	Switzerland
	l'Union européenne, l'UE	European Union, EU

USEFUL WORDS (*feminine*)

	l'Algérie	Algeria
	l'Allemagne	Germany
les	Antilles	West Indies
	l'Australie	Australia
	l'Autriche	Austria
la	Chine	China
	l'Écosse	Scotland
	l'Espagne	Spain
la	Grèce	Greece
la	:Hollande	Holland
	l'Inde	India
	l'Irlande (du Nord)	(Northern) Ireland
	l'Italie	Italy
la	Norvège	Norway
la	Nouvelle-Zélande	New Zealand
la	Pologne	Poland
la	Roumanie	Romania
la	Russie	Russia
la	Suède	Sweden
la	Tunisie	Tunisia

NATIONALITIES

ESSENTIAL WORDS *(masculine)*

un	**Africain**	an African
un	**Américain**	an American
un	**Anglais**	an Englishman
un	**Asiatique**	an Asian
un	**Belge**	a Belgian
un	**Britannique**	a Briton
un	**Canadien**	a Canadian
un	**Européen**	a European
un	**Français**	a Frenchman
un	**Suisse**	a Swiss

USEFUL PHRASES

il est anglais, c'est un Anglais he is English
elle est anglaise, c'est une Anglaise she is English
le paysage anglais the English countryside
une ville anglais an English town
un Canadien français a French Canadian

ESSENTIAL WORDS *(feminine)*

une	**Africaine**	an African
une	**Américaine**	an American
une	**Anglaise**	an Englishwoman, an English girl
une	**Asiatique**	an Asian
une	**Belge**	a Belgian
une	**Britannique**	a Briton, a British girl *or* woman
une	**Canadienne**	a Canadian
une	**Européenne**	a European
une	**Française**	a Frenchwoman, a French girl
une	**Suisse**	a Swiss girl *or* woman

USEFUL PHRASES

je suis américain – je parle anglais I am American – I speak English
une Canadienne française a French Canadian
je suis Américaine I am American
un étranger (une étrangère) a foreigner
à l'étranger abroad, overseas; la nationalité nationality

USEFUL WORDS *(masculine)*

un **Allemand**	a German
un **Algérien**	an Algerian
un **Antillais**	a West Indian
un **Arabe**	an Arab
un **Australien**	an Australian
un **Chinois**	a Chinese
un **Écossais**	a Scot
un **Espagnol**	a Spaniard
un **Gallois**	a Welshman
un **Grec**	a Greek
un **:Hollandais**	a Dutchman
un **Indien**	an Indian
un **Irlandais**	an Irishman
un **Italien**	an Italian
un **Japonais**	a Japanese
un **Marocain**	a Moroccan
un **Néo-Zélandais** *(pl inv)*	a New Zealander
un **Pakistanais**	a Pakistani
un **Polonais**	a Pole
un **Russe**	a Russian
un **Tchèque**	a Czech
un **Tunisien**	a Tunisian
un **Turc**	a Turk
un **Vietnamien**	a Vietnamese

USEFUL WORDS (feminine)

une	Allemande	a German
une	Algérienne	an Algerian
une	Antillaise	a West Indian
une	Arabe	an Arab
une	Australienne	an Australian
une	Chinoise	a Chinese
une	Écossaise	a Scot
une	Espagnole	a Spaniard
une	Galloise	a Welshwoman, a Welsh girl
une	Grecque	a Greek
une	:Hollandaise	a Dutchwoman, a Dutch girl
une	Indienne	an Indian
une	Irlandaise	an Irishwoman, an Irish girl
une	Italienne	an Italian
une	Japonaise	a Japanese
une	Marocaine	a Moroccan
une	Néo-Zélandaise (pl ~s)	a New Zealander
une	Pakistanaise	a Pakistani
une	Polonaise	a Pole
une	Russe	a Russian
une	Tchèque	a Czech
une	Tunisienne	a Tunisian
une	Turque	a Turk
une	Vietnamienne	a Vietnamese

ESSENTIAL WORDS (*masculine*)

	l'air	air
un	arbre	tree
le	bois	wood
le	bruit	noise
le	champ	field
le	chasseur	hunter
le	château (*pl* -x)	castle
le	chemin	path, way
le	fermier	farmer
le	marché	market
le	pays	country; district
le	paysan	countryman, farmer
le	paysage	scenery
le	pique-nique (*pl* ~s)	picnic
le	pont	bridge
le	ruisseau	stream
le	sentier	track
le	terrain	soil; ground
le	touriste	tourist
le	village	village

USEFUL PHRASES

en plein air in the open air

je connais le chemin du village I know the way to the village

faire un tour en bicyclette to go cycling

les gens du pays the locals

nous avons fait un pique-nique we went for a picnic

ESSENTIAL WORDS *(feminine)*

une	auberge de jeunesse	youth hostel
la	barrière	gate; fence
la	camionnette	van
la	campagne	country
la	canne	walking stick
la	ferme	farm, farmhouse
la	forêt	forest
la	montagne	mountain
la	pierre	stone, rock
la	promenade	walk
la	randonnée	hike
la	rivière	river
la	route	road
la	terre	earth, ground
la	tour	tower
la	touriste	tourist
la	vallée	valley

USEFUL PHRASES

à la campagne in the country
aller à la campagne to go into the country
habiter à la campagne/en ville to live in the country/in town
cultiver la terre to cultivate the land

IMPORTANT WORDS *(masculine)*

un	**agriculteur**	farmer
les	**campagnards**	country people
le	**fleuve**	river
le	**gendarme** *(m+f)*	police officer
le	**lac**	lake
le	**sommet**	top *(of hill)*

USEFUL WORDS *(masculine)*

le	**bâton**	stick
le	**blé**	wheat
le	**buisson**	bush
le	**caillou** *(pl -x)*	pebble
un	**étang**	pond
le	**foin**	hay
le	**fossé**	ditch
le	**:hameau** *(pl -x)*	hamlet
le	**marais**	marsh
le	**moulin (à vent)**	(wind)mill
le	**piège**	trap
le	**poteau** *(pl -x)* **indicateur**	signpost
le	**poteau** *(pl -x)* **télégraphique**	telephone pole
le	**pré**	meadow
le	**sentier**	path

USEFUL PHRASES

agricole agricultural
paisible, tranquille peaceful
au sommet de la colline at the top of the hill
tomber dans un piège to fall into a trap

IMPORTANT WORDS (feminine)

	l'agriculture	agriculture
une	auberge	inn
la	botte (de caoutchouc)	rubber boot
la	chaussée	road surface
la	colline	hill
la	feuille	leaf
la	paysanne	countrywoman
la	poussière	dust
la	propriété	property, estate
la	tranquillité	peace

USEFUL WORDS (feminine)

la	boue	mud
la	bruyère	heather
la	carrière	quarry
la	caverne	cave
la	chasse	hunting; shooting
la	chaumière	(thatched) cottage
la	chute d'eau	waterfall
la	:haie	hedge
les	jumelles	binoculars
la	lande	moor
la	mare	pond
la	moisson	harvest
la	plaine	plain
la	récolte	crop, harvest
la	rive	bank (of river)
les	ruines	ruins
la	source	spring, source
les	vendanges	grape harvest

USEFUL PHRASES

s'égarer to lose one's way
faire la moisson to bring in the harvest
faire les vendanges to harvest the grapes

ESSENTIAL WORDS *(masculine)*

	l'**âge**	age
un	**air**	appearance
les	**cheveux**	hair
les	**yeux**	eyes

USEFUL PHRASES

affreux(euse) hideous
agité(e) agitated
aimable nice
amusant(e) amusing, entertaining
barbu(e) bearded, with a beard
beau handsome; belle beautiful
bête stupid
calme calm
chauve bald
court(e) short
dégoûtant(e) disgusting
désagréable unpleasant
drôle funny
dynamique dynamic
formidable great
gai(e) cheerful
gentil(le) kind
grand(e) tall
gros(se) fat
heureux(euse) happy
impoli(e) rude
intelligent(e) intelligent
jeune young
joli(e) pretty
laid(e) ugly
long(ue) long
maigre skinny
malheureux(euse) unhappy, unfortunate
méchant(e) naughty
mignon(ne) cute

ESSENTIAL WORDS *(feminine)*

la	barbe	beard
la	couleur	color
la	larme	tear
les	lunettes	glasses
la	moustache	mustache
la	personne	person
la	pièce d'identité	ID
la	taille	height, size; waist

USEFUL PHRASES

mince **slim**

nerveux(euse) **nervous, tense**

optimiste/pessimiste **optimistic/pessimistic**

petit(e) **small, little**

poli **polite**

sage **well-behaved**

sérieux(euse) **serious**

timide **shy**

vieux, vieille **old**

elle a l'air triste **she looks sad**

il pleurait **he was crying**

il souriait **he was smiling**

il avait les larmes aux yeux **he had tears in his eyes**

un homme de taille moyenne **a man of average height**

je mesure/je fais 1 mètre 70 **I am 1 meter 70 tall**

de quelle couleur sont tes yeux/tes cheveux ? **what color are your eyes/ is your hair?**

j'ai les cheveux blonds **I have fair hair**

j'ai les yeux bleus/verts **I have blue eyes/green eyes**

les cheveux bruns **dark *or* brown hair**

les cheveux châtains **chestnut-colored hair**

les cheveux frisés **curly hair**

les cheveux roux/noirs/blancs **red/black/gray hair**

les cheveux teints **dyed hair**

IMPORTANT WORDS (*masculine*)

le	bouton	pimple
le	caractère	character, nature
le	regard	look
le	sourire	smile
le	teint	complexion

USEFUL WORDS (*masculine*)

le	défaut	fault
le	dentier	false teeth, dentures
le	géant	giant
le	geste	gesture
le	grain de beauté	mole, beauty mark
le	poids	weight

USEFUL PHRASES

il a bon caractère he is good-tempered
il a mauvais caractère he is bad-tempered
avoir le teint pâle to have a pale complexion
porter des lunettes/des lentilles to wear glasses/contact lenses

IMPORTANT WORDS *(feminine)*

la	**beauté**	beauty
la	**curiosité**	curiosity
une	**expression**	expression
une	**habitude**	habit
	l'**humeur**	mood
la	**laideur**	ugliness
les	**lentilles (de contact)**	contact lenses
la	**qualité**	(good) quality
la	**voix**	voice

USEFUL WORDS *(feminine)*

la	**boucle**	curl
la	**cicatrice**	scar
les	**fossettes**	dimples
la	**frange**	bangs
la	**permanente**	perm
la	**ressemblance**	resemblance
les	**rides**	wrinkles
les	**taches de rousseur**	freckles
la	**timidité**	shyness

USEFUL PHRASES

je suis toujours de bonne humeur **I am always in a good mood**
il est de mauvaise humeur **he is in a bad mood**
il s'est mis en colère **he got angry**
elle ressemble à sa mère **she looks like her mother**
il se ronge les ongles **he bites his nails**

ESSENTIAL WORDS (*masculine*)

	l'allemand	German
	l'alphabet	alphabet
	l'anglais	English
	l'apprentissage	apprenticeship; learning
le	camarade de classe	classmate
le	carnet	notebook
le	club	club
le	collège	middle school
le	concert	concert
le	copain	pal
les	cours	lessons
le	crayon	pencil
le	dessin	drawing
le	devoir	test
les	devoirs	homework
le	directeur	principal, headmaster
le	dortoir	dormitory
un	échange	exchange
un	écolier	schoolboy
un	élève	student, schoolboy
un	emploi du temps	timetable
	l'enseignement	education, teaching
	l'espagnol	Spanish
un	étudiant	student
un	examen	exam
un	examen blanc	mock exam
un	exposé	presentation
le	français	French
le	groupe	group
le	gymnase	gym(nasium)
	l'italien	Italian
le	laboratoire	laboratory
le	livre	book
le	lycée	secondary school, high school
le	self	cafeteria

ESSENTIAL WORDS (*feminine*)

la	biologie	biology
la	camarade de classe	classmate
la	cantine	cafeteria
la	carte	map
la	chimie	chemistry
la	classe	class; grade; classroom
la	copine	pal
la	directrice	principal, headmistress
une	école	school
une	école maternelle	kindergarten
une	école primaire	elementary school
une	écolière	schoolgirl
	l'éducation physique	PE
	l'électronique	electronics
une	élève	student, schoolgirl
	l'EPS	PE
une	erreur	mistake
	l'étude (de)	study (of)
les	études	studies
une	étudiante	student
une	excursion	trip, outing
une	expérience	experiment
la	faute	mistake
la	géographie	geography
la	gomme	eraser
les	grandes vacances	summer vacation
la	gymnastique	gym(nastics)
	l'histoire	history; story
	l'informatique	computer studies
la	journée	day
les	langues (vivantes)	(modern) languages
la	leçon	lesson
la	lecture	reading
les	mathématiques	mathematics
les	maths	math
la	matière	(school) subject
la	musique	music

ESSENTIAL WORDS *(masculine continued)*

le	**mot**	word
un	**ordinateur**	computer
le	**prix**	prize
le	**professeur**	teacher
le	**professeur des écoles**	elementary school teacher
les	**progrès**	progress
le	**résultat**	result
le	**semestre**	semester
le	**tableau (noir)**	blackboard
le	**travail**	work
les	**travaux manuels**	handicrafts
les	**travaux pratiques**	practical class
le	**trimestre**	term

USEFUL PHRASES

travailler to work

apprendre to learn

étudier to study

depuis combien de temps apprenez-vous le français ? how long have you been learning French?

apprendre qch par cœur to learn sth by heart

j'ai des devoirs tous les jours I have homework every day

ma petite sœur va à l'école – moi, je vais au collège my little sister goes to elementary school – I go to middle school

enseigner le français to teach French

le professeur d'allemand the German teacher

j'ai fait des progrès en maths I have made progress in math

passer un examen to take an exam

être reçu(e) à un examen to pass an exam

échouer à un examen to fail an exam

avoir la moyenne to get a passing grade

ESSENTIAL WORDS *(feminine continued)*

la	natation	swimming
la	note	grade
la	phrase	sentence
la	physique	physics
la	piscine	swimming pool
la	professeur	teacher
la	professeur des écoles	elementary school teacher
la	question	question
la	récréation	recess
la	rentrée (des classes)	beginning of the semester
la	réponse	answer
la	salle de classe	classroom
la	salle des professeurs	teachers' lounge
les	sciences	science
une	université	college
les	vacances	vacation

USEFUL PHRASES

facile/difficile easy/difficult
intéressant(e) interesting
ennuyeux(euse) boring
lire to read; écrire to write
écouter to listen (to)
regarder to look at, watch
répéter to repeat
répondre to reply
parler to speak
elle est première/dernière de la classe she is first/last in the class
entrer en classe to go into the classroom
faire une erreur to make a mistake
corriger to correct
j'ai fait une faute de grammaire I made a grammatical mistake
j'ai eu une bonne note I got a good grade
répondez à la question ! answer the question!

IMPORTANT WORDS (*masculine*)

le baccalauréat, le bac	baccalaureate diploma/exam
le bulletin	report
le bureau	office
le certificat	certificate
le classeur	folder, file
le concours	competitive exam
le conseil de classe	teachers' meeting (*to discuss progress of students*)
le couloir	corridor
le diplôme	diploma
le dossier	file
un écrit	written exam
un instituteur	elementary school teacher
le jour de congé	day off
un oral	oral exam
le papier	paper
le règlement	rules

USEFUL PHRASES

mon ami prépare son bac my friend is taking the baccalaureate exam

les Français ont congé le mercredi après-midi French children have
   Wednesday afternoons off

réviser ses leçons to review

je vais réviser la leçon demain I'll go over the lesson again tomorrow

IMPORTANT WORDS *(feminine)*

une	**absence**	absence
une	**appréciation**	comment *(from teacher)*
la	**conférence**	lecture
la	**cour (de récréation)**	playground, schoolyard
une	**institutrice**	elementary school teacher
les	**langues anciennes**	ancient languages
une	**LV1 (langue vivante 1)**	first foreign language studied
une	**LV2 (langue vivante 2)**	second foreign language studied
la	**mention**	grade
la	**règle**	rule; ruler
la	**traduction**	translation
la	**trousse**	pencil case
la	**version**	translation (from foreign language)

USEFUL PHRASES

en sixième 6th grade
en cinquième 7th grade
en quatrième 8th grade
en troisième 9th grade, high school freshman
en seconde 10th grade, sophomore
en première 11th grade, junior
en terminale 12th grade, senior

présent(e) present
absent(e) absent
punir un élève to punish a student
mettre une colle à qn to give sb detention
taisez-vous ! be quiet!
levez la main ! put your hand up!

USEFUL WORDS (*masculine*)

le	Bic®	ballpoint pen
le	brouillon	rough copy
le	cahier	notebook
le	calcul	sum
le	cartable	book bag
le	collège technique	vocational school
le	correcteur (liquide)	correction fluid
le	dictionnaire	dictionary
un	examinateur	examiner
un	exercice	exercise
le	feutre	felt-tip pen
le	grec	Greek
un	inspecteur	school inspector
un	internat	boarding school
un	interne	boarder
le	latin	Latin
le	lycéen	high school student
le	manuel	textbook
le	pensionnaire	boarder
le	principal	principal (*of collège*)
le	professeur principal	homeroom teacher
le	proviseur	principal (*of lycée*)
le	pupitre	desk
le	rang	row (*of seats etc*)
le	russe	Russian
le	stylo bille	ballpoint pen
le	stylo feutre	felt-tip pen
le	surveillant	supervisor
le	tableau interactif	interactive whiteboard, Smartboard®
le	taille-crayon (*pl* ~s)	pencil sharpener
le	test	test
le	thème	prose translation
le	trimestre	term
le	vestiaire	coatroom
le	vocabulaire	vocabulary

USEFUL WORDS *(feminine)*

	l'algèbre	algebra
	l'arithmétique	arithmetic
la	calculatrice, la calculette	calculator
la	colle	detention; difficult question
la	composition	essay; class exam
la	conduite	behavior
la	craie	chalk
la	distribution des prix	prize-giving
une	école maternelle	kindergarten
une	école normale	teachers' college
	l'écriture	handwriting
	l'encre	ink
une	épreuve	test
la	faculté, la fac	college; faculty
la	feuille de présence	absence sheet
la	géométrie	geometry
la	grammaire	grammar
une	inspectrice	school inspector
	l'instruction religieuse	religious instruction
une	interne	boarder
la	lycéenne	high school student
la	menuiserie	shop class
la	moyenne	average grade
	l'orthographe	spelling
la	poésie	poetry, poem
la	punition	punishment
la	retenue	detention
la	sacoche	book bag
les	sciences naturelles	biology, natural history
la	serviette	briefcase
la	surveillante	supervisor
la	tache	blot
la	tâche	task

ESSENTIAL WORDS *(masculine)*

	l'air	air
les	animaux	animals
les	arbres	trees
le	bois	wood
un	écologiste	environmentalist
	l'environnement	environment
les	fruits	fruit
le	gas-oil	diesel
le	gaz	gas *(natural or bottled)*
les	gaz d'échappement	exhaust fumes
les	habitants	inhabitants
le	journal *(pl* journaux)	newspaper
les	légumes	vegetables
le	monde	world
le	pays	country
les	poissons	fish
le	temps	weather; time
le	trou	hole
les	Verts	the Greens *(political party)*
le	verre	glass

IMPORTANT WORDS *(masculine)*

	l'aluminium	aluminum
	l'avenir	future
le	climat	climate
le(s)	dégât(s)	damage
le	détergent	detergent
un	événement	event
le	fleuve	river
le	gouvernement	government
le	lac	lake
le	parc éolien	wind farm
le	polluant	pollutant

ESSENTIAL WORDS *(feminine)*

les	bouteilles	bottles
la	carte	map
la	côte	coast
	l'eau	water
	l'écologie	ecology
une	éolienne	wind turbine
une	espèce	species
	l'essence	gasoline
les	fleurs	flowers
une	île	island
la	mer	sea
la	montagne	mountain
la	plage	beach
les	plantes	plants
la	pluie	rain
la	pollution	pollution
la	question	question
la	région	region, area
la	rivière	river
la	température	temperature
la	terre	earth
une	usine	factory
la	voiture	car

IMPORTANT WORDS *(feminine)*

la	centrale nucléaire	nuclear plant
la	chaleur	heat
la	crise	crisis
la	forêt	forest
la	lessive	laundry detergent; laundry
la	planète	planet
la	solution	solution
la	taxe	tax
la	zone	zone

USEFUL WORDS (*masculine*)

les	**aliments bio**	organic food
un	**aérosol**	aerosol
le	**canal** (*pl* canaux)	canal
les	**CFC**	CFC
le	**chercheur**	researcher
le	**combustible**	fuel
le	**continent**	continent
les	**déchets nucléaires/ industriels**	nuclear/industrial waste
le	**dépotoir**	dumping ground
le	**désert**	desert
le	**développement durable**	sustainable development
un	**écosystème**	ecosystem
un	**engrais (chimique)**	(chemical) fertilizer
un	**océan**	ocean
les	**OGM**	GMO
le	**pot catalytique**	catalytic converter
le	**produit**	product
les	**produits chimiques**	chemicals
le	**réchauffement planétaire**	global warming
le	**recyclage**	recycling
les	**scientifiques**	scientists
l'	**univers**	universe

USEFUL PHRASES

il est très écolo he's very environmentally minded
un produit écologique an eco-friendly product
à l'avenir in the future
polluer to pollute; détruire to destroy
contaminer to contaminate
interdire to ban
sauver to save
recycler to recycle
vert(e) green

USEFUL WORDS *(feminine)*

la	catastrophe	disaster
la	couche d'ozone	ozone layer
	l'énergie éolienne	wind power
	l'énergie nucléaire	nuclear power
une	énergie renouvelable	renewable energy
la	forêt tropicale humide	tropical rainforest
la	lune	moon
la	marée noire	oil spill
la	nocivité	harmfulness
les	pluies acides	acid rain
la	pollution sonore	noise pollution
la	population	population
les	vidanges	sewage

USEFUL PHRASES

biodégradable biodegradable

nocif(ive) pour l'environnement harmful to the environment

biologique organic

l'essence sans plomb unleaded gasoline

les espèces en voie de disparition endangered species

ESSENTIAL WORDS (*masculine*)

les	**adultes**	adults
	l'âge	age
le	**bébé**	baby
le	**cousin**	cousin
un	**enfant**	child
le	**fiancé**	fiancé
le	**fils** [fis]	son
le	**frère**	brother
le	**garçon**	boy
les	**gens**	people
le	**grand-père** (*pl* ~s~s)	grandfather
les	**grands-parents**	grandparents
un	**homme**	man
le	**jeune homme**	youth, young man
les	**jeunes**	young people
le	**mari**	husband
le	**nom**	name
le	**nom de famille**	surname, last name
le	**nom de jeune fille**	maiden name
un	**oncle**	uncle
le	**papa**	daddy
le	**parent**	relative
les	**parents**	parents
le	**père**	father
le	**prénom**	first *or* Christian name

USEFUL PHRASES

quel âge avez-vous ? how old are you?
j'ai 15 ans – il a 40 ans I'm 15 – he is 40
comment vous appelez-vous ? what is your name?
je m'appelle Robert my name is Robert
il s'appelle Jean-Pierre his name is Jean-Pierre
fiancé(e) engaged
marié(e) married
divorcé(e) divorced
séparé(e) separated
épouser qn, se marier avec qn to marry sb
se marier to get married; divorcer to get divorced

ESSENTIAL WORDS *(feminine)*

la	cousine	cousin
la	dame	lady
une	enfant	child
la	famille	family
la	femme	woman; wife
la	fiancée	fiancée
la	fille	daughter; girl
les	gens	people
la	grand-mère (*pl* ~s~s)	grandmother
les	grandes personnes	grown-ups
la	maman	mommy
la	mère	mother
la	personne	person
la	sœur	sister
la	tante	aunt

USEFUL PHRASES

plus jeune/âgé que moi younger/older than me
as-tu des frères et sœurs ? do you have any brothers or sisters?
j'ai un frère et une sœur I have one brother and one sister
je n'ai pas de frères/de sœurs I don't have any brothers/sisters
je suis enfant unique I am an only child
toute la famille the whole family
grandir to grow
vieillir to get old
je m'entends bien avec mes parents I get along well with my parents
ma mère travaille my mother works

IMPORTANT WORDS (*masculine*)

un	adolescent	teenager
le	beau-père (*pl* ~x~s)	father-in-law; stepfather
le	célibataire	bachelor
l'	époux	husband
le	neveu	nephew
le	petit-fils [pətifis] (*pl* ~s~)	grandson
les	petits-enfants [pətizɑ̃fɑ̃]	grandchildren
le	veuf	widower
le	voisin	neighbor

USEFUL WORDS (*masculine*)

le	beau-fils [bofis] (*pl* ~x~s)	son-in-law; stepson
le	beau-frère (*pl* ~x~s)	brother-in-law
le	couple	couple
le	demi-frère (*pl* ~s)	stepbrother
le	filleul	godson
le	gendre	son-in-law
le	gosse	kid
les	jumeaux	twins
le	marié	bridegroom
les	nouveaux mariés	newlyweds
un	orphelin	orphan
le	parrain	godfather
le	retraité	pensioner
le	surnom	nickname
les	triplés	triplets
le	vieillard	old man

USEFUL PHRASES

naître to be born
vivre to live
mourir to die
je suis né(e) en 1990 I was born in 1990
ma grand-mère est morte my grandmother is dead
elle est morte en 1995 she died in 1995

IMPORTANT WORDS *(feminine)*

une	**adolescente**	teenager
les	**allocations familiales**	child benefit
la	**belle-mère** *(pl ~s~s)*	mother-in-law; stepmother
la	**célibataire**	single woman
une	**épouse**	wife
la	**jeune fille au pair**	au pair
la	**jeunesse**	youth
la	**nièce**	niece
la	**petite-fille** *(pl ~s~s)*	granddaughter
la	**veuve**	widow
la	**voisine**	neighbor

USEFUL WORDS *(feminine)*

la	**belle-fille** *(pl ~s~s)*	daughter-in-law; stepdaughter
la	**belle-sœur** *(pl ~s~s)*	sister-in-law
la	**demi-sœur** *(pl ~s)*	stepsister
la	**femme au foyer**	housewife
la	**filleule**	goddaughter
la	**gosse**	kid
la	**jeune mariée**	bride
les	**jumelles**	twins, twin sisters
la	**marraine**	godmother
la	**nurse**	nanny
une	**orpheline**	orphan
la	**retraitée**	pensioner
la	**vieillesse**	old age

USEFUL PHRASES

il/elle est célibataire he/she is single
il est veuf he is a widower
elle est veuve she is a widow
je suis le cadet (la cadette) I am the youngest
je suis l'aîné(e) I am the eldest
ma sœur aînée my elder sister

ESSENTIAL WORDS *(masculine)*

un	**agriculteur**	farmer
un	**animal** *(pl* animaux)	animal
le	**bœuf** [bœf] *(pl* -s [bø])	ox
le	**cabri**	kid
le	**canard**	duck
le	**champ**	field
le	**chat**	cat
le	**cheval** *(pl* chevaux)	horse
le	**chien**	dog
le	**chien de berger**	sheepdog
le	**cochon**	pig
le	**dindon**	turkey
le	**fermier**	farmer
le	**mouton**	sheep
le	**poulet**	chicken
le	**veau** *(pl* -x)	calf
le	**village**	village

IMPORTANT WORDS *(masculine)*

un	**agneau** *(pl* -x)	lamb
le	**coq**	rooster
le	**paysan**	countryman
le	**tracteur**	tractor

USEFUL PHRASES

l'agriculture biologique organic farming
un champ de blé a wheatfield
s'occuper des animaux to look after the animals
rentrer la moisson to bring in the harvest

ESSENTIAL WORDS *(feminine)*

une	**agricultrice**	farmer
la	**barrière**	gate; fence
la	**brebis**	ewe
la	**camionnette**	van
la	**campagne**	country
une	**exploitation agricole**	farm
la	**ferme**	farm, farmhouse
la	**fermière**	farmer's wife
la	**forêt**	forest
la	**jument**	mare
la	**poule**	hen
la	**serre**	greenhouse
la	**terre**	earth, ground
la	**truie**	sow
la	**vache**	cow

IMPORTANT WORDS *(feminine)*

la	**colline**	hill
la	**paysanne**	countrywoman

USEFUL PHRASES

vivre à la campagne to live in the country
travailler dans une ferme to work on a farm
faire la récolte to bring in the crops
faire les foins to make hay
les poulets élevés en plein air free range chickens
les œufs de poules élevées en plein air free range eggs

USEFUL WORDS (*masculine*)

un	âne	donkey
le	bélier	ram
le	berger	shepherd
le	bétail	cattle
le	blé	wheat
le	chevreau (*pl* -x)	kid
un	élevage	cattle farm
un	engrais	fertilizer
un	épouvantail	scarecrow
un	étang	pond
le	foin	hay
le	fossé	ditch
le	fumier	manure
le	grain	grain, seed
le	grenier	loft
le	:hangar	shed, barn
le	maïs [ma-is]	maize
le	marché	market
le	moulin (à vent)	(wind)mill
le	paysage	landscape
le	porc [pɔʀ]	pig
le	poulailler	henhouse
le	poulain	foal
le	poussin	chick
le	pré	meadow
le	puits	well
le	raisin	grape
le	seigle	rye
le	sillon	furrow
le	silo	silo
le	sol	ground, earth
le	taureau (*pl* -x)	bull
le	troupeau (*pl* -x)	(*sheep*) flock; (*cattle*) herd

USEFUL WORDS *(feminine)*

	l'avoine	oats
la	basse-cour *(pl ~s~s)*	farmyard
la	boue	mud
la	céréale	cereal crop
la	charrette	cart
la	charrue	plow
la	chaumière	(thatched) cottage
la	chèvre	goat
une	échelle	ladder
une	écurie	stable
une	étable	cowshed
la	foire	fair
la	grange	barn
la	laine	wool
la	lande	moor, heath
la	meule de foin	haystack
la	moisson	harvest
la	moissonneuse-batteuse *(pl ~s~s)*	combine harvester
une	oie	goose
	l'orge	barley
la	paille	straw
la	porcherie	pigsty
la	récolte	crop
les	vendanges	grape harvest, grape picking
la	vigne	vine

ESSENTIAL WORDS (*masculine*)

les	fruits de mer	seafood
le	poisson	fish
le	poisson rouge	goldfish

IMPORTANT WORDS (*masculine*)

le	crabe	crab
un	insecte	insect

USEFUL WORDS (*masculine*)

un	aquarium	aquarium
le	brochet	pike
le	cafard	cockroach
le	calmar	squid
le	criquet	cricket
le	frelon	hornet
le	grillon	cricket
le	:haddock	haddock
le	:hareng	herring
le	:homard	lobster
le	merlan	whiting
le	moucheron	midge
le	moustique	mosquito
le	papillon	butterfly
le	papillon de nuit	moth
le	poulpe	octopus
le	requin	shark
le	saumon	salmon
le	têtard	tadpole
le	thon	tuna
le	ver	worm
le	ver à soie	silkworm

USEFUL PHRASES

nager to swim
voler to fly
nous allons à la pêche we're going fishing

ESSENTIAL WORDS (*feminine*)

l'eau	water

IMPORTANT WORDS (*feminine*)

la	mouche	fly
la	sardine	sardine
la	truite	trout

USEFUL WORDS (*feminine*)

une	abeille	bee
une	aile	wing
une	anguille	eel
une	araignée	spider
la	bête à bon Dieu	ladybug, ladybird
la	chenille	caterpillar
la	cigale	cicada
la	coccinelle [kɔksinɛl]	ladybug, ladybird
la	crevette	shrimp
la	fourmi	ant
la	grenouille	frog
la	guêpe	wasp
une	huître	oyster
la	langouste	crayfish
les	langoustines	scampi
la	libellule	dragonfly
la	méduse	jellyfish
la	morue	cod
la	moule	mussel
la	pieuvre	octopus
la	puce	flea
la	punaise	bug
la	sauterelle	grasshopper
la	sole	sole

USEFUL PHRASES
une piqûre de guêpe a wasp sting
une toile d'araignée a spider's web

ESSENTIAL WORDS (*masculine*)

	l'alcool	alcohol
un	apéritif	aperitif
le	bar	bar
le	beurre	butter
le	bifteck	steak
le	bœuf	beef
le	bol	bowl
les	bonbons	candy
le	café	coffee; coffee shop
le	café au lait	milky coffee
le	café-crème	coffee with milk
le	chocolat (chaud)	(hot) chocolate
le	cidre	cider
le	coca	Coke®
le	couteau (*pl* -x)	knife
le	croissant	croissant
le	croque-monsieur (*pl inv*)	toasted ham-and-cheese sandwich
le	cuisinier	cook
le	déjeuner	lunch
le	demi	half-pint
le	dessert	dessert
le	dîner	dinner
le	fromage	cheese
un	fruit	piece of fruit
les	fruits	fruit
les	fruits de mer	seafood
le	garçon (de café)	waiter
le	gâteau (*pl* -x)	cake
le	:hamburger	hamburger
les	:hors-d'œuvre	appetizers
le	jambon	ham
le	jus de fruit	fruit juice
le	lait	milk
les	légumes	vegetables
le	menu	fixed-price menu
un	œuf [œf] (*pl* ~s [ø])	egg

ESSENTIAL WORDS *(feminine)*

	l'addition	check
une	assiette	plate
la	baguette	French loaf
la	bière	beer
la	boisson	drink
la	boîte	can; box
la	bouteille	bottle
la	carte	menu
les	céréales	cereal
la	confiture	jam
la	confiture d'oranges	marmalade
la	conserve	home-canned food
la	crêpe	pancake
les	crudités	mixed salad
la	cuiller, la cuillère	spoon
	l'eau (minérale)	(mineral) water
une	entrecôte	(entrecôte) steak
une	entrée	first course
la	faim	hunger
la	fourchette	fork
les	frites	fries, French fries
la	glace	ice cream
	l'huile	oil
la	limonade	lemonade
une	olive	olive
une	omelette	omelet
la	pâtisserie	pastry; patisserie
la	poissonnerie	fish shop
les	pommes frites	fries, French fries
la	quiche	quiche
la	salade	salad
la	saucisse	sausage
la	soif	thirst
la	soucoupe	saucer
la	soupe	soup
la	table	table
la	tasse	cup

ESSENTIAL WORDS *(masculine continued)*

un	œuf à la coque	soft-boiled egg
un	œuf dur	hard-boiled egg
le	pain	bread
le	pain grillé	toast
le	pain au chocolat	chocolate-filled croissant
le	pâté	pâté
le	patron	owner
le	petit déjeuner	breakfast
le	pique-nique *(pl ~s)*	picnic
le	plat	dish; course
le	plat du jour	today's special
le	plateau *(pl ~x)*	tray
les	plats cuisinés	ready-made meals
le	poisson	fish
le	porc [pɔʀ]	pork
le	potage	soup
le	poulet (rôti)	(roast) chicken
le	quart	quarter *(bottle/liter etc)*
le	repas	meal
le	restaurant	restaurant
le	riz	rice
le	rôti	roast
le	sandwich [sɑ̃dwitʃ]	sandwich
le	saucisson	salami
le	sel	salt
le	self	cafeteria
le	service	service
le	steak [stɛk]	steak
le	sucre	sugar
le	thé	tea
le	veau	veal
le	verre	glass
le	vin	wine
le	vinaigre	vinegar
le	yaourt	yogurt

ESSENTIAL WORDS (feminine continued)

la	tranche (de)	slice (of)
la	vaisselle	dishes
la	viande	meat

IMPORTANT WORDS (feminine)

la	brasserie	restaurant
la	cafétéria	cafeteria
la	carafe	carafe, jug
les	chips	chips
la	côte de porc	pork chop
la	crème	cream
la	cuiller à café/à dessert/ à soupe	teaspoon/dessert spoon/ tablespoon
la	farine	flour
la	grillade	grilled meat
la	mayonnaise	mayonnaise
la	merguez	spicy sausage
la	moutarde	mustard
une	odeur	smell
la	pizza	pizza
la	pression	draft beer
la	recette	recipe
la	serveuse	waitress
la	tarte	tart
la	terrine	pâté
la	théière	teapot
la	vanille	vanilla

IMPORTANT WORDS (*masculine*)

	l'agneau	lamb
	l'ail	garlic
le	chariot	shopping cart
le	chef (*m+f*)	chef
le	choix	choice
le	couvert	cover charge; place setting
les	escargots	snails
le	goût	taste
le	goûter	snack
le	lapin	rabbit
le	mouton	mutton
le	parfum	flavor
le	pichet	pitcher, jug
le	poivre	pepper
le	pourboire	tip
le	prix fixe	set price
le	prix net	inclusive price
le	serveur	waiter
le	sirop	syrup; cordial
le	supplément	extra charge

USEFUL WORDS (*masculine*)

le	bouchon	cork
le	cacao	cocoa
le	casse-croûte (*pl inv*)	snack
le	champagne	champagne
le	citron pressé	freshly squeezed lemon juice
le	cognac	brandy
le	foie	liver
le	gibier	game
le	glaçon	ice cube
le	ketchup	ketchup
le	lard	bacon
les	lardons	diced bacon
le	miel	honey
un	ouvre-boîtes (*pl inv*)	can opener
le	panaché	shandy (*beer mixed with pop*)

USEFUL WORDS *(feminine)*

une	assiette anglaise	selection of cold cuts
la	biscotte	Melba toast
la	brioche	bun
la	carte des vins	wine list
la	côtelette	chop
la	crème anglaise	custard
la	crème Chantilly	whipped cream
la	cruche	pitcher, jug
les	cuisses de grenouille	frogs' legs
la	gelée	Jell-O®
une	infusion	herbal tea
la	margarine	margarine
la	miette	crumb
les	moules	mussels
la	nappe	tablecloth
la	nourriture	food
la	paille	straw
les	pâtes	pasta
la	purée	mashed potatoes
les	rillettes	potted meat (*made of pork or goose*)
la	sauce	sauce; gravy
la	serviette	napkin
la	tartine	piece of bread and butter
la	tisane	herbal tea
les	tripes	tripe
la	vinaigrette	vinaigrette dressing
la	volaille	poultry

USEFUL PHRASES

cuisiner to cook
manger to eat
boire to drink
avaler to swallow
mon plat préféré my favorite dish
qu'est-ce que tu bois ? what are you having to drink?
c'est bon it's nice

USEFUL WORDS *(masculine continued)*

le	**petit pain**	roll
le	**ragoût**	stew
les	**rognons**	kidneys
le	**rosbif**	roast beef
le	**thermos**	thermos
le	**tire-bouchon** *(pl ~s)*	corkscrew
un	**toast**	slice of toast
le	**whisky**	scotch; bourbon

USEFUL PHRASES

déjeuner **to have lunch**
dîner **to have dinner**
goûter qch **to taste sth**
ça sent bon ! **that smells good!**
le vin blanc/rosé/rouge **white/rosé/red wine**
un steak saignant/à point/bien cuit **a rare/medium/well-done steak**
avoir faim **to be hungry**
avoir soif **to be thirsty**
mettre le couvert, mettre la table **to set the table**
débarrasser **to clear the table**
faire la vaisselle **to do the dishes**
nous goûtons en rentrant de l'école **we have a snack when we come back from school**
prendre le petit déjeuner **to have breakfast**
délicieux(ieuse) **delicious**
dégoûtant(e) **disgusting**
bon appétit ! **enjoy your meal!**
à votre santé ! **cheers!**
l'addition, s'il vous plaît ! **the check please!**
est-ce que le service est compris ? **is service included?**
"service (non) compris" **"service (not) included"**
manger au restaurant **to eat out**
inviter qn à déjeuner **to invite sb to lunch**
prendre l'apéritif **to have drinks**

SMOKING

le	**briquet**	lighter
le	**tabac**	tobacco; smoke shop
le	**cendrier**	ashtray
le	**cigare**	cigar
une	**allumette**	match
la	**cigarette**	cigarette
la	**pipe**	pipe

USEFUL PHRASES

une boîte d'allumettes **a box of matches**
avez-vous du feu ? **do you have a light?**
allumer une cigarette **to light up**
"défense de fumer" **"no smoking"**
je ne fume pas **I don't smoke**
j'ai arrêté de fumer **I've stopped smoking**
fumer est très mauvais pour la santé **smoking is very bad for you**

ESSENTIAL WORDS (*masculine*)

un	appareil-photo (*pl ~s~s*)	camera
	l'argent de poche	pocket money
le	baby-sitting	babysitting
le	babyfoot	foosball
le	baladeur	personal stereo
le	billet	ticket
le	CD	CD
le	chanteur	singer
le	cinéma	movie theater
le	club	club
le	concert	concert
le	correspondant	penpal
le	disque	record
le	DVD	DVD
les	échecs	chess
le	film	movie
le	:hobby	hobby
	l'internet	Internet
le	jeu (*pl -x*)	game
le	jeu vidéo	video game
le	journal (*pl* journaux)	newspaper
le	lecteur de CD/DVD/MP3	CD/DVD/MP3 player
le	magazine	magazine
le	membre	member
le	musée	museum; art gallery
le	passe-temps (*pl inv*)	hobby
le	programme	program
le	roman	novel
le	roman policier	detective novel
le	spectacle	show
le	sport	sports
le	(téléphone) portable	cell (phone)
le	temps libre	free time
le	théâtre	theater
le	week-end (*pl ~s*)	weekend

ESSENTIAL WORDS *(feminine)*

la	bande dessinée	comic strip
la	brochure	leaflet
les	cartes	cards
la	cassette	cassette
la	chaîne de télévision	TV channel
la	chanson	song; singing
la	chanteuse	singer
la	console de jeu	game console
la	correspondante	penpal
la	danse	dance; dancing
la	distraction	entertainment
une	excursion	trip, outing
la	fête	party
les	informations	news
	l'informatique	computing
la	lecture	reading
la	musique (pop/classique)	(pop/classical) music
la	patinoire	skating rink
la	photo	photo
la	presse	the press
la	promenade	walk
la	publicité	publicity
la	radio	radio
la	revue	magazine
la	télé(vision)	TV, television
la	vedette (de cinéma) *(m+f)*	(movie) star

USEFUL PHRASES

je sors avec mes amis I go out with my friends
je lis les journaux, je regarde la télévision I read the newspapers,
  I watch television
bricoler to do DIY
faire du baby-sitting to babysit
je joue au football/au tennis/aux cartes I play soccer/tennis/cards
zapper to channel-surf

IMPORTANT WORDS *(masculine)*

un	appareil-photo numérique	digital camera
le	caméscope	camcorder
le	concours	competition
le	dessin animé	cartoon
le	disque compact	compact disc, CD
le	feuilleton	serial; soap
le	graveur de CD/DVD	CD/DVD writer
le	jouet	toy
les	loisirs	leisure activities
le	magnétoscope	video recorder
le	PC	PC, personal computer
le	petit ami	boyfriend
le	site web	website
le	SMS	text message
le	tricot	knitting

USEFUL WORDS *(masculine)*

le	blog	blog
le	chat [tʃat]	chat; chatroom
un	éclaireur	scout
le	fan [fan]	fan
le	:hit-parade	charts
le	jeu de société	board game
les	mots croisés	crossword puzzle(s)
le	scout	scout
le	skate(board)	skateboard
le	vidéoclub	video shop

USEFUL PHRASES

passionnant(e) **exciting**
ennuyeux(euse) **boring**
amusant(e) **funny**
pas mal **not bad, quite good**
danser **to dance**
faire des photos **to take photos**
je m'ennuie **I'm bored**

IMPORTANT WORDS *(feminine)*

les	**actualités**	news
une	**affiche**	notice; poster
la	**bande**	tape
la	**collection**	collection
une	**émission**	program
une	**exposition**	exhibition
la	**maison des jeunes**	youth club
la	**peinture**	painting
la	**pellicule**	film *(for camera)*
la	**petite amie**	girlfriend
la	**petite annonce**	ad, classified
la	**randonnée**	hike
la	**réunion**	meeting
la	**soirée**	evening

USEFUL WORDS *(feminine)*

la	**boîte de nuit**	night club
la	**chorale**	choir
la	**colonie de vacances**	summer camp
la	**diapositive**	photographic slide
une	**éclaireuse**	scout
la	**méchanique**	mechanics
la	**photographie**	photograph; photography
la	**planche de skate**	skateboard

USEFUL PHRASES

aller en boîte to go clubbing

on se réunit le vendredi we meet on Fridays

je fais des économies pour m'acheter un lecteur MP3 I'm saving up to buy an
    MP3 player

j'aimerais faire le tour du monde I'd like to go round the world

ESSENTIAL WORDS *(masculine)*

un	abricot	apricot
un	ananas	pineapple
le	citron	lemon
un	fruit	piece of fruit
les	fruits	fruit
le	marron (grillé)	(roasted) chestnut
le	pamplemousse	grapefruit
le	raisin	grape(s)
le	raisin sec	raisin

IMPORTANT WORDS *(masculine)*

un	arbre fruitier	fruit tree
le	melon	melon

USEFUL WORDS *(masculine)*

un	avocat	avocado
le	cassis	blackcurrant
le	kiwi	kiwi
le	noyau *(pl* -x)	stone *(in fruit)*
le	pépin	pip *(in fruit)*
le	pruneau *(pl* -x)	prune

ESSENTIAL WORDS *(feminine)*

la	**banane**	banana
la	**cerise**	cherry
la	**fraise**	strawberry
la	**framboise**	raspberry
une	**orange**	orange
la	**peau**	skin
la	**pêche**	peach
la	**poire**	pear
la	**pomme**	apple
la	**tomate**	tomato

USEFUL WORDS *(feminine)*

la	**baie**	berry
la	**cacahuète**	peanut
la	**datte**	date
la	**figue**	fig
la	**grenade**	pomegranate
la	**groseille**	currant
la	**groseille à maquereau**	gooseberry
la	**mandarine**	tangerine
la	**mûre**	blackberry
la	**myrtille**	blueberry
la	**noisette**	hazelnut
la	**noix**	nut; walnut
la	**noix de cajou**	cashew
la	**noix de coco**	coconut
la	**prune**	plum
la	**rhubarbe**	rhubarb
la	**vigne**	vine

USEFUL PHRASES

un jus d'orange/d'ananas **an orange/a pineapple juice**
une grappe de raisin **a bunch of grapes**
mûr(e) **ripe**
pas mûr(e) **unripe**
peler un fruit **to peel a fruit**
glisser sur une peau de banane **to slip on a banana skin**

ESSENTIAL WORDS *(masculine)*

un	abat-jour	lampshade
le	congélateur	freezer
le	fauteuil	armchair
le	freezer	freezer
le	frigidaire	refrigerator
le	frigo	refrigerator
le	lit	bed
le	meuble	piece of furniture
les	meubles	furniture
le	miroir	mirror
le	placard	cupboard
le	radiateur	heater
le	radio-réveil	clock radio
le	rayon	shelf
le	téléphone	telephone
le	transistor	transistor

IMPORTANT WORDS *(masculine)*

un	appareil	appliance
un	aspirateur	vacuum cleaner
le	buffet	sideboard
le	bureau (pl -x)	desk
le	canapé	sofa
le	coffre	chest
le	four à micro-ondes	microwave oven
le	lave-vaisselle	dishwasher
le	lecteur de CD/DVD	CD/DVD player
le	magnétophone	tape recorder
le	piano	piano
le	portable	cell phone; laptop
le	sèche-linge	clothes dryer
le	tableau (pl -x)	picture
le	téléphone sans fil	cordless phone

ESSENTIAL WORDS *(feminine)*

une	armoire	wardrobe
la	bouilloire	kettle
la	chaîne (stéréo)	stereo system
la	chaise	chair
la	cuisinière (électrique/à gaz)	(electric/gas) range
la	glace	mirror
la	lampe	lamp
la	machine à laver	washing machine
la	pendule	clock
la	pièce	room
la	radio	radio
la	table	table
la	télévision	television

IMPORTANT WORDS *(feminine)*

la	bibliothèque	bookcase
la	peinture	painting
la	radio numérique (DAB)	digital radio
la	table basse	coffee table

USEFUL WORDS (*masculine*)

le	berceau (*pl* -x)	cradle
le	cadre	frame
le	camion de déménagement	moving van
le	déménagement	move
le	déménageur	mover
le	fer à repasser	iron
le	four	oven
le	home cinéma	home theater system
le	lampadaire	floor lamp
le	lit d'enfant	crib
les	lits superposés	bunk beds
le	matelas	mattress
le	mobilier	furniture
le	pèse-personne	scale
le	portemanteau (*pl* –x)	coat hanger; coat rack; hat stand
le	robot ménager	food processor
le	répondeur	answering machine
le	sèche-cheveux (*pl inv*)	hair-dryer
le	secrétaire	writing desk
le	siège	seat
le	store	blind
le	tabouret	stool
le	tapis	rug
le	tiroir	drawer
les	volets	shutters

USEFUL PHRASES

un appartement meublé a furnished apartment
allumer/éteindre le radiateur to switch on/off the heater
j'ai fait mon lit I've made my bed
s'asseoir to sit down
mettre qch au four to put sth in the oven
tirer les rideaux to draw the curtains
fermer les volets to close the shutters

USEFUL WORDS *(feminine)*

une	antenne	aerial
une	antenne parabolique	satellite dish
la	caméra vidéo	video camera, camcorder
la	chaîne compacte	stereo system
la	coiffeuse	dressing table
la	commode	chest of drawers
une	enceinte	loudspeaker
une	étagère	shelves
la	lampe halogène	halogen lamp
la	machine à coudre	sewing machine
la	machine à écrire	typewriter
la	moquette	fitted carpet
la	planche à repasser	ironing board
la	table de chevet	nightstand
la	table roulante	cart, table on wheels
la	télécommande	remote control

USEFUL PHRASES

c'est un 4 pièces it's a 4-room apartment
à table ! dinner (or lunch etc) is ready!

ESSENTIAL WORDS

les Alpes *(fpl)*	the Alps
l'Atlantique *(m)*	the Atlantic
Bordeaux	Bordeaux
la Bourgogne	Burgundy
la Bretagne	Brittany
Bruxelles	Brussels
la Côte d'Azur	the Cote d'Azur
l'est *(m)*	the east
la Loire	the Loire
Lyon	Lyons
Marseille	Marseilles
le Massif Central	the Massif Central
la Méditerranée	the Mediterranean
le Midi	the South of France
le nord	the north
la Normandie	Normandy
l'ouest *(m)*	the west
Paris	Paris
les Pyrénées *(fpl)*	the Pyrenees
le Rhône	the Rhone
la Seine	the Seine
le sud	the south

IMPORTANT WORDS

Québec	Quebec *(city)*
le Québec	Quebec *(state)*

USEFUL WORDS

Alger	Algiers
Anvers	Antwerp
Athènes	Athens
Barcelone	Barcelona
Berlin	Berlin
Le Caire	Cairo
la capitale	the capital
le chef-lieu	the main town
la Corse	Corsica
l'Extrême-Orient (m)	the Far East
Genève	Geneva
les îles (fpl) Britanniques	the British Isles
le Jura	the Jura Mountains
le lac Léman	Lake Geneva
Londres	London
Moscou	Moscow
le Moyen-Orient	the Middle East
le Pacifique	the Pacific
Pékin	Beijing
le Pôle nord/sud	the North/South Pole
le Proche-Orient	the Near East
la Sardaigne	Sardinia
Varsovie	Warsaw
Venise	Venice
Vienne	Vienna
les Vosges (fpl)	the Vosges Mountains

USEFUL PHRASES

aller à New York/en Bourgogne to go to New York/to Burgundy

aller dans le Midi to go to the South of France

je viens de New York/du Massif Central I come from New York/the Massif Central

au nord in or to the north; au sud in or to the south

à l'est in or to the east; à l'ouest in or to the west

GREETINGS
bonjour hello
salut hi; goodbye
ça va ? how are you?
ça va (*in reply*) fine
enchanté(e) pleased to meet you
allô hello (*on telephone*)
bonsoir good evening; good night
bonne nuit good night (*when going to bed*)
au revoir goodbye
à demain see you tomorrow
à bientôt, à tout à l'heure see you later
adieu farewell

BEST WISHES
bon anniversaire happy birthday
joyeux Noël merry Christmas
bonne année happy New Year
joyeuses Pâques happy Easter
meilleurs vœux best wishes
bienvenue welcome
félicitations congratulations
bon appétit enjoy your meal
bon courage all the best
bonne chance good luck
bon voyage have a good trip
à tes (*or* **vos**) **souhaits** bless you (*after a sneeze*)
à la tienne (*or* **la vôtre**) cheers (*when initiating or accepting a toast*)
à ta (*or* **votre**) **santé** cheers (*when initiating or accepting a toast*)

SURPRISE

mon Dieu my goodness
comment ?, hein ?, quoi ? what?
ah bon oh, I see
ça, par exemple well, well
sans blague (?) really(?)
ah oui ?, c'est vrai ?, vraiment ? really?
tu rigoles, tu plaisantes you're kidding
quelle chance ! what a stroke of luck!
tiens ! well, well!

POLITENESS

excusez-moi I'm sorry, excuse me
s'il vous (*or* te) plaît please
SVP please
merci thank you
non merci no thank you; **oui merci** yes please
de rien, je vous en prie, il n'y a pas de quoi not at all, it's quite all right,
  don't mention it
volontiers gladly

AGREEMENT

oui yes
bien sûr of course
d'accord OK
bon fine

DISAGREEMENT

non no
máis non no (*contradicting a positive statement*)
si yes (*contradicting a negative statement*)
bien sûr que non of course not
jamais de la vie not on your life
pas du tout not at all
au contraire on the contrary
ça, par exemple well I never
quel culot what a nerve
mêlez-vous de vos affaires mind your own business

DIFFICULTIES

au secours help
au feu fire
aïe ouch
hélas alas
pardon (I'm) sorry, excuse me, I beg your pardon
je m'excuse I'm sorry
je regrette I'm sorry
désolé(e) I'm (really) sorry
c'est dommage, quel dommage what a pity
zut bother
j'en ai marre I'm fed up
je n'en peux plus I can't stand it any more
oh là là oh dear
quelle horreur how awful

ORDERS

attention be careful
halte-là stop
hep *or* **eh, vous là-bas** hey, you there
fiche le camp get lost
chut shhhh
ça suffit that's enough
défense de fumer no smoking
allons go on, come on
allons-y let's go
allez-y, vas-y go ahead

OTHERS

aucune idée no idea
peut-être perhaps, maybe
je ne sais pas I don't know
vous désirez ? can I help you?
voilà there, there you are
j'arrive just coming
ne t'en fais pas don't worry
ce n'est pas la peine it's not worth it
à propos by the way
dis donc (*or* **dites donc**) by the way
chéri(e) darling
le (*or* **la**) **pauvre** poor thing
tant mieux so much the better
ça m'est égal I don't mind
tant pis too bad
cela dépend that depends
que faire ? what shall I (or we) do?
à quoi bon ? what's the point?
ça m'embête it bothers me
ça m'agace it gets on my nerves

ESSENTIAL WORDS *(masculine)*

un	accident	accident
le	dentiste *(m+f)*	dentist
le	docteur *(m+f)*	doctor
un	hôpital *(pl hôpitaux)*	hospital
un	infirmier	(male) nurse
le	lit	bed
le	malade	patient
le	médecin *(m+f)*	doctor
le	rendez-vous *(pl inv)*	appointment
le	ventre	stomach

IMPORTANT WORDS *(masculine)*

un	antiseptique	antiseptic
le	brancard	stretcher
le	cabinet (de consultation)	surgery
le	cachet	tablet
le	comprimé	tablet
le	coton hydrophile	absorbent cotton
le	coup de soleil	sunburn
le	médicament	medicine, drug
le	pansement	dressing; bandage
le	patient	patient
le	pharmacien	pharmacist
le	plâtre	plaster cast
le	remède	medicine
un	rhume	cold
le	sang	blood
le	sirop	syrup
le	sparadrap	Band Aid®

USEFUL PHRASES

il y a eu un accident **there's been an accident**
être admis(e) à l'hôpital **to be admitted to the hospital**
vous devez rester au lit **you must stay in bed**
être malade, être souffrant(e) **to be ill**
se sentir mieux **to feel better**
soigner **to look after**

ESSENTIAL WORDS (feminine)

une	aspirine	aspirin
une	infirmière	nurse
la	pastille	lozenge
la	pharmacie	pharmacy
la	santé	health
la	température	temperature

IMPORTANT WORDS (feminine)

une	allergie	allergy
une	ambulance	ambulance
une	assurance	insurance
la	blessure	injury, wound
la	chambre d'hôpital	hospital room
la	clinique	clinic, private hospital
la	crème	cream, ointment
la	cuillerée	spoonful
la	diarrhée	diarrhea
la	douleur	pain
la	grippe	flu
une	insolation	sunstroke
la	maladie	illness
la	médecine	medicine (science)
une	opération	operation
une	ordonnance	prescription
la	patiente	patient
la	pilule	pill; the Pill
la	piqûre	injection; sting
les	urgences	emergency room

USEFUL PHRASES

je me suis blessé(e), je me suis fait mal I have hurt myself
je me suis coupé le doigt I have cut my finger
je me suis foulé la cheville I have sprained my ankle
il s'est cassé le bras he has broken his arm
je me suis brûlé I have burnt myself
j'ai mal à la gorge/mal à la tête/ mal au ventre I've got a sore throat/
    a headache/a stomachache
avoir de la température or de la fièvre to have a temperature

USEFUL WORDS *(masculine)*

un	abcès	abscess
un	accès	seizure
	l'acné	acne
le	bandage	bandage
le	bleu	bruise
le	cancer	cancer
le	choc	shock
le	dentier	false teeth, dentures
le	fauteuil roulant	wheelchair
le	fortifiant	tonic
le	microbe	germ
le	nerf	nerve
les	oreillons	mumps
le	poison	poison
le	pouls [pu]	pulse
les	premiers secours	first aid
les	premiers soins	first aid
le	préservatif	condom
le	régime	diet
le	repos	rest
le	rhume des foins	hay fever
le	SAMU	emergency medical service
le	sida	AIDS
le	stress	stress
le	vertige	dizzy spell

USEFUL PHRASES

j'ai sommeil I'm sleepy
j'ai mal au cœur I'm nauseous
maigrir to lose weight
grossir to put on weight
avaler to swallow
saigner to bleed
vomir to vomit
être en forme to be in good shape
se reposer to rest

USEFUL WORDS *(feminine)*

une	angine	tonsillitis
une	appendicite	appendicitis
la	béquille	crutch
la	cicatrice	scar
la	coqueluche	whooping cough
la	crise cardiaque	heart attack
une	écharde	splinter
une	égratignure	scratch
une	épidémie	epidemic
la	grossesse	pregnancy
la	guérison	recovery
la	migraine	migraine
la	nausée	nausea
la	plaie	wound
la	pommade	ointment
la	radio	X-ray
la	rougeole	measles
la	rubéole	German measles
la	toux	cough
la	transfusion	blood transfusion
la	varicelle	chickenpox
la	variole	smallpox

USEFUL PHRASES

guérir to cure; to get better
grièvement blessé(e) seriously injured
êtes-vous assuré(e) ? are you insured?
je suis enrhumé(e) I have a cold
ça fait mal ! that hurts!
respirer to breathe
s'évanouir to faint
tousser to cough
mourir to die
perdre connaissance to lose consciousness
avoir le bras en écharpe to have one's arm in a sling

ESSENTIAL WORDS *(masculine)*

un	ascenseur	elevator
les	bagages	luggage
le	balcon	balcony
le	bar	bar
le	bruit	noise
le	chèque	check
le	client	guest
le	confort	comfort
le	déjeuner	lunch
le	directeur	manager
un	escalier	stairs
un	étage	floor; story
le	garçon	waiter
le	grand lit	double bed
un	hôtel	hotel
les	lits jumeaux	twin beds
le	numéro	number
le	passeport	passport
le	petit déjeuner	breakfast
le	porteur	porter
le	prix	price
le	réceptionniste	receptionist
le	repas	meal
le	restaurant	restaurant
le	rez-de-chaussée	ground floor
le	séjour	stay
le	tarif	rates
le	téléphone	telephone
les	WC	restrooms

USEFUL PHRASES

je voudrais réserver une chambre I would like to reserve a room
une chambre avec douche/avec salle de bains a room with a shower/
with a bathroom
une chambre pour une personne a single room
une chambre pour deux personnes a double room

ESSENTIAL WORDS *(feminine)*

	l'addition	bill
les	arrhes [aʀ]	deposit
la	chambre	room
la	clé, clef	key
la	cliente	guest
la	date	date
la	directrice	manager
la	douche	shower
	l'entrée	entrance
la	fiche	form
	l'hospitalité	hospitality
la	monnaie	change
la	note	bill
la	nuit	night
la	pension	guesthouse
la	pension complète	full board
la	piscine	swimming pool
la	réception	reception
la	réceptionniste	receptionist
la	réservation	reservation, booking
la	salle de bains	bathroom
la	serviette (de toilette)	towel
la	serveuse	waitress
la	sortie de secours	fire escape
la	télévision	television
les	toilettes	toilets
la	valise	suitcase
la	vue	view

USEFUL PHRASES

avez-vous une pièce d'identité ? do you have any ID?
à quelle heure est le petit déjeuner ? what time is breakfast served?
faire la chambre to clean the room
"ne pas déranger" "do not disturb"

IMPORTANT WORDS (masculine)

un	accueil	welcome
le	bouton	light switch
le	cabinet de toilette	bathroom
le	digicode	entry code
les	draps	sheets
le	guide	guidebook
le	pourboire	tip
le	prix net	inclusive price
le	reçu	receipt

USEFUL WORDS (masculine)

le	cuisinier	cook
le	hall	foyer
un	hôtelier	hotelier
le	maître d'hôtel	head waiter
le	parking	parking lot
le	pensionnaire	guest (at guesthouse)
le	sommelier	wine waiter

USEFUL PHRASES

occupé(e) occupied

libre vacant

propre clean

sale dirty

dormir to sleep

se réveiller to wake

"tout confort" "with all facilities"

pourriez-vous me réveiller à 7 heures demain matin ? I'd like a 7 a.m. alarm call tomorrow morning, please

une chambre donnant sur la mer a room overlooking the sea

IMPORTANT WORDS *(feminine)*

une	**auberge**	inn
la	**carte magnétique**	electronic key card
la	**demi-pension** *(pl ~s)*	half-board
la	**femme de chambre**	chambermaid
la	**réclamation**	complaint
la	**pension de famille**	guesthouse
la	**pensionnaire**	guest (at guesthouse)

USEFUL PHRASES

chambre avec demi-pension room with breakfast and dinner provided

on se met à la terrace ? shall we sit outside?

on nous a servis à la terrasse we were served outside

un hôtel 3 étoiles a three-star hotel

TTC (toutes taxes comprises) inclusive of tax

ESSENTIAL WORDS (*masculine*)

un	appartement	apartment
un	ascenseur	elevator
le	balcon	balcony
le	bâtiment	building
le	chauffage central	central heating
le	confort	comfort
un	escalier	stairs
un	étage	floor; story
	l'extérieur	exterior
le	garage	garage
un	grand ensemble	housing development
un	HLM (habitation à loyer modéré)	subsidized housing
un	immeuble	apartment building
	l'intérieur	interior
le	jardin	garden; yard
le	meuble	piece of furniture
les	meubles	furniture
le	mur	wall
le	numéro de téléphone	phone number
le	parking	parking lot
le	rez-de-chaussée (*pl inv*)	ground floor
le	salon	living room
le	séjour	living room
le	sous-sol (*pl* ~s)	basement
le	terrain	lot
le	village	village

USEFUL PHRASES

quand je rentre à la maison when I go home
regarder par la fenêtre to look out of the window
chez moi/toi/nous at my/your/our house
déménager to move
louer un appartement to rent an apartment

ESSENTIAL WORDS *(feminine)*

une	adresse	address
une	allée	avenue, drive
une	avenue	avenue
la	cave	cellar, basement
la	chambre (à coucher)	bedroom
la	clé, clef	key
la	cuisine	kitchen
la	douche	shower
	l'entrée	entrance
la	fenêtre	window
une	HLM (habitation à loyer modéré)	subsidized housing
la	maison	house
la	pièce	room
la	porte	door
la	porte d'entrée	front door
la	rue	street
la	salle à manger	dining room
la	salle de bains	bathroom
la	salle de séjour	living room
la	salle	room
les	toilettes	bathroom
la	ville	town
la	vue	view

USEFUL PHRASES

j'habite un appartement/une maison I live in an apartment/a house

en haut upstairs

en bas downstairs

au rez-de-chaussée on the ground floor

à la maison at home

IMPORTANT WORDS *(masculine)*

	l'ameublement	furniture
le	cabinet de toilette	bathroom
le	concierge	caretaker
le	couloir	corridor
le	débarras	storage closet
le	déménagement	move
	l'entretien	upkeep
le	gîte	vacation home
le	logement	accommodations
le	loyer	rent
le	meublé	furnished apartment
le	palier	landing
le	propriétaire	owner; landlord
le	toit	roof
le	voisin	neighbor

USEFUL WORDS *(masculine)*

le	bureau	study
le	carreau *(pl* -x)	tile; windowpane
le	décor	decoration
le	grenier	attic
le	locataire	tenant; lodger
le	parquet	parquet floor
le	pavillon	house
le	plafond	ceiling
le	plancher	floor
le	seuil	doorstep
le	store	blind
le	studio	studio apartment
le	tuyau *(pl* -x)	pipe
le	vestibule	hall
le	volet	shutter

USEFUL PHRASES

frapper à la porte to knock at the door
on a sonné that's the doorbell

IMPORTANT WORDS *(feminine)*

la	**cheminée**	chimney; fireplace
la	**concierge**	caretaker
la	**cour**	yard
la	**femme de ménage**	cleaner
la	**fumée**	smoke
la	**pelouse**	lawn
la	**propriétaire**	owner; landlady
la	**voisine**	neighbor

USEFUL WORDS *(feminine)*

une	**antenne**	aerial
une	**ardoise**	slate
la	**chambre d'amis**	guestroom
la	**chaudière**	boiler
la	**façade**	front *(of house)*
la	**:haie**	hedge
la	**locataire**	tenant; lodger
la	**loge**	caretaker's room
la	**lucarne**	skylight
la	**mansarde**	attic
la	**marche**	step
la	**ménagère**	housewife
la	**paroi**	partition
la	**porte-fenêtre** *(pl ~s~s)*	French window
la	**sonnette**	doorbell
la	**tuile**	roof tile
la	**vitre**	window pane

USEFUL PHRASES

de l'extérieur from the outside
à l'intérieur on the inside
jusqu'au plafond up to the ceiling

ESSENTIAL WORDS *(masculine)*

le	bouton	light switch
le	cendrier	ashtray
le	dentifrice	toothpaste
le	drap	sheet
un	essuie-mains *(pl inv)*	hand towel
un	évier	sink
le	gaz	gas
le	lavabo	washbasin
le	magnétophone à cassettes	cassette recorder
le	magnétoscope	video recorder
le	ménage	housework
le	miroir	mirror
un	oreiller	pillow
le	placard	cupboard
le	plateau *(pl* -x)	tray
le	poster [pɔstɛʀ]	poster
le	radiateur	heater
le	réveil	alarm clock
les	rideaux	curtains
le	robinet	faucet
le	savon	soap
le	tableau	picture
le	tapis	rug
le	téléviseur	television set
le	transistor	transistor

USEFUL PHRASES

prendre un bain, se baigner to take a bath
prendre une douche to take a shower
faire le ménage to do the housework
j'aime faire la cuisine I like cooking

ESSENTIAL WORDS *(feminine)*

une	armoire	wardrobe
la	baignoire	bathtub
la	balance	bathroom scale
la	boîte aux lettres	mailbox
la	brosse	brush
la	cafetière	coffee pot; coffee maker
la	casserole	saucepan
la	couverture	blanket
la	cuisinière	range
la	douche	shower
	l'eau	water
	l'électricité	electricity
la	glace	mirror
la	lampe	lamp
la	lumière	light
la	machine à laver	washing machine
la	photo	photo
la	poubelle	garbage can
la	serviette	towel; napkin
la	télévision	television
la	vaisselle	dishes

USEFUL PHRASES

regarder la télévision to watch television
à la télévision on television
allumer/éteindre la télé to switch on/off the TV
jeter qch à la poubelle to throw sth away
faire la vaisselle to do the dishes

IMPORTANT WORDS *(masculine)*

un	**aspirateur**	vacuum cleaner
le	**bidet**	bidet
le	**four**	oven
le	**lave-vaisselle** *(pl inv)*	dishwasher
le	**linge**	linens; laundry

USEFUL WORDS *(masculine)*

le	**balai**	broom
le	**bibelot**	ornament
le	**chiffon**	dustcloth
le	**cintre**	coat hanger
le	**coussin**	cushion
le	**couvercle**	lid
le	**fer à repasser**	iron
le	**four à micro-ondes**	microwave oven
le	**grille-pain** *(pl inv)*	toaster
un	**interrupteur**	switch
le	**mixeur**	blender
le	**moulin à café**	coffee grinder
le	**papier peint**	wallpaper
le	**seau** *(pl -x)*	pail
le	**torchon**	dishcloth
le	**traversin**	bolster
le	**vase**	vase

USEFUL PHRASES

brancher/débrancher to plug in/to unplug
passer l'aspirateur to vacuum
faire la lessive to do the washing

IMPORTANT WORDS *(feminine)*

une	ampoule électrique	lightbulb
la	baignoire	bathtub
la	femme de ménage	cleaner
la	lessive	laundry detergent; laundry
la	peinture	paint; painting
la	poêle [pwal]	frying pan
la	poussière	dust
la	prise de courant	electrical outlet
la	recette	recipe
la	serrure	lock

USEFUL WORDS *(feminine)*

la	bouilloire	kettle
la	cocotte-minute® *(pl ~s~)*	pressure cooker
la	corbeille à papier	wastepaper basket
la	couette	comforter
la	couverture chauffante	electric blanket
la	descente de lit	bedside rug
une	échelle	ladder
une	éponge	sponge
la	moquette	fitted carpet
les	ordures	garbage
la	planche à repasser	ironing board
la	poignée	handle
la	tapisserie	wallpaper

USEFUL PHRASES

balayer to sweep (up)
nettoyer to clean
ranger ses affaires to put away one's things
laisser traîner ses affaires to leave one's things lying around

ESSENTIAL WORDS *(masculine)*

un	**abonnement (téléphonique)**	phone contract
un	**appel**	call
le	**billet**	ticket; banknote
le	**bureau** (*pl* -x) **de change**	foreign exchange
le	**centime (d'euro)**	euro cent
le	**chèque**	check
le	**code postal**	postcode, zip code
le	**colis**	parcel
le	**courriel**	email
le	**cybercafé**	internet café
un	**dollar**	dollar
un	**employé**	counter clerk
un	**euro**	euro
le	**facteur**	letter carrier
le	**fax**	fax; fax machine
le	**franc suisse**	Swiss franc
le	**guichet**	counter
un	**indicatif**	area code
le	**justificatif**	written proof
un	**mail**	email
le	**numéro**	number
un	**opérateur**	phone company
le	**paquet**	parcel
le	**passeport**	passport
le	**prix**	price
les	**renseignements**	information; directory assistance
le	**répondeur**	answering machine
le	**SMS**	text message
le	**stylo**	ballpoint pen
le	**syndicat d'initiative**	tourist information office
le	**tarif**	(postage) rate
le	**téléphone**	telephone
le	**(téléphone) fixe**	landline
le	**(téléphone) portable**	cell (phone)
le	**timbre**	stamp

USEFUL PHRASES

la banque la plus proche the nearest bank

je voudrais encaisser un chèque/changer de l'argent I would like to cash
  a check/change some money

ESSENTIAL WORDS *(feminine)*

une	adresse	address
les	arrhes	deposit
la	banque	bank
la	boîte aux lettres	mailbox
la	boîte vocale	voicemail
la	caisse	checkout
la	carte d'identité	ID card
la	carte postale	postcard
une	enveloppe	envelope
une	erreur	mistake
la	factrice	letter carrier
la	fiche	form
la	lettre	letter
la	monnaie	change
la	pièce d'identité	ID
la	poste	post office
la	réduction	discount
la	réponse	reply
la	signature	signature
la	sonnerie	ringtone
la	tonalité	dial tone

USEFUL PHRASES

un coup de téléphone *or* de fil a phone call

téléphoner à qn to call sb

décrocher to lift the receiver

composer le numéro to dial (the number)

allô – ici Jean *or* c'est Jean à l'appareil hello – this is Jean

la ligne est occupée the line is engaged

ne quittez pas hold the line

je me suis trompé(e) de numéro I got the wrong number

raccrocher to hang up

je voudrais appeler à l'étranger I'd like to make an international phone call

IMPORTANT WORDS *(masculine)*

un	annuaire	telephone directory
le	carnet de chèques	checkbook
le	chèque de voyage	traveler's check
le	compte (en banque)	(bank) account
le	coup de téléphone	phone call
le	courrier	mail
le	courrier électronique	email
le	crédit	credit
le	domicile	home address
le	formulaire	form
le	haut débit	broadband
les	objets trouvés	lost and found
le	paiement	payment
le	papier à lettres	stationery
le	portefeuille	wallet
le	porte-monnaie *(pl inv)*	wallet
le	supplément	extra charge
le	taux de change	exchange rate
le	télégramme	telegram

USEFUL WORDS *(masculine)*

un	accusé de réception	acknowledgement of receipt
le	cadran	dial
le	combiné	receiver
le	destinataire	addressee
l'	expéditeur	sender
un	identifiant	login
un	imprimé	printed matter
le	mandat	postal order
le	mot de passe	password
le	papier d'emballage	wrapping paper
le	récepteur	receiver
le	standardiste	operator
le	tampon	stamp

IMPORTANT WORDS *(feminine)*

la	**cabine téléphonique**	phone booth
la	**carte bancaire**	bank card
la	**Carte bleue**®	debit card
la	**carte SIM**	SIM card
la	**carte téléphonique**	phone card
la	**dépense**	expense
la	**fente**	slot
la	**levée**	collection
une	**opératrice**	operator
la	**pièce jointe**	attachment
la	**poste restante**	general delivery
la	**récompense**	reward
la	**taxe**	tax

USEFUL WORDS *(feminine)*

la	**boîte postale**	PO box
la	**communication interurbaine**	long distance call
la	**communication locale**	local call
la	**lettre recommandée**	registered letter
la	**standardiste**	switchboard operator
la	**télécarte**®	phone card

USEFUL PHRASES

j'ai perdu mon portefeuille I've lost my wallet
remplir une fiche to fill in a form
en majuscules in block letters
téléphoner en PCV to make a collect call

GENERAL SITUATIONS

quelle est votre adresse ? what is your address?
comment cela s'écrit ? how do you spell that?
avez-vous la monnaie de 10 euros ? do you have change for 10 euros?
écrire to write
répondre to reply
signer to sign
est-ce que vous pouvez m'aider ? can you help me please?
pour aller à la gare ? how do I get to the train station?
tout droit straight ahead
à droite to or on the right; à gauche to or on the left

LETTERS

Cher Robert Dear Robert
Chère Anne Dear Anne
Monsieur Dear Sir
Madame (or Mademoiselle) Dear Madam
amitiés best wishes
bien affectueusement love from
bien amicalement or cordialement kind regards
bons baisers love and kisses
veuillez agréer mes (or nos) salutations distinguées yours faithfully
je vous prie d'agréer, Monsieur (or Madame), l'expression de mes
   sentiments les meilleurs yours sincerely
TSVP see other side

CELL PHONES

envoyer un SMS à qn to text sb
envoyer un MMS photo à qn to send a picture message
envoyer un MMS vidéo à qn to send a video message
télécharger une sonnerie to download a ringtone
Je ne te capte plus ! You're breaking up!
Je n'ai plus de crédit. I'm out of credit.
Je n'ai pas de réseau. I can't get a signal.

EMAIL

composer un mail to compose an email
envoyer un mail à qn to send an email to sb
faire suivre un mail to forward an email
joindre un fichier à un mail to attach a file to an email
répondre à un mail to reply to an email

ESSENTIAL WORDS *(masculine)*

un	accident	accident
un	agent (de police)	policeman, police officer
le	cambriolage	burglary
le	commissariat de police	police station
un	incendie	fire
le	problème	problem

IMPORTANT WORDS *(masculine)*

un	avocat	lawyer
le	cambrioleur	burglar
le	constat	report
le	consulat	consulate
le	coupable	culprit
le(s)	dommage(s)	damage
un	espion	spy
le	gendarme	policeman, police officer
le	gouvernement	government
les	impôts	income tax
le	mort	dead man
le	piratage	hacking
le	porte-monnaie *(pl inv)*	wallet
le	portefeuille	wallet
le	poste de police	police station
le	propriétaire	owner
le	pyromane	arsonist
le	sans-papiers *(pl inv)*	undocumented person
le	témoin	witness
le	viol	rape
le	vol	robbery
le	voleur	thief

USEFUL PHRASES

voler to steal; to rob
cambrioler to burglarize
on m'a volé mon portefeuille ! someone has stolen my wallet!
contre la loi illegal
ce n'est pas de ma faute it's not my fault
au secours ! help!

ESSENTIAL WORDS (feminine)

la	**faute**	fault
	l'**identité**	identity
la	**pièce d'identité**	ID
la	**vérité**	truth
la	**victime**	victim

IMPORTANT WORDS (feminine)

une	**amende**	fine
une	**armée**	army
une	**avocate**	lawyer
la	**bande**	gang
la	**coupable**	culprit
la	**fraude**	fraud
la	**fraude fiscale**	tax evasion
la	**gendarmerie**	police station
les	**incivilités**	antisocial behavior
la	**manifestation**	demonstration
la	**mort**	death
la	**morte**	dead woman
la	**peine de mort**	death penalty
la	**permission**	permission
la	**police d'assurance**	insurance policy
la	**propriétaire**	owner
la	**récompense**	reward
	l'**usurpation d'identité**	identity theft
la	**violence**	violence

USEFUL PHRASES

au voleur ! stop thief!
au feu ! fire!
haut les mains ! hands up!
braquer une banque to hold up a bank
police-secours emergency services
incarcérer to imprison
innocent(e) innocent
s'évader to escape

USEFUL WORDS (*masculine*)

un	assassin	murderer
le	butin	loot
le	cadavre	corpse
le	coup (de feu)	(gun)shot
le	courage	bravery
le	crime	crime
le	criminel	criminal
le	dealer	drug dealer
le	détective privé	private detective
le	détournement d'avion	plane hijacking
le	drogué	drug addict
un	enlèvement	kidnapping
un	escroc [ɛskʀo]	crook
le	flic	cop
le	fusil [fyzi]	gun
le	gangster	gangster
le	garde	guard
le	gardien	guard; warden
le	:héros	hero
le	:hold-up (*pl inv*)	hold-up
le	juge	judge
le	jury	jury
le	meurtre	murder
le	meurtrier	murderer
un	otage	hostage
le	palais de justice	law courts
le	pirate de l'air	hijacker
le	policier	policeman, police officer
le	prisonnier	prisoner
le	procès	trial
le	PV	fine
le	reportage	report
le	revolver [ʀevɔlvɛʀ]	revolver
le	sauvetage	rescue
le	témoignage	evidence
le	témoin	witness
le	terrorisme	terrorism
le	terroriste	terrorist
le	tribunal	court
le	voyou	hooligan

USEFUL WORDS *(feminine)*

	l'accusation	the prosecution
une	accusation	charge; accusation
une	arme	weapon
une	arrestation	arrest
la	bagarre	fight
la	bombe	bomb
la	cellule	cell
la	défense	defense
la	déposition	statement
la	dispute	argument
la	droguée	drug addict
les	drogues	drugs
une	émeute	uprising
une	enquête	inquiry
une	évasion	escape
	l'héroïne	heroine; heroin
	l'incarcération	imprisonment
la	loi	law
une	ordonnance	police order
la	preuve	proof
la	prison	prison
la	rafle	raid
la	rançon	ransom
la	tentative	attempt

USEFUL PHRASES

une attaque à main armée a hold-up
enlever un enfant to abduct a child
se battre to fight
une bande de voyous a bunch of hooligans
en prison in prison
arrêter to arrest
inculper to charge
être en détention provisoire to be remanded in custody
mettre qn en examen to indict sb
prendre la fuite to run away

ESSENTIAL WORDS (*masculine*)

l'acier	steel
l'argent	silver
le bois	wood
le caoutchouc	rubber
le coton	cotton
le cuir	leather
le fer	iron
le gas-oil	diesel
le gaz	gas
le métal (*pl* métaux)	metal
l'or	gold
le plastique	plastic
le tissu	fabric
le verre	glass

IMPORTANT WORDS (*masculine*)

l'acier inoxydable	stainless steel
l'aluminium	aluminum
le carton	cardboard
l'état	condition
le fer forgé	wrought iron
le papier	paper
le synthétique	synthetics
le tissu	fabric

USEFUL PHRASES

une chaise de *or* en bois a wooden chair
une boîte en plastique a plastic box
une bague d'or *or* en or a gold ring
en bon état in good condition
en mauvais état in bad condition

ESSENTIAL WORDS (feminine)

la	**fourrure**	fur
la	**laine**	wool
la	**pierre**	stone

IMPORTANT WORDS (feminine)

la	**brique**	brick
la	**soie**	silk

USEFUL PHRASES

un manteau en fourrure **a fur coat**
un pull en laine **a wool sweater**
rouillé(e) **rusty**

USEFUL WORDS (*masculine*)

	l'acrylique	acrylic
le	béton	concrete
le	bronze	bronze
le	caoutchouc [kautʃu]	rubber
le	caoutchouc mousse	foam rubber
le	carton	cardboard
le	charbon	coal
le	ciment	cement
le	cristal	crystal
le	cuivre	copper
le	cuivre jaune	brass
le	daim	suede
	l'étain	tin; pewter
le	fer	iron
le	fer-blanc	tin, tinplate
le	fil	thread
le	fil de fer	wire
le	lin	linen
le	liquide	liquid
le	marbre	marble
les	matériaux	materials
	l'osier	wickerwork
le	plâtre	plaster
le	plomb	lead
le	satin	satin
le	tweed	tweed
le	velours	velvet
le	velours côtelé	corduroy

USEFUL WORDS *(feminine)*

	l'**argile**	clay
la	**cire**	wax
la	**colle**	glue
la	**dentelle**	lace
une	**étoffe**	material
la	**faïence**	ceramics
la	**ficelle**	string
la	**paille**	straw
la	**porcelaine**	china
la	**toile**	linen; canvas

ESSENTIAL WORDS *(masculine)*

le	chef d'orchestre	conductor
le	groupe	group
un	instrument de musique	musical instrument
le	musicien	musician
un	orchestre	orchestra
le	piano	piano
le	violon	violin

USEFUL WORDS *(masculine)*

un	accord	chord
un	accordéon	accordion
un	alto	viola
un	archet	bow
le	basson	bassoon
le	bâton	conductor's baton
le	biniou	Breton bagpipes
les	bois	woodwind
le	clairon	bugle
le	cor d'harmonie	French horn
les	cuivres	brass
un	enregistrement numérique	digital recording
un	étui	case
un	harmonica	harmonica
le	:hautbois	oboe
le	jazz [dʒaz]	jazz
le	microphone	microphone
le	minidisque	minidisc
un	orgue	organ
le	pupitre	music stand
le	saxophone	saxophone
le	solfège	music theory
le	soliste	soloist
le	studio d'enregistrement	recording studio
le	tambour	drum
le	tambourin	tambourine
le	triangle	triangle
le	trombone	trombone
le	violoncelle	cello

ESSENTIAL WORDS (feminine)

la	batterie	drums, drum kit
la	clarinette	clarinet
la	flûte	flute
la	flûte à bec	recorder
la	guitare	guitar
la	musique	music

USEFUL WORDS (feminine)

la	composition	composition
la	contrebasse	double bass
la	corde	string
les	cordes	brass
la	cornemuse	bagpipes
les	cymbales	cymbals
la	fanfare	brass band; fanfare
la	grosse caisse	bass drum
la	:harpe	harp
la	note	note
la	soliste	soloist
la	sono	sound system
la	table de mixage	(mixing) deck
la	touche	(piano) key
la	trompette	trumpet

USEFUL PHRASES

jouer or interpréter un morceau to play a piece
jouer fort/doucement to play loudly/softly
jouer juste/faux to play in tune/out of tune
jouer du piano/de la guitare to play the piano/the guitar
faire de la batterie to play drums
Luc à la batterie Luc on drums
travailler son piano to practice the piano
est-ce que tu joues dans un groupe ? do you play in a band?
une fausse note a wrong note

CARDINAL NUMBERS

zéro	0	zero
un (m), une (f)	1	one
deux	2	two
trois	3	three
quatre	4	four
cinq	5	five
six	6	six
sept	7	seven
huit	8	eight
neuf	9	nine
dix	10	ten
onze	11	eleven
douze	12	twelve
treize	13	thirteen
quatorze	14	fourteen
quinze	15	fifteen
seize	16	sixteen
dix-sept	17	seventeen
dix-huit	18	eighteen
dix-neuf	19	nineteen
vingt	20	twenty
vingt et un	21	twenty-one
vingt-deux	22	twenty-two
vingt-trois	23	twenty-three
trente	30	thirty
trente et un	31	thirty-one
trente-deux	32	thirty-two
quarante	40	forty
cinquante	50	fifty
soixante	60	sixty
soixante-dix	70	seventy
soixante-et-onze	71	seventy-one
quatre-vingts	80	eighty
quatre-vingt-un	81	eighty-one
quatre-vingt-dix	90	ninety
quatre-vingt-onze	91	ninety-one
cent	100	one hundred

CARDINAL NUMBERS *(continued)*

cent un	101	a hundred and one
cent deux	102	a hundred and two
cent dix	110	a hundred and ten
cent-quatre-vingt-deux	182	a hundred and eighty-two
deux cents	200	two hundred
deux cent un	201	two hundred and one
deux cent deux	202	two hundred and two
trois cents	300	three hundred
quatre cents	400	four hundred
cinq cents	500	five hundred
six cents	600	six hundred
sept cents	700	seven hundred
huit cents	800	eight hundred
neuf cents	900	nine hundred
mille	1000	one thousand
mille un	1001	a thousand and one
mille deux	1002	a thousand and two
deux mille	2000	two thousand
deux mille deux	2002	two thousand and two
dix mille	10000	ten thousand
cent mille	100000	one hundred thousand
un million	1000000	one million
deux millions	2000000	two million

USEFUL PHRASES

mille euros **a thousand euros**
un million de dollars **one million dollars**
trois virgule deux (3,2) **three point two (3.2)**

ORDINAL NUMBERS

premier(ière)	$1^{er}, 1^{ère}$	first
deuxième	2^e	second
troisième	3^e	third
quatrième	4^e	fourth
cinquième	5^e	fifth
sixième	6^e	sixth
septième	7^e	seventh
huitième	8^e	eighth
neuvième	9^e	ninth
dixième	10^e	tenth
onzième	11^e	eleventh
douzième	12^e	twelfth
treizième	13^e	thirteenth
quatorzième	14^e	fourteenth
quinzième	15^e	fifteenth
seizième	16^e	sixteenth
dix-septième	17^e	seventeenth
dix-huitième	18^e	eighteenth
dix-neuvième	19^e	nineteenth
vingtième	20^e	twentieth
vingt et unième	21^e	twenty-first
vingt-deuxième	22^e	twenty-second
trentième	30^e	thirtieth
trente et unième	31^e	thirty-first
quarantième	40^e	fortieth
cinquantième	50^e	fiftieth
soixantième	60^e	sixtieth
soixante-dixième	70^e	seventieth
quatre-vingtième	80^e	eightieth
quatre-vingt-dixième	90^e	ninetieth
centième	100^e	hundredth

ORDINAL NUMBERS *(continued)*

cent unième	101^e	hundred and first
cent-dixième	110^e	hundred and tenth
deux centième	200^e	two hundredth
trois centième	300^e	three hundredth
quatre centième	400^e	four hundredth
cinq centième	500^e	five hundredth
six centième	600^e	six hundredth
sept centième	700^e	seven hundredth
huit centième	800^e	eight hundredth
neuf centième	900^e	nine hundredth
millième	1000^e	thousandth
deux millième	2000^e	two thousandth
millionième	1000000^e	millionth
deux millionième	2000000^e	two millionth

FRACTIONS

un(e) demi(e)	$\frac{1}{2}$	a half
un(e) et demi(e)	$1\frac{1}{2}$	one and a half
deux et demi(e)	$2\frac{1}{2}$	two and a half
un tiers	$\frac{1}{3}$	a third
deux tiers	$\frac{2}{3}$	two thirds
un quart	$\frac{1}{4}$	a quarter
trois quarts	$\frac{3}{4}$	three quarters
un sixième	$\frac{1}{6}$	a sixth
trois et cinq sixièmes	$3\frac{5}{6}$	three and five sixths
un douzième	$\frac{1}{12}$	a twelfth
sept douzièmes	$\frac{7}{12}$	seven twelfths
un centième	$\frac{1}{100}$	a hundredth
un millième	$\frac{1}{1000}$	a thousandth

USEFUL PHRASES

une assiette de a plate of
une bande de a group of
beaucoup de lots of
une boîte de a can of; a box of
un bol de a bowl of
une bouchée de a mouthful of
un bout de papier a piece of paper
une bouteille de a bottle of
cent grammes de a hundred grams of
une centaine de (about) a hundred
une cuillerée de a spoonful of
un demi de bière half a liter of beer
une demi-douzaine de half a dozen
un demi-litre de half a liter of
tous (f toutes) les deux both of them
une dizaine de (about) ten
une douzaine de a dozen
une foule de loads of
un kilo de a kilo of
à quelques kilomètres de a few kilometers from
un litre de a liter of
une livre de à pound of
un mètre de a meter of

USEFUL PHRASES

à quelques mètres de a few meters from
des milliers de thousands of
la moitié de half of
un morceau de gâteau a piece of cake
une paire de a pair of
un paquet de a packet of
un peu de a little
une pile de a pile of
la plupart de or des most (of)
plusieurs several
une poignée de a handful of
une portion de a portion of
un pot de a pot or tub or jar of
une quantité de a lot of, many
un quart de a quarter of
un tas de a heap of, heaps of
une tasse de a cup of
un tonneau de a barrel of
une tranche de a slice of
trois quarts de three quarters of
un troupeau de a herd of (cattle); a flock of (sheep)
un verre de a glass of

ESSENTIAL WORDS (*masculine*)

le **bijou** (*pl* -x)	jewel
le **bracelet**	bracelet
le **dentifrice**	toothpaste
le **déodorant**	deodorant
le **gant de toilette**	washcloth
le **maquillage**	makeup
le **miroir**	mirror
le **parfum**	perfume
le **peigne**	comb
le **rasoir**	razor
le **shampooing** [ʃɑ̃pwɛ̃]	shampoo

USEFUL WORDS (*masculine*)

un **après-rasage**	aftershave
le **bigoudi**	curler
le **blaireau** (*pl* -x)	shaving brush
le **bouton de manchette**	cufflink
le **collier**	necklace
le **diamant**	diamond
le **dissolvant**	nail polish remover
les **effets personnels**	personal effects
le **fard**	makeup
le **fard à paupières**	eye shadow
le **fond de teint**	foundation
le **kleenex**®	tissue
le **papier hygiénique**	toilet paper
le **pendentif**	pendant
le **porte-clefs** (*pl inv*)	key ring
le **poudrier**	(powder) compact
le **rimmel**	mascara
le **rouge à lèvres**	lipstick
le **sèche-cheveux**	hairdryer
le **vernis à ongles**	nail polish

ESSENTIAL WORDS *(feminine)*

la	**bague**	ring
la	**brosse à dents**	toothbrush
la	**chaîne**	chain
la	**chaînette**	chain
la	**crème de beauté**	face cream
une	**eau de toilette**	eau de toilette
la	**glace**	mirror
la	**montre**	watch
la	**pâte dentifrice**	toothpaste

USEFUL WORDS *(feminine)*

une	**alliance**	wedding ring
la	**boucle d'oreille** (*pl* ~s d'oreille)	earring
la	**broche**	brooch
la	**coiffure**	hairstyle
la	**crème à raser**	shaving cream
une	**éponge**	sponge
la	**gourmette**	chain bracelet
la	**manucure**	manicure
la	**mousse à raser**	shaving cream
la	**perle**	pearl
la	**poudre**	face powder
la	**trousse de toilette**	toilet bag

USEFUL PHRASES

se maquiller to put on one's makeup
se démaquiller to take off one's makeup
se coiffer to do one's hair
se peigner to comb one's hair
se raser to shave
se brosser les dents to brush one's teeth

ESSENTIAL WORDS *(masculine)*

un	**arbre**	tree
le	**jardin**	garden
le	**jardinage**	gardening
le	**jardinier**	gardener
les	**légumes**	vegetables
le	**soleil**	sun

IMPORTANT WORDS *(masculine)*

le	**banc**	bench
le	**bouquet de fleurs**	bunch of flowers
le	**buisson**	bush
le	**gazon**	lawn

USEFUL PHRASES

planter **to plant**
désherber **to weed**
offrir un bouquet de fleurs à qn **to give sb a bunch of flowers**
tondre le gazon **to mow the lawn**
"défense de marcher sur le gazon" **"keep off the grass"**
mon père aime jardiner **my father likes gardening**

ESSENTIAL WORDS *(feminine)*

une	abeille	bee
la	branche	branch
la	feuille	leaf
la	fleur	flower
	l'herbe	grass
la	pelouse	lawn
la	plante	plant
la	pluie	rain
la	rose	rose
la	terre	earth, ground

IMPORTANT WORDS *(feminine)*

la	barrière	gate; fence
la	culture	cultivation
la	guêpe	wasp
les	mauvaises herbes	weeds
	l'ombre	shade; shadow
la	plate-bande *(pl ~s~s)*	flowerbed
la	racine	root

USEFUL PHRASES

les fleurs poussent the flowers are growing
par terre on the ground
arroser les fleurs to water the flowers
cueillir des fleurs to pick flowers
se mettre à l'ombre to go into the shade
rester à l'ombre to remain in the shade
à l'ombre d'un arbre in the shade of a tree

USEFUL WORDS *(masculine)*

un	arbuste	shrub, bush
un	arrosoir	watering can
le	bassin	(ornamental) pool
le	bourgeon	bud
le	bouton-d'or *(pl ~s~)*	buttercup
le	chèvrefeuille	honeysuckle
le	chrysanthème	chrysanthemum
le	coquelicot	poppy
le	crocus	crocus
le	feuillage	leaves
	l'hortensia	hydrangea
le	jardin potager	vegetable garden
le	lierre	ivy
le	lilas	lilac
le	lis [lis]	lily
le	muguet	lily of the valley
un	œillet	carnation
un	outil	tool
le	papillon	butterfly
le	parterre	flowerbed
le	pavot	poppy
le	perce-neige *(pl inv)*	snowdrop
le	pissenlit	dandelion
le	pois de senteur	sweet pea
le	rosier	rose bush
le	sol	earth, soil
le	tournesol	sunflower
le	tronc	trunk *(of tree)*
le	tuyau d'arrosage	hose
le	ver	worm
le	verger	orchard

USEFUL WORDS *(feminine)*

une	allée	path
la	baie	berry
la	brouette	wheelbarrow
la	clôture	fence
une	épine	thorn
les	graines	seeds
la	:haie	hedge
la	jacinthe	hyacinth
la	jonquille	daffodil
la	marguerite	daisy
une	orchidée	orchid
la	pâquerette	daisy
la	pensée	pansy
la	pivoine	peony
la	primevère	primrose
la	rocaille	rockery
la	rosée	dew
la	serre	greenhouse
la	tige	stalk
la	tondeuse	lawn mower
la	tulipe	tulip
la	violette	violet

ESSENTIAL WORDS *(masculine)*

le baigneur	swimmer
le bateau (*pl* -x) de pêche	fishing boat
le bikini	bikini
le bord de la mer	seaside
le maillot (de bain)	swimming trunks *or* swimsuit
le pêcheur	fisherman
le pique-nique (*pl* -s)	picnic
le port	port, harbor
le quai [ke]	quay
le slip de bain	swimming trunks

IMPORTANT WORDS *(masculine)*

le château (*pl* -x) de sable	sandcastle
le coup de soleil	sunburn
le crabe	crab
le fond	bottom
l'horizon	horizon
le mal de mer	seasickness
le matelas pneumatique	air mattress
le sable	sand
le vacancier	vacationer

USEFUL PHRASES

au bord de la mer **at the seaside**
à l'horizon **on the horizon**
il a le mal de mer **he is seasick**
nager **to swim**
se noyer **to drown**
je vais me baigner **I'm going for a swim**
plonger dans l'eau **to dive into the water**
flotter **to float**

ESSENTIAL WORDS *(feminine)*

la	côte	coast
	l'eau	water
une	île	island
les	lunettes de soleil	sunglasses
la	mer	sea
la	natation	swimming
la	pierre	stone
la	plage	beach
la	promenade	walk
la	serviette	towel

IMPORTANT WORDS *(feminine)*

la	chaise longue	deckchair
la	crème solaire	sunscreen
la	planche à voile	windsurfing (board)
la	traversée	crossing

USEFUL PHRASES

au fond de la mer **at the bottom of the sea**
à la plage **on the beach; to the beach**
faire la traversée en bateau **to go across by boat**
se bronzer **to get a tan**
être bronzé(e) **to be tanned**
il sait nager **he can swim**

USEFUL WORDS (*masculine*)

	l'air marin	sea air
un	aviron	oar
le	bac	ferry
le	caillou (*pl* -x)	pebble
le	cap [kap]	headland
le	coquillage	shell
le	courant	current
un	équipage	crew
les	flots	waves
le	gouvernail	rudder
le	maître nageur	lifeguard
le	marin	sailor
le	mât	mast
le	matelot	sailor
le	naufrage	shipwreck
les	naufragés	shipwrecked people, castaways
un	océan	ocean
le	parasol	parasol
le	pavillon	flag
le	pédalo	pedal boat
le	phare	lighthouse
le	port de plaisance	marina
le	radeau (*pl* -x)	raft
le	rivage	shore
le	rocher	rock
le	seau (*pl* -x)	bucket
le	vaisseau (*pl* -x)	vessel
le	vapeur	steamer

USEFUL WORDS (feminine)

les	algues	seaweed
une	ancre	anchor
la	baie	bay
la	barque	small boat
la	bouée	buoy
la	cargaison	cargo
la	ceinture de sauvetage	lifebelt
la	croisière	cruise
	l'écume	foam
une	embouchure	mouth (of river)
une	épave	wreck
la	falaise	cliff
une	insolation	sunstroke
la	jetée	pier
les	jumelles	binoculars
la	marée	tide
la	marine	navy
la	mouette	seagull
la	passerelle	gangway; bridge (of ship)
la	pelle	spade
la	rame	oar
la	vague	wave
la	voile	sail; sailing

USEFUL PHRASES

j'ai eu une insolation I had sunstroke
à marée basse/haute at low/high tide
faire de la voile to go sailing

ESSENTIAL WORDS *(masculine)*

un	achat	purchase
	l'argent	money
le	billet de banque	banknote
le	boucher	butcher
le	boulanger	baker
le	bureau (*pl* -x) de poste	post office
le	bureau de tabac	smoke shop
le	cadeau (*pl* -x)	gift
le	centime (d'euro)	euro cent
le	centre commercial	mall, shopping center
le	charcutier	pork butcher
le	chèque	check
le	chéquier	checkbook
le	client	customer
un	dollar	dollar
un	épicier	grocer
un	euro	euro
le	fleuriste	flower shop
le	grand magasin	department store
un	hypermarché	supermarket
le	magasin	store
le	magasin de chaussures	shoe store
le	marché	market; deal
le	prix	price
le	rayon	department
les	soldes	sales
le	souvenir	souvenir
le	supermarché	supermarket
le	tabac	smoke shop
le	vendeur	salesclerk

ESSENTIAL WORDS *(feminine)*

une	agence de voyages	travel agency
	l'alimentation	food
la	banque	bank
la	boucherie	butcher shop
la	boulangerie	bakery
la	boutique	small shop
la	caisse	check-out
la	Carte bleue®	debit card
la	carte de crédit	credit card
la	charcuterie	pork butcher
la	cliente	customer
une	épicerie	grocery store, deli
la	liste	list
la	monnaie	change
la	parfumerie	perfume shop/department
la	pâtisserie	cake shop
la	pharmacie	pharmacy
la	pointure	(shoe) size
la	poste	post office
la	réduction	discount
la	taille	size
la	vendeuse	salesclerk

USEFUL PHRASES

acheter/vendre to buy/sell
ça coûte combien ? how much does this cost?
ça fait combien ? how much does that come to?
je l'ai payé(e) 5 euros I paid 5 euros for it
chez le boucher/le boulanger at the butcher/bakery

IMPORTANT WORDS (*masculine*)

un	article	article
le	coiffeur	hairdresser
le	commerçant	storekeeper
le	commerce	business
le	commerce équitable	fair trade
le	comptoir	counter
le	cordonnier	shoe repair man
un	escalier roulant	escalator
le	gérant	manager
le	marchand de fruits	fruit seller
le	marchand de légumes	greengrocer
le	marché aux puces	flea market
le	portefeuille	wallet
le	porte-monnaie (*pl inv*)	wallet
le	pressing	dry cleaner
le	reçu	receipt

USEFUL PHRASES

je ne fais que regarder I'm just looking
c'est trop cher it's too expensive
quelque chose de moins cher something cheaper
c'est bon marché it's cheap
"payez à la caisse" "pay at the checkout"
c'est pour offrir ? would you like it gift-wrapped?
il doit y avoir une erreur there must be some mistake

IMPORTANT WORDS *(feminine)*

la	**bibliothèque**	library
la	**brocante**	secondhand store
la	**calculette**	calculator
la	**cordonnerie**	shoe repair shop
la	**grande surface**	supermarket
la	**librairie**	bookstore
la	**marque**	brand
la	**promotion**	special offer
la	**réclamation**	complaint
la	**vitrine**	store window

USEFUL PHRASES

avec ça ? **anything else?**

SA (société anonyme) **Inc.**

SARL (société à responsabilité limitée) **limited liability company**

et Cie **& Co.**

"en vente ici" **"on sale here"**

une voiture d'occasion **a used car**

en promotion **on sale**

USEFUL WORDS *(masculine)*

un	agent immobilier	real estate agent
le	bijoutier	jeweler
le	coloris	color
le	confiseur	confectioner
le	disquaire	record dealer
un	horloger	watchmaker
le	libraire	bookseller
le	marchand de journaux	newsagent
un	opticien	optician
le	poissonnier	fishmonger
le	produit	product; *(pl)* produce
le	quincaillier	hardware dealer
le	rabais	discount
le	vidéoclub	video rental store
le	voyagiste	travel agent

USEFUL PHRASES

faire du lèche-vitrines **to go window shopping**
heures d'ouverture **business hours**
payer cash **to pay cash**
payer par chèque **to pay by check**

USEFUL WORDS (*feminine*)

une	agence immobilière	real estate agency
la	bijouterie	jewelry store
la	blanchisserie	laundry
la	caisse d'épargne	savings bank
les	commissions	shopping
la	confiserie	candy store
une	course	errand
les	courses	shopping
la	devanture	store window; display
la	droguerie	hardware store
une	encolure	collar size
une	horlogerie	watchmaker
les	marchandises	goods, merchandise
la	papeterie	office supply store
la	queue [kø]	line, queue
la	quincaillerie	hardware store
la	succursale	branch
la	teinturerie	dry cleaner
la	vente	sale

USEFUL PHRASES
en vitrine **in the window**
faire les courses **to go shopping**
dépenser **to spend**

ESSENTIAL WORDS *(masculine)*

le	badminton	badminton
le	ballon	ball *(large)*
le	baseball	baseball
le	basket	basketball
le	billard	billiards
le	but [byt]	goal
le	champion	champion
le	championnat	championship
le	cyclisme	cycling
le	football	soccer
le	golf	golf
le	:hockey	hockey
le	jeu *(pl* -x)	game; play
le	joueur	player
le	match *(pl* matches)	match
le	résultat	result, score
le	rugby	rugby
le	ski	skiing; ski
le	ski nautique	water skiing
le	sport	sport
le	stade	stadium
le	tennis	tennis; tennis court
le	terrain	ground; pitch
le	volley	volleyball

USEFUL PHRASES

jouer au baseball/au tennis to play baseball/tennis
marquer un but/un point to score a goal/a point
marquer les points to keep the score
le champion du monde the world champion
gagner/perdre un match to win/lose a match
faire match nul to draw
mon sport préféré my favorite sport

ESSENTIAL WORDS *(feminine)*

	l'aérobic	aerobics
la	balle	ball *(small)*
la	championne	champion
une	équipe	team
	l'équitation	horseback riding
la	gymnastique	gymnastics
la	joueuse	player
la	natation	swimming
la	partie	game
la	pêche	fishing
la	piscine	swimming pool
la	planche à voile	windsurfing (board)
la	promenade	walk
la	voile	sailing

USEFUL PHRASES

égaliser to equalize, to tie up

courir to run

sauter to jump

lancer, jeter to throw

battre qn to beat sb

s'entraîner to train

Paris Saint-Germain mène par 2 à 1 Paris Saint-Germain is leading by 2 goals to 1

une partie de tennis a tennis match

il fait partie d'un club he belongs to a club

aller à la pêche to go fishing

aller à la piscine to go to the swimming pool

sais-tu nager ? can you swim?

faire du sport to do sport

faire une promenade en vélo to go cycling

faire de la voile to go sailing

faire du footing/de l'alpinisme to go jogging/climbing

USEFUL WORDS (*masculine*)

un	adversaire	opponent
	l'alpinisme	mountaineering
un	arbitre	referee; (*tennis*) umpire
	l'athlétisme	athletics
	l'aviron	rowing
le	catch	wrestling
le	champ de course	race course
le	championnat	championship
le	chronomètre	stopwatch
le	débutant	beginner
le	détenteur du titre	titleholder
un	entraîneur	trainer, coach
le	filet	net
le	footing	jogging
le	gardien de but	goalkeeper
le	javelot	javelin
les	Jeux olympiques	Olympic Games
le	jogging	jogging; tracksuit
le	maillot	jersey
le	parapente	paragliding
le	patin (à glace)	(ice) skate; (ice) skating
les	rollers	roller skates
le	saut en hauteur	high jump
le	saut en longueur	long jump
le	score	score
le	spectateur	spectator
le	squash	squash
le	tir	shooting
le	tir à l'arc	archery
le	toboggan	toboggan; water slide

IMPORTANT WORDS *(feminine)*

la	boule	bowl; billiard ball
les	boules	bowls
la	course	race
les	courses	horseracing
la	défense	defense
la	piste	ski slope; track
la	rencontre	match

USEFUL WORDS *(feminine)*

les	baskets	sneakers, running shoes
la	boxe	boxing
la	canne à pêche	fishing rod
la	chasse	hunting
la	coupe	cup
une	éliminatoire	heat
	l'escrime	fencing
une	étape	stage
la	finale	final
la	gagnante	winner
la	luge	sled; sledding
la	lutte	wrestling
la	mêlée	scrum
la	mi-temps *(pl inv)*	half-time
la	patinoire	skating rink
la	perdante	loser
la	plongée	diving
la	prolongation	overtime
la	raquette	racket
la	station de sports d'hiver	winter sports resort
les	tennis	tennis shoes
la	tribune	stand

ESSENTIAL WORDS *(masculine)*

un	**acteur**	actor
le	**balcon**	dress circle
le	**billet**	ticket
le	**cinéma**	movie theater
le	**cirque**	circus
le	**clip vidéo**	music video
le	**clown** [klun]	clown
le	**comédien**	actor
le	**comique**	comedian
le	**costume**	costume
le	**film**	movie
le	**guichet**	box office
un	**opéra**	opera
un	**orchestre**	orchestra
le	**programme**	program
le	**public**	audience
le	**rideau** (*pl* -x)	curtain
le	**spectacle**	show
le	**théâtre**	theater
le	**western**	western

USEFUL PHRASES

aller au théâtre/au cinéma to go to the theater/to the movies
réserver une place to book a seat
un fauteuil d'orchestre a seat in the orchestra
mon acteur préféré/actrice préférée my favorite actor/actress
pendant l'entracte during the intermission
entrer en scène to come on stage
jouer le rôle de to play the part of

ESSENTIAL WORDS *(feminine)*

une	**actrice**	actress
une	**ambiance**	atmosphere
la	**comédienne**	actress
la	**comique**	comedienne
la	**musique**	music
la	**pièce** (de théâtre)	play
la	**place**	seat
la	**salle**	auditorium; audience
la	**séance**	performance; showing
la	**sortie**	exit
la	**vedette** *(m+f)* **de cinéma**	movie star

USEFUL PHRASES

jouer **to play**
danser **to dance**
chanter **to sing**
tourner un film **to shoot a movie**
"prochaine séance: 21 heures" **"next showing: 9 p.m."**
"version originale" **"in the original language"**
"sous-titré" **"subtitled"**
"complet" **"full house"**
applaudire **to clap**
bis ! **encore!**
bravo ! **bravo!**
un film d'amour/de science fiction **a romance/a science fiction movie**
un film d'adventure/d'horreur **an adventure/horror movie**

IMPORTANT WORDS *(masculine)*

l'acteur principal	leading man
le ballet	ballet
un entracte	intermission
le maquillage	makeup
un ouvreur	usher
le pourboire	tip
le sous-titre *(pl ~s)*	subtitle
le titre	title

USEFUL WORDS *(masculine)*

les applaudissements	applause
le décor	scenery
le dramaturge	playwright
un écran	screen
le feuilleton	serial
le foyer	foyer, lobby
le metteur en scène	producer
le parterre	stalls, orchestra
le personnage	character *(in play)*
le poulailler	*the highest and cheapest seats in the theater*
le producteur	producer
le projecteur	spotlight
le réalisateur	director
le régisseur	stage manager
le rôle	part
le scénario	script
le soap	soap (opera)
le souffleur	prompter
le spectateur	member of the audience
le texte	script, lines
le vestiaire	checkroom

IMPORTANT WORDS (feminine)

	l'actrice principale	leading lady
une	affiche	notice; poster
la	comédie	comedy
la	critique	review; critics
la	location	booking; box office
une	ouvreuse	usherette

USEFUL WORDS (feminine)

la	comédie musicale	musical
la	corbeille	circle
les	coulisses	wings
la	distribution	cast (on program)
une	estrade	platform
la	farce	farce
la	fosse d'orchestre	orchestra pit
une	intrigue	plot
les	jumelles de théâtre	opera glasses
la	loge	box
la	mise en scène	production
la	première	first night
la	rampe	footlights
la	répétition	rehearsal
la	répétition générale	dress rehearsal
la	représentation	performance
la	scène	stage; scene
la	tragédie	tragedy

ESSENTIAL WORDS (*masculine*)

un	**an**	year
un	**après-midi** (*pl inv*)	afternoon
un	**instant**	moment
le	**jour**	day
le	**matin**	morning
le	**mois**	month
le	**moment**	moment
le	**quart d'heure**	quarter of an hour
le	**réveil**	alarm clock
le	**siècle**	century
le	**soir**	evening
le	**temps**	time
le	**week-end** (*pl ~s*)	weekend

USEFUL PHRASES

à midi at noon
à minuit at midnight
après-demain the day after tomorrow
aujourd'hui today
avant-hier the day before yesterday
demain tomorrow
hier yesterday
il y a 2 jours 2 days ago
dans 2 jours in 2 days
huit jours a week
quinze jours two weeks
tous les jours every day
quel jour sommes-nous ? what day is it?
le combien sommes-nous ? what's the date?
en ce moment at the moment
3 heures moins le quart a quarter to 3
3 heures et quart a quarter after 3
au 21ème siècle in the 21st century
hier soir last night, yesterday evening

ESSENTIAL WORDS *(feminine)*

une	**année**	year
une	**après-midi** *(pl inv)*	afternoon
une	**demi-heure** *(pl ~s)*	half an hour
une	**heure**	hour
	l'**heure**	time *(in general)*
la	**journée**	day
la	**matinée**	morning
la	**minute**	minute
la	**montre**	watch
la	**nuit**	night
la	**pendule**	clock
la	**quinzaine**	two weeks
la	**seconde**	second
la	**semaine**	week
la	**soirée**	evening

USEFUL PHRASES

l'année dernière/prochaine **last/next year**

dans une demi-heure **in half an hour**

une/deux/trois fois **once/twice/three times**

plusieurs fois **several times**

3 fois par an **3 times a year**

9 fois sur 10 **9 times out of 10**

il était une fois **once upon a time there was**

10 à la fois **10 at the same time**

quelle heure est-il ? **what time is it?**

avez-vous l'heure ? **have you got the time?**

il est 6 heures/6 heures moins 10/6 heures et demie **it is 6 o'clock/10 to 6/
half past 6**

il est 14 heures pile **it is 2 o'clock sharp**

tout à l'heure *(past)* **a short while ago**; *(future)* **soon**

tôt, de bonne heure **early**; tard **late**

cette nuit *(past)* **last night**; *(to come)* **tonight**

620 time

IMPORTANT WORDS (*masculine*)

l'avenir	future
le lendemain	next day
le retard	delay; lateness

USEFUL WORDS (*masculine*)

le cadran	face (*of clock*)
le calendrier	calendar
le chronomètre	stopwatch
le futur	future; future tense
le Moyen-Âge	Middle Ages
le passé	past; past tense
le présent	present (time); present tense

USEFUL PHRASES

après-demain the day after tomorrow
avant-hier the day before yesterday
le surlendemain two days later
la veille the day before
à l'avenir in the future
un jour de congé a day off
un jour férié a national holiday
un jour ouvrable a weekday
par un jour de pluie on a rainy day
au lever du jour at dawn
le lendemain matin/soir the following morning/evening
à présent now
vous êtes en retard you are late

USEFUL WORDS *(feminine)*

une	**aiguille**	hand (*of clock*)
une	**année bissextile**	leap year
la	**décennie**	decade
une	**époque**	era; time
	l'**horloge**	(large) clock
une	**horloge normande**	grandfather clock

USEFUL PHRASES

vous êtes an avance you are early
cette montre avance/retarde this watch is fast/slow
arriver à temps, arriver à l'heure to arrive on time
combien de temps ? how long?
le 3e millénaire the third millennium
faire la grasse matinée to sleep in
d'une minute à l'autre any minute now
aujourd'hui en huit a week today
la veille au soir the night before
à cette époque at that time

ESSENTIAL WORDS *(masculine)*

un	**atelier**	workshop
le	**bricolage**	DIY
le	**bricoleur**	handyman
un	**outil**	tool

USEFUL WORDS *(masculine)*

le	**cadenas**	padlock
le	**chantier**	construction site
le	**ciseau** (*pl* -x)	chisel
les	**ciseaux**	scissors
le	**clou**	nail
un	**échafaudage**	scaffolding
un	**élastique**	rubber band
un	**escabeau** (*pl* -x)	stepladder
le	**fil de fer (barbelé)**	(barbed) wire
le	**foret**	drill
le	**marteau** (*pl* -x)	hammer
le	**marteau-piqueur** (*pl* ~x ~s)	pneumatic drill
le	**pic**	pickax
le	**pinceau** (*pl* -x)	paintbrush
le	**ressort**	spring
le	**scotch**	Scotch tape®
le	**tournevis**	screwdriver

USEFUL PHRASES

faire du bricolage to do odd jobs
enfoncer un clou to hammer in a nail
"attention peinture fraîche" "wet paint"
peindre to paint; tapisser to wallpaper

ESSENTIAL WORDS *(feminine)*

la	**clé, clef**	key; wrench
la	**corde**	rope
la	**machine**	machine

USEFUL WORDS *(feminine)*

une	**aiguille**	needle
la	**bêche**	spade
la	**boîte à outils**	toolbox
la	**clef anglaise**	wrench
la	**colle**	glue
une	**échelle**	ladder
la	**fourche**	pitchfork
la	**lime**	file
la	**pelle**	shovel
la	**perceuse**	drill
la	**pile**	battery
les	**pinces**	pliers
la	**pioche**	pickax
la	**planche**	plank
la	**punaise**	thumbtack
la	**scie**	saw
la	**serrure**	lock
la	**vis** [vis]	screw

USEFUL PHRASES

"chantier interdit" "construction site: keep out"
pratique handy
couper to cut; réparer to repair
visser to screw (in); dévisser to unscrew

ESSENTIAL WORDS (*masculine*)

un	agent (de police)	policeman, police officer
un	arrêt de bus	bus stop
le	bâtiment	building
le	bureau (*pl* -x) de poste	post office
le	bureau (*pl* -x)	office
le	centre-ville (*pl* ~s~s)	downtown, town center
le	cinéma	movie theater
le	coin	corner
le	commissariat	police station
les	environs	surroundings
un	habitant	inhabitant
un	HLM (habitation à loyer modéré)	subsidized housing
un	hôtel	hotel
un	hôtel de ville	town hall
un	immeuble	apartment building
le	jardin public	park
le	magasin	store
le	marché	market
le	métro	subway
le	musée	museum; art gallery
le	parc	park
le	parking	parking lot
le	piéton	pedestrian
le	pont	bridge
le	quartier	district
le	restaurant	restaurant
le	sens interdit	one-way street
le	taxi	taxi
le	théâtre	theater
le	tour	tour
le	touriste	tourist

ESSENTIAL WORDS *(feminine)*

une	**auto**	car
la	**banlieue**	suburbs
la	**banque**	bank
la	**boutique**	(small) store
la	**cathédrale**	cathedral
une	**église**	church
la	**gare**	train station
la	**gare routière**	bus station
une	**HLM (habitation à loyer modéré)**	subsidized housing
la	**laverie automatique**	coin laundry
la	**mairie**	town hall
la	**piscine**	swimming pool
la	**place**	square
la	**police**	police
la	**pollution**	air pollution
la	**poste**	post office
la	**route**	road
la	**rue**	street
la	**station de taxis**	taxi stand
la	**station-service** *(pl ~s~)*	gas station
la	**tour**	tower
une	**usine**	factory
la	**ville**	town, city
la	**voiture**	car
la	**vue**	view

USEFUL PHRASES

je vais en ville I'm going into town
au centre-ville downtown
sur la place in the square
une rue à sens unique a one-way street
traverser la rue to cross the street
au coin de la rue at the corner of the street
habiter en banlieue to live in the suburbs

IMPORTANT WORDS *(masculine)*

le	carnet de tickets	book of tickets
le	carrefour	intersection
le	château *(pl* -x)	castle
le	distributeur de billets	ticket machine
un	embouteillage	traffic jam
un	endroit	place
le	jardin zoologique	zoo
le	kiosque (à journaux)	newsstand
le	lieu *(pl* -x)	place
le	maire	mayor
le	monument	monument
le	parcmètre	parking meter
le	passant	passerby
le	sens unique	one-way street
le	temple	Protestant church
le	trottoir	sidewalk

USEFUL PHRASES

marcher to walk

prendre le bus/le métro to take the bus/the subway

acheter un carnet de tickets to buy a book of 10 tickets

composter to punch *(ticket)*

IMPORTANT WORDS *(feminine)*

une	affiche	notice; poster
la	bibliothèque	library
la	chaussée	road
la	circulation	traffic
la	déviation	detour
la	mosquée	mosque
la	rue principale	main street
la	synagogue	synagogue
la	vieille ville	old town
la	zone bleue	restricted parking zone
la	zone industrielle	industrial zone
la	zone piétonne	pedestrian area

USEFUL PHRASES

industriel(le) industrial
historique historic
joli(e) pretty
laid(e) ugly
propre clean
sale dirty

USEFUL WORDS (*masculine*)

un	abribus	bus shelter
un	arrondissement	district
un	autobus	bus
le	bistrot	coffee shop
le	bus	bus
le	cimetière	cemetery
le	citadin	citizen
le	citoyen	citizen
le	conseil municipal	town council
le	défilé	parade
le	dépliant	leaflet
un	édifice	building
un	égout	sewer
le	faubourg	suburb
le	gratte-ciel (*pl inv*)	skyscraper
le	panneau (*pl* -x)	roadsign
le	passage clouté	crosswalk
le	pavé	cobblestone
le	refuge	traffic island
les	remparts	ramparts
le	réverbère	street lamp
le	sondage d'opinion	opinion poll
le	square	square
le	virage	bend

USEFUL WORDS (*feminine*)

une	agglomération	built-up area
la	camionnette de livraison	delivery van
la	caserne de pompiers	fire station
la	cité universitaire	(student) residence halls
les	curiosités	sights, places of interest
la	flèche	arrow
la	foule	crowd
la	galerie	art gallery
la	grand-rue	main street
une	impasse	dead end
la	piste cyclable	cycle path
la	population	population
la	prison	prison
la	queue [kø]	line, queue
la	statue	statue
la	voiture d'enfant	baby carriage

ESSENTIAL WORDS (*masculine*)

un	aller-retour	round-trip ticket
un	aller simple	one-way ticket
les	bagages	luggage
le	billet	ticket
le	compartiment	compartment
le	départ	departure
le	douanier	customs officer
le	frein	brake
le	guichet	ticket office
l'	horaire	timetable, schedule
le	mécanicien	train engineer
le	métro	subway
le	numéro	number
les	objets trouvés	lost and found
le	passeport	passport
le	plan	map
le	pont	bridge
le	porteur	porter
le	prix du billet	fare
le	prix du ticket	fare
le	quai [ke]	platform
les	renseignements	information
le	retard	delay
le	sac	bag
le	supplément	extra charge
le	taxi	taxi
le	TGV	high-speed train
le	ticket	ticket
le	train	train
le	train express	fast train
le	train rapide	express train
le	vélo	bike
le	voyage	journey
le	voyageur	traveler

ESSENTIAL WORDS *(feminine)*

une	arrivée	arrival
la	bicyclette	bicycle
la	classe	class
la	consigne	baggage check
la	consigne automatique	baggage locker
la	correspondance	connection
la	direction	direction
la	douane	customs
une	entrée	entrance
la	gare	train station
la	ligne	line
la	place	seat
la	réduction	discount
la	réservation	reservation
la	salle d'attente	waiting room
la	sortie	exit
la	station de métro	subway station
la	station de taxis	taxi stand
la	valise	suitcase
la	voie	track, line
la	voiture	passenger car

USEFUL PHRASES

réserver une place to reserve a seat
payer un supplément to pay an extra charge
faire/défaire ses bagages to pack/unpack
prendre le train to take the train
manquer le train to miss the train
monter dans le train/bus to get onto the train/bus
descendre du train/bus to get off the train/bus
c'est libre ? is this seat free?

IMPORTANT WORDS (*masculine*)

le	**chemin de fer**	railroad
le	**conducteur**	driver
le	**contrôleur**	conductor
un	**escalier roulant**	escalator
le	**pourboire**	tip
le	**tarif**	fare
le	**wagon-lit** (*pl* ~s~s)	sleeping car
le	**wagon-restaurant** (*pl* ~s~s)	dining car

USEFUL WORDS (*masculine*)

le	**chef de gare**	stationmaster
le	**chef de train**	conductor
le	**cheminot**	railroad worker
le	**coup de sifflet**	whistle
le	**déraillement**	derailment
un	**indicateur**	timetable
le	**passage à niveau**	grade crossing
les	**rails**	rails
le	**signal d'alarme**	alarm
le	**train de marchandises**	freight train
le	**trajet**	trip
le	**wagon**	railcar

USEFUL PHRASES

le train est en retard the train is late

un compartiment fumeur/non-fumeur a smoking/non-smoking
   compartment

"défense de se pencher au dehors" "do not lean out of the window"

IMPORTANT WORDS *(feminine)*

la	barrière	barrier
la	couchette	sleeping car
la	destination	destination
la	durée	length (of time)
la	frontière	border
la	portière	train door
la	SNCF	French Railways

USEFUL WORDS *(feminine)*

la	banquette	seat
la	carte d'abonnement	season ticket
la	carte jeune	young persons' discount card
une	étiquette	baggage label
la	locomotive	locomotive
la	malle	trunk
la	salle d'attente	waiting room
la	sonnette d'alarme	alarm
la	voie ferrée	(railroad) line *or* track

USEFUL PHRASES

je t'accompagnerai à la gare I'll go to the train station with you
je viendrai te chercher à la gare I'll come and pick you up at the train station
le train de 10 heures à destination de Paris/en provenance de Paris
the 10 a.m. train to/from Paris

ESSENTIAL WORDS (*masculine*)

un	arbre	tree
le	bois	wood

USEFUL WORDS (*masculine*)

un	abricotier	apricot tree
un	arbre fruitier	fruit tree
le	bouleau (*pl* -x)	birch
le	bourgeon	bud
le	buis	box (shrub)
le	buisson	bush
le	cerisier	cherry tree
le	châtaignier	chestnut tree
le	chêne	oak
un	érable	maple
le	feuillage	foliage
le	figuier	fig tree
le	frêne	ash
le	:hêtre	beech
le	:houx	holly
un	if	yew
le	marronnier	chestnut tree
le	noyer	walnut tree
un	oranger	orange tree
un	orme	elm
le	pêcher	peach tree
le	peuplier	poplar
le	pin	pine
le	platane	plane tree (*sycamore*)
le	poirier	pear tree
le	pommier	apple tree
le	rameau (*pl* -x)	branch
le	sapin	fir tree
le	saule pleureur	weeping willow
le	tilleul	lime tree
le	tronc	trunk
le	verger	orchard
le	vignoble	vineyard

ESSENTIAL WORDS *(feminine)*

la	**branche**	branch
la	**feuille**	leaf
la	**forêt**	forest

USEFUL WORDS *(feminine)*

	l'**aubépine**	hawthorn
la	**baie**	berry
	l'**écorce**	bark
la	**racine**	root

ESSENTIAL WORDS *(masculine)*

le	**champignon**	mushroom
le	**chou** *(pl* -x)	cabbage
le	**chou-fleur** *(pl* ~x~s)	cauliflower
le	**:haricot**	bean
le	**:haricot vert**	green bean
les	**légumes**	vegetables
un	**oignon** [ɔɲɔ̃]	onion
les	**petits pois**	peas

USEFUL WORDS *(masculine)*

	l'**ail** [aj]	garlic
un	**artichaut**	artichoke
le	**brocoli**	broccoli
le	**céléri**	celery
les	**choux de Bruxelles**	Brussels sprouts
le	**concombre**	cucumber
le	**cresson**	watercress
le	**maïs** [mais]	corn
les	**épinards**	spinach
le	**navet**	turnip
le	**persil** [pɛrsi]	parsley
le	**poireau** *(pl* -x)	leek
le	**poivron**	(sweet) pepper
le	**radis**	radish

USEFUL PHRASES
cultiver des légumes **to grow vegetables**
un épi de maïs **corn on the cob**

ESSENTIAL WORDS *(feminine)*

la	**carotte**	carrot
les	**crudités**	mixed raw vegetables
la	**pomme de terre**	potato
	(*pl* ~s de terre)	
la	**salade (verte)**	(green) salad
la	**tomate**	tomato

USESFUL WORDS *(feminine)*

les	**asperges**	asparagus
une	**aubergine**	eggplant
la	**betterave**	beet
la	**chicorée**	chicory
la	**courge**	squash
la	**courgette**	zucchini
une	**endive**	chicory
la	**laitue**	lettuce

USEFUL PHRASES

des carottes râpées **grated carrots**
biologique **organic**
végétarien(ne) **vegetarian**

ESSENTIAL WORDS *(masculine)*

	l'arrière	back
un	autobus	bus
un	autocar	coach
	l'avant	front
un	avion	plane
le	bateau *(pl -x)*	boat
le	bateau à rames/à voile	rowboat/sailboat
le	bus	bus
le	camion	truck
le	car	intercity bus
le	casque	helmet
le	ferry	ferry
un	hélicoptère	helicopter
un	hovercraft	hovercraft
le	métro	subway
le	mobile home	trailer, mobile home
le	moyen de transport	means of transportation
le	poids lourd	heavy load vehicle
le	prix du billet	fare
le	risque	risk
le	scooter	scooter
le	taxi	taxi
le	train	train
les	transports publics	public transportation
le	véhicule	vehicle
le	vélo	bike
le	vélomoteur	moped

USEFUL PHRASES

voyager to travel
il est allé à Paris en avion he flew to Paris
prendre le bus/le métro/le train to take the bus/the subway/the train
faire de la bicyclette to go cycling
on peut y aller en voiture you can go there by car

ESSENTIAL WORDS *(feminine)*

la	**bicyclette**	bicycle
la	**camionnette**	van
la	**caravane**	camping trailer
la	**distance**	distance
la	**moto**	motorbike
la	**voiture**	car

IMPORTANT WORDS *(feminine)*

une	**ambulance**	ambulance
la	**dépanneuse**	tow truck
la	**voiture de pompiers**	fire engine

USEFUL PHRASES

dépanner qn to repair sb's car
une voiture de location a rental car
une voiture de sport a sports car
une voiture de course a race car
une voiture de fonction a company car
"voitures d'occasion" "used cars"
démarrer to start, to move off

USEFUL WORDS (*masculine*)

un	aéroglisseur	hovercraft
le	bac	ferry
le	bateau-mouche (*pl* ~x~s)	tour boat in Paris
le	break [bʀɛk]	station wagon
le	bulldozer [buldozɛʀ]	bulldozer
le	camion-citerne (*pl* ~s~s)	tanker
le	canoë [kanɔe]	canoe
le	canot	rowboat
le	canot de sauvetage	lifeboat
le	char (d'assaut)	tank
le	cyclomoteur	moped
un	hydravion	seaplane
le	navire	ship
un	ovni (objet volant non identifié)	UFO (unidentified flying object)
le	paquebot	cruise ship
le	pétrolier	oil tanker (*ship*)
le	planeur	glider
le	porte-avions (*pl inv*)	aircraft carrier
le	remorqueur	tug
le	semi-remorque (*pl* ~s)	tractor-trailer, semi
le	sous-marin (*pl* ~s)	submarine
le	téléphérique	cable car
le	télésiège	chairlift
le	tram	streetcar, tram
le	vaisseau (*pl* -x)	vessel
le	vapeur	steamer
le	vélomoteur	moped
le	yacht [jɔt]	yacht

USEFUL WORDS *(feminine)*

la	camionnette de livraison	delivery van
la	charrette	cart
la	fusée	rocket
la	jeep	jeep
la	locomotive	locomotive
la	mobylette	moped
la	péniche	barge
la	remorque	trailer
la	soucoupe volante	flying saucer
la	vedette	speedboat
la	voiture d'enfant	baby carriage

ESSENTIAL WORDS (*masculine*)

	l'air	air
	l'automne	fall, autumn
le	brouillard	fog
le	bulletin de la météo	weather report
le	ciel	sky
le	climat	climate
le	degré	degree
	l'est	east
	l'été	summer
le	froid	cold
	l'hiver	winter
le	nord	north
le	nuage	cloud
	l'ouest	west
le	parapluie	umbrella
le	printemps	spring
le	soleil	sun; sunshine
le	sud	south
le	temps	weather
le	vent	wind

USEFUL PHRASES

quel temps fait-il ? what's the weather like?
il fait chaud/froid it's hot/cold
il fait beau it's a lovely day
il fait mauvais (temps) it's a horrible day
en plein air in the open air
il y a du brouillard it's foggy
30° à l'ombre 30° in the shade
écouter la météo or les prévisions to listen to the weather forecast
pleuvoir to rain
neiger to snow
il pleut it's raining
il neige it's snowing

ESSENTIAL WORDS *(feminine)*

la	**glace**	ice
la	**météo**	weather forecast
la	**neige**	snow
la	**pluie**	rain
la	**région**	region, area
la	**saison**	season
la	**température**	temperature

USEFUL PHRASES

le soleil brille the sun is shining
le vent souffle the wind is blowing
il gèle it's freezing
geler to freeze
fondre to melt
ensoleillé sunny
orageux(euse) stormy
pluvieux(euse) rainy
frais (fraîche) cool
variable changeable
humide humid
le ciel est couvert the sky is overcast

USEFUL WORDS *(masculine)*

un	**arc-en-ciel** *(pl* arcs-en-ciel)	rainbow
le	**baromètre**	barometer
le	**changement**	change
le	**chasse-neige** *(pl inv)*	snowplow
le	**clair de lune**	moonlight
le	**coucher de soleil**	sunset
le	**courant d'air**	draft
le	**crépuscule**	twilight
le	**dégel**	thaw
le	**déluge**	downpour
un	**éclair**	flash of lightning
le	**flocon de neige**	snowflake
le	**gel**	frost
le	**givre**	frost
le	**glaçon**	icicle
un	**orage**	thunderstorm
un	**ouragan**	hurricane
le	**paratonnerre**	lightning rod
le	**rayon de soleil**	ray of sunshine
le	**tonnerre**	thunder
le	**verglas**	black ice

IMPORTANT WORDS *(feminine)*

une	amélioration	improvement
une	averse	shower
la	chaleur	heat
une	éclaircie	sunny spell
la	fumée	smoke
la	poussière	dust
les	précipitations	rainfall
les	prévisions (météorologiques)	(weather) forecast
la	tempête	storm
la	visibilité	visibility

USEFUL WORDS *(feminine)*

l'	atmosphère	atmosphere
l'	aube	dawn
la	brise	breeze
la	brume	mist
la	canicule	heatwave
la	chute de neige	snowfall
la	congère	snowdrift
la	flaque d'eau	puddle
la	foudre	lightning
la	gelée	frost
la	goutte de pluie	raindrop
la	grêle	hail
une	inondation	flood
la	rafale	gust of wind
la	rosée	dew
la	sécheresse	drought
les	ténèbres	darkness
la	vague de chaleur	heatwave

ESSENTIAL WORDS (*masculine*)

le	bureau (*pl*-x)	office
le	dortoir	dormitory
le	drap	sheet
le	lit	bed
les	lits superposés	bunk beds
le	petit déjeuner	breakfast
le	repas	meal
le	séjour	stay
le	silence	silence
le	tarif	rate(s)
le	visiteur	visitor
les	WC	toilets

IMPORTANT WORDS (*masculine*)

le	guide	guidebook
le	linge	linens; laundry
le	règlement	rules
le	sac à dos	backpack
le	sac de couchage	sleeping bag

ESSENTIAL WORDS *(feminine)*

une	AJ	youth hostel
une	auberge de jeunesse	youth hostel
la	carte	map; card
la	cuisine	kitchen; cooking
la	douche	shower
la	nuit	night
la	poubelle	garbage can
la	salle à manger	dining room
la	salle de bains	bathroom
la	salle de jeux	game room
les	toilettes	toilets
les	vacances	vacation

IMPORTANT WORDS *(feminine)*

la	carte d'adhérent	membership card
la	randonnée	hike

USEFUL PHRASES

passer une nuit à l'auberge de jeunesse to spend a night at the youth hostel
je voudrais louer un sac de couchage I would like to rent a sleeping bag
il n'y a plus de place there's no more room

The vocabulary items on pages 648 to 677 have been grouped under parts of speech rather than topics because they can apply in a wide range of circumstances. Use them just as freely as the vocabulary already given.

CONJUNCTIONS

> **What is a conjunction?**
> A **conjunction** is a word such as *and*, *but*, *or*, *so*, *if*, and *because* that links two words or phrases, or two parts of a sentence, for example, *Diane* _and_ *I have been friends for years; I left* _because_ *I was bored.*

alors que while
aussi … que as … as
avant de + *infinitive* before
car because
cependant however
c'est-à-dire that is to say
comme as
comment how
depuis que since
dès que as soon as
donc so; then
et and
et alors ? so what!
lorsque when
maintenant que now (that)
mais but
ne … que only
ni … ni neither … nor

or now
ou or
ou … ou either … or
ou bien or
parce que because
pendant que while
pourquoi why
pourvu que + *subj* provided that, so long as
puisque since, because
quand when
que that; than
si if
sinon otherwise
tandis que while
tant que so long as
vu que in view of the fact that

ADJECTIVES

> **What is an adjective?**
> An **adjective** is a describing word that tells you more about a person
> or thing, such as their appearance, color, size, or other qualities,
> for example, *pretty*, *blue*, *big*.

abordable affordable

abrégé(e) shortened

absurde absurd

accueillant(e) welcoming

actif, active active

actuel(le) present

aérien(ne) aerial

affectueux(euse) affectionate

affreux(euse) dreadful

âgé(e) old

agité(e) restless; stormy (*sea*)

agréable pleasant

agricole agricultural

aigu, aiguë acute; piercing

aimable kind, nice

aîné(e) elder, eldest

amer, amère bitter

amoureux(euse) in love

amusant(e) entertaining

ancien(ne) old; former

animé(e) busy

annuel(le) annual

anonyme anonymous

anxieux(euse) anxious, worried

appliqué(e) diligent

apte capable

arrière: siège *m* **arrière** back seat

assis(e) sitting, seated

aucun(e) no, not any

automatique automatic

autre other

avant: siège *m* **avant** front seat

avantageux(euse) good value

barbu bearded

bas(se) low

beau (bel), belle beautiful

bête silly

bien fine, well; comfortable

bienvenu(e) welcome

bizarre strange, odd

blessé(e) injured

bon(ne) good

bon marché *inv* cheap

bordé(e) de lined with

bouillant(e) boiling

bouleversé(e) upset

bref, brève brief

brillant(e) bright, brilliant; shiny

bruyant(e) noisy

calme calm

capable capable

carré(e) square

catholique Catholic

célèbre famous

certain(e) sure

chaque each

chargé(e) de loaded with;
  responsible for

charmant(e) delightful
chaud(e) warm, hot
cher, chère dear; expensive
chic smart
choquant(e) shocking
chouette brilliant
chrétien(ne) Christian
clair(e) clear; light
classique classical
climatisé(e) air-conditioned
commode convenient
complet, complète complete; full
compliqué(e) complicated
composé(e) de comprising
compréhensif(ive) understanding
compris(e) understood; included
confortable comfortable
constipé(e) constipated
contemporain(e) contemporary
content(e) happy
continuel(le) continuing
convenable suitable
correct(e) correct
couché(e) lying down
courageux(euse) brave, courageous
court(e) short
couvert(e) de covered with
créé(e) created, established
cruel(le) cruel
cuit(e) cooked
culturel(le) cultural
curieux(euse) curious, strange
dangereux(euse) dangerous
debout standing (up)
décevant(e) disappointing

déchiré(e) torn
découragé(e) discouraged
déçu(e) disappointed
défendu(e) forbidden
dégoûté(e) disgusted
délicat(e) delicate
délicieux(euse) delicious
dernier, dernière last, latest
désagréable unpleasant
désert(e) deserted
désespéré(e) desperate
désolé(e) desolate, sorry
détestable ghastly
détruit(e) destroyed
différent(e) different
difficile difficult
digne worthy
direct(e) direct
disponible available
distingué(e) distinguished
distrait(e) absentminded
divers(e) different
divertissant(e) entertaining
divin(e) divine
divisé(e) divided
doré(e) golden; gilt
doux, douce gentle; sweet; soft
droit(e) straight; right(hand)
drôle funny
dur(e) hard
économique economic; economical
effrayé(e) frightened
égal(e) equal; even
électrique electric
élégant(e) elegant
élevé(e) high; **bien élevé(e)**

well-mannered

embêtant(e) annoying

enchanté(e) delighted

énervé(e) irritated; nervous

ennuyé(e) bothered

ennuyeux(euse) boring

énorme huge

ensoleillé(e) sunny

entendu(e) agreed

entier, entière whole

épais(se) thick

épouvantable terrible

épuisé(e) exhausted

essentiel(le) essential

essoufflé(e) out of breath

étendu(e) stretched out

étonnant(e) astonishing

étonné(e) astonished

étrange strange

étranger, étrangère foreign

étroit(e) narrow

éveillé(e) awake

évident(e) obvious

exact(e) exact

excellent(e) excellent

expérimenté(e) experienced

extraordinaire extraordinary

fâché(e) angry

facile easy

faible weak

fatigant(e) tiring

fatigué(e) tired

faux, fausse false, wrong

favori(te) favorite

fermé(e) closed

féroce fierce

fier, fière proud

fin(e) fine; thin

final(e) final

fondé(e) founded

formidable tremendous

fort(e) strong; hard

fou, folle mad

fragile fragile; frail

frais, fraîche fresh, cool

froid(e) cold

furieux(euse) furious

futur(e) future

gai(e) cheerful

gauche left(hand)

général(e) general

généreux(euse) generous

génial(e) brilliant

gentil(le) kind, nice

gonflé(e) swollen

gracieux(euse) graceful

grand(e) big; tall

gratuit(e) free

grave serious

gros(se) big; fat

habile skilful

habitué(e) à used to

habituel(le) usual

haut(e) high; tall

heureux(euse) happy

historique historical

honnête honest

identique identical

illuminé(e) lit; floodlit

illustré(e) illustrated

imaginaire imaginary

immense huge

immobile motionless
important(e) important
impossible impossible
impressionnant(e) impressive
imprévu(e) unforeseen
inattendu(e) unexpected
incapable(de) incapable (of)
inconnu(e) unknown
incroyable unbelievable
indispensable indispensable
industriel(le) industrial
inondé(e) flooded
inquiet, inquiète worried
insouciant(e) carefree
insupportable unbearable
intelligent(e) intelligent
interdit(e) prohibited
intéressant(e) interesting
interminable endless
international(e) international
interrompu(e) interrupted
inutile useless
irrité(e) annoyed
isolé(e) isolated
jeune young
jaloux(ouse) jealous
joli(e) pretty
joyeux(euse) merry, cheerful
juif, juive Jewish
juste just; correct
lâche cowardly
laid(e) ugly
large wide; broad
léger, légère light
lent(e) slow
leur/leurs their

libre free
local(e) local
long(ue) long
lourd(e) heavy
magique magical
magnifique magnificent
maigre thin
malade sick
malheureux(euse) unhappy,
   unfortunate
malhonnête dishonest
mauvais(e) bad
mécanique mechanical
méchant(e) naughty
mécontent(e) unhappy
médical(e) medical
meilleur(e) better, best
même same
merveilleux(euse) marvelous
militaire military
minable pathetic
mince slim
mobile mobile; moving; movable
moche ugly
moderne modern
moindre least
mon/ma/mes my
montagneux(euse) mountainous
mort(e) dead
mouillé(e) wet
mouvementé(e) lively
moyen(ne) average
mû, mue (par) moved (by)
multicolore multicolored
muni(e) de provided with
municipal(e) municipal, town

mûr(e) ripe
musclé(e) muscular
musical(e) musical
musulman(e) Muslim
mystérieux(euse) mysterious
natal(e) native
national(e) national
naturel(le) natural
né(e) born
nécessaire necessary
négatif(ive) negative
nerveux(euse) nervous
net(te) clear
neuf, neuve new
nombreux(euse) numerous
normal(e) normal
notre/nos our
nouveau (nouvel), nouvelle new
noyé(e) drowned
obligatoire compulsory
obligé(e) de obliged to
occupé(e) taken; busy; engaged
officiel(le) official
ordinaire ordinary
original(e) original
orné(e) de decorated with
outré(e) outraged
ouvert(e) open
paisible peaceful
pâle pale
pareil(le) similar, same
paresseux(euse) lazy
parfait(e) perfect
particulier, particulière particular; private
passionnant(e) exciting

passionné(e) passionate
patient(e) patient
pauvre poor
pénible painful
permanent(e) permanent
perpétuel(le) perpetual
personnel(le) personal
petit(e) small, little
pittoresque picturesque
plat(e) flat
plein(e) (de) full (of)
plusieurs several
pneumatique inflatable
poli(e) polite; polished
populaire popular
portatif(ive) portable
positif(ive) positive
possible possible
pratique practical; handy
précédent(e) previous
précieux(euse) precious
précis(e) precise
préféré(e) favorite
premier, première first
pressant(e) urgent
pressé(e): être pressé(e) to be in a hurry
prêt(e) ready
primaire primary
privé(e) private
privilégié(e) privileged
prochain(e) next
proche nearby; close
profond(e) deep
propre own; clean
protestant(e) Protestant

prudent(e) cautious
public, publique public
publicitaire advertising, promotional
quel(le) what
quelque(s) some
rafraîchissant(e) refreshing
rangé(e): bien rangé(e) neat and tidy·
rapide fast
rare rare
ravi(e) delighted
récent(e) recent
reconnaissant(e) grateful
rectangulaire rectangular
réel(le) real
religieux(euse) religious
réservé(e) reserved
responsable (de) responsible (for)
rêveur(euse) dreamy
riche rich
ridicule ridiculous
rond(e) round
rusé(e) cunning
sage well-behaved; wise
sain et sauf safe and sound
sale dirty
sanitaire sanitary
satisfait(e) (de) satisfied (with)
sauvage wild
scolaire school (*year etc*)
sec, sèche dry
second(e) second
secondaire secondary
secret, secrète secret
semblable similar

sensible sensitive
sérieux(euse) serious
serré(e) tight
seul(e) alone
sévère severe
simple simple
sincère sincere
sinistre sinister
situé(e) situated
social(e) social
solennel(le) solemn
solide solid
sombre dark
son/sa/ses his, her, its, one's
soudain(e) sudden
souriant(e) smiling
sous-marin(e) underwater
spécial(e) special
suivant(e) following
suivi(e) de followed by
super super
superbe magnificent
supérieur(e) upper; advanced
supplémentaire extra
sûr(e) sure
surprenant(e) surprising
sympa(thique) nice, likeable
technique technical
tel(le) such
temporaire temporary
terrible terrible
théâtral(e) theatrical
tiède lukewarm
timide shy
ton/ta/tes your
touristique tourist (*area etc*)

tout/toute/toutes all
traditionnel(le) traditional
tranquille quiet, peaceful
trempé soaked
triste sad
troublé(e) disturbed
typique typical
uni(e) plain
unique only; unique
urbain(e) urban
urgent(e) urgent
utile useful
valable valid

varié(e) varied; various
vaste vast
véritable real
vide empty
vieux (vieil), vieille old
vif, vive bright
vilain(e) naughty; ugly; nasty
violent(e) violent
vivant(e) alive; lively
voisin(e) neighboring
votre/vos your
vrai(e) real, true

ADVERBS AND PREPOSITIONS

What is an adverb?
An **adverb** is a word used with verbs to give information on where, when or how an action takes place, for example, *here*, *today*, *quickly*. An adverb can also add information to adjectives and other adverbs, for example, *extremely quick*, *very quickly*.

What is a preposition?
A **preposition** is one word such as *at*, *for*, *with*, *into*, or *from*, or words such as *in front of* or *near to*, which are usually followed by a noun or a pronoun.

Prepositions show how people and things relate to the rest of the sentence, for example, *She's at home; It's for you; You'll get into trouble; It's in front of you*.

à to, at
abord: d'abord first, at first;
  tout d'abord first of all;
  aux abords de alongside
absolument absolutely
actuellement at present
admirablement admirably
afin de so as to
ailleurs elsewhere;
  d'ailleurs moreover
ainsi thus;
  ainsi que as well as
alors then
anxieusement anxiously
après after;
  après-demain the day after
  tomorrow;
  d'après according to
assez fairly, quite;

assez de enough
aujourd'hui today
auparavant previously
auprès de next to
aussi also, too; as
aussitôt at once
autant (de) as much; as many;
  d'autant plus (que) all the more
  (since)
autour (de) around
autrefois formerly
autrement otherwise; differently;
  autrement dit in other words;
autrement que other than
avance: à l'avance in advance;
  d'avance in advance
avant (de) before
avec with
bas: en bas downstairs, at the bottom

beaucoup a lot; much;
 beaucoup de a lot of; many
bien well;
 bien entendu of course
bientôt soon
bord: à bord (de) on board;
 au bord de beside
bout: au bout de after; at the end of
bref in short
brusquement suddenly
cependant however
certainement certainly
chez at (or to) the house;
 chez moi/toi/lui/elle
 at my/your/his/her house
combien (de) how much,
 how many
comme as, like;
 comme d'habitude as usual;
 comme toujours as usual
comment how
complètement completely
compris: y compris including
conséquent: par conséquent
 as a result
continuellement continually
contraire: au contraire on the
 contrary
contre against;
 ci-contre opposite;
 par contre on the other hand
côté: à côté de next to, beside;
 de ce côté (de) on this side (of);
 de l'autre côté (de) on the other
 side (of);
 juste à côté next door
couramment fluently

cours: au cours de during
dans in, into
davantage (de) more
de of, from
debout standing
dedans inside
dehors outside
déjà already
demain tomorrow;
 après-demain the day after
 tomorrow
depuis since, for
derrière behind
dès from; dès que as soon as
dessous underneath;
 ci-dessous below;
 en-dessous de below
dessus on top;
 au-dessus (de) above;
 ci-dessus above
devant in front (of)
doucement gently
droit: tout droit straight (on)
droite: à droite on the right,
 to the right
dur hard
effet: en effet indeed
également also; equally
encore still; again;
 encore une fois once again
enfin at last
énormément (de) a lot (of)
ensemble together
ensuite then
entièrement entirely
entre between
environ about

éventuellement possibly
évidemment obviously
exactement exactly
exprès on purpose
extérieur: à l'extérieur (de) outside
extrêmement extremely
face à faced with;
  en face (de) opposite
facilement easily
façon: de façon à so as to
fidèlement faithfully
finalement in the end; after all
fort hard
franchement frankly
gauche: à gauche on the left,
  to the left
général: en général usually
généralement generally
gentiment nicely
grâce à thanks to
gravement gravely; seriously
guère: ne ... guère hardly
habitude: d'habitude usually;
  comme d'habitude as usual
hasard: par hasard by chance;
  au hasard at random
haut: en haut (de) at the top (of);
  de haut en bas from top to bottom
heure: à l'heure on time;
  de bonne heure early
heureusement fortunately
hier yesterday;
  avant-hier the day before
  yesterday
ici here
immédiatement immediately
importe: n'importe où anywhere

intellectuellement intellectually
intérieur: à l'intérieur (de) inside
jadis formerly, once
jamais ever;
  ne ... jamais never
jusque: jusqu'à until;
  jusqu'ici so far, until now;
  jusque-là until then
justement exactly
là there; là-bas over there;
  là-haut up there
légèrement slightly
lendemain:
  le lendemain the next day;
  le lendemain matin the next
  morning
lentement slowly
loin (de) far (from)
long: le long de along
longtemps for a long time
lourdement heavily
maintenant now
mal badly
malgré in spite of
malheureusement unfortunately
manuellement manually
maximum: au maximum
  at the maximum
même same; even;
  même pas not even;
  quand même even so
mentalement mentally
mieux better; le mieux best
milieu: au milieu de in the middle of
moins less, minus;
  moins de less than, fewer than;
  au moins at least;

du moins at least

mystérieusement mysteriously

naturellement of course, naturally

nerveusement nervously

normalement normally

notamment especially

nouveau: de nouveau again

nulle part nowhere

ne ... nullement in no way

où where;

  n'importe où anywhere

outre: en outre furthermore

paisiblement peacefully

par by; through;

  par terre on the ground;

  par-dessous under;

  par-dessus over

parfaitement perfectly

parfois sometimes

parmi among

part: à part apart (from);

  nulle part nowhere;

  quelque part somewhere

particulier: en particulier
in particular

particulièrement particularly

partiellement partially

partir: à partir de from

partout everywhere

pas: pas du tout not at all;

  pas loin de not far from;

  pas mal de a lot of

patiemment patiently

peine: à peine scarcely, hardly,
barely

pendant during, for

peu: peu à peu little by little;

à peu près about, approximately

peut-être perhaps, maybe

poliment politely

plus [plys]:

  deux plus deux two plus two;

  en plus moreover;

  de plus moreover;

  de plus en plus [dəplyzãply] more
and more;

plus [ply]:

  plus de (pommes) no more
(apples);

  plus de (dix) more than (ten);

  ne ... plus no more, no longer;

  plus tard later;

  non plus neither, either;

  moi non plus ! me neither!

plutôt rather

pour for; in order to

pourtant yet, nevertheless

près de near

présent: à présent at present

presque almost, nearly

proximité: à proximité de
near to

puis then

quand when;

  quand même however, even so,
nevertheless

quant à (moi) as for (me)

quelquefois sometimes

quelque part somewhere

rapidement quickly

rarement rarely

récemment recently

régulièrement regularly

retard: en retard late

sans without;
   sans cesse incessantly
sauf except
selon according to
sérieusement seriously
seulement only
simplement simply
soigneusement carefully
soudain suddenly
sous under
souvent often
sur on
sûrement certainly
sur-le-champ at once
surtout especially
tant de so much, so many
tard late;
   plus tard later;
   trop tard too late
tellement so; so much
temps: de temps en temps
   from time to time;
   de temps à autre from time to
   time;

en même temps at the same time
tôt early;
   trop tôt too soon, too early;
   le plus tôt possible as soon as
   possible
toujours always; still
tout: en tout in all;
   tout d'abord first of all;
   tout à coup suddenly;
   tout à fait completely, quite;
   tout près (de) very near;
   tout de suite at once
travers: à travers through
très very
trop too; too much;
   trop de too much, too many
uniquement only
un à un one by one
vers towards; about (of time)
vite quickly, fast
vraiment really
y there, to that place, in that place

SOME EXTRA NOUNS

> **What is a noun?**
> A **noun** is a naming word for a living being, a thing, or an idea,
> for example, *woman, Andrew, desk, happiness.*

un accent accent
un accord agreement
un accueil reception
une action action
une activité activity
les affaires *fpl* things
l'âge *m* age
l'air *m* air
une ambition ambition
une âme soul
un ami friend
une amie friend
l'amour *m* love
l'angoisse *f* anguish, distress
une annonce advertisement
une antenne parabolique
  satellite dish
l'argent *m* silver; money
l'arrière *m* back, rear
un article article
l'attention *f* attention;
  à l'attention de for the attention of
un attrait attraction
un avantage advantage
une aventure adventure
un avis notice; opinion;
  à mon avis in my opinion
le bain bath
la barrière gate; fence
la bataille battle

le bâton stick
la beauté beauty
la bêtise stupidity
le bien good
la bise kiss
le bonheur happiness
le bonhomme de neige snowman
la boue mud
la bousculade bustle
le bout end, ending
la brochure brochure
le bruit noise
le budget budget
le but aim; goal
le calme peace, calm
le candidat candidate
le canif penknife
le caractère character, nature
la carte d'identité ID card
le cas case; **en cas de** in case of;
  en tout cas in any case
la catastrophe disaster
le/la catholique Catholic
la cause cause;
  à cause de because of
le centimètre centimeter
le centre center
le cercle circle
le chagrin distress
la chance luck

la chapelle chapel
le chapitre chapter
le charme charm
le chef boss
le chiffre figure
le choix choice
la chose thing
le/la chrétien(ne) Christian
le chuchotement whispering
la civilisation civilization
le classement classification
la cloche bell
le clocher steeple
le coin corner
la colère anger
la colonne column
le commencement beginning
la compagne companion
le compagnon companion
la comparaison comparison
le compte calculation
la confiance confidence
le confort comfort
la conscience conscience
le conseil advice
la construction construction
le contraire the opposite
la copie copy
la corbeille basket
la corde rope
le/la correspondant(e)
  correspondent
le côté side
le coup blow, bang, knock
le courage courage, bravery
le cours course, lesson

la coutume custom
le couvent convent
la crainte fear
le cri cry
le croix cross
la cuisine kitchen; cuisine
la culture culture
le curé vicar, priest
la curiosité curiosity
le danger danger
les débris mpl wreckage
le début beginning
la décision decision
les dégâts mpl damage
le délai time limit
le déodorant deodorant
le désarmement disarmament
le désastre disaster
le désavantage disadvantage
le désir wish
le désordre disorder
le destin destiny
le détail detail
la détresse distress
Dieu God
la différence difference;
  quelle est la différence
  entre X et Y? what is the difference
  between X and Y?
la difficulté difficulty
la dimension dimension
la direction direction
la discipline discipline
la dispute argument
la distance distance
le distributeur dispenser
le documentaire documentary

la **documentation** documentation
le **doute** doubt;
   sans doute no doubt; probably
le **drapeau** flag
le **droit** right
la **droite** the right
la **durée** time
un **échange** exchange;
   en échange de in exchange for
une **échelle** ladder
l'**économie** f economy; saving
un **effet** effect
un **effort** effort
un **électeur** elector
une **élection** election
l'**élégance** f elegance
un **endroit** place
l'**énergie** f energy
l'**enfance** f childhood
un **ennemi** enemy
l'**ennui** m boredom; problem
une **enseigne** sign
un **ensemble** group
l'**enthousiasme** m enthusiasm
un **entretien** conversation;
   interview
les **environs** mpl surrounding
   district
l'**épaisseur** f thickness
une **erreur** mistake
l'**espace** m space
une **espèce** sort; species;
   en espèces in cash
un **espoir** hope
l'**essentiel** m the main thing
une **étape** stage, step; stop
un **état** state

l'**étendue** f extent
une **étoile** star
l'**étonnement** m astonishment
un **événement** event
un **excès** excess
un **exemple** example;
   par exemple for example
l'**exil** m exile
une **expérience** experience;
   experiment
un **expert** expert
une **explication** explanation
une **exposition** exhibition
un **extrait** extract
la **fabrication**
la **façon** way;
   de cette façon in this way
le **fait** fact
la **famille** family
la **fanfare** brass band; fanfare
la **faute** fault;
   c'est de ma faute it's my fault
la **fermeture** closure
le **feu** fire
la **fin** end
la **flèche** arrow
la **foi** faith
la **fois** time
la **folie** madness
le **fond** background; bottom
la **force** strength
la **forme** shape
la **foule** crowd
la **fraîcheur** freshness
les **frais** mpl expenses
la **gaieté, la gaîté** gaiety
la **gauche** the left

le gaz gas
le genre type, kind, sort
la gentillesse kindness
le goût taste; chacun son goût
   each to his own
le gouvernement government
la grandeur size
le gros lot first prize
le groupe group
la guerre war
le guide guide
une habileté f skill
une habitude habit
l'harmonie f harmony
le :haut-parleur
   (pl haut-parleurs) loudspeaker
la :hauteur height
l'honneur m honor
les honoraires mpl fees
la :honte shame
l'humeur f mood
l'humour f humor
l'hygiène f hygiene
une idée idea
un/une idiot(e) idiot
une image picture
l'imagination f imagination
un/une imbécile idiot
un/une immigré(e) immigrant
l'importance f importance
une impression impression
un/une inconnu(e) stranger
un inconvénient disadvantage
les informations fpl news
un inspecteur inspector
les instructions fpl instructions

l'intérêt m interest
une interruption break,
   interruption
une interview interview
une invitation invitation
la jalousie jealousy
la joie joy
le jouet toy
le jour day
le journal (pl journaux) newspaper
le/la juif, (juive) Jew
la largeur width
la larme tear
le lecteur reader
la légende legend, caption
le lever de soleil sunrise
le lieu place;
   au lieu de instead of
la ligne line
la limite boundary, limit
la liste list
la littérature literature
la location rental
le loisir leisure
la longueur length
la Loterie nationale National
   Lottery
la lumière light
la lune moon
la lutte struggle
le machin thing, contraption
le magazine magazine
la malchance bad luck
le malheur misfortune
la manière way
le manque (de) lack (of)

le **maximum** maximum
le **mélange** mixture
le **membre** member
la **mémoire** memory
le **mensonge** lie
la **messe** mass
la **méthode** method
le **mieux** best
le **milieu** middle
le **minimum** minimum
le **Ministère de** the Ministry of
le **mot** word; message
le **moyen (de)** the means (of);
　au **moyen de** by means of
le/la **musulman(e)** Muslim
le **mystère** mystery
le **niveau** (*pl* -x) level
le **nom** name
le **nombre** number
la **nourriture** food
la **nouvelle** (piece of) news
une **objection** objection
un **objet** object
l'**obscurité** *f* darkness
une **observation** remark
une **occasion** opportunity;
　occasion
les **œuvres** *fpl* works
une **ombre** shadow
une **opinion** opinion
un **ordre** order
l'**orgueil** *m* pride
l'**ouverture** *f* opening
la **page** page
la **paire** pair
la **paix** peace

le **panier** basket
le **panneau** (*pl* -x) sign, notice
le **pari** bet
la **parole** word
la **part** part; **de la part de** from
la **partie** part
le **pas** footstep
la **patience** patience
le **pays** country
la **peine** difficulty; sentence
la **pensée** thought
la **permission** permission
la **perruque** wig
la **personne** person
le **pétrole** oil, petroleum; kerosene
le **peuple** nation
la **phrase** sentence
la **pièce (de 10 centimes)**
　(10-centime) coin
la **pile** battery
la **plaisanterie** joke
le **plaisir** pleasure
le **plan** plan; map;
　au **premier plan** in the foreground;
　à l'**arrière plan** in the background
le **plateau** (*pl* -x) tray; plateau
la **plupart de** most (of)
le **poids** weight
le **point** point, mark; period
le **point de vue** point of view
la **politesse** politeness
la **politique** politics
le **pont** bridge, deck
portée: à portée de la main
　within arm's reach
le **portrait** portrait

la **position** position
la **possibilité** possibility,
 opportunity
la **poupée** doll
la **poussière** dust
le **pouvoir** power
les **préparatifs** *mpl* preparations
la **préparation** preparation
la **présence** presence
le **pressentiment** feeling
le **principe** principle;
 en **principe** in principle
le **problème** problem
le **produit** product; produce
la **profondeur** depth
le **projet** plan
la **propreté** cleanliness
la **prospérité** prosperity
les **provisions** provisions
la **prudence** caution
la **publicité** publicity
la **qualité** quality
la **question** question
la **queue** tail
le **raccourci** shortcut
la **raison** reason
le **rapport** connection
la **reine** queen
la **religion** religion
les **remerciements** *mpl* thanks
le **remue-ménage** commotion
la **rencontre** meeting
le **rendez-vous** appointment
les **renseignements** *mpl*
 information
la **réponse** reply

la **reprise** resumption
la **réputation** reputation
le **rescapé** survivor
le **réseau** (*pl* -x) network
la **résolution** resolution
le **respect** respect
les **restes** *mpl* remains
le **résultat** result
le **résumé** summary
le **retour** return;
 de **retour** back
la **réussite** success
le **rêve** dream
la **révolution** revolution
le **roi** king
le **ruisseau** stream
le **rythme** rhythm
la **saleté** dirtiness
le **salon de beauté** beauty salon
le **sang-froid** calm
le **sanglot** sob
le **schéma** diagram
le **seau** pail
le **secours** help
le **secret** secret
la **section** section
la **sécurité** security
le **séjour** stay
la **sélection** selection
la **semaine** week
le **sens** sense
la **sensation** feeling
la **série** series
le **service** service;
 de **service** on duty
le **signe** sign

le **silence** silence
la **situation** situation
la **société** society
la **solution** solution
la **somme** sum
le **son** sound
le **sort** fate
la **sorte** sort, kind
le **soupçon** suspicion
le **sourire** smile
le **souvenir** souvenir; memory
le **spectateur** spectator
le/la **stagiaire** trainee
le **style** style
le **succès** success
la **sueur** sweat
le **sujet** subject;
　au **sujet de** about
la **surprise** surprise
la **surveillance** supervision; watch
le **système** system
la **tache** stain
la **tâche** task
le **talent** talent
le **tas** heap, pile
le **taux de change** exchange rate
la **taxe** tax
le **téléscope** telescope
le/la **téléspectateur(trice)** viewer
la **tentative** attempt

le **terme** term, expression
le **texte** text
la **théorie** theory
la **timidité** shyness
le **tour** turn; trick; **c'est ton tour**
　it's your turn
le **tournoi** tournament
la **tragédie** tragedy
le **traitement** treatment; salary
le **transistor** transistor
le **tremblement de terre**
　earthquake
la **tristesse** sadness
le **tube** tube; hit song
le **type** type; guy
le **va-et-vient** coming and going
la **valeur** value
la **vapeur** steam
la **veine** luck
la **version** version
le **verso** back (of page)
la **victoire** victory
la **vie** life
les **vœux** *mpl* wishes
le **voyage** journey
la **vue** view; **de vue** by sight;
　en vue de with a view to

VERBS

> **What is a verb?**
> A **verb** is a word which describes what somebody or something does, what they are, or what happens to them, for example, *play, be, disappear.*

abandonner to abandon
abîmer to spoil, to damage
aboutir to end
s'abriter to shelter
accepter to accept
accompagner to go with
accomplir to accomplish
s'accoutumer à to become
  accustomed to
accrocher to hang (up); to catch
  (*à* on)
accueillir to welcome
accuser to accuse
acheter to buy
achever to finish
admettre to admit
admirer to admire
adorer to adore
s'adresser à to apply to; to speak to
afficher to display
affirmer to maintain, to assert
agacer to irritate
agir to act, to behave;
  il s'agit de it is a question of
s'agrandir to grow
aider qn à to help sb to
aimer to like, to love;
  aimer bien to like;
  aimer mieux to prefer

ajouter to add
aller to go;
  aller chercher qn to go and meet sb;
s'en aller to go away
allumer to switch on; to light
amener to bring
s'amuser to enjoy oneself
annoncer to announce
annuler to cancel
s'apercevoir de to notice
appartenir (à) to belong (to)
appeler to call;
  s'appeler to be called
apporter to bring
apprécier to appreciate
apprendre (à faire) to pretend
  (to do sth)
apprendre qch à qn to teach sb sth
s'approcher de to approach
approuver to approve
appuyer to press;
  s'appuyer to lean
arracher to pull out; to snatch;
  to tear
s'arranger: cela
  s'arrangera it will be all right
arrêter to stop; to arrest;
  s'arrêter to stop
arriver to arrive; to happen
s'asseoir to sit down

assister à to attend, to be
  present at, to go to

assurer to assure; to insure

attacher to tie, to fasten

attaquer to attack

atteindre to reach

attendre to wait (for)

attirer to attract

attraper to catch

augmenter to increase

(s')avancer to go forward

avoir to have;
  avoir l'air to seem;
  avoir besoin de to need;
  avoir chaud/froid to be hot/cold;
  avoir envie de to want to; avoir
  l'habitude de to be in the habit of;
  avoir honte (de) to be ashamed (of);
  avoir l'intention de to intend to;
  avoir lieu to take place;
  avoir du mal à to have difficulty in;
  en avoir marre to be fed up;
  avoir peur to be afraid;
  avoir raison/tort to be
  right/wrong

avouer to confess

baisser to lower

balbutier to stammer

barrer to block

bâtir to build

battre to beat;
  se battre to fight

bavarder to chat

bloquer to block

bouger to move

bouleverser to upset

bricoler to putter about,

to do odd jobs

briller to shine

briser to break

brûler to burn

(se) cacher to hide

(se) calmer to calm down

casser to break

causer to cause; to chat

cesser (de) to stop

changer to change;
  changer d'avis to change one's
  mind

chanter to sing

charger to load

chasser to chase (off);
  to get rid of

chauffer to heat up

chercher to look for

choisir to choose

chuchoter to whisper

circuler to move

cirer to polish

cocher to tick

collaborer to collaborate

collectionner to collect

coller to stick

commander to order

commencer (à) to begin (to)

compenser to compensate for

comporter to comprise

composer to compose; to make up;
  to dial

composter to date-stamp;
  to punch

comprendre to understand

compter to count; to intend to

concerner to concern

conclure to conclude
condamner to condemn;
  to sentence
conduire to drive;
  se conduire to behave
confectionner to make
confirmer to confirm
connaître to know
consacrer to devote
conseiller to advise
conserver to keep
considérer to consider
consister to consist
consommer to consume
constater to establish
constituer to make up
construire to build
consulter to consult
contacter to get in touch with
contempler to contemplate
contenir to contain
continuer to continue
convenir to be suitable
copier to copy
corriger to correct
se coucher to go to bed;
  to lie down
coudre to sew
couler to flow
couper to cut (off)
courir to run
coûter to cost
couvrir to cover
craindre to fear
créer to create
creuser to dig
crier to shout

critiquer to criticize
croire to believe
cueillir to pick
cultiver to grow
danser to dance
se débrouiller to manage
décevoir to disappoint
déchirer to tear
décider (de) to decide (to);
  se décider (à) to make up one's
  mind (to)
déclarer to declare
découper to cut up
se décourager to become
  discouraged
découvrir to discover
décrire to describe
défendre to forbid; to defend
dégager to clear
se déguiser to dress up
demander to ask;
  demander à qn de faire qch to ask
  sb to do sth;
  se demander to wonder
demeurer to live
démolir to demolish
dépasser to overtake
se dépêcher to hurry
dépendre de to depend on
déplaire: cela me déplaît
  I don't like it
déposer to put down
déranger to disturb
désapprouver to disapprove of
descendre to come or go down;
  to get off; to take down
déshabiller to undress

désirer to desire, to want
désobéir to disobey
dessiner to draw
détester to hate
détourner to divert
détruire to destroy
développer to develop
devenir to become
deviner to guess
devoir to have to (*must*)
différer (de) to be different (from)
diminuer to reduce
dire to say, to tell
diriger to direct;
  se diriger vers to go towards
discuter to discuss
disparaître to disappear
se disputer to argue
distinguer to distinguish
distribuer to distribute
diviser to divide
dominer to dominate
donner to give
donner sur to overlook
dormir to sleep
se doucher to take a shower
douter (de) to doubt
dresser to set up;
  se dresser to stand (up)
durer to last
échanger to exchange
s'échapper (de) to escape (from)
éclairer to light (up)
éclater de rire to burst out laughing
économiser to save
écouter to listen (to)

écraser to crush;
  s'écraser to crash
s'écrier to cry out
écrire to write;
  s'écrire to write to each other;
  ça s'écrit comment ? how do you spell it?
effacer to erase
effectuer to carry out
effrayer to frighten
s'élancer to rush forward
élever to erect; to bring up;
  s'élever to rise
emballer to wrap (up)
embrasser to kiss
emmener to take
empêcher (de) to prevent (from)
employer to use
emporter to take
emprunter qch à qn to borrow sth from sb
encourager qn à faire encourage sb to do
s'endormir to fall asleep
enfermer to imprison
s'enfuir to flee
enlever to take away; to take off
s'ennuyer to be bored
enregistrer to record
entasser to stack
entendre to hear;
  qu'entendez-vous par... ? what do you mean by ...?;
  entendre parler de to hear about;
  s'entendre to agree
entourer (de) to surround (with)
entrer (dans) to go *or* come in(to)

envahir to invade
envelopper to wrap (up)
envoyer to send
épeler to spell
éprouver to experience
espérer to hope
essayer (de faire qch) to try
  (to do sth)
essuyer to wipe
établir to establish, to set up
étaler to spread out
éteindre to put out; to switch off
s'étendre to stretch out
étonner to astonish;
  s'étonner to be astonished
étouffer to suffocate
être to be;
  être d'accord to agree;
  être assis(e) to be sitting;
  être obligé(e) de to be obliged to;
  être sur le point de to be just
    about to;
  être de retour to be back;
  être en train de faire qch to be
    doing sth
étudier to study
(s')éveiller to wake up
éviter (de faire) to avoid (doing)
exagérer to exaggerate
examiner to examine
s'excuser (de) to apologize (for)
exister to exist
expliquer to explain
exprimer to express
fabriquer to make
se fâcher to become angry
faillir: il a failli tomber

he almost fell
faire to do; to make;
  faire attention to be careful;
  faire la bise à qn to kiss sb on the
    cheek;
  faire chaud/froid to be hot/cold;
  faire la connaissance de to meet;
  faire entrer quelqu'un to let
    somebody in;
  se faire couper les cheveux
    to have one's hair cut;
  faire halte to stop;
  faire du mal (à) to harm;
  faire partie de to belong to;
  faire la queue to queue;
  faire de son mieux (pour) to do
    one's best (to);
  faire une promenade to go for a
    walk;
  faire semblant de to pretend to;
  faire signe to signal, to wave; **faire
    un stage** to go on a training course
falloir to be necessary;
  il faut one must
féliciter to congratulate
fermer to close, to shut;
  fermer à clef to lock
figurer to imagine
finir to finish
fixer to stare at; to fix
flâner to stroll
fonctionner to work;
  faire fonctionner to operate
former to form
fouiller to search
fournir to provide
frapper to hit, to knock
fréquenter to frequent; to see

gagner to win; to earn
garantir to guarantee
garder to keep
gâter to spoil;
  se gâter to go wrong
gémir to groan
gêner to bother
glisser to slip, to slide
gratter to scratch
grimper to climb
guetter to watch
habiter to live (in);
  s'habituer à to get used to
hésiter to hesitate
heurter to bump into
ignorer not to know
imaginer to imagine
imprimer to print
indiquer qch à qn to inform sb
  of sth
s'inquiéter to worry
inscrire to write down;
  s'inscrire to register
installer to put in;
  s'installer to settle
s'instruire to educate oneself
insulter to insult
interdire to prohibit;
  "interdit de fumer"
  "no smoking"
intéresser to interest;
  s'intéresser à qch to be interested
  in sth
interroger to question
interrompre to interrupt
interviewer to interview
introduire to introduce

inventer to invent
inviter to invite
jeter to throw (away)
joindre to join
jurer to swear
laisser to leave; to let; to allow;
  laisser tomber to drop
lancer to throw
(se) laver to wash
lever to lift; to raise;
  se lever to get up; to stand up
lire to read
loger (chez) to live (with)
louer to hire, to rent
lutter to struggle
manœuvrer to operate
manquer to miss; to be lacking
marcher to walk; to work
se marier (avec qn) to marry (sb)
marquer to mark; to write down;
  to score
mêler to mix; se mêler (à qch)
  to get involved (in sth)
menacer to threaten
mener to lead
mentir to lie
mériter to deserve
mesurer to measure
mettre to put (on); to take;
  mettre qch au point to finalize
  sth; to perfect sth;
  mettre qn à la porte to throw
  sb out;
  se mettre à l'abri to take shelter;
  se mettre en colère to get angry;
  se mettre en route to set off
monter to come or go up;

to get into
montrer to show
se moquer de to make fun of
mordre to bite
multiplier to multiply
noter to write down; to mark
nourrir to feed
obliger qn à faire to force sb to do
observer to observe; to keep
obtenir to obtain, to get
s'occuper de to attend to
offrir to give
s'opposer à to be opposed to
ordonner to order
organiser to organize
orner (de) to decorate (with)
oser (faire qch) to dare (to do sth)
oublier to forget
ouvrir to open
paraître to appear
parier (sur) to bet (on)
parler to speak, to talk
partager to share
participer (à) to take part (in)
partir to leave, to go away
passer to pass; to spend (*time*);
  passer un examen to sit an exam;
  se passer to happen
passionner to fascinate
payer to pay
peindre to paint
pénétrer (dans) to enter
penser (à) to think (about)
perdre to lose;
  perdre qn de vue to lose sight
  of sb
permettre (à qn de faire)

to allow (sb to do)
persuader to persuade
peser to weigh
photographier to photograph
placer to place, to put
se plaindre (de) to complain (about)
plaire (à) to please;
  cela me plaît I like that
plaisanter to joke
pleurer to cry
plier to fold
porter to carry; to wear; to take
poser to put (down);
  poser des questions to ask
  questions
posséder to own
poursuivre to pursue
pousser to push; to grow
pouvoir to be able to
pratiquer to play; to practice
précipiter to hurl;
  se précipiter dans to rush into
prédire to predict
préférer to prefer
prendre to take;
  prendre qch à qn to take sth
  from sb;
  prendre part à to take part in;
  prendre soin (de) to take care (to)
préparer to prepare
présenter to present; to introduce;
  se présenter to appear;
  to introduce oneself
prêter qch à qn to lend sb sth
prévoir to foresee
prier to request;
  je vous en prie please, don't

mention it

priver qn de qch to deprive sb of sth

produire to produce;
  se produire to happen

profiter (de) to take advantage (of)

se promener to go for a walk

promettre (à qn de faire qch)
  to promise (sb to do sth)

prononcer to pronounce

proposer (de faire) to suggest
  (doing)

protéger to protect

protester to protest

prouver to prove

provoquer to cause

se quereller to quarrel

quitter to leave

raccommoder to mend

raconter to tell

ralentir to slow down

ramasser to pick up

ramener to bring or take back

ranger to tidy

se rappeler to remember

rapporter to report; to bring back

rassurer to reassure

rater to miss; to fail

rattraper qn to catch up with sb

recevoir to receive

réchauffer to warm (up)

recommander to recommend;
  to register

recommencer to begin again

reconnaître to recognize

recouvrir (de) to cover (with)

reculer to move back; to reverse

redescendre to come or go down

again

refaire to do again

refermer to close again

réfléchir to think

refuser (de) to refuse (to)

regagner to go back to

regarder to look (at)

régler to adjust; to settle

regretter (que) to be sorry (that)

rejoindre to join; to catch up

se relever to get up again

relier to connect

relire to read again

remarquer to notice

rembourser to refund

remercier (de) to thank (for)

remettre to put back; to postpone

remplacer to replace

remplir (de) to fill (with)

remuer to stir

rencontrer to meet;
  se rencontrer to meet

rendre to give back;
  rendre visite à to visit;
  se rendre to give oneself up;
  se rendre à to visit;
  se rendre compte to realize

renseigner to inform;
  se renseigner (sur) to inquire
  (about)

rentrer to go back (in)

renverser to run over;
  to spill; to knock over

renvoyer to expel, to dismiss;
  to send back

réparer to repair

repasser to iron

répéter to repeat
répondre to answer
se reposer to rest
reprendre to resume
représenter to represent
réserver to book
résoudre to solve
respecter to respect
ressembler à to look like
rester to stay
retenir to book
retourner to return;
  se retourner to turn round
retrouver to meet; to find (again)
se réunir to meet
réussir (à faire) to succeed
  (in doing)
réveiller to wake up;
  se réveiller to wake up
révéler to reveal
revenir to come back
rêver to dream
revoir to see again;
  au revoir goodbye
rire to laugh
risquer (de) to risk
rougir to blush
rouler to drive (along)
saisir to grasp
salir to dirty
saluer to greet
sauter to jump
sauver to save;
  se sauver to run off
savoir to know
sécher to dry
secouer to shake

sélectionner to select
sembler to seem
sentir to smell; to feel;
  se sentir (mal) to feel (ill)
séparer to separate
serrer to tighten;
  se serrer la main to shake hands
se servir to help oneself;
  se servir de qch to use sth
siffler to whistle
signaler to point out
signer to sign
soigner to look after
sonner to ring
sortir to go or come out;
  to take out
se soucier de to worry about
souffrir to suffer
souhaiter to wish
soulager to relieve
soulever to lift
soupçonner to suspect
soupirer to sigh
sourire to smile
se souvenir de qch to remember sth
sucer to suck
suffire to be sufficient
suggérer to suggest
suivre to follow
supposer to suppose
surprendre to surprise
sursauter to jump
se taire to be quiet;
  taisez-vous ! be quiet!
téléphoner (à) to phone
tendre to hold out
tenir to hold

tenter de to attempt to
(se) terminer to finish
tirer to pull; to shoot
tomber to fall;
  laisser tomber to drop;
  tomber en panne to break down
toucher to touch
tourner to turn; to shoot;
  se tourner vers to turn towards
traduire to translate
trahir to betray
traîner to drag
travailler to work
traverser to cross; to go through;
  to go over
trembler to shake
tricher to cheat
tromper to deceive;
  se tromper to be mistaken
troubler to worry
trouver to find;

se trouver to be situated
tuer to kill
unir to unite
utiliser to use
vaincre to conquer
valoir to be worth
vendre to sell
venir to come;
  venir de faire qch to have just
  done sth
vérifier to check
verser to pour
visiter to visit
vivre to live
voir to see
voler to steal; to fly
vouloir to want;
  vouloir bien faire to be happy
  to do;
  vouloir dire to mean
voyager to travel

ENGLISH
INDEX

The words on the following pages cover all of the ESSENTIAL
and IMPORTANT NOUNS in the book.

firefighter 476, 478
fireplace 567
firework; firework display 472
first course 533
first name 522
fish 458, 518, 530, 534
fish shop 533
fisherman 600
fishing 611
fishing boat 600
flashlight 475
flat tire 463, 485
flavor 536
flea market 606
flight 454
flight attendant 455, 477
floor 560, 564
flour 535
flower shop 604
flower(s) 519, 597
flowerbed 597
flu 557
flute 587
fly 531
foal 458
fog 642
folder 514
food 605
foosball 540
foot 466

forecast 643, 645
forehead 466
foreign exchange 572
forest 503, 519, 527, 635
fork 475, 533
form 561, 573, 574
France 497
fraud 579
free time 540
freeway 483
freezer 546
French 510
Frenchman 498
Frenchwoman 499
Friday 470
fries 533
front 638
front door 565
fruit 518, 532, 544
fruit juice 532
fruit seller 606
fruit tree 544
frying pan 571
full board 561
fur 459, 583
furnished apartment 566
furniture 546, 564, 566
future 478, 518, 620
game 540, 610, 611

game console 541
game room 475, 647
gang 579
garage 482, 564
garage owner 476, 482
garbage can 475, 569, 647
garden 564, 596
gardener 596
gardening 596
garlic 536
gas 474, 483, 484, 518, 568, 582
gas cooker 547
gas pump 485
gas station 483, 625
gas station attendant 484
gate 503, 527, 597
gear 463, 485
general delivery 575
geography 511
gift 472, 604
girl 523
girlfriend 543
glass 518, 534, 582
glasses 507
glove 488
goal 610
goalkeeper 612
goat 461

potato 637
power steering 483
practical class 512
prescription 557
present 472, 604
presentation 510
president 478, 479
press 541
price 560, 572, 604
principal 510, 511
printer 495
prize 512
problem 578
profession 477
program 494, 540, 543, 614
programmer 494
progress 512
property 505
publicity 541
public transportation 638
puppy 458
purchase 604
purse 488
Pyrenees 550
quality 509
quarter 534
quarter of an hour 618
quay 600
Quebec 550

question 513, 519
quiche 533
rabbit 458, 536
race 613
radio 541, 547
railroad 632, 633
rain 519, 597, 643
raincoat 488
rainfall 645
raise 479
raisin 544
range 547, 569
rape 578
raspberry 545
rate(s) 646
razor 594
reading 511, 541
ready-made meals 534
receipt 562, 606
reception 561
receptionist 477, 560, 561
recipe 535, 571
record 540
recorder 540, 587
red light 482
refrigerator 546
region 519, 643
relative 522
rent 566
reply 573

report 514, 578
reservation 455, 561, 631
restaurant 534, 535, 560, 624
restricted parking zone 485, 627
restroom 562
result 512, 610
retirement 477
review 617
reward 575, 579
Rhone 550
rice 534
right of way 485
ring 595
ringtone 573
risk 638
river 503, 504, 518, 519
road 483, 503, 625, 627
road accident 484
road map 483
road surface 505
roast 534
roast chicken 534
robbery 578
rock 503
roof 566
room 475, 547, 561, 565

Merriam-Webster's Best-Selling Bilingual Dictionaries

The perfect companions to foreign language learning references

ISBN: 978-0-87779-917-7
MASS-MARKET PAPERBACK
SRP: $5.99

ISBN: 978-0-87779-166-9
JACKETED HARDCOVER
SRP: $19.95

ISBN: 978-0-87779-916-0
MASS-MARKET PAPERBACK
SRP: $6.50

ISBN: 978-0-87779-165-2
JACKETED HARDCOVER
SRP: $19.95

Other French and Spanish titles from Merriam-Webster

MERRIAM-WEBSTER'S NOTEBOOK FRENCH-ENGLISH DICTIONARY
ISBN: 978-0-87779-673-2
PAPERBACK, 3-HOLE PUNCHED
SRP: $4.95

MERRIAM-WEBSTER'S POCKET FRENCH-ENGLISH DICTIONARY
ISBN: 978-0-87779-518-6
FLEXIBLE PAPERBACK
SRP: $4.95

ISBN: 978-0-87779-890-3

DICCIONARIO ESPAÑOL-INGLÉS MERRIAM-WEBSTER
ISBN: 978-0-87779-920-7
MASS-MARKET PAPERBACK
SRP: $6.50

DICCIONARIO MERRIAM-WEBSTER DE SINÓNIMOS Y ANTÓNIMOS EN INGLÉS
ISBN: 978-0-87779-852-1
MASS-MARKET PAPERBACK
SRP: $6.50

JUEGO DE DICCIONARIOS MERRIAM-WEBSTER (pictured) Especially for Spanish speakers.
Set includes: Diccionario Español-Inglés Merriam-Webster (bilingual); The Merriam-Webster Dictionary (English); and Diccionario Merriam-Webster de Sinónimos y Antónimos en Inglés (English synonyms for Spanish speakers).
ISBN: 978-0-87779-890-3
MASS-MARKET PAPERBACKS
SRP: $19.50

MERRIAM-WEBSTER'S NOTEBOOK SPANISH-ENGLISH DICTIONARY
ISBN: 978-0-87779-672-5
PAPERBACK, 3-HOLE PUNCHED
SRP: $4.95

MERRIAM-WEBSTER'S POCKET SPANISH-ENGLISH DICTIONARY
ISBN: 978-0-87779-519-3
FLEXIBLE PAPERBACK
SRP: $5.95

MERRIAM-WEBSTER'S ENGLISH & SPANISH REFERENCE SET
Set includes: The Merriam-Webster Dictionary (English); The Merriam-Webster Thesaurus (English); and Merriam-Webster's Spanish-English Dictionary (bilingual).
ISBN: 978-0-87779-897-2
MASS-MARKET PAPERBACKS
SRP: $18.99